CLASSICAL
Music

An essential guide to the world's finest music

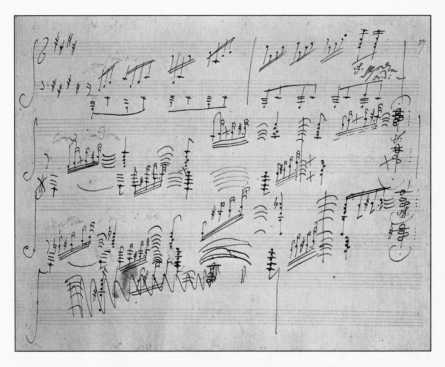

A part of the manuscript of Beethoven's well-known Moonlight Sonata.

Open-air concert at London's Kenwood House.

CLASSICAL Music

An essential guide to the world's finest music

Peter Gammond

HARMONY BOOKS

NEW YORK

Copyright © 1988 by Salamander Books Ltd.

Published in 1989 in the United States of America by Harmony Books, a division of Crown Publishers, Inc., 225 Park Avenue South, New York, New York 10003.

This edition originally published as *The Encyclopedia of Classical Music* in 1988 in Great Britain by Salamander Books Ltd.

Library of Congress Cataloging-in-Publication Data
Gammond, Peter.
 The harmony illustrated encyclopedia of classical music.
 Bibliography: p.
 1. Music—History and criticism. I. Title.
ML160.G227 1988   780'.3   88-23750
ISBN 0-517-57094-7
10 9 8 7 6 5 4 3 2 1

CREDITS

Editor: Richard Collins
Designer: Mark Holt
Line diagrams: Ralph Stobart
(© Salamander Books Ltd)
Map artwork: Janos Marffy
(© Salamander Books Ltd)
Picture researchers: Andrea Stern, Vanessa Whinney
Filmset by SX Composing Ltd
Colour reproduction by Kentscans Ltd
Printed in Belgium by Proost International Book Production, Turnhout

CONTRIBUTORS

PETER GAMMOND. Editor and general filler-in. The author of over thirty books on music including such varied items as *The Illustrated Encyclopedia of Recorded Opera, The Bluffer's Guide to Music, The Guinness Jazz A-Z, The Bluffer's Guide to Jazz, Duke Ellington, Scott Joplin and the Ragtime Era, Opera on Compact Disc, Schubert* and *The Magic Flute.*

JOHN CRABBE. Gramophone and Composers. For many years the Editor of *Hi-Fi News* (later *Hi-Fi News & Record Review*) and author of *Hi-Fi in the Home, Hector Berlioz: Rational Romantic* and *Beethoven's Empire of the Mind.*

JOHN FREESTONE. Opera. Well-known lifelong contributor and reviewer to many books and periodicals on opera and joint author of *Caruso: His Recorded Legacy.* Only surviving pupil of Marchesi and a student with Maggie Teyte.

ROBERT HARDCASTLE. Composers. Director of Discourses Ltd and promoter of their 'All About Music' series. Involved in publishing, writing and the musical life of Tunbridge Wells.

CHRISTOPHER HEADINGTON. Chamber music, Composers, Instruments, Choral, etc. Composer and pianist and a pupil of Benjamin Britten. Author of *The Performing World of the Musician, Bodley Head History of Western Music, The Orchestra and its Instruments, Illustrated Dictionary of Musical Terms, Listeners Guide to Chamber Music, Britten* and *Opera: A History.*

PETER HERRING. The Orchestra. Freelance musical journalist and photographer. Editor of *Hi-Fi Sound* for ten years, contributing editor to *Which Compact Disc?* and author of *Classical Music on Compact Disc.*

Right: *Gennady Rozhdestvensky (b. Russia 1931), presently chief conductor, BBC Symphony Orchestra.*

CONTENTS

This latest addition to the Salamander 'Encyclopedia' series (which covers both classical and popular music) attempts to fill a possible gap in the music-lover's and student's requirements by tackling music from a categorical and technical viewpoint. Whereas the previous volumes on Opera and Classical Music were mainly biographical and discographical, this volume is designed to give the reader a practical introduction to music by covering it from all obvious aspects, first explaining its history and growth and then backing this up with selective material on composers, their works, operas, conductors and singers that will help the searcher to find the way in to a balanced appreciation of the whole classical music scene.

We begin with a look at the central interest of musical appreciation, the orchestra, first looking at its history and development and then giving brief histories of the great orchestras of the world. This is backed up by a consideration of the role of the conductor with an appreciation of fifty well-known practitioners. A wide selection of the most important orchestral works is broken down into symphonies, concertos and other kinds of orchestral works and, finally, some ballet scores which are enjoyed for their musical qualities.

The world of opera is then similarly sub-divided into a concise history, a survey of some of the most popular works in the opera repertoire backed up by our own reckoning of the Top 60 (which should prove controversial) and a biographical survey of leading opera singers and conductors and a look at some of the world's principal, and favourite, opera houses.

We turn to the composer and how he works, considering the rival attractions of abstract and programme music, ancient and modern, with a look at the modes of music-making that operate in the Eastern World. This is backed up by a wide survey of composers dealt with under nationalities which gives a chance to sum up the importance of national characteristics.

Chamber music is a special consideration. How do we define it and what are its most important works and which are its leading protagonists? This led us to the instruments themselves, with a survey of modern and ancient species, a special look at the keyboard categories and the organ, backed up with a list of works. We have not forgotten the popular fields of choral music and song which are similarly broken down into histories and

biographical surveys – not forgetting the accompanist. A look into the special world of early music is followed by a brief consideration of music itself, something of its elements, its language and a look at a musical score.

The private means of listening to and studying music are of great importance today and we summarise the aid to appreciation that the gramophone has brought. We end with a useful glossary of musical terms.

It may be stating the obvious to say that the most important person in music is the composer. Nevertheless it is possible in the clamour of claims to our attention that come from highly paid performers, organisers and establishments, not to mention the pressures of business and publicity, for the composer to be half forgotten; sometimes ending up with the smallest billing on the poster. As a re-assertion of the composer's eminence we scatter through the book nearly a hundred illustrated inserts which it is hoped add to its attractiveness and usefulness as a handy reference. An attempt has been made to place these in an appropriate position but, as someone may well point out, this was not always possible.

I must end by thanking a knowledgeable and helpful team (each indicated throughout by their initials) who have made this survey more thorough by their expert participation. Christopher Headington [CH], a practising composer himself, has provided his special insight in several of the main sections, Peter Herring [PH] who dealt with the orchestra, John Freestone [JF] our opera specialist, John Crabbe [JC] who dealt with the gramophone and, along with Robert Hardcastle [RH], provided many of the useful composer inserts that occur throughout the book. Final thanks to a patient and tolerant editor, Richard Collins, who made the compilation of the book as near to a pleasure as hard work can be.

**Peter Gammond
Shepperton, 1988**

Below: *Leopold Stokowski conducting the London Philharmonic Orchestra.*

PART ONE

THE ORCHESTRA

The London Philharmonic, one of the world's greatest orchestras, founded by Sir Thomas Beecham in 1932.

For as long as man has had music, players have joined together to exploit and enjoy the contrasts between their instruments and the blends of sounds that they can produce together. Musical 'groups' are mentioned in the Bible and in the writings of Ancient Greece, and are depicted in Egyptian wall-paintings. In medieval times secular music was played by bands of musicians whose instruments were based on strings, wind and percussion. Gradually, this music-making became more organised, first in Italy and then in France, Germany, the Netherlands and Britain. In 1571, London had its 'waits', a group of musicians retained by the city to play at ceremonial events. Numerous documents from the fifteenth and sixteenth centuries mention the gathering together of often large numbers of players to perform at great occasions, and by the late sixteenth century ensembles akin to our notion of an 'orchestra' had been established in France. We also know that in 1576 orchestras composed of bowed viols, lutes, recorders, organs and voices were performing in London, while the King of France later had his own resident band of twenty-two violins and twelve wind instruments.

Lesser royal courts of Europe also engaged large numbers of musicians: while in the service of the Duke of Mantua, Claudio Monteverdi could accompany his operas (such as *Orfeo*) with strings, flutes, hautbois (oboes),

Above: *Town waits, or civic minstrels, were permanently employed by larger cities. This wash drawing of 17th century waits is attributed to Marcellus Laroon (c. 1649-1702).*

Below: *As well as playing concerts, Haydn's orchestra at Esterház played in the private theatre, here as pit orchestra for* L'incontro improvisso *in 1773.*

cornets, trumpets, trombones, harp, organ and harpsichord, and produce a wealth of sonorities and instrumental colours with these forces.

This pre-eminence of the strings stemmed from musical practicality: it was the one family of instruments able to produce a wholly homogenous sound and so supply the basic fabric of the orchestra. The strings were also the most responsive instruments in terms of dynamic range, able to express every nuance of sound from the very soft to the very loud. Also fundamental to the Baroque orchestra was the *continuo* which more or less supplied the underpinning bass line to the music. This role was allocated to a keyboard instrument, either harpsichord or organ.

Italian composers, principally Antonio Vivaldi and Arcangelo Corelli, used this framework for their many hundreds of concertos, taking the string writing to new expressive heights. In the main, the solo role in these concertos was taken by the violin which, during this period in Italy, had reached a pinnacle of design, construction and performance. However, other instruments — flute, oboe, cello and so forth — were not

Below: *The orchestra and performers in Westminster Abbey during a commemorative performance celebrating the 100th anniversary of Handel's birth in 1785.*

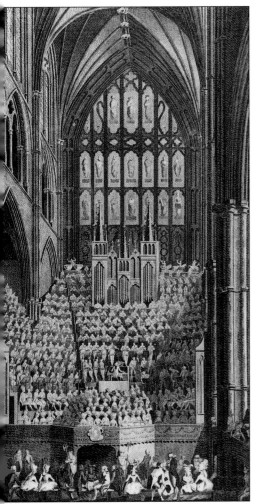

neglected, either in their technical development, or in the skills required to play them.

Among aristocratic families the 'resident orchestra' became an essential part of social entertainment. There was increasing use of instruments in church music, both Catholic and Protestant, and the growing number of theatres and opera houses also required 'house musicians'. Music was no longer an exclusive pleasure: public concerts, albeit held in drawing-rooms of large houses and mansions were accessible to all that could afford them. At first they were organised by music-lovers on a purely amateur basis, but it was not long before the professional impresario appeared on the scene with such ideas as subscription concerts where patrons were invited to underwrite the performances in advance, thus guaranteeing that at least the costs were covered.

Public concerts reached America (then a British colony) in the 1730s, first in Boston and then in New York. The orchestra was similarly spreading its wings. Its size had been limited by the size and the acoustic of the available auditoria. Composers such as Bach wrote the orchestral parts of their scores to match the players available to them. They also had to be conscious of the widely varying abilities of those players, especially as some of their noble patrons were amateur musicians. There are several instances of very simple accompanying roles in Bach's music for instruments known to have been played by his employers.

The change from 'chamber' orchestra to something resembling today's symphony orchestra came in the mid-eighteenth century: in 1743, the first ensemble of symphony orchestra proportions was formed at the court of the Elector Palatine, Duke Karl Theodor at Mannheim in Germany. That same year the oldest orchestra still in existence made its first appearance. Known initially as the *Grosses Concert* and later as the *Liebhaber-Concerte*, in 1781 this orchestra acquired a new home, a room especially converted for it, at the Cloth Merchants' Hall in Leipzig: a building which, in German, translates as *Gewandhaus*. The Leipzig Gewandhaus Orchestra remains one of the major orchestras of the German Democratic Republic (although it now occupies a purpose-built concert hall).

At Mannheim and Leipzig the format of the 'classical' orchestra was established. The principal constituent was still a large body of strings: violins, violas, cellos amd basses, plus pairs of oboes and horns. Other instruments were incorporated as required, also in pairs — flutes and bassoons at the high and low ends of the woodwind scale, trumpets, and kettledrums. All this would be familiar to today's audiences; less so would be the keyboard player — using either harpsichord or fortepiano — who, in conjunction with the leader of the first violin group, would control the orchestra.

Antonio VIVALDI
(1678-1741)

Son of Giovanni Battista Vivaldi, violinist at St Mark's, Venice. Two of his three brothers, both redheads like himself, were known to the local police for 'brawling and unseemly conduct'. He was ordained in 1703, but after two years he gave up saying Mass because of a chest complaint, a decision which in later life brought him into serious conflict with the church authorities. From 1704 to 1740 he taught the violin at one of the four famous orphanages which occupied an important place in Venetian musical life. He gave recitals, played the violin in operatic performances and produced his first opera *Ottone in Villa* at Vicenza in 1713, following this a year later with his first opera in Venice, *Orlando finto pazzo*. His famous work *Le quattro stagione (The Four Seasons)* was published in 1725. He travelled widely and his music was admired throughout Europe: among his appreciative contemporaries was J.S. Bach, who transcribed a number of his compositions. Vivaldi's output was prodigious, but for many years was out of favour. A major revival in recent years has been given added impetus by the growing interest in the performance of baroque music on authentic instruments of the period. Vivaldi's genius as a composer of opera and of sacred and secular choral works, as well as music for stringed instruments, is now universally recognised. R.H.

The keyboard-led orchestra, perhaps forty-strong, would have been accepted by Haydn as it was by Handel, even though the orchestra itself went through important changes between the career peaks of these two composers. By Mozart's time, the distinctive tone colour of the clarinet had been added to the orchestral palette, while Beethoven's Fifth introduced trombones into the symphony for the first time.

The keyboard *continuo* role had become obsolete and the early years of the nineteenth century saw composers such as Mendelssohn, Berlioz and Weber conducting their works standing in front of the orchestra, a practice which has continued ever since. With the likes of Berlioz the complement of the orchestra was both enlarged and extended.

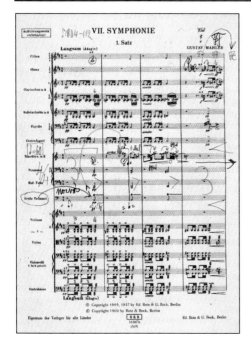

Above: *Score of the first page of Gustav Mahler's Symphony No. 7, written in 1906, whose added colours and divided textures match the big scale of his symphonic works and their romantic character.*

Above: *Igor Stravinsky (1882-1971) was one of the last of the dying breed of 'great' composers surviving into the 20th century and writing in every possible musical form, from chamber music to opera.*

Right: *The London Philharmonic Orchestra away from the concert platform and acting as pit orchestra at a performance at the famous festival opera house, Glyndebourne, founded in 1934.*

'Optional extras' included increasing the range of the woodwind section with the tiny piccolo and the mighty double-bassoon, adding the deep voice of the tuba to the brass or the glittering harp behind the strings. The two kettledrums could be complemented with bass drum, snare drum, triangle and cymbals (although Haydn, Mozart and Beethoven had already introduced such additional percussion, Haydn's *Military* Symphony and Beethoven's Ninth Symphony being good examples).

With larger halls came larger audiences and the finance to sustain greater orchestral forces, an opportunity which composers did not ignore, with its potential for increased dramatic impact. They were helped to a large extent by the instrument-makers who had been able to enhance the projection and volume possible from woodwind and brass.

The period between 1840 and 1900 saw the founding of many of the world's great symphony orchestras. Both the Vienna Philharmonic and the New York Philharmonic gave their first concerts in 1842, followed by the Boston Symphony in 1881. The splendid orchestras of Amsterdam and Berlin were formed in the 1880s, the prestigious Chicago Symphony in 1891. An indication of the growing power and influence of the United States was the arrival of the Los Angeles Philharmonic, the Pittsburg Symphony and the Philadelphia orchestras all in the space of four years between 1896 and 1900.

In most respects, the orchestra of the second half of the nineteenth century is the one we know today, the orchestra of Brahms, Verdi and Wagner, whose influence pervaded music as no other even if it provoked a counter-reaction. Not only would the sound of the instruments be recognisable to us, so would the layout of the orchestra. First and second violins would generally be split to the right and left of the conductor (it is only comparatively recently that all the violins would have been grouped to his left). Violas would be placed centrally, between the violins, with the cellos to the right. The violins themselves were now in sub-groups so that more notes of a chord could be divided among them.

Woodwind would be arranged behind the strings, the highest sounding on the left, the lowest on the right, which ensured that they would not be drowned by the powerful brass contingent behind: horns to the left, trumpets, trombones and tuba to the right. Centrally, at the very back sat the kettledrums, with whatever other percussion had been specified alongside. Although larger and more diverse than anything they could have envisaged, the governing musical principles behind this layout would have been self-evident to Bach, Handel and even Monteverdi before them.

The last decades of the nineteenth century also saw the flourishing of national styles in music, a deliberate break with the dominating Austro-German tradition. Russian composers especially augmented orchestral colour with a wide range of Oriental effects, both real and fanciful. Later, Gustav Mahler provoked comment and not a little derision by calling for all manner of bizarre effects – either in terms of new 'instruments', or ways of playing existing ones – in works such as his Sixth and Seventh Symphonies. Mahler, like Richard Strauss, wrote for huge orchestras.

A counter-reaction to this kind of scale and opulence was predictable. In many ways, Stravinsky's *The Rite of Spring*, first performed in 1913, was a turning-point: still a large orchestra, but a new kind of music. But whatever musical course the orchestra may have taken after this point remains pure conjecture: World War I had an economic impact on Western Europe, particularly Germany, which inevitably took its toll on the arts. Extravagant orchestral works were no longer cost-effective. Meanwhile, those such as Anton Webern were demonstrating how musical notes as well as pound or dollar notes could be employed more economically. 'Big' symphonies, concerts and tone-poems were still being written, largely in response to commissions from the United States, yet a major figure such as Stravinsky, primarily for musical reasons, had quit dense orchestral textures for an altogether leaner brand of neo-Classicism.

In retrospect, orchestral music pre-1914 either attained its zenith or, some would argue, a dose of indigestion from over-indulgence from which it has never recovered. Very few major symphony orchestras have been founded in the past seventy years: the Cleveland Orchestra and the Suisse Romande Orchestra both date from 1918; the BBC Symphony Orchestra from 1930, followed by the London Philharmonic Orchestra in 1932. Also in Britain, the Philharmonia was formed in 1945 and the Royal Philharmonic two years later, while the Paris Orchestra was established as recently as 1967.

Modern composers have composed substantially for the symphony orchestra and often on a large scale. They have also intro-

Hector BERLIOZ
(1803-69)

Son of a provincial French doctor with a practice near Grenoble, Berlioz was destined for the medical profession. However, after his first year in Paris he gave up medicine and became a music student instead, learning to play the flute, the flageolet and the guitar. In 1826 he entered the Paris Conservatoire, and a year later saw Charles Kemble and his company in a production of *Hamlet* at the Odéon, where he fell violently in love with an Irish actress, Harriet Smithson, who played Ophelia. From this point on, his life, as related in his own *Memoirs*, is that of an archetypal Romantic hero. Beset by financial difficulties he was obliged to write reviews and articles to augment his income, a task he loathed but did supremely well. The power and originality of his music and the brilliance of his orchestration were not appreciated by his contemporaries, and even today his genius is more widely recognized outside France than it is within. 'Berlioz . . . a genius without talent', said Bizet. 'A monster', declared Debussy, 'he is not a musician at all.' And even mild-mannered Ravel once described him as 'the worst musician among musical geniuses'. But after hearing *Les Troyens*, the Requiem, or any other of his stunning masterpieces, who can doubt that Hector Berlioz is, in fact, the greatest Frenchman of them all? R.H.

duced yet more fresh sounds, some generated electronically; this kind of development will certainly continue. All kinds of percussion instruments have now assumed an importance in many new compositions which would have astounded Mahler and possibly Bartók.

The most remarkable recent development in performance has been the enthusiastic and zealous return to the practices of earlier centuries. The 'authenticity' movement has strengthened thanks to the persuasive advocacy of orchestras such as the Academy of Ancient Music, the English Concert, and the Orchestra of the 18th century, and the efforts of conductors such as Nikolaus Harnoncourt, Christopher Hogwood, Trevor Pinnock, John Eliot Gardiner and Frans Bruggen. What began as an eccentric sideshow has now

attained a following and a momentum such that now the 'modern' versions of Bach, Handel and Vivaldi are the 'oddities'.

The quest for authenticity in terms of instrumental forces, instrumental sound, fidelity to the score and sympathetic acoustic now extends through Haydn and Mozart to Beethoven and conductors such as Christopher Hogwood see no reason for it not to eventually encompass the early Romantics such as Berlioz and Schumann. There are sufficient historical differences between performance then and performance now to justivy the effort.

This is not to say that the great symphony orchestras will be forced to stop playing Beethoven, Mozart and the like in the 'traditional' (i.e. modern!) manner: there are still plenty of listeners to whom the sound of

vibrato-less violins and valveless horns is anathema. However, it is also the case that life for the major orchestras is becoming increasingly difficult, with an ever-increasing reliance on subsidies and sponsorship. It is unlikely that any of the great symphony orchestras currently exists purely on its income from paying customers at concerts. External support is vital, as is income from recording, which in the case of certain British orchestras means undertaking virtually any kind of session work from film scores to the backing on pop records.

Just as Bach and Mozart would no doubt readily come to terms with the conception of the modern symphony orchestra, they would not be at all surprised to find that patronage – even if from the most unlikely sources – was just as vital as it ever was. P.H.

The work of many orchestras is heard and appreciated today by way of the greater mobility of the modern orchestra, which now tours the world to make concert appearances, and by way of the gramophone record. Maybe the search for accuracy and recorded perfection has led, as some assert, to a greater uniformity of sound and maybe the eccentricities of the Beechams and Toscaninis are no longer as common a trait. Nevertheless, there is still much national and individual character to be found. With apologies for omissions, we list some of the great orchestras of the world.

ACADEMY OF ANCIENT MUSIC
United Kingdom

Specialist 'authentic performance' orchestra founded in 1974 by conductor Christopher Hogwood and taking its name from an eighteenth-century 'early music' band. Dedicated to performing the music of the Baroque and Classical periods as it would have been heard at the time of composition, both in terms of style and instrumentation.

ACADEMY OF ST MARTIN-IN-THE-FIELDS
United Kingdom

Players due to give solo recitals at the church off London's Trafalgar Square elected instead to combine forces under the aegis of violinist Neville Marriner. Since 1959 has made an impressive reputation in Bach, Handel, Haydn and Mozart, and also in more modern music – Stravinsky and Bartók, for example.

BAVARIAN RADIO SYMPHONY ORCHESTRA
West Germany

One of several fine orchestras based around West German broadcasting stations, the Bavarian RSO dates from 1949. Eugen Jochum was its principal conductor until 1961, then Rafael Kubelik until 1981. Britain's Sir Colin Davis took over in 1984.

Above: *The Academy of St Martin-in-the-Fields first caught the public ear with a fresh and lively sound. Under its musical director, Sir Neville Marriner, it continually widens its musical horizon.*

BBC SYMPHONY ORCHESTRA
United Kingdom

Formed 1930, with an inspired choice of music director in Adrian Boult. He took the orchestra into the top flight and became its permanent conductor, although there were many famous guests: Richard Strauss, Felix Weingartner, Bruno Walter and, in 1935, Arturo Toscanini. Resident orchestra at the London Prom season and currently directed by Soviet conductor Gennady Rozhdestvensky.

Below: *The BBC Symphony Orchestra was founded in 1930 and first directed by the late Sir Adrian Boult. Its activities go far beyond broadcasting and are especially appreciated at the yearly Proms.*

BERLIN PHILHARMONIC ORCHESTRA
West Germany

Fifty-four musicians quit the Bilseseche Kapelle orchestra in 1882 to become the Philharmonic under impresario Hermann Wolf and music director Franz Wüllner. Soon became Berlin's best orchestra and conductors included Tchaikovsky, Brahms, Grieg and Richard Strauss. International reputation forged under Arthur Nikisch and widened by his successor, Wilhelm Furtwängler.

Its Philharmonie Hall was destroyed in 1944, but post-war concerts commenced early in 1945, with Furtwängler returning as chief conductor two years later. At his death in 1954, orchestra began its now thirty-four year association with Herbert von Karajan. A new Philharmonie Hall was opened in West Berlin in 1963.

BOSTON SYMPHONY ORCHESTRA
United States of America

The Boston banker Henry Lee Higginson formed the orchestra in 1881 with an endowment of around $1 million, then brought in Sir George Henschel as its first conductor. Superb Boston Symphony Hall, seating over 2,500, opened 1900.

Boston Symphony became first US orchestra to make a recording (1917) and in 1919 Pierre Monteux was appointed chief conductor. Succeeded by Serge Koussevitzky in 1924, during whose twenty-five year tenure the orchestra's Berkshire Music Center at Tanglewood, Massachusetts, was established. Concerts are held there every summer, and the BSO is also known for its 'Pops' concerts.

CHICAGO SYMPHONY ORCHESTRA
United States of America

Formed 1891, the Chicago Orchestra moved to its 2,600-seat Orchestra Hall in 1904 with Theodore Thomas its principal conductor. Thomas died the following year and from 1906 the orchestra was renamed in his honour, reverting to the Chicago Symphony Orchestra in 1909. There have been several famous music directors: Rafael Kubelik from 1950 to 1953, Fritz Reiner 1953-63, and responsible for some of the orchestra's greatest recordings) and, from 1969, Sir Georg Solti who has kept it in the very front rank.

CITY OF BIRMINGHAM SYMPHONY ORCHESTRA
United Kingdom

The first permanent orchestra of Britain's second city dates from 1920: a local musician augmented a police band with a string section! A grant from the city council established the orchestra for a five-year trial period and its first concert was conducted by Sir Edward Elgar.

Johann Christian BACH
(1735-82)

The youngest son of Johann Sebastian Bach and Anna Magdalena, he was taught music by his father and later by his elder brother Carl Philipp Emanuel. In 1756 (the year Mozart was born) he went to study in Bologna where he wrote church music and in 1760 he was appointed organist at Milan Cathedral. His close contacts with Italian music were to colour his music from now on. His first opera was produced in Turin in 1761 and the following year he went to London where he was to spend the rest of his life – to become known as the 'English Bach'. In 1763 he produced his first London opera and became music-master to Queen Charlotte. It was his court position that made him responsible for the welfare of the Mozart family when they visited England 1764-5 and he became a close friend and mentor of the young composer. The influence of Bach's elegantly Italianate style can be seen in the early orchestral and operatic works of Mozart. J. C. Bach's writing was always stylish and tuneful but even today remains somewhat under-rated; his popularity in his lifetime gradually eroded by the growing reputations of Haydn and Mozart and the subsequent dominance of Beethoven. During his London heyday he was called upon to provide music for all kinds of social occasions, including the supply of songs to be sung at the famous Vauxhall Gardens. Bach also contributed three sets of fine and careful settings of popular lyrics.P.G.

Below: *The Berlin Philharmonic Orchestra, founded in 1882, is one of the great orchestras of the world, latterly asserting its supremacy under the autocratic leadership of Herbert von Karajan.*

Above: *The great Hungarian-born conductor Sir Georg Solti has been moulding the Chicago Symphony Orchestra to international standards since 1969.*

Going full-time in 1944, the orchestra took the title of CBSO four years later and gave its first London concert. Made great strides under Louis Frémaux from 1969 to 1978 and is currently enjoying great success and acclaim under Simon Rattle.

CLEVELAND ORCHESTRA
United States of America

Founded 1918, its first music director was Nikolai Sokoloff. In 1933 Arthur Rodzinski replaced him, remaining ten years. Came to the fore under George Szell (1946-70) and has remained there under the guidance of Lorin Maazel.

The Cleveland enjoys the excellent acoustics of the Severance Hall, built 1931, for its winter concerts and in the summer performs at the no less splendid Blossom Music Center, where seating for over 4,500 is augmented by surrounding lawns with room for another 13,000.

CONCERTGEBOUW ORCHESTRA, AMSTERDAM
The Netherlands

The acoustically magnificent Concertgebouw Hall was opened in 1888, and the resident orchestra formed soon after by Willem Kes. An international reputation was established by Willem Mengelberg who replaced Kes and remained in charge until 1941. Mengelberg directed the then novel Mahler festival in 1920 and among guest conductors in the twenties and thirties were Richard Strauss, Walter, Beecham, Boult and Stravinsky.

Bernard Haitink became music director in 1961, sharing the post with Jochum for three years. By his departure in 1987, Haitink had spread the fame of the Concertgebouw far and wide through his concerts and recordings.

CZECH PHILHARMONIC ORCHESTRA
Czechoslovakia

The Czech Philharmonic started life as the orchestra of the Prague National Opera, before becoming an independent body in 1909. Its reputation was forged during directorship of Václav Talich (1919-41). Reformed in 1945, its most notable incumbents included Rafael Kubelik, Karel Ančerl and, from 1968, Vaclav Neumann.

DETROIT SYMPHONY ORCHESTRA
United States of America

The name dates back to 1875, but the present organisation was founded in 1914. It ceased working twice during the 1940s but reformed in 1951 under the direction of Paul Paray who enhanced the orchestra's standing until his retirement in 1962. In 1970, the Detroit Symphony Youth Orchestra was formed and, more recently, the DSO has received much acclaim for its work under Antal Dorati.

DRESDEN STAATSKAPELLE
East Germany

History can be traced back to the court orchestra of the Elector of Saxony, formed in 1548. In 1617 Heinrich Schütz became its *Kapellmeister* for fifty-five years. Two centuries later, Carl Maria von Weber occupied the same post and, through him, Dresden became centre of German opera, responsible for three Wagner premières.

In 1872, Emstron Schuch became conductor, and the Staatskapelle's standing was confirmed under Fritz Busch and Karl Böhm. Both city and orchestra rose from the ashes after World War II and, with conductors such as Keilberth, Kempe and Sanderling, became the leading orchestra of the German Democratic Republic. Current music director is the Swede, Herbert Blomstedt, and the Staatskapelle has also made several fine recordings under Britain's Sir Colin Davis.

ENGLISH CHAMBER ORCHESTRA
United Kingdom

Origins were in the fifties when Baroque music specialist Arnold Goldsborough gave viola player Quintin Ballardie the task of organising an orchestra on his behalf. The Goldsborough Orchestra broadened its activities, becoming the English Chamber Orchestra in 1960. The following year came its first major tour, and first recording, both with Colin Davis and a fruitful relationship was soon formed with Benjamin Britten and the Aldeburgh Festival. There was a complete cycle of the Mozart piano concertos for HMV, with Daniel Barenboim both soloist and conductor (since followed by one with Murray Perahia in the same roles).

The ECO has toured widely, with notable appearances in Vienna, Salzburg and Moscow. It has also been a regular visitor to the major British festivals and, as London's only full-time chamber orchestra, stages its own concert season each year. Jeffrey Tate became its principal conductor in 1985.

GOTHENBURG SYMPHONY ORCHESTRA
Sweden

Its birthdate of 1905 makes the Gothenburg orchestra one of Scandinavia's oldest and it quickly acquired a reputation under the leadership of composer and conductor Wilhelm Stenhammer. Soon, Sibelius and Nielsen were making guest appearances conducting their own works and other well-known visitors have included Barbirolli, Furtwängler, von Karajan, Kleiber, Sargent, Solti and Walter. From 1982, conductor-in-chief has been Estonian émigré Neeme Järvi, who has made a series of outstanding Sibelius recordings.

HALLÉ ORCHESTRA
United Kingdom

With the distinction of being the oldest professional symphony orchestra in Britain, for four decades Manchester's Hallé was owned and run by its founder, Charles Hallé. On his death, the burghers of Manchester determined to keep the orchestra going and engaged Hans Richter as successor. Richter stayed for twelve years, to be followed by Michael Balling (1912-24) and then Hamilton Harty, who made Hallé Britain's premier orchestra between 1920 and 1933, a tradition continued under Sir John Barbirolli from 1943. Barbirolli guided the Hallé for twenty-seven years; on his death, James Loughran became only the sixth principal conductor in over 100 years of music-making.

LONDON SYMPHONY ORCHESTRA
United Kingdom

Forty-six players in Henry Wood's Promenade Concert Orchestra broke away to form the LSO, giving a début concert in 1904 and making it the oldest of London's 'big four' orchestras. Hans Richter was the conductor and, within two years, the LSO was well established on the British music scene and abroad. Elgar and Nikisch became principal conductors, and the orchestra subsequently worked frequently with maestros such as Beecham, Koussevitzky, Krips, Mengelberg, Solti, Szell, Walter and Weingartner and, of course, with

Above: *The London Philharmonic Orchestra, founded 1932, became self-governing during the Second World War with members of the orchestra on its directorial board and able to choose its conductors.*

many distinguished soloists.

Claudio Abbado appointed principal conductor 1979, becoming music director from 1983 to 1987. New incumbent is American Michael Tilson Thomas.

The LSO has toured since 1906 and should, in 1912, have travelled to the USA on board the ill-fated *Titanic* but had to cancel the booking. Since then, three major world tours (last in 1983) and the only UK orchestra to appear at the Salzburg Festival.

ISRAEL PHILHARMONIC ORCHESTRA
Israel

The orchestra is older than Israel itself: under the name Palestine Symphony Orchestra, it was formed 1936 by Polish violinist Bronislaw Huberman and some of the finest Jewish musicians in Europe whom he persuaded to emigrate. Altogether, seventy performers, including refugees already in the country, came under the baton of William Steinberg, although the inaugural concert was conducted by no less than Toscanini.

Gives concerts in over a dozen centres throughout Israel but has a permanent home in the less than flattering acoustic of the Mann Auditorium in Tel Aviv. Zubin Mehta became IPO's music adviser in 1969 and its director in 1977, and the orchestra also has a special relationship with Leonard Bernstein who conducted its 1986 European tour.

LEIPZIG GEWANDHAUS ORCHESTRA
East Germany

The world's oldest true orchestra, having given concerts during the time of Bach in the Cloth Merchants' Hall (*Gewandhaus*) in

Georg Philipp TELEMANN
(1681-1767)

Telemann is one of those composers whose prolific output prompts the question, at what point does musical facility become merely facile and nothing else?' 'He could write a motet for eight voices more quickly than one could write a letter', said Handel disapprovingly, and most modern critics agree that although much of Telemann's music has charm and is full of skilful counterpoint, it is superficial in nature and lacks weight. After forty operas, forty-four Passions, innumerable trio sonatas, suites, flute quartets and 600 overtures in the Italian style, such judgements do not come altogether as a surprise, although they are perhaps a little hard on a composer who has provided some of the most popular trumpet concertos in the standard repertoire, no more virtuoso than many others in that particular tradition. German by birth, Telemann was a self-taught composer and organist who, in 1721, was offered the post of cantor at the Thomaskirche in Leipzig, but decided instead to go to the Johanneum in Hamburg where a higher salary was on offer. Here he remained until his death. The Leipzig vacancy went to the runner-up on the list, a rather less impressive candidate who gave his name as Johann Sebastian Bach. R.H.

Above: *The New York Philharmonic Orchestra was founded in 1842. A distinguished succession of conductors has included Weingartner, Strauss, Mahler, Toscanini, Barbirolli and Bernstein.*

Leipzig. Later conductors included Mendelssohn and the name was retained even when the orchestra moved into a purpose-built concert hall in 1885.

LENINGRAD PHILHARMONIC ORCHESTRA
Russia

With its roots in the court orchestra of the czars, the Leningrad Philharmonic was founded in 1921. Its principal music directors have been Nikolai Malko (1926-9), Alexander Gauk (1930-33), and Yevgeny Mravinsky whose fifty-year tenure was ended only by his death in January 1988. Between 1941 and 1960, Mravinsky shared the post with Kurt Sanderling and the orchestra has also been associated with Arvid Jansons and Temirkanov. The former's son, Mariss Jansons, conducted the Leningraders in recent concerts in the west.

Mravinsky and his orchestra were entrusted by Shostakovich with the first performances of eight of his symphonies.

LONDON PHILHARMONIC ORCHESTRA
United Kingdom

After formation in 1932, the LPO dominated the London concert scene for the remainder of the decade: its founder, Sir Thomas Beecham, had succeeded in creating an orchestra to rival those of Berlin, New York and Vienna. During the war, the players formed a co-operative to stage concerts and the LPO remains self-governing to this day.

Post-war years saw many notable guest conductors, with Eduard van Beinum enjoying two highly successful spells as principal

conductor. Sir Adrian Boult enjoyed a long association with the LPO, as have Bernard Haitink and Sir Georg Solti, who was made conductor emeritus in 1983. That same year, Klaus Tennstedt began another vintage era.

Two notable firsts for the LPO are the first tour of the USSR by a British orchestra (1956) and the first tour of China by any Western orchestra (1982). Back home, the LPO has been resident orchestra at the Glyndebourne Festival Opera.

LOS ANGELES PHILHARMONIC ORCHESTRA
United States of America

Formed in 1919, principal conductors have included Arthur Rodzinski (1929-33), Otto Klemperer (1933-9), Eduard van Beinum (1956-9), Zubin Mehta (1962-77) and Carlo Maria Giulini (1978-86). Under Mehta and Giulini, the LAPO returned to the front rank of the world's orchestras and maintains that status under André Previn, current music director. Toured Europe, India and Iran with Mehta in 1967.

MONTREAL SYMPHONY ORCHESTRA
Canada

Along with the Toronto Symphony, the principal Canadian orchestra. Had its roots in several organisations, with the émigré Belgian violinist Joseph Goulet conducting a Montreal Symphony Orchestra for some years after 1897. Modern orchestra dates back to 1930 and founding by music scholar Douglas Clarke, while the rival Concerts Symphoniques de Montreal was formed five years later. Clarke's orchestra folded 1941 and resources were combined. Present name dates only from 1954 and among its conductors have been Klemperer, Markevich, Mehta and Frühbeck de Burgos. Since 1978 under Charles Dutoit, orchestra has become a polished, world-class outfit with a host of

superlative recordings to its name for the UK Decca label.

NEW YORK PHILHARMONIC ORCHESTRA
United States of America

America's oldest symphony orchestra, founded in 1842 as the Philharmonic Society of New York. Early music directors included Leopold Damrosch and Theodore Thomas (who later found fame with the Chicago Symphony as well). During the first two decades of this century, conductors included Sir Henry Wood, Felix Weingartner, Richard Strauss and – most notably – Gustav Mahler. Mengelberg enjoyed an eight-year tenure from 1922 to 1930, sharing part of it with Toscanini; Barbirolli was in charge from 1943 to 1947, and Mitropoulus and Stokowski jointly from 1958 to 1969. Many memorable concerts and recordings with Leonard Bernstein (1971-7), who has recently revived his association with the New Yorkers.

PARIS ORCHESTRA
France

When the Conservatoire Concerts Orchestra was disbanded in 1967, the Paris Orchestra emerged from the ashes to at last give the French capital an orchestra of international ranking. First principal conductor Charles Munch, followed by von Karajan in 1969, Solti in 1971 and, most recently, Daniel Barenboim.

OSLO PHILHARMONIC ORCHESTRA
Norway

Edvard Grieg co-founded and conducted in 1870, but it was another forty years before the Oslo orchestra was established as a permanent body. Over the past twenty years has broadened activities under conductors such as Herbert Blomstedt and Okku Kamu. Moved into the new Oslo Concert Hall in 1977, and in the past nine years under the directorship of Mariss Jansons has received wide international acclaim.

PHILADELPHIA ORCHESTRA
United States of America

Founded 1900, orchestra's reputation established under Stokowski (1912-38). Ormandy co-conducted with Stokowski between 1936 and 1938, then succeeded him, remaining as music director for forty years. Under Stokowski, the Philadelphia introduced many major twentieth-century works to American audiences. In 1981, Riccardo Muti took over as principal conductor and maintained the high standards of his predecessors.

Above: *The Orchestre de Paris has operated in its present form since 1967, being established as a top orchestra under such conductors as Munch, Karajan, Solti and (seen here) Barenboim.*

PHILHARMONIC ORCHESTRA
United Kingdom

Dating from 1945, perhaps the first orchestra created primarily for recording. The idea of impresario Walter Legge, he attracted conductors such as Cantelli, Furtwängler, Giulini, von Karajan, Richard Strauss and Toscanini, but most productive association was with Klemperer.

In 1964, the orchestra became self-governing, calling itself the New Philharmonia (it reverted to the original name 1977). The American Lorin Maazel was associated principal conductor under Klemperer from 1971 to 1973, and Riccardo Muti became principal after Klemperer's death in 1973, where he remained until 1982. The controversial Giuseppe Sinopoli took over in 1984.

PITTSBURGH SYMPHONY ORCHESTRA
United States of America

Formed 1895 and gave promenade concerts under composer-conductor Victor Herbert from 1898 to 1904. Guest conductors included Elgar and Richard Strauss, but concerts ceased 1910. Revival 1926 and reorganisation under Klemperer (1937) was followed by a purple patch under Reiner from 1938 to 1948. William Steinberg enhanced the orchestra's reputation during a 24-year tenure; it continues to flourish under Previn.

ROYAL LIVERPOOL PHILHARMONIC ORCHESTRA
United Kingdom

The Royal Liverpool Philharmonic Society dates back to 1840. First conductor of inter-

Below: *The RPO was founded by Sir Thomas Beecham in 1947 who, with his own choice of musicians, created an orchestral sound entirely his own.*

Dennis BRAIN
(1921-1957)

Scion of a celebrated family of English horn players, Dennis Brain was educated at St Paul's School and at the Royal Academy of Music in London. Here he studied with his distinguished father Aubrey who was principal horn with the BBC Symphony Orchestra until 1945. Aubrey Brain's elder brother, Alfred, was himself principal horn with the Queen's Hall Orchestra under Sir Henry Wood, before emigrating in 1923 to the USA where he joined the Damrosch Orchestra. The young Dennis Brain made his public début in 1938 in a Bach series with his father and the Busch Chamber Players, and went on to perform with a number of leading instrumental groups including the Lener,

Griller and Busch quartets. Like his father he preferred a French horn to the more usual German instrument, and displayed an astonishing virtuosity and purity of tone throughout the whole of its compass. At the outbreak of war he joined the RAF and soon emerged as principal horn with the Central Band. After he was demobilised his career blossomed rapidly: he became first horn of the Royal Philharmonic Orchestra. In addition he appeared frequently on the concert platform as soloist, and founded his own wind ensemble. Many composers wrote music for him, notably Benjamin Britten (*Serenade for tenor, horn and strings*), Elizabeth Lutyens and Paul Hindemith. R.H.

Arcangelo CORELLI
(1653-1713)

Corelli started his musical training at a very early age in Faenza before moving to Bologna, whilst still only thirteen years old, in order to study the violin. Four years later he joined the Accademia Filharmonica, and then made a number of visits to France and Germany during which he achieved considerable fame as a virtuoso. By his early thirties he had settled in Rome under the protection of his rich and gifted patron Cardinal Pietro Ottobani. His Opus 1, a set of twelve sonatas, published in 1681, enhanced his reputation still further, and his gentle upbringing, amiable disposition and formidable array of talents won him a favoured position in Roman society. He especially enjoyed the company of many of the leading painters of his day, and with their help he assembled a collection of valuable pictures which included at least one Breughel. Corelli's major contribution to the development of European music is twofold. As a great performer he laid the foundations for the future development of violin technique, and as a composer he established in his chamber sonatas and *concerti grossi* a basic style upon which this particular form of composition was to flourish significantly in the years ahead. Corelli died in Rome, a much admired and respected figure, not long before his sixtieth birthday. R.H.

national note Max Bruch (1880-83), followed by twelve years under Charles Hallé. Sargent conducted for six years between 1942 and 1948, followed by Hugo Rignold (1948-54) and John Pritchard (1955-63). RLPO's reputation confirmed under directorship of Sir Charles Groves (1963-77), both in concert and on record, and maintained by Walter Weller (1977-80), David Atherton (1980-83) and more recently Marek Janowski and Libor Pesek. Original Philharmonic Hall (1894) was one of finest in Europe but burnt down in 1933 to be replaced by current venue.

ROYAL PHILHARMONIC ORCHESTRA
United Kingdom

More so than the LPO (which he also founded), the RPO will always be associated with Beecham, principal conductor from 1947 to 1961. During that time RPO was a regular guest at the Glyndebourne Festival and became first British orchestra to tour the USA since 1912 when it did so in 1950. Beecham's standards maintained under Kempe, Dorati, Weller and, most recently, Previn.

SCOTTISH NATIONAL ORCHESTRA
United Kingdom

History goes back to the Scottish Orchestra of 1891. George Henschel principal conductor for first four years, then Max Bruch from 1898 to 1900. Other notable incumbents have been Barbirolli (1933-6), Szell, (1936-9) and Susskind (1946-52). Renamed SNO in 1950, came to prominence from 1959 under Sir Alexander Gibson who enlarged repertory, including premières of works by Henze and Stockhausen; Neeme Järvi arrived in 1984 and took the orchestra to new artistic heights, but left abruptly early 1988.

SUISSE ROMANDE ORCHESTRA
Switzerland

Forever associated with Swiss conductor Ernest Ansermet who formed orchestra in 1918 and remained principal conductor until 1966. He was followed by Paul Kletzki (1967-9), Wolfgang Sawallisch (1970-80)

and, in recent years, by Horst Stein and Armin Jordan. The principal Swiss orchestra, the Suisse Romande is based in Geneva.

VIENNA PHILHARMONIC ORCHESTRA
Austria

One of the top four or five among the world's orchestras, the VPO can trace its origins back to 1833 when players from the Vienna Opera Orchestra joined together to give orchestral concerts. But it took nine years for the orchestra to be officially formed, the first concert taking place in 1842. In 1870, the VPO moved into the magnificent Grosser Saal of the Musikverein which has been its home since. Brahms and Wagner conducted in the 1870s and permanent conductors have included Furtwängler, Mahler, Richter, Walter and Weingartner.

Lately has been conducted by Böhm, von Karajan, Bernstein and present director of the Vienna State Opera, Claudio Abbado. Regularly appears at the Staatsoper and at the Salzburg Festival.

Below: *The Vienna Philharmonic Orchestra was officially formed in 1842 and its luscious sound has worked in the service of the Viennese musical heritage ever since. Leonard Bernstein conducts.*

PROFILE OF AN ORCHESTRA

Unofficially known as London's 'fifth orchestra' (after the four major symphony orchestras), the English Chamber Orchestra is also the capital's only full-time chamber orchestra. The enthusiastic patron of the orchestra's society is HRH The Prince of Wales and, uniquely perhaps, the ECO's founder and one of the directors, Quintin Ballardie, still occupies the first desk among the orchestra's violas. The advantage in terms of communication between players and administrators is, to say the least, considerable.

The ECO is administered from an office in west London by a staff of six. A key figure is the 'fixer' whose responsibility it is to ensure the players are in the right place at the right time. Planning the orchestra's activities starts many years in advance. The bigger tours are pencilled in three to four years ahead, overseas tours perhaps two years and London concerts eighteen months in advance (though only a year for the Promenade concert season).

As the months go by, the advance diary gradually fills up. There will be recording sessions – sometimes as many as one or two a month – but these are not booked as far ahead as concerts. The ECO has avoided any exclusive contracts in order to be free to work with any of the major recording companies. Touring occupies up to fifteen weeks a year, but two months is ideal from the musicians' point of view, and as far as programming goes the aim is to have an interesting mix from a wide-ranging repertoire that will appeal both to those who hear it and those who play it.

In October 1987, for example, the orchestra's players received the long-term schedule for 1988. This is updated with monthly 'definitive' schedules, although the 'fixer' will have booked players well before those appear. He is in constant liaison with the administration team, both working from a fully-detailed daily schedule.

Deciding the content of the programmes is a matter for discussion between the orchestra and the promoters. Promoters will approach the ECO with ideas and guidelines, including how much the concerts should cost. Of course, the players have plenty of suggestions for music they would like to do, often new or difficult works which inevitably require more rehearsal time. It can also be difficult persuading promoters to accept unusual repertoire, one of the advantages of the ECO's annual London concert series. With up to twenty concerts a year, this provides an opportunity for the orchestra to do the works it wants to do, programmes which can then be taken on tour abroad and at home, and to other festivals. A theme for the 1988 concert series, for instance, was 'The Italian Inspiration' which included many rarely heard delights by Cavalli, Cherubini, Cimarosa, Monteverdi, Rossini and others interspersed with Italian-influenced works by composers as far apart as Haydn and Hans Werner Henze.

Sponsorship for these 'Italian' concerts came, for example, from Italian banks, but the ECO is nothing like as dependent on public or private finance as other orchestras. That said, it would still expect to lose around £5,000 on even a sell-out concert in London's major chamber and Baroque music venue, the Queen Elizabeth Hall. The whole concert series, without the sponsorship actively sought by the directors of the ECO Society, would incur operating losses in the region of at least £100,000.

Public funding is received, but by the English Chamber Orchestra and its Music Society, not by the English Chamber Orchestra Ltd, which runs as a company like any other with all the usual freedoms. There is a similar distinction in the United States where the English Chamber Orchestra Society of America assists in obtaining the sponsorship that is essential for any North American tour.

Putting a price on what it costs to run an orchestra such as the ECO is difficult: basically, the orchestra needs to sell itself for what it costs, but it aims for between 400 and 450 'work periods' per year. Each 'work period' consists of three hours, as specified by the Musicians' Union; a concert consists of two such periods – one for rehearsal, one for performance. Currently, the ECO is averaging 430 work periods each year, which is more than most symphony orchestras.

Although its players are full-time, they are not salaried in the usual sense: put simply, if the orchestra is not playing, it does not get paid. There is a range of fees, with the concert payments above the Musicians' Union rates. The principals of the orchestra command more, as do players required to do 'semi-solos' – the horns in Bach's first Brandenburg concerto, for example. The average fee in the profession might be £65 per concert (for six hours' work), and in a recording session, a principal would receive around £55.

Among the ECO's recording projects have been three complete cycles of the

Mozart piano concertos, with soloists Daniel Barenboim, Murray Perahia and, currently, Mitsuko Uchida. It has been vital in all of these that certain key instrumentalists – notably the wind principals – are present for every session even if the whole cycle takes several years to complete.

All the ECO's players own their instruments, although the orchestra has its own harpsichord and, rather more surprisingly, a contra-bassoon: a rare beast that they even hire out to other orchestras!

With a top-quality violin costing between £15,000 and £20,000 it is not surprising that, wherever possible, the instruments travel as the players' personal luggage, even if it means buying airline seats for the cellos. If circumstances do not allow that, they go in the hold in special fibreglass cases.

More valuable than the instruments, though, are the players and the ECO has a very informal system of recruiting new talent. There are no 'audition days' as other orchestras hold. Musicians may come along for auditions, but generally reliance is put on personal recommendations from existing players or elsewhere within the music business. Informal auditions may be held during rehearsal breaks; promising players will work with the orchestra and its opinions sought, both as to musical ability and perception, and personality. The players simply have to be good – they cannot 'hide' in a comparatively small ensemble like the ECO – and they need to fit in as people. Choice of players is the most important decision for the orchestra: they make the sound, without which you do not have an orchestra.

Far left: *Quintin Ballardie, the founder and a director of the English Chamber Orchestra, is also the leader of the viola section. The orchestra made its first visit to the USA in 1968.*

Near left: *The English Chamber Orchestra has frequently been partner to the famous Russian cellist, Mstislav Rostropovich, first working with him to give the first performance of Britten's Cello Symphony in 1963.*

Right: *The ECO with Heinz Holliger (oboe) and conducted by Raymond Leppard in London's Westminster Abbey where, in 1985, they gave a Handel Tercentenary Concert which was broadcast live on British television and radio.*

The ECO has no formal contracts with its players, instead a nucleus of musicians who are 'members'. There are also 'regular non-members' and some repertoire does require extras to be brought in. But the core of the orchestra is stable and bound by its commitment as 'members': it would do no one's reputation any favours if they suddenly took advantage of the informal arrangement and left.

The ECO's founder, Quintin Ballardie, has a knack of finding good players and keeping them, and this has been the orchestra's recipe for success. Under him, all the players are guided and handled as individuals, and the players themselves have a say in who conducts them. For the first twenty-five years of its existence, the ECO did not have a principal conductor, but in its silver jubilee year, 1985, it did appoint Jeffrey Tate to that post. Prior to that it had been conducted by many great names, including the composers Benjamin Britten and William Walton (the ECO makes regular appearances at the Aldeburgh Festival founded by Britten).

Early in 1988, another typically busy year lay ahead for the English Chamber Orchestra with its own concert series augmented by visits to the USA, Bahamas, Spain, Germany, Majorca, Belgium, Switzerland, Italy and Portugal; and appearances at major festivals around the world, including five performances of *Così fan tutte* at Aix-en-Provence under Jeffrey Tate. Meanwhile, back in London W.5., the scores will be coming out of the library for the next concerts, the monthly diary will be on its way to all players, and dates will be going into the diary for 1992. . . . P.H.

Otto NICOLAI
(1810-49)

The single work on which Nicolai's international fame rests is his opera *The Merry Wives of Windsor*, the tuneful overture to which is still frequently performed. The plot closely follows Shakespeare's original comedy, but without Bardolph and Pistol, while the music itself is in the very best German comic opera tradition, holding its place in the popular repertoire despite the success of Verdi's later work, *Falstaff*, based on the same subject. As to the man himself, Otto Nicolai was born in Königsburg and, after an unhappy childhood, ran away from home at the age of sixteen. He was lucky enough to find a protector who sent him to Berlin to study music. In 1833 he went to Rome as organist to the Prussian Embassy and four years later he was appointed *Kapellmeister* at the Kärntnertor Theatre in Vienna. After returning to Rome in 1838 he started to compose a series of operas very much in accordance with the taste and the conventions of that time. In 1841 he went back to Vienna to take up a post as *Kapellmeister* to the Court Opera, where his work as a conductor won him considerable renown. Other compositions by Nicolai include a symphony, a Requiem and a 'Te Deum'. R.H.

The Church was the first centre of organised music. In charge would be the cantor and, in the absence of any printed scores, his was the responsibility of teaching, by ear, the liturgical chant to his choir. His only guide was a sequence of marks or symbols above the words of the biblical text indicating the accents, inflections and suggested melody to accompany these words. The rhythm, however, was free, requiring the cantor to use some kind of technique, usually hand gestures, to keep his singers together.

By the tenth century, the four-line stave distinguishing high and low had come into being and the symbols above the biblical text became a standardised system of notation indicating the melody. Later, the notes came to be varied to indicate time and the cantor now had a 'score' whose indications he had to convey to his singers. There were no bar lines, though, and the rhythmic pulse, the 'beat', still had to be set and maintained visually.

In the seventeenth century, it was commonplace to accompany voices with instruments and the job of unifying the forces had become considerably more complex. The cantor (a role that Bach performed, for example) would now direct from a keyboard instrument and beat time with a tightly rolled piece of paper in one hand (and by stamping his foot when occasion demanded). His roll of paper would also suggest the character of the music to some extent.

Eventually the paper was replaced by a stick, but the practice of literally beating time, either on the floor if the stick was long enough, or on a desk or music stand was still the most used. Hardly surprisingly audiences came to resent his noisy intrusion on the music and it was replaced by a wholly visual, largely silent use of gesture.

Responsibilities for controlling the orchestra were now shared between the *Kapellmeister* on the keyboard (he was often the composer, too) and the leader of the all-important violins, in German the *Konzertmeister* (concert-master), a term which sums up his role. They would dictate the pace of the performance together, the *Konzertmeister* using his violin bow. It was not a wholly satisfactory arrangement and, as the keyboard contribution became redundant (except in concertante works), the single figure of the conductor emerged to take sole charge of controlling the orchestra.

It was a change that coincided with the time of Haydn, Mozart and Beethoven. Haydn was known to have directed his London performances in the 1790s from the keyboard in conjunction with the violinist Salomon. Mozart also led from the keyboard, but Beethoven conducted from a podium in front of the orchestra, often visually conveying the emotions in his music as well as the musical essentials.

Not all conductors used the stick or baton: many relied on their hands, as some do today. Rapidly the notion of the conductor came to be accepted, if grudgingly by downgraded first violins and keyboard players!

Some composers proved to be very good conductors both of their own music and that of others: Mendelssohn is a leading example although there is evidence to suggest that he thought it necessary only to set the opening tempo for each movement and then leave the musicians to get on with the performance, occasionally jumping up to indicate things which he may not have written into the score.

The first to fit our modern conception of the conductor-as-interpreter was Hans von Bülow (1830-94). With von Bülow, according to his fellow-conductor Felix Weingartner, 'musical sensationalism began', and with the coming of professional symphony orchestras came the need for permanent principal conductors. Styles varied, and continue to do so: there are the autocrats, the musical dictators, and there are those that prefer to rely on the sound musical instincts of their players.

As the nineteenth century wore on and travel became easier, so it became commonplace for conductors to switch appointments many times during their careers, both within Europe and, increasingly, the United States. Today, it is usual for the top-ranking conductors to hold several different posts at once, guaranteeing to spend a certain amount of time with each one every year. Whether this is conducive to high standards of music-making is debatable. Certainly rehearsal time becomes limited (though not quite as much as it has been in some previous decades) and American orchestras, at least, have assistant conductors able to do a lot of the preparatory work with the orchestra prior to the arrival of the principal.

Styles of conducting vary considerably. There are those who emote violently and perspiringly on the podium leaving the audience in no doubt about what they feel the music is conveying. This can become an imposition between audience and music and is often abhorred by the orchestra which is looking for musical direction not a display of histrionics.

Other conductors move hardly at all on the podium, merely indicating what is required from the players with clear-cut effective gestures: Sir Adrian Boult was the epitome of this style, and it did nothing to diminish the emotional impact of his performances. Perhaps some audiences feel that unless a conductor sheds a few pounds in weight during a symphony, they will not have had value for money!

Certainly the cult of the conductor has now reached an absurd level with the promotion of the maestro image, often to the detriment of music-making. Recording companies as much as concert promoters are to blame for this state of affairs, and it has to be concluded that major appointments may now be made more on a conductor's commercial viability than his musical potential.

Reading the accompanying biographies, it will become apparent that there is no fixed path to becoming a conductor. Many would study conducting as part of a course at a music academy or conservatory. Others have graduated from being instrumentalists. In recent years, conducting competitions and scholarships have set many of today's major names on their way to success. More rarely, prominent instrumentalists – Vladimir Ashkenazy is a prime instance – have graduated into conducting with equal facility.

There are schools specifically for conducting though doing well in them is no guarantee of a career. The post of *répétiteur* at opera houses, someone who does the basic coaching of singers in a score, has been a stepping-off point for the likes of Sir Georg Solti and most of the major European and North American (but regrettably not British) orchestras still have the post of 'assistant conductor'. With the job of rehearsing the

Left: 'Family concert at Château Renescure', by an anonymous French or Flemish painter, nicely encapsulates the family group enjoying music together. The central figure, the conductor, is shown beating time to the music with a rolled up manuscript.

Below: Hans Schliessmann's 1901 caricature of Gustav Mahler portrays him as 'Ein Hypermoderner Dirigent' – an ultramodern conductor – conducting his Symphonia diabolica. Despite being a caricature, it gives a good idea of the multi-talented Mahler's ability.

Gustav MAHLER
(1860-1911)

In the world of music there have been few developments more remarkable than the growth of Mahler's reputation during the latter part of the present century. As Michael Kennedy has acutely observed: 'He championed the younger generation during his lifetime and became their idol after his death'. What makes it even more remarkable is the comparatively small output on which Mahler's formidable reputation rests: nine symphonies (ten if Cooke's version is included), *Das Lied von der Erde*, a cantata, a couple of song cycles, various songs and arrangements and a handful of chamber works. Mahler started to learn the piano at the age of six, gave his first public recital when he was ten, and five years later entered the Vienna Conservatoire. He started conducting in 1880, taking up appointments in Leipzig, Budapest, Hamburg and elsewhere. In 1897 he became director of the Vienna Court Opera, where he was responsible for a 'glorious decade' of operatic productions which set the seal on his reputation as the leading conductor of his day. After a dispute in 1907 he resigned and, despite failing health, made a triumphant début in the USA where, in 1909 he became conductor of the re-organised New York Philharmonic Orchestra. His work as a composer won him few admirers during his lifetime, but he took comfort in the conviction that 'my time will come'. How right he was. R.H.

Kapellmeister Kappelmann dirigirt seine Symphonie diabolica.

separate sections of the orchestra before they come together under the baton of the principal conductor, this is always a good grounding.

First and foremost, the role of the conductor is to unify the orchestra and the sound it creates, and also to set a clear beat for all the musicians to follow. The same number of bars must be at the same tempo, in approximately the same key and with the right dynamics.

Tempo is indicated with the right hand, through up, down and sideways movements corresponding to the composer's indications. The right (baton) hand also gestures strong accents and can signal entries to specific instruments, the left hand conveys 'interpretation': a gesture to indicate too loud or too soft, and all manner of subtle indications to the orchestra.

First and foremost, though, the conductor has four basic instructions to convey. The first, as mentioned, is tempo and the second, dynamics – the volume of sound. The third is *rubato*, changes from the fixed tempo: a little quicker here, a slight delay there, but always maintaining the basic pulse. Finally there is phrasing, which is much to do with understanding and feeling for what the composer wants: where to emphasise, where to stress.

There is much more, all adding up to why no two conductors will perform a work in precisely the same way, despite the notes, tempos, rhythms and dynamics all being carefully laid down by the composer. If there is one prerequisite of 'interpretation' it is surely that the music should flow and that its overall structure should remain intact. It is all very well bringing out the details of the score – it is part of the conductor's job – but this can become obsessive and lead to the indulging of 'harmonic corners'. There must be clarity and, naturally, the conductor must be able to instill a degree of discipline (although surely stop short of striking fear in his players!). It is also possible to 'over-interpret' and ruin the flow of the music with a surfeit of meaningful gestures. The best conductors get the results they want without this; indeed, it is true to say that you should not notice the best conductors until the end of the performance. Chances are they will not then have come between you and the music. P.H.

The conductor has become as important in modern times, at least to the publicist and the general public, as the composer. His role at first, as orchestras got larger, was simply to act as a time-beater to keep the orchestra together. With the advent of the romantic age and the greater possibilities of interpretation, the conductor added new dimensions to musical performance and the world became aware of how much a great conductor could enhance and vary a performance. From then on we didn't just listen to Beethoven's symphonies but to the interpretation by X or Y or Z; and recordings increased our ability to choose. The careers and achievements of fifty leading conductors are presented in detail in the following pages.

Claudio ABBADO (b. 1933) Italy

Born into a musical family – his father a violinist and teacher and his brother a composer and pianist – Claudio Abbado was taught piano by his father before entering the Milan Conservatory. In 1955, he left for the Vienna Academy of Music to study conducting and three years later won the coveted Koussevitzky prize. This led to conducting engagements throughout Italy and a spell teaching at the Parma Conservatory.

The breakthrough for Abbado came in 1963 with the winning of the Mitropoulos Prize and its five-month tenure with the New York Philharmonic. His reputation grew rapidly and in 1965 he conducted at the prestigious Salzburg Festival, the same year making his British début with the Hallé Orchestra. Renowned for his interpretations of opera as well as the orchestral repertoire, Abbado returned to Italy in 1969 to become resident conductor (later musical director) of the La Scala Orchestra in his native Milan.

Since 1966, Abbado has enjoyed a profitable relationship with the London Symphony Orchestra, including the first appearance by any British orchestra at the Salzburg Festival (1973). Additionally, he was appointed principal conductor of the Vienna Philharmonic in 1971. Recently, Abbado has made some notable appearances with the European Youth Orchestra, but has now relinquished his LSO post to concentrate on his new role with the Vienna State Opera.

Ernest ANSERMET (1883-1969) Switzerland

Best known for his work with the Orchestre de la Suisse Romande, which he founded in 1918, Ansermet began life as a mathematics professor, only turning to conducting after musical studies with Ernest Bloch, the composer, and the conductors Artur Nikisch and Felix Mottl. Renowned by his interpretations of Stravinsky's 'Russian' ballets and the music of Debussy and Ravel, Ansermet was much associated with Diaghilev's Ballets

Above: *The great Italian tradition in conducting, established by such figures as Toscanini, De Sabata and Giulini, is continued by Claudio Abbado, currently conducting with the Vienna State Opera.*

Russes between 1915 and 1923, with whom he made many guest appearances in Paris, London, Italy, Spain, South America and the USA from 1915 to 1923 after Stravinsky had brought them together. In 1918 he gave the first performance of Stravinsky's *L'Histoire du Soldat*. He was a considerable composer himself and a persistent opponent of the twelve-tone technique. After a brilliant list of recordings in early LP days he retired from conducting in 1967.

Sir John BARBIROLLI (1899-1970) England

Born in London (a fact which made his interpretation of Vaughan Williams's *London Symphony* very special indeed), Barbirolli studied at Trinity College, London, and then at the Royal Academy of Music until 1917. He had already made his début as a cellist in 1910 and in 1915 became a member of the Queen's Hall orchestra. His conducting career flourished from 1920 and in 1937 he replaced Toscanini as chief conductor of the New York Philharmonic. Six years later, in the midst of war, he returned to Britain to begin a long and productive association with Manchester's Hallé Orchestra. Barbirolli also conducted many other major orchestras and made enduring recordings of Brahms, Mahler and Italian opera, as well as music of his fellow-countrymen, Elgar, Delius and Vaughan Williams. He was knighted in 1949.

Sir Thomas BEECHAM (1879-1961) England

One of music's personalities, Sir Thomas Beecham's career has yielded a rich fund of anecdotes. He came from St Helens in Lancashire, a member of the famous pharmaceutical family. After studying at Oxford, he took up conducting locally in 1899, making his London début in 1905. He soon became known for his advocacy of new and unfamiliar music, as well as affectionate performances of Haydn, Mozart and Schubert. His greatest achievement was to bring the music of the then unknown Frederick Delius to the attention of concert-goers, a mission which reached fulfilment in the Delius Festival of 1929. Three years later, Beecham founded the London Philharmonic Orchestra and, during World War II, conducted widely in North America and Australia. Returning to Britain, he formed the Royal Philharmonic Orchestra in 1947 and with them enjoyed an active conducting career right up to his death. It included many early stereo recordings for the HMV label, including Delius interpretations which have never been surpassed.

Leonard BERNSTEIN (b. 1918) USA

Of Russian descent, America's most famous musician was born in Lawrence, Massachusetts. He studied piano at Harvard and, with the composer Walter Piston, composition, graduating in 1939. There were further studies at the Curtis Institute, although it was not as a classical musician that Bernstein was making a name but as a jazz pianist.

He became assistant to Serge Koussevitzky at the Boston Symphony, but achieved virtually overnight fame with his first major appearance with the New York Philharmonic in 1943. Bernstein received glowing reviews after taking over at short notice from a visiting conductor who had fallen ill.

Bernstein's relationship with the NYPO was a long and fruitful one: he was their chief conductor from 1958 until 1969, and all the time his composing career similarly flourished (most notably with *West Side Story, Candide, The Chichester Psalms* and the ballet *Fancy Free*).

More recently, Bernstein has been most active with Israel and Vienna Philharmonics, performing a repertoire that stretches from the Viennese classics through Brahms and Mahler (whose music he has always had an intuitive sympathy for) to Shostakovich. A strong believer in live concert recording, Bernstein's interpretations are seldom less than controversial: deeply intense to some, self-indulgent to others. Few other conductors have succeeded in exciting quite such extremes of admiration and antipathy.

Karl BÖHM (1894-1981) Austria

One of this century's finest conductors of the Austro-German classics, Karl Böhm was born in Graz and studied both music and law in Vienna. His conducting reputation was forged in leading European opera houses such as Dresden (1934-43) and Vienna, where

Above: *A handful of composers have managed to combine their creative work with the busy life of a conductor and become equally eminent in that role. One such man is Leonard Bernstein.*

Below: *Another leading conductor/composer is the Frenchman Pierre Boulez. He combines his enthusiasm for contemporary music with a firm grasp of older styles.*

Aaron COPLAND
(b. 1900)

Born in Brooklyn of Russian parents, Copland is the first American composer to have won a truly international reputation. His ballet scores *Billy the Kid, Rodeo* and *Appalachian Spring* have all won permanent places in the orchestral repertoire, while his fantasy based on Mexican tunes, *El Salon Mexico*, has become a firm favourite with audiences all over the world. Copland studied first with Rubin Goldmark and then (1921) with Nadia Boulanger in Paris. In a deliberate attempt to break free from an exclusively European tradition, many of his earlier works draw heavily on jazz idioms. There followed a more austere style, reminiscent of Schoenberg, but many of Copland's later compositions seem to reflect his determination to bridge the gap between modern music and popular taste. His works include a number of symphonic pieces, an opera *The Tender Land* (1954), several suites, some chamber music, including a duo for flute and piano written in memory of Stravinsky, songs, solo piano pieces and music written for the cinema, including *Of Mice and Men* and *Our Town*. He now prefers conducting to composing, and has done a great deal as a writer, teacher and lecturer to promote American music overseas, winning many honours and awards in recognition of his work. R.H.

he enjoyed two fruitful periods between 1943-5 and 1954-6.

However, Böhm will be best remembered for his many great performances with the Vienna Philharmonic, particularly in Mozart (including the operas), Beethoven and Wagner (a memorable *Tristan*).

Pierre BOULEZ (b. 1925) France

As well as being a major contemporary composer, Boulez has also attained high status as an interpreter, particularly of Stravinsky and the music of his teacher, Olivier Messiaen. There have also been great performances of the 'second Viennese school' – Berg, Schoenberg and Webern – and, more surprisingly, some outstanding Wagner productions, including the *Ring*.

Born in Montbrison, Boulez's studies with

Messiaen were at the Paris Conservatory from where he emerged with the *Premier Prix* in 1946. He has been principal conductor of the New York Philharmonic (1969-77) and of the BBC Symphony, and from 1977 Director of IRCAM (Institute Recherche et Coordination Acoustique et Musique), one of the most active organisations supporting and encouraging contemporary music.

Sir Adrian BOULT (1889-1983) England

Born in Chester into a shipping family, Boult was educated at Westminster School and Christ Church, Oxford, where he gained a Doctorate of Music. After studying with Nikisch at the Leipzig Conservatory during 1912-13, he joined the staff of the Royal Opera House Covent Garden in 1914, making his conducting debut four years later. In

1920, his unequalled affinity for British music was established by a performance of Elgar's Second Symphony which was the first to get to the heart of this great work. There was a six-year spell with the Birmingham City Orchestra between 1924 and 1930, followed by the most significant appointment of his career, musical director of the BBC. At the time, the BBC Symphony Orchestra was being formed and, after its first, outstanding concerts under Boult's baton, he was appointed its chief conductor. Through Boult's efforts, the BBC SO became one of Europe's finest bands and attracted many notable guest conductors.

When the BBC ungraciously and unwisely enforced retirement on Boult in 1950, he joined the London Philharmonic and spent thirty more glorious years conducting this and the London Symphony orchestra.

Above: *Colin Davis, knighted in 1980 for his services to British music, has made his mark as a Mozartian and as a champion of such divergent composers as Berlioz and Tippett.*

Right: *The Hungarian conductor Antal Dorati has worked with leading orchestras in Europe and the USA, and made recordings of the complete Haydn symphonies.*

Joseph JOACHIM
(1831-1907)

Hungarian violinist, conductor and composer who at a very early age was trained by the leader of the Pest Opera Orchestra, and whose exceptional talent was recognised by Mendelssohn. After making his début in London in 1844 he returned to Leipzig for further study with Mendelssohn and David. In 1849 he became leader of the Weimar Court Orchestra where Liszt had settled, and four years later he accepted the post of *Konzertmeister* and solo violinist to the Hanoverian court, where he remained until 1866. During this time he made regular appearances in England at the Monday Popular Concerts, at the Crystal Palace and provincial concert halls. He also married the contralto Amalie Weiss, but the marriage was not a success and the breakdown led to a breach with his close friend Brahms, who had earlier dedicated his violin concerto to Joachim. In 1868 he went to Berlin as the head of the newly established *Hochschule für ausübende Tonkunst*, and formed the Joachim Quartet the following year. His interpretations of the Beethoven violin concerto and of Bach's solo sonatas were regarded by his contemporaries as models, and his technical mastery was unsurpassed. His own compositions had much in common with the music of Schumann, although the influence of Brahms can also be clearly discerned. R.H.

Such is Boult's association with British music – he gave the premières of a notable array of works by Bliss, Delius, Holst, Ireland and Vaughan Williams – it is often overlooked that he also introduced a great deal of new European music to British audiences: the first London performances of Mahler's Ninth Symphony, Berg's *Wozzeck* and Schoenberg's Variations for Orchestra.

Sir Colin DAVIS (b. 1927) England

After studying the clarinet at the Royal College of Music, Davis conducted the Kalmar Orchestra and the Chelsea Opera Group in his early twenties. An appearance at the new Royal Festival Hall followed in 1952. After touring with a Russian ballet company and conducting opera at Oxford and Cambridge, he was appointed assistant conductor of the BBC Scottish Orchestra in 1957. There were also appearances in North America, with the Canadian Broadcasting Corporation Symphony Orchestra in 1959 and the Minneapolis Orchestra.

Appointed music director of London's Sadler's Wells in 1961, he held the post for four years before joining the English Chamber Orchestra as principal conductor. In 1967 came the conductorship of the BBC Symphony Orchestra, then the music directorship of Covent Garden Opera.

Davis names Mozart and Stravinsky as his favourite composers. He has made many fine recordings of their music and of Britten, Berlioz and Tippett. Recently he has been active with the Concertgebouw Orchestra, Amsterdam, and the Dresden Staatskapelle.

Antal DORATI (b. 1906) Hungary

Born in Budapest, Dorati studied at its Academy of Music with Bartók and Kodály. He first conducted in 1918 and, after World War II, applied for American citizenship. His US début came in 1948 with the Minneapolis Symphony.

A fine arranger as well as conductor, Dorati was chief conductor of the BBC Symphony from 1963 to 1967 and, during the seventies, achieved a notable gramophone first by recording for the first time all 104 symphonies of Haydn for Decca. Most of Dorati's recent work has been done with the Sinfonia Hungarica in Germany.

Charles DUTOIT (b. 1936) Switzerland

At Lausanne Conservatory (the town of his birth), Dutoit studied first violin and theory and then conducting. He obtained a diploma in the latter after a period in Geneva. Further study encompassed viola and instrumentation, while his conducting skills were refined under the guidance of Alceo Galliera and, at Tanglewood, with Charles Munch. Back in Switzerland, amateur conducting engagements came in the late fifties and early sixties and, in 1964, Dutoit was appointed second conductor of the Berne Symphony Orchestra, succeeding Paul Kletzki as its principal conductor three years later.

During the seventies, Dutoit's reputation increased throughout Europe, notably for his interpretations of Stravinsky. However, there is no doubt that his finest work is now coming with the Montreal Symphony Orchestra, which he has conducted in an outstanding series of recordings of, among others Ravel, Respighi and Berlioz, as well as Stravinsky, for the Decca label.

Wilhelm FURTWÄNGLER (1886-1954)
Germany

It was as an interpreter of the German classics that Furtwängler became one of the dominant figures of twentieth-century music. His career started in 1905, as *répétiteur* at the Breslau Stadttheater. A first concert in 1906 included nothing less than the Bruckner Ninth and in the ensuing three years Furtwängler developed his conducting skills under Felix Mottl at the Munich Court Opera. After a year as third conductor at the Strasbourg Opera, his first major appointment was as director of the Lübeck Opera between 1911 and 1915. This was followed by five years at the Mannheim Opera and, after concerts in Frankfurt and Berlin, he succeeded Artur Nikisch as conductor of both the Berlin Philharmonic and the Leipzig Gewandhaus Orchestras.

Furtwängler's interpretations were stimulating and controversial and reached an even wider audience in 1926 when he made his first recording, with the Berlin Philharmonic, of Beethoven's Fifth Symphony. The next year he was appointed music director of the Vienna Philharmonic, and in 1928 conducted one of the great performances of *Tristan* at Bayreuth.

1933 saw his first clash with the Nazis as, first, he protested about the purge of Jewish musicians and, second, refused to give the Nazi salute at concerts. When Hindemith's *Mathis der Maler* was banned the following year, Furtwängler supported the composer and resigned all his posts.

An invitation to succeed Toscanini as chief conductor of the New York Philharmonic had to be withdrawn after protests within the United States and, although he conducted at London's Covent Garden in 1937, Furtwängler was effectively confined to Germany, where he spent the war years composing two symphonies before fleeing to Switzerland in 1945.

He gave his first post-war concerts in 1947 and in 1950 revived Wagner's *Ring* at La Scala, Milan. The reopening of the Bayreuth Theatre was marked with a performance of Beethoven's Ninth Symphony (currently on record) and in 1952, Furtwängler regained his directorship of the Berlin Philharmonic. Although severely ill during 1953, he came back to conduct nine different orchestras between March and September and 1954, including appearances at Bayreuth, Salzburg and Lucerne festivals.

His last years were marred by increasing deafness. On his death in 1955 his post with the Berlin Philharmonic was taken over by Karajan.

Above: *The Dutch conductor Bernard Haitink left the great Concertgebouw Orchestra of Amsterdam in 1987, after a performance of Mahler's 9th, to take over as artistic director at Covent Garden.*

Carlo Maria GIULINI (b. 1914) Italy

Born in Barletta, Giulini studied viola and conducting at the Academy of St Cecilia in Rome, then continued his tuition in the latter with the composer Alfredo Casella. However, it was not until after World War II that he secured his first appointments of note, first working for Italian radio and then becoming conductor of the Radio Milan Orchestra in 1950. While in Milan, Giulini made his La Scala début during the 1951-2 season and his reputation as a conductor not only of Italian opera, but also of Mozart, grew rapidly.

His recordings of Verdi and Mozart, made during the 1960s for HMV, remain among the very finest in the catalogue and more recently Giulini has been working with the Berlin, Chicago and Vienna Philharmonics in Beethoven, Bruckner and Mahler. During his tenure as chief conductor, Giulini was responsible for greatly improving and revitalising the Los Angeles Philharmonic.

Bernard HAITINK (b. 1929)
The Netherlands

Haitink first studied conducting under Felix Hupka in his native Amsterdam, then with Ferdinand Leitner where his talents earned him in 1955 the post of second conductor with the Netherlands Radio Union. This gave him co-responsibility for four Dutch radio orchestras. His relationship with Amsterdam's Concertgebouw Orchestra began in 1956 and, after a short period as principal conductor of the Netherlands Radio Phil-

Johannes BRAHMS
(1833-97)

Son of a double-bass player in the Hamburg State Theatre, Brahms was taught to play the violin by his father and took piano lessons from Otto Cossel, making his public début at the age of fifteen. During his early years he made a meagre living by playing in taverns and dance halls, and it was not until Joachim gave him letters of introduction to Liszt and Schumann that his career as a professional composer started to unfold. In 1860 he signed a manifesto against the 'new music' methods of Liszt and his followers, thereby sowing the seeds of the fruitless and bitter controversy between himself and Wagner. In 1862 he first visited Vienna, where he held various musical appointments and spent most of the rest of his life. Brahms never forgot his humble origins and made few attempts to overcome his lack of social poise, cultivating instead an uncouth manner and untidy appearance as he grew older. He destroyed a great deal of his work but what remains is impressive enough: he was a master of every form except opera and his music represents a perfect marriage between romantic expression and classical structure. His orchestral and chamber music, his sonatas, songs and organ works may not have heralded a new dawn, but they certainly brought the old era to an overwhelming and triumphant conclusion. R.H.

harmonic, he became co-conductor with Jochum of the Concertgebouw in 1961.

With Jochum's departure in 1964 Haitink became its sole conductor and, three years later, added the posts of principal conductor and artistic advisor to the London Philharmonic to his duties. He proved himself an outstanding interpreter of Mahler and Bruckner and, surprisingly perhaps, of Debussy and Ravel. His talents for opera were also recognised and, in 1972, Haitink made the first of many appearances at the Glyndebourne Opera, conducting Mozart's *Die Entführung aus dem Serail*. He became the artistic director at Glyndebourne in 1979.

With a performance of Mahler's Ninth Symphony, Haitink finally parted company with the Concertgebouw in 1987 to take over as artistic director at Covent Garden.

Above: *The Russian conductor Jascha Horenstein came back into favour in the 1960s with some fine recordings of the Mahler symphonies, made on his return to Europe after a wartime spent in America.*

Jascha HORENSTEIN (1899-1973) Russia

Born in Kiev, Horenstein's career took off in Vienna, in the time of Richard Strauss, Felix Weingartner and Wilhelm Furtwängler. He made his conducting début with the Vienna Symphony Orchestra and, throughout his life, came to conduct most of the world's major orchestras. There were also notable opera productions at Covent Garden, La Scala and the Berlin Staatsoper. He was responsible for the first French performance of Janáček's *From the House of the Dead* in 1955, and the American première of Busoni's *Dr Faustus* in 1964. However, he will best be remembered for his interpretations of Mahler, Bruckner and the 'second Viennese school' of Berg, Schoenberg and Webern.

Eugen JOCHUM (1902-1987) Germany

Born in Babenhausern, Jochum studied piano and organ at the Augsburg Conservatory from 1914 to 1922, then went on to spend two more years learning composition at the Munich Academy of Music. His first professional posts were as *répétiteur* in Munich and then Kiel, following which he was invited to conduct at Mannheim and Duisburg. Jochum's first major appointment was as director of the Hamburg State Opera from 1934 to 1945, and from 1949 he conducted the Munich Radio Orchestra. As an interpreter, he excelled in the Austro-German clas-

sics and towards the end of his career recorded a fine Beethoven cycle for the HMV label.

Herbert von KARAJAN (b. 1908) Austria

Arguably the most famous conductor of the past twenty-five years, Karajan was born in Salzburg into a family which had both Austrian and Macedonian roots. After four years of piano lessons, the eight-year-old Karajan began studies at the Salzburg Mozarteum, and was giving piano recitals at fourteen. In 1925, he went to Vienna to study at

Below: *Herbert von Karajan took over the Berlin Philharmonic in 1955 after the death of Furtwängler and built a musical empire of his own with a staggering schedule of performances and recordings.*

the Technical High School, the University and the Academy of Music. At his graduation in 1928, he conducted the Academy orchestra in Rossini's *William Tell* overture and the following year gave his first concert with the Mozarteum Orchestra in Salzburg. An appointment as conductor at the Ulm Stadttheater quickly followed and in 1935, Karajan became the youngest musical director in Germany when he secured that post, and that of head of opera at Aachen shortly after conducting a memorable performance there of Beethoven's *Fidelio*. He successfully conducted the opera again in 1937, this time at the Berlin Staatsoper and his work with this company was to continue through the war years. From 1941, he also took charge of the Berlin Staatskapelle.

Prevented from conducting in the immediate post-war years, he revived his career in Vienna and Salzburg, then conducted in Buenos Aires and Milan. In 1951, he collaborated with Wieland Wagner in staging the reborn Bayreuth Festival.

With the death of Furtwängler in 1954, and an American tour which Karajan conducted with great brilliance, the Berlin Philharmonic Orchestra appointed him as conductor for life, a relationship which has continued – with one much-publicised disagreement – for over thirty years, during which Karajan has perfected the beauty of tone as well as the precision for which the Berliners are renowned.

Karajan has also been very active in Vienna, where he directed the State Opera from 1957 to 1963 and has frequently worked with the Vienna Philharmonic Orchestra. Since 1967, he has conducted at the Salzburg Summer Festivals, and at the Easter Festivals (which he founded). He takes courses for young conductors in Berlin and, in 1968, founded the International Karajan Foundation which finances competitions for youth orchestras and conductors and the training of instrumentalists.

Over the years, Karajan has dominated the catalogue of Germany's Deutsche Grammophon record label and, more recently, has built up a multi-media organisation around himself and his orchestra. His repertoire stretches from Bach to Webern, although solidly based on the German classics.

Rudolf KEMPE (1910-76) Germany

The oboe was Kempe's instrument: after a childhood spent in a small town near Dresden, he became first oboe with the Leipzig Gewandhaus Orchestra in 1929. He turned to conducting in 1936 but World War II slowed his career and it was not until 1949 that he secured the major position of director of the Dresden State Opera. After three years there, he moved to Munich in a similar capacity.

The mid-fifties found Kempe in New York, conducting at the Metropolitan Opera and he was to enjoy considerable success at most of

Above: *The German conductor Rudolf Kempe died in 1976 leaving a fine legacy of recordings, notably those of the music of Richard Strauss, including a highly praised set of the orchestral works.*

the world's major opera houses: there were many successful visits to London's Covent Garden and Kempe had a profitable period as music director of the Royal Philharmonic Orchestra. A technically excellent conductor, Kempe's repertoire was wide, but it is without doubt his peerless interpretations of Richard Strauss's operas and tone-poems which will be best remembered.

István KERTÉSZ (1929-73) Hungary

Following violin and piano lessons as a child, Kertész continued to study violin and composition at the Franz Liszt Academy in his home city of Budapest, where his teachers included the composer Zoltan Kodály. A significant influence on his development as a conductor was Otto Klemperer, who was in charge at the Budapest Opera during Kertész's youth.

Kertész himself joined that company in 1955 after a two-year period as resident conductor in Györ, but left Hungary for Germany after the 1956 uprising.

First music director at Augsburg (1958-63), and then Cologne, he made his British début with the Royal Liverpool Philharmonic in 1960, and toured the USA for the first time the following year with the Hamburg Radio Symphony Orchestra.

Kertész achieved some notable firsts: he introduced Benjamin Britten's *War Requiem* and *Billy Budd* to Germany and Austria and

made the first complete recordings in the west of Bartók's *Bluebeard's Castle* and his mentor Kodály's *Háry János*. His cycle of the Dvořák symphonies for the UK Decca label remains one of the very finest ever made.

Erich KLEIBER (1890-1956) Austria

Although born in Vienna, Kleiber studied in Prague and went on to become chorus master of the city's German Opera. His first major post was as director of the Berlin Staatsoper, which he held from 1923 to 1935, finally quitting as a protest against the Nazis. He then lived principally in Argentina, where his son Carlos – a notable conductor today – was born. A great Beethoven interpreter, several of Erich Kleiber's performances of the symphonies continue to be available on record.

Otto KLEMPERER (1885-1973) Germany

One of the greatest conductors of this century, Klemperer enjoyed a long if not entirely untroubled career that culminated in a glorious Indian summer with London's Philharmonia Orchestra, and one which yielded many unforgettable concerts and great recordings, most still available on the HMV label.

Born in Breslau, he was first taught by his mother then studied in Frankfurt and Berlin. He became acquainted with Gustav Mahler and it was on the latter's recommendation that Klemperer was appointed conductor at the German National Theatre in Prague during 1907. Klemperer's reputation was made in opera, at Hamburg, Strasbourg, Cologne and Wiesbaden, where his revelatory productions of *Fidelio* and *Don Giovanni* were acclaimed. This led to him becoming

Below: *The brilliant career of Hungarian conductor István Kertész was curtailed when he was drowned when swimming on holiday in Israel. His fine recordings with the LSO on Decca are still treasured.*

*Anton BRUCKNER
(1824-96)*

The life and work of Anton Bruckner are evidence enough that simplicity of manner and of spirit should never be confused with simplicity of mind, for while the composer remained a simple countryman all his life, his great symphonies, with their complexity of organisation and of structure, reveal a very high degree of musical sophistication and insight. Although he was the son of a village schoolmaster and showed early musical talent, he received no formal training before the age of eleven. He joined the choir of St Florian's monastery and in 1840 went to Linz to train as a teacher, returning to the monastery as an assistant teacher in 1845. His spare time was devoted to composition and to the organ, of which he became a master. In 1855 he was appointed organist of Linz Cathedral, and took lessons in counterpoint and harmony to such good effect that he eventually became a professor in these subjects at the Vienna Conservatoire. His determination to master the art of composition in all its aspects inevitably made him a late starter, and recognition did not come until the last years of his life. In all, Bruckner wrote eleven symphonies (one incomplete), a great deal of choral music on the same scale and of the same grandeur as his orchestral works, and two pieces for string quintet. R.H.

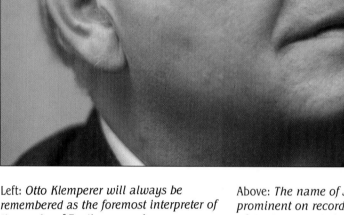

Left: *Otto Klemperer will always be remembered as the foremost interpreter of the works of Beethoven and as a conductor who worked closely with Mahler.*

Above: *The name of Josef Krips was prominent on recordings in the early days of the LP, notably in the classic Viennese repertoire. He was conductor of the Vienna State Opera, 1933-8.*

chief conductor of the new 'people's opera' in Berlin, the Kroll, where his innovatory productions, especially of Wagner, provoked both praise and opposition.

However, within two weeks of Hitler's accession to power, Klemperer along with many other Jewish intellectuals (although he had converted to Catholicism in 1917), left Germany, first for Switzerland and then the United States. While there, he miraculously survived a brain tumour, but was left partly paralysed for the rest of his life.

Returning to Europe in 1946, Klemperer took over at the Budapest Opera, a successful if often stormy tenure which lasted until 1950. The producer, Walter Legge, who had founded the Philharmonia Orchestra in London, persuaded Klemperer to become its principal conductor in 1954 and so began the most productive period of his career, despite illness and injury (he was badly burned in a fire). In 1961, Klemperer made his Covent Garden début – at the age of seventy-six! – conducting *Fidelio* and, despite increasing physical restrictions, went on conducting and recording for several more years.

Although his interpretations were always controversial – he was renowned for slow tempos and made clarity of sound his first priority, well above tonal beauty – their integrity could never be doubted. He was at his best in Beethoven, Mozart, Brahms, Schubert and the symphonies and song cycles of Mahler.

He was also a considerable composer and recorded several of his own works.

Serge KOUSSEVITZKY (1874-1951) **Russia**

Koussevitzky is best remembered now not so much as an outstanding conductor, but for the Natalie Koussevitzky Foundation which he established in 1942 as a memorial to his first wife and which, by 1965, had commissioned no less than 135 new works from contemporary composers. These include some of the major compositions of this century, Bartók's *Concerto for Orchestra* and Messiaen's *Turangalîla* Symphony among them.

A virtuoso on the double-bass, Koussevitzky studied in Moscow before joining the Russian Imperial Orchestra. He later toured Europe as a double-bass soloist before forming his own orchestra and taking up conducting in the United States with the Boston Symphony Orchestra, which he conducted for twenty-five years up to 1949.

Clemens KRAUSS (1893-1954) **Austria**

Born in Vienna, Krauss studied at its conservatoire and began his conducting career at various provincial opera houses in both Germany and Austria. His first major post was with the Vienna State Opera (1922), followed by responsibility for the Museum Concerts at Frankfurt in 1924. Between 1929 and 1936 Krauss was successively director of the Vienna State and then Berlin State Operas, before moving on to Munich. He enjoyed a close association with Richard Strauss which included providing the libretto for Strauss's opera *Capriccio*.

Josef KRIPS (1902-74) **Austria**

While a violinist in the Vienna Volksoper Orchestra, Krips became a pupil of Felix Weingartner and started his conducting

---

Vladimir ASHKENAZY
(b. 1937)

Gifted Russian pianist and conductor. His parents were both professional pianists so he was inducted at an early age, afterwards studying at the Moscow Conservatory. His career was launched by a series of competitive achievements – Second Prize in the International Chopin Competition in Warsaw in 1955; First Prize in the Queen Elizabeth of Belgium International Competition in Brussels in 1956; and joint First Prize (with John Ogdon) in the Tchaikovsky International Competition in Moscow in 1962. He had been to the USA in 1958 and came to England in 1963. As befits a notable prizewinner

he has a remarkable technical control but adds to this the great intelligence and sensibility that has put him in the ranks of the finest pianists of this century. A great exponent of Chopin but equally fine in Beethoven (with recordings of all the piano concertos) and a persuasive interpreter of Scriabin and other modern composers. He gradually moved into conducting with especially fine interpretations of Russian composers but also covering a wide repertoire; and in 1981 he was appointed principal guest conductor of the London Philharmonic Orchestra. P.G.

Pyotr Ilyich TCHAIKOVSKY
(1840-93)

The story of Tchaikovsky's life is as colourful and as dramatic as his music. Born of a well-to-do provincial family, he read law before joining the St Petersburg Conservatory to study music. In 1866 he went to Moscow where he was appointed professor of harmony at the new Conservatory under Nikolai Rubinstein. Here he completed his First Symphony and an opera (The Voyevoda). Three more operas and his ever popular B flat minor piano concerto followed, then in 1877 he entered into a disastrous marriage with one of his pupils, which lasted exactly a week and brought him to the brink of suicide. But shortly afterwards his wealthy patroness, Madame von Meck, gave Tchaikovsky an annual allowance which enabled him to give up teaching, to concentrate on composition and to travel extensively. There followed a relatively happy and fruitful period during which many of his major works appeared, although his moods continued to fluctuate between extreme elation and deep depression without apparent cause. Undoubtedly a repressed homosexuality was at the heart of his tempestuous nature and probably led to his final ruin, for recent evidence suggests that he took his own life to avoid scandal and did not die accidentally after drinking contaminated water, as in the accepted version. R.H.

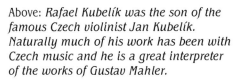

Above: *Rafael Kubelík was the son of the famous Czech violinist Jan Kubelík. Naturally much of his work has been with Czech music and he is a great interpreter of the works of Gustav Mahler.*

career in 1921. In 1924, he took up an appointment at the opera house at Aussig in Czechoslovakia but, after only a year there, moved on to the Dortmund Opera and then to the Hoftheater in Karlsrühe.

What should have been the pinnacle of his early career – the post of permanent conductor with the Vienna State Opera and a professorship at the Vienna Academy – was abruptly terminated by the war. But, after 1945, Krips was able to play a major role in the revival of Viennese musical life.

He conducted the London Symphony Orchestra between 1950 and 1954, making his American début in 1953. This led to an appointment as musical director of the Buffalo Philharmonic and the conducting of many Beethoven festivals both in New York and London. Although a Beethoven specialist, Krips also recorded a notable Schubert Ninth Symphony for the UK Decca company.

Rafael KUBELÍK (b. 1914) Czechoslovakia

After studying at the Prague Conservatory, Kubelík made his conducting début with the Czech Philharmonic in 1934, becoming its chief conductor between 1942 and 1948 after a spell at the National Theatre in Brno. In 1950, he was appointed principal conductor of the Chicago Symphony and a return to Europe in 1953 was followed with the post of music director at Covent Garden from 1955 to 1958. Also an ambitious composer – Kubelík has an opera and a choral symphony to his name – from 1961 he enjoyed a very success-

Above: *Lorin Maazel was born in France of American parents but went to the USA as a child and showed an early musical talent. He had conducted several leading American orchestras before he was twelve.*

ful period as conductor of the Bavarian Radio Symphony Orchestra, recording a memorable Mahler cycle with them.

James LEVINE (b. 1943) USA

Born in Cincinatti, Levine made his début as a pianist with the city's orchestra at the age of ten. He went on to study piano and conducting at the Juilliard School in New York and in 1964 was asked to become assistant conductor of the Cleveland Orchestra by its director, George Szell. Levine stayed with the Cleveland for six years, simultaneously becoming director of the University Circle Orchestra.

In 1971, he made his Metropolitan Opera début in New York with Puccini's *Tosca*, and the Met made him its principal conductor in 1973. Additionally during the seventies, Levine assumed the directorships of two American festivals and, in Britain, conducted the Welsh National Opera (a début with Verdi's *Aida* in 1970) and at Covent Garden in 1973. A memorable *Otello* followed in Hamburg in 1975 and Levine has subsequently worked with both the Vienna and the Berlin Philharmonic Orchestra. His repertoire stretches from Mozart to Mahler and the 'second Viennese school', but opera remains the core of his work.

Lorin MAAZEL (b. 1930) USA

A musical prodigy, at the age of only nine, Maazel conducted the Interlochen Orchestra at the New York World's Fair. Born in Paris to

American parents, he was educated in the United States and followed his New York début by sharing a concert with Leopold Stokowski at the Hollywood Bowl. Two years later, Toscanini invited him to conduct the NBC Symphony Orchestra and the precocious Maazel subsequently led the New York Philharmonic and the Cleveland Orchestras.

While studying at Pittsburgh University – not music, but languages, mathematics and philosophy – Maazel became a violinist with the Pittsburgh Symphony, later becoming an apprentice conductor with the orchestra during 1949-50. The next year, Serge Koussevitzky invited him to the Berkshire Music Center at Tanglewood as conducting fellow and Maazel combined this appointment with studies of Baroque music in Italy.

His reputation quickly spread to Europe and, in 1960, he became the first American (and the youngest ever conductor) to perform at Bayreuth. For a time, Maazel was associated principal conductor of London's Philharmonia under Otto Klemperer and has been variously artistic director of the West Berlin Opera and music director of the Berlin Radio Symphony, and conducted the major orchestras of London, Paris and Vienna.

More recently, he has taken the Cleveland Orchestra on several major international tours and appeared at festivals such as Edinburgh, Lucerne and Salzburg, as well as the Metropolitan Opera in New York and La Scala, Milan.

Sir Charles MACKERRAS (b. 1925) Australia

Mackerras studied at the Sydney Conservatory before becoming first oboe of the Sydney Symphony Orchestra. He began his conducting career in Australia before coming to Britain in 1946. During 1947 and 1948, he furthered his studies with the eminent Czech conductor Vaclav Talich in Prague and also developed an affinity for Czech music, particularly the operas of Janáček. Back in Britain, Mackerras was engaged by the Sadler's Wells Opera Company, later becoming its principal conductor. He has enjoyed worldwide success principally as an opera conductor, and his work with Janáček has been enthusiastically acknowledged by the Czechs themselves.

Sir Neville MARRINER (b. 1924) England

Although he has broadened his musical base of late, Marriner remains best known for his work with the Academy of St Martin-in-the-Fields, the chamber orchestra he founded in 1959.

Lincoln-born, Marriner's studies at the Royal College of Music were interrupted by war service. After a year at the Paris Conservatory, the immediate post-war years saw him teaching at Eton College. He then became second violin in the Martin String Quartet, later co-forming the Jacobean Ensemble with early music specialist Thurston Dart. From 1949 to 1959, Marriner taught violin at the Royal College of Music in London, as well as playing with the London Symphony and Philharmonia orchestras, but his conducting ambitions had been fired and lessons were taken with Pierre Monteux in the United States.

The Academy of St Martin-in-the-Fields, with its repertoire of Bach, Vivaldi, Haydn and

Above: *Zubin Mehta left a possible medical career in India to study the double bass and conducting in Vienna. Since when he has become a leading international conductor and recording artist.*

Mozart, provided the ideal vehicle for Marriner's conducting talents, although he remained principal second violin with the LSO until 1968.

In 1969, he became music director of the Los Angeles Chamber Orchestra, and for three years (1975-7) organised London's South Bank Summer Music Festivals. Much of Marriner's recent work has been with the Minnesota Orchestra, of which he has been music director since 1978.

Zubin MEHTA (b. 1936) India

Son of the violinist Mehlia Mehta, it was from his father that the Bombay-born Mehta received his first tuition. Conducting studies were pursued in Vienna from 1954, and rewarded when he won the competition for young conductors in Liverpool, England. In 1959, Mehta guest-conducted the Vienna Philharmonic, an orchestra he has been associated with ever since. His career has taken him throughout Europe and the United States and in 1961 he became music director of the Los Angeles Philharmonic for a highly successful period.

Dmitri MITROPOULOS (1896-1960) Greece

Athens Conservatory, Brussels and Berlin were where Mitropoulos learnt his trade, along with five years on the staff of the Berlin Opera. He then returned to his native Athens to take over as conductor of its municipal orchestra.

Back in Berlin, he made his conducting début there in 1930 and, in 1936, went to the United States as guest conductor of the Boston Symphony Orchestra. The next year, he took the post of conductor with the Minneapolis Symphony, a tenure which lasted until 1949 when he joined the New York Philharmonic, becoming its music director in 1950.

It was with these two great American orchestras that Mitropoulos's lasting reputation was made. He successfully introduced many new works into their repertoires, making a pioneering recording of Shostakovich's Tenth Symphony in 1954. Mitropoulos also broke new ground with concert performances of the great operas, and made many memorable appearances at New York's Metropolitan Opera. He became an American citizen in 1946.

Pierre MONTEUX (1875-1964) France

Renowned as the conductor who gave the first performances of virtually all the great ballets commissioned by Diaghilev for his Ballets Russes, Monteux hailed from Paris and studied violin and composition at the conservatory there, winning the *premier prix* for violin in 1896. After a spell playing viola in the Colonne Orchestra, Monteux began conducting for Diaghilev in 1911 and in the ensu-

Below: *Neville Marriner had the best of all groundings as an orchestral violinist before he rose to fame with the Academy of St-Martin-in-the-Fields, London, which he organised in 1959.*

ing years gave the premières of Stravinsky's *Petrouchka* and *The Rite of Spring*, Ravel's *Daphnis et Chloé* and Debussy's *Jeux*. He conducted all over the world, but most specifically as principal conductor of the San Francisco Symphony Orchestra from 1936 to 1952. Although best remembered for his performances of the music of his fellow-countrymen, Debussy and Ravel, as well as Stravinsky, Monteux also had a fine feel for the German repertoire.

Yevgeni MRAVINSKY (1906-88) **Russia**

Legendary conductor of the Leningrad Philharmonic right up to his recent death, Mravinsky was born in the city and graduated from the conducting class at the conservatory in 1931. After winning the All-Union Conductors' Competition in Moscow in 1938, he returned to Leningrad to take up the conductorship of its orchestra and, over the years, built it up to be the finest in the Soviet Union, and one of the very best in the world.

Mravinsky was Shostakovich's favourite conductor of his works and gave the premières of several of the fifteen symphonies. The Eighth was dedicated to him by the composer, and memorably played by the Leningrad Philharmonic under Mravinsky at London's Royal Festival Hall in 1960. It is a pity that the West did not get to hear more of both Mravinsky and his orchestra and there are, sadly, comparatively few recordings to remember him by.

Charles MUNCH (1891-1968) **France**

Munch studied at the conservatory in his home town of Strasbourg before going to

Below: *Pierre Monteux will ever be remembered as the director of such important premières as* Petrouchka, Le Sacre de Printemps, Le Rossignol, Daphnis et Chloé *and* Jeux.

Paris and Berlin for tuition in the violin. He returned to Strasbourg to teach violin from 1919 to 1925, additionally leading the city's orchestra. He became leader of the Leipzig Gewandhaus Orchestra in 1926, making his Paris début as conductor in 1932. His finest work, however, was done with the Boston Symphony Orchestra, where he became conductor in 1949.

Arthur NIKISCH (1855-1922) **Hungary**

One of the most revered conductors of the late nineteenth/early twentieth centuries, Nikisch first learnt violin in Vienna and played in the Court Orchestra there from 1874 to 1877. But by 1878, he was conducting at the Leipzig Opera, spending ten years there before taking up a four-year tenure with the Boston Symphony Orchestra. Returning to Europe in 1893, he joined the Budapest Opera, then went on to conduct both the Leipzig Gewandhaus and Berlin Philharmonic Orchestras to great acclaim.

Eugene ORMANDY (1899-1985) **Hungary**

Born in Budapest, Ormandy was taught violin by his father, going on to study the instrument at the city's Royal Academy of Music. He graduated in 1917, becoming first violin in the Blüthner Orchestra in Berlin. In 1921, he emigrated to the United States, eventually becoming an American citizen, and after ten years in various posts was appointed conductor of the Minneapolis Symphony Orchestra. In 1938, he began a famous relationship with the Philadelphia Orchestra, becoming its chief conductor and continuing to head the orchestra for the rest of his life.

Below: *Eugene Ormandy had much to live up to when he succeeded Leopold Stokowski as conductor of the Philadelphia Orchestra, but in 42 seasons he built up an equal reputation.*

*Emmanuel CHABRIER
(1841-94)*

Not a one-work man but two – the evocative and brilliantly orchestrated rhapsody *España*, which he wrote after a visit to Spain in 1883, and the delightful *Marche Joyeuse*, guaranteed to add sparkle to the dullest of orchestral programmes. Chabrier was a largely self-taught pianist and composer who included among his friends Manet, Verlaine and fellow-musicians Duparc, d'Indy and Fauré. He remained a civil servant with the Ministry of the Interior until he was thirty, and then became assistant choirmaster to Lamoureux in Paris. It was a performance of Wagner's *Tristan und Isolde* at Munich which led to his decision to devote the rest of his life entirely to music, although his passion for Wagner was curiously at odds with his own musical temperament which was full of verve, wit and spontaneity. He wrote two operettas and a remarkable comic opera *Le Roi malgré lui*, as well as two choral pieces, some piano music and a number of songs. His work was greatly admired by later French composers, including Satie and Ravel, who freely acknowledged a considerable debt to him. The latter years of Chabrier's life were overshadowed by a mental collapse which led to his death at the comparatively early age of fifty-three. R.H.

Above: *Seiji Ozawa is the first Japanese conductor to build an international reputation as an interpreter of Western music, making his mark latterly with the famous Boston Symphony Orchestra.*

Below: *André Previn was a jazz pianist and a film composer in the USA before he had the temerity to come to Britain to forge a career as a classical conductor, his triumphs mainly achieved with the LSO.*

Above: *The latest public favourite and a brilliant conductor is Simon Rattle who has preferred to mould the City of Birmingham Orchestra into a superb unit rather than accept more glamorous posts.*

Seiji OZAWA (b. 1935) Japan

Although Japan has produced a number of famous instrumentalists in recent times, Ozawa remains by far the most successful of conductors to have emerged.

However, when he entered the Toho School in Tokyo, his intention was to become a pianist. But when both index fingers were broken in a sporting accident, circumstances forced a change of direction and he took up composition and conducting. His first concerts were with Japanese orchestras and, in 1959, Ozawa left for Europe where he collected first prize at the Besançon conductors' competition. Charles Munch, one of the judges, arranged further study in the USA where Ozawa proceeded to win the Koussevitzky Award and then a scholarship which took him to Berlin to work with von Karajan.

In 1961, he accompanied Leonard Bernstein and the New York Philharmonic on its tour to Japan, becoming assistant conductor of the orchestra for the 1961-2 season.

Ozawa's career continued its rapid progress: he became music director of the Chicago Symphony's Ravinia Festival from 1964 to 1968, and of the Toronto Symphony Orchestra between 1965 and 1970, moving to San Francisco and the co-direction of the Boston Symphony's Berkshire Festival. The latter led to his appointment first as music advisor, and then music director (1973) of the Boston Orchestra.

André PREVIN (b. 1929) USA

Born Andreas Ludwig Priwin, he studied piano in Berlin (where he was born) and Paris before emigrating with his family to the United States in 1939 and taking American nationality in 1943.

After studying composition, Previn became a fine jazz pianist and orchestrator and was appointed music director to MGM studios. Tuition in conducting commenced in 1951, with Pierre Monteux, and he subsequently left MGM to take up a career as concert pianist and conductor. Previn's conducting début came in 1963 with the St Louis Symphony and his first major appointment was as conductor-in-chief of the Houston Orchestra between 1967 and 1970.

In 1969, he began a long and very fruitful association with the London Symphony Orchestra, becoming its principal conductor for ten years and then its conductor emeritus. The combination produced outstanding recordings of Holst, Rachmaninov, Vaughan Williams and Walton among others and Pre-

vin's popular appeal did much for music as a whole in Britain. He was artistic director of London's South Bank Summer Music Festivals from 1972 to 1974 before taking up the post of principal conductor of the Pittsburgh Orchestra in 1976.

Previn still makes occasional concert and recording appearances as a pianist, as well as composing accompanying scores and more serious works.

Simon RATTLE (b. 1955) England

Rattle studied conducting at the Royal Academy of Music, having learnt piano and played percussion with the city orchestra of his native Liverpool. After taking first prize in the John Player International Conductors' Competition in 1974, he spent three years as assistant conductor of the Bournemouth Symphony Orchestra and the Bournemouth Sinfonietta. Similar posts with the Royal Liverpool Philharmonic and BBC Scottish Symphony Orchestras followed, but Rattle gave up both in 1980 to take on the role of principal conductor and artistic advisor to the City of Birmingham Symphony Orchestra, which under his aegis has become an orchestra of world ranking.

Rattle combines his Birmingham post with that of principal guest conductor of the Rotterdam Philharmonic and Los Angeles Philharmonic Orchestras, and artistic director of the London Choral Society. He also works frequently with the London Sinfonietta and Philharmonia Orchestras.

Considered the most promising of young British conductors, Rattle made his American début in 1979 with the Los Angeles Orchestra and has since conducted in Chicago, Cleveland, San Francisco and Toronto. Elsewhere, he has appeared in Ger-

Above: *Gennady Rozhdestvensky was conductor of the USSR State Radio Orchestra 1961-74, his reputation abroad being built up by some fine recordings of Russian music on the Melodiya label.*

Below: *Sir Malcolm Sargent, a great favourite with the British public and a fine conductor in the British choral tradition, aptly ended his career as the director of the famous Albert Hall Promenade Concerts.*

Jean SIBELIUS
(1865-1957)

The great national hero of Finland, whose music is now enjoying a revival after a period of neglect following his death. He started writing music as a child, long before receiving any formal instruction, and then went on to study the piano and the violin. In 1885 he enrolled at Helsinki University to read law, but a year later changed to musical composition and the violin. His first successes came in 1892 with a choral symphony *Kullervo* and the tone poem *En Saga*, which were soon followed by the four Lemminkäinen *Legends*. Official recognition came early in his career, for in 1897 the Finnish government awarded an annual state pension to enable him to devote himself to full time composition. His tone poem *Finlandia* appeared two years later, to become virtually a national anthem, and his first symphony, a highly original work which nevertheless owes much to Russian romanticism as exemplified by Tchaikovsky. Other major works followed during the next twenty years showing remarkable originality of form and structure as well as a complete mastery of the orchestra. Yet it is wrong to think of Sibelius and his music in, as so many do, monumental, somewhat bleak, terms. He was by no means as unbending as his rather grim, forbidding photographs suggest, and there are many delights to be found in his lighter pieces and in his incidental music, of which he wrote a considerable amount. R.H.

many, Scandinavia, Holland and Israel, making his first appearance with Britain's Glyndebourne opera in 1975 and working regularly with it since. For three years, from 1980 to 1983, he was artistic director of the South Bank Summer Music Festival in London.

Rattle's repertoire is ever-widening, but he has displayed a special affinity for Mahler, Britten, Sibelius, Nielsen and Messiaen as well as contemporary music.

Fritz REINER (1881-1963) Hungary

Born and educated in Budapest, Reiner held conducting posts in the Hungarian capital and elsewhere in Europe before assuming the conductorship of the Cincinatti Orchestra in 1922. Ten years with the Pittsburgh Symphony (1938-48) were followed by a period at the New York Metropolitan Opera and, from 1953, the post of principal conductor of the Chicago Symphony Orchestra, with whom Reiner made many fine recordings for RCA Victor. He still made occasional appearances in Europe, most notably at the reopening of the Vienna Opera in 1955 where he conducted Wagner's *Die Meistersinger*.

Gennady ROZHDESTVENSKY (b. 1931)
Russia

Rozhdestvensky was taught conducting by his father, who was a professor at the Moscow Conservatory. Piano tuition came from the great Soviet player, Lev Oborin. While still a student, Rozhdestvensky conducted Tchaikovsky's *Nutcracker* at the Bolshoi and, at his graduation, was already known both in the Soviet Union and abroad.

For some twenty years, he was principal conductor at the Bolshoi Theatre in Moscow,

and at the end of his time there, in 1970, was awarded the Lenin Prize. From 1961, Rozhdestvensky had also been principal conductor of the Symphony Orchestra of All-Union Radio and Television.

More recently, his work has been concentrated in the West, as artistic director of the Stockholm Philharmonic and as chief conductor of the BBC Symphony Orchestra, a post he has held with considerable success since 1978.

Sir Malcolm SARGENT (1895-1967)
England

One of the most popular figures of British music, Sargent was born in the Lincolnshire market town of Stamford and studied at the

Royal College of Organists, winning the Sawyer Prize in 1910. The following year, he returned to his native fen country to become the assistant organist of Peterborough Cathedral, moving on to nearby Melton Mowbray in 1914.

After service in World War I, Sargent took a Doctor of Music degree at Durham University and made his début as a conductor, and with one of his own compositions, at a Henry Wood Promenade Concert in 1921. As well as teaching at the Royal College of Music, he conducted round the world including, from 1927 to 1930, work with the Diaghilev Ballet Company.

Sargent is best remembered, though, for his performances at the London Promenade Concerts which, in his capacity as chief conductor of the BBC Symphony Orchestra, he made his own from 1950 right up to his death in 1967.

Sir Georg SOLTI (b. 1912) **Hungary**

At an age when many have retired, Solti remains as active as ever, conducting both opera and orchestral music with equal relish. Born in Budapest, he studied at its conservatory with three of Hungary's great composers: Bartók, Kodály and Dohnányi. Originally a pianist, he became a *répétiteur* with the Budapest Opera and went on to assist Toscanini at the Salzburg Festivals of 1936/7.

At the outbreak of war, Solti left Hungary for Switzerland where he remained active both as conductor and pianist, winning the first prize for piano at the 1942 Concours Internationale in Geneva. He then returned triumphantly as director of the Munich Opera in 1946. Six years there were followed by nine at the Frankfurt Opera and then an enormously successful decade (1961-71) at London's Covent Garden.

Solti has also proved a memorable music director of the Chicago Symphony Orchestra for many years, both on concert and on record (many great performances for the Decca label). And it was for Decca that Solti made his historic first studio recording – with the Vienna Philharmonic – of the complete *Ring* cycle.

Leopold STOKOWSKI (1882-1977) **England**

Son of a Polish father and Irish mother, Stokowski was born in London and studied at the Royal College of Music and at Oxford, Paris and Munich. His first employment came as an organist, first in London then in New York but

Below: *Hungarian Georg Solti has become very much a part of the British musical scene and also a favourite in the USA. His memorial will remain the first complete recording of Wagner's* Ring *cycle.*

he turned to conducting in 1908, becoming conductor of the Cincinatti Symphony Orchestra the following year. In 1912, a fruitful association with the Philadelphia Orchestra commenced, and Stokowski boldly introduced much new music into his concerts.

Between 1942 and 1943, he was joint conductor of the NBC Symphony Orchestra with Toscanini and, two years later, took over as music director of the Hollywood Bowl Orchestra. Subsequently, there was the music directorship of the New York Philharmonic in the 1949-50 season, and the conductorship of the Houston Symphony from 1955.

Stokowski made many arrangements for orchestra (not always to the benefit of the music, it must be added), but also did much to popularise classical music. Ever an exciting conductor, he was giving concerts and making recordings right up to the last years of his life.

George SZELL (1897-1970) **Hungary**

A child prodigy, Szell came to Vienna first to study composition but when a career in this field did not materialise, turned to conducting. A Berlin début came in 1914, and through the influence of Richard Strauss he obtained an appointment in Strasbourg towards the end of World War I. During the early twenties, he worked in Prague, Darmstadt and Düsseldorf before becoming principal conductor at the Berlin State Opera from 1924 to 1930. The last three of those years were also spent teaching at the Berlin Hochschule für Musik.

Six years in Prague were followed by two with the Scottish National Orchestra before Szell emigrated to the United States. There he was guest conductor with the NBC Symphony during 1941-2 and in the ensuing four years conducted both the New York Philharmonic and at the Metropolitan Opera. It was with the Cleveland Orchestra, however, that Szell did his best work. Although something of an autocrat, he nevertheless

Above: *The Hungarian conductor George Szell had a reputation as a disciplinarian but also achieved some fine and sensitive performances with the Cleveland Orchestra.*

obtained wonderful results with the orchestra, many of which can still be appreciated on record.

Klaus TENNSTEDT (b. 1926) **Germany**

One of the great Mahler interpreters of the present day, Tennstedt came from Merseburg to study at Leipzig. From 1948, he led the orchestra at the Municipal Theatre in Halle, eventually becoming its principal conductor. Other major appointments within the German Democratic Republic included director of the Dresden Opera, but in 1971 he moved to Sweden, working first with the Swedish Radio Symphony Orchestra and then at the Kiel Opera in West Germany. During 1974, Tennstedt made his North American début with the Boston and Toronto Symphony Orchestras, and in 1976 began what was to prove a happy association with the London music scene. Although appointed chief conductor of the North German Radio Symphony Orchestra and chief guest conductor of the Minnesota Orchestra in 1979, Tennstedt's finest achievements have been as principal conductor of the London Philharmonic Orchestra, a post which ill-health may sadly force him to relinquish.

Arturo TOSCANINI (1867-1957) **Italy**

If there is one conductor known to all, it is Toscanini. Equally at home in all schools of music, he achieved worldwide fame early, becoming chief conductor of La Scala, Milan, at only thirty-one.

He was born in Parma and after tuition there and in Paris became a cellist. He suffered from myopia and so developed a perfect memory, which astonished a Rio de Janeiro audience one evening when, at a moment's notice, he took over from an ailing

Above: *The great Italian conductor Arturo Toscanini excelled in the world of opera and presided over the first performances of* I Pagliacci *and* La Bohème.

conductor to conduct Verdi's *Aida* without a score. From this sensational début, engagements came in Italy and in 1898 he was appointed to the top job in La Scala.

In 1907, he became chief conductor of the Metropolitan Opera in New York and, from then on, his activities centred on the United States, although he continued to conduct at major European festivals such as Salzburg. Later, he formed the NBC Symphony Orchestra and, with them, placed many of his unique interpretations on record.

Bruno WALTER (1876-1962) **Germany**

A conductor who excelled in Beethoven, Brahms, Mahler and Mozart, Walter's real name was Schlesinger. Berlin-born, he studied at the city's Stern Conservatory, making his conducting début in Cologne in 1894. He went on to conduct opera at Hamburg, Breslau, Pressburg, Riga and Berlin, coming to Vienna in 1901 and forging a close friendship with Mahler. Walter stayed in Vienna until 1912, when he was offered the directorship of the Munich opera, a post he held until 1922.

From 1925 until 1933, he conducted at the Stadtische Oper in Berlin and, for the last four of those years, was employed as music director of the Leipzig Gewandhaus Concerts. Walter also conducted German opera with great success at Covent Garden in London from 1924 to 1931, and made his presence felt at the Salzburg Festival.

He left Germany for Austria in 1933, but after a period as artistic director of the Vienna Opera, the Anschluss of 1938 saw Walter leave first for France and then, in 1939, for the USA.

From 1941, he conducted frequently at the Metropolitan Opera in New York, only returning to Europe to guest-conduct after the war.

In his later years, Walter conducted the Columbia Symphony Orchestra in a wonderful legacy of recordings, most still available.

Günter WAND (b. 1912) **Germany**

Little known outside Germany until recent years, Wand is one of the most stimulating and independent interpreters of the German classics, especially Brahms and Bruckner. Born in Elberfeld, he spent twenty-eight years as conductor of the Gürzenich Orchestra in Cologne and more recently has been active with the North German Radio Symphony Orchestra. Wand prefers working with provincial orchestras such as these where he can be given the time he feels needed to properly mould an interpretation in rehearsal. Justification has come in the shape of a Deutscher Schallplattenpreis for his recordings of the Bruckner Fifth and Eighth Symphonies, and a Preis der Schallplattenkritik for the entire Bruckner cycle.

Sir Henry WOOD (1869-1944) **England**

Immortalized in the annual series of London Promenade Concerts which bears his name, Wood was born in London and was on the way to a career as an organist at the age of ten. Studies at the Royal Academy of Music were followed by a début conducting opera in 1919. Six years later came the appointment that was to occupy him for the next fifty years, when he began conducting promenade concerts in London's Queen's Hall. Wood also conducted at many other festivals and introduced much music that was previously unknown to British audiences into his programmes. He received his knighthood in 1911. P.H.

Below: *Sir Henry Wood, forever immortalised as the founder of the Queen's Hall Promenade Concerts, here rehearses Sibelius's* En Saga *in the Duke's Hall at the Royal Academy of Music in London.*

Sergei Sergeyevich PROKOFIEV (1891-1953)

Another infant prodigy, Prokofiev started to learn the piano at the age of three, wrote his first opera when he was nine years old, and went on to the St Petersburg Conservatory to study music under Glière, Liadov and Rimsky-Korsakov. He published several works while he was still a student, and in 1914 he came to London to work with Diaghilev. In 1917 he composed his brilliant *Classical Symphony*, and then went to America where he performed his own compositions and was commissioned by the Chicago Opera to write *The Love of Three Oranges*. He settled in Paris from 1920 onwards, where he wrote three ballets for Diaghilev and attended performances of some of his orchestral pieces. Prokofiev chose an inopportune time to return to Russia in 1933, but undaunted by the new, harsh doctrine of 'social realism' he turned his attention to the cinema, producing splendid scores for *Alexander Nevsky* and *Lieutenant Kije*. Ballet music for *Romeo and Juliet* belongs to this same period as does his delightful orchestral guide *Peter and the Wolf*. In 1941 he started work on his major opera, *War and Peace*, which he continued to revise up to his death, and in 1944 he completed the fifth of his seven symphonies. Four years later Prokofiev was forced to write an open letter to the Union of Soviet Composers apologising for his lapse into 'formalism'. R.H.

The term symphony derives from the Greek – *sym* (together) and *phonos* (sound) – and since the time of Beethoven has been regarded as the highest, most intellectually demanding form of orchestral music. Originally, the description *sinfonia* was applied to all kinds of music, often an instrumental interlude in an opera or oratorio (Handel's *Messiah* for example). During the eighteenth century, it became a musical form in its own right, particularly in Italy and Germany, and now consisting of three separate movements. Elements of the dance suite and divertimento were incorporated, such as the minuet and the familiar four-movement 'classical' symphony began to evolve.

Chief among the new 'symphonists' was Haydn, soon followed by Mozart who had been influenced by the sinfonias of Bach's son C.P.E. Bach. In the main, they adhered to a strict four-movement format: the first movement was worked through in *sonata* form – exposition, development, recapitulation – and at a moderately fast tempo. The second movement was in sharp contrast, usually slow and perhaps romantic or melancholy in feel, while the third was based on the minuet. This was invariably the lightest, most carefree of the four. The fourth movement was again quick, but may have included a theme and variations, for example.

Beethoven 'dramatised' the symphony and enlarged its ambition. He was followed by the nineteenth-century 'Romantics', Mendelssohn, Schumann, Brahms and then by the 'nationalists'. The culmination came in the vast symphonic canvases of Mahler and Bruckner, after which many composers dispensed with the form.

In the twentieth century, the symphony has been pronounced dead many times but stubbornly refuses to die, even though notions of what can be termed a symphony differ widely. We have seen 'conventional' symphonies from such as Prokofiev, Shostakovich and Sibelius, and less conventional interpretations from Stravinsky and Britten. The form still continues to attract and stimulate composers. P.H.

Ludwig van BEETHOVEN (1770-1827)
Germany

Symphony No. 1 in C, Op. 21
(first performed Vienna, 1800)
Symphony No. 2 in D, Op. 36
(first performed Vienna, 1803)
Symphony No. 3 in E♭, Op. 55
Eroica (first performed Vienna, 1805)
Symphony No. 4 in B♭, Op. 60
(first performed Vienna, 1807)
Symphony No. 5 in C minor, Op. 67
(first performed Vienna, 1808)
Symphony No. 6 in F, Op. 68
Pastoral (first performed Vienna, 1808)
Symphony No. 7 in A, Op. 92
(first performed Vienna, 1813)

Symphony No. 8 in F, Op. 93
(first performed Vienna, 1814)
Symphony No. 9 in D minor, Op. 125
Choral (first performed Vienna, 1824)

For over one hundred and fifty years the nine symphonies of Ludwig van Beethoven have remained the hub of the symphonic repertoire. Their stature has rarely, if ever, been questioned and their popularity has never waned. If Mozart perfected the 'classical style' in his later symphonies and concertos, Beethoven took it into another realm, harnessing and mastering every classical device to achieve previously unheard – and unimagined – levels of expression that add up to the first philosophy of life in music.

The timing may have been unintentional, but it was appropriate that the first symphony should make its debut in 1800: a new century and, in the aftermath of the French Revolution, the beginnings of a new social order throughout Europe. The excitement, optimism, new-found confidence and turmoil are all mirrored in the symphonies, the first eight of which were accomplished in the space of fifteen years. At least three, and arguably four, of these can justifiably be said to have taken the symphony – and music – into new dimensions.

Although the First Symphony nods quite plainly in the direction of Mozart and Haydn, its exuberance is a foretaste of what was to come. A brief slow introduction leads into a

Dimitri SHOSTAKOVICH
(1906-75)

International fame came to Shostakovich at an early age when his powerful and mature First Symphony was performed in Leningrad, and later in Moscow, in 1926. He had studied at the Leningrad Conservatory under Glazunov, among others, and was regarded as extremely sound, both technically as a musician and politically as an avowed Communist. But many of the works following his initial success, notably the next two symphonies, were disappointing, and it was not until 1934 that he scored his next major triumph with the opera *Lady Macbeth of Mtsensk*, which was first performed in Leningrad and created a sensation. His ballets *The Nose, The Age of Gold, Bright Stream* and *The Bolt* together with a number of film scores belong to this same period, and his career seemed set fair when, in January 1936, his work was savagely attacked in the Soviet newspaper *Pravda*. The overt eroticism of *Lady Macbeth* offended Stalin and other officials. A long process of rehabilitation, followed by a further period in disgrace, had little effect on his prodigious creativity (15 symphonies, 6 concertos of various kinds, 5 operas, and a vast number of orchestral, instrumental and chamber works). The music of Shostakovich is the music of extremes – from powerful tragedy to quirky and bizarre humour, from almost unbearable emotional intensity to Mahlerian banality. No wonder that he is regarded by many as the greatest composer this century has produced. R.H.

Left: Painting by Carl Schloesser 'Beethoven at the piano in his work-room'; the conventional vision of the genius at work, far removed from the happenings of ordinary life.

Above: The famous title page of the MS of Beethoven's Symphony No. 3, 'Sinfonia Eroica'. A tribute to Napoleon Bonaparte, his name was angrily obliterated after he proclaimed himself emperor.

breezy allegro. The slow movement has grace and elegance, but the succeeding 'minuet' is that in name alone, with its quicker, one-in-a-bar beat. After the well-judged hesitancy of its opening bars, the finale launches into five minutes of bubbling high spirits.

There is no lack of wit or good humour in the Second Symphony either, yet as he worked on it Beethoven was learning the awful truth of his deafness, the despair he felt finding voice in the near-suicidal outpourings of the *Heilgenstadt Testament*. Expansive, confident and – according to one contemporary critic 'striving too hard to be new' – there is no hint of this in any of the Second's four movements. For the first time in any symphony, the third is labelled 'scherzo' rather than minuet, while the slow movement cossets the ear with its serene melody (which became popular enough to be arranged as a song) and its rich ornamentation. In sharp contrast, the opening flourish of the fourth verges on the comic, yet the working-through of this musical 'banana skin' is quite remarkable. Beethoven is thought to have drafted and re-drafted the score of the Second Symphony three times before declaring himself satisfied.

But it was with his Third Symphony that Beethoven can fairly be said to have changed the course of music – and changed it for good. In its scale and in what it sought to express, the *Sinfonia Eroica* broke new ground. For the first time music gave voice to a radical kind of idealism: the opening bars

audibly seem to break free from invisible bonds to relish their freedom.

Originally, the *Eroica* had a hero: Napoleon Bonaparte who, to many Europeans (if not the British) appeared the embodiment of the 'age of revolution'. He certainly earned the admiration of Beethoven who, on the title page wrote: 'Grand Symphony entitled Bonaparte', only to tear it out on hearing that Napoleon had declared himself Emperor. To Beethoven, taking such a title sadly proved that the Frenchman was every bit as vain and despotic as the autocratic nobility he had been busily deposing.

The second movement of the *Eroica* is marked *marcia funebre*, yet is not so much a funeral march as a mighty oration. At its climax, the main theme undergoes fugal treatment of awesome power and complexity: Beethoven at his craggiest, granite-like best.

Quite why he then chose to follow the playful scherzo with a set of variations on the theme from his ballet music *Prometheus* has never been established: was there any significance in the choice of this mythological figure who stole fire from heaven and gave it to mankind?

Despite its generally sunny disposition, the Fourth Symphony is far from being the 'lightweight' it is often made out to be. True, the adagio is Beethoven at his most charming and romantic, with the most beguiling melody for clarinet, but there are tragic undertones which are not far removed from the funeral march of the *Eroica*.

All are dispelled, though, with the boisterous third movement and the jovial finale which includes much marvellous writing for woodwind in its fast-flowing stream of ideas.

While writing the Fourth Symphony, Beethoven put to one side other symphonic sketches which had occupied him since completing the *Eroica* in 1804. The gestation of what has become the most famous symphony in all music was to occupy four years and it was not until December 1808 that the Fifth was ready for performance. It was not an auspicious debut, with scrappy playing forcing the composer, who was conducting, to halt the proceedings at one stage. The symphony, with its familiar four-note 'call to attention' – the originality of which we now take for granted – survived this fiasco to become one of the cornerstones of music.

Yet the originality of the opening was but one aspect which must have amazed that first Viennese audience: the darkly sinister scherzo which suddenly erupts into blazing triumph remains one of the most stunning transitions anywhere, musically notable for its first use of symphonic trombones.

Incredibly that same evening, the audience saw the symphony take a second new direction. The Sixth was also heard for the first time. Subtitled 'Pastoral symphony, or Recollections of country life', it gave pictorial descriptions to each of the five movements (also a fresh departure), events such as peasants' merrymaking (complete with musicians playing out of time!) and a summer thunderstorm. Beethoven was at pains to call the work 'an expression of feeling' rather than a landscape in music, but he had nevertheless set a pattern for all the 'programme' symphonies that were to follow.

With the Seventh, he returned to 'abstract' music, although Richard Wagner was surely right when he described the work as 'the apotheosis of the dance'. That kind of pulse permeates all four movements, from the cheerful 6/8 rhythm of the first, through the more dignified step of the second to the whirling vigour and riotous exuberance of the third and fourth. In contrast, the Eighth, with its reversion to minuet tempo for the third movement, seems both more relaxed and more traditional. It is also comparatively short, barely longer than the First Symphony at around twenty-six minutes. Nevertheless, this delightful work is still full of original touches and it was one the composer was especially fond of.

Ten years were to elapse between the Eighth and Ninth Symphonies, a period during which Beethoven's reputation rose to the giddy heights it has occupied ever since. But it was also a period in which encroaching deafness virtually ended his performing activities and, not surprisingly, brought about a physical as well as psychological withdrawal from society. In that context, the achievement of the Ninth Symphony is all the more astounding.

In its last movement, it introduced voices – both solo and choral – into a symphony for the first time, with a principal theme almost as well known as that of the first movement of the Fifth: the 'Joy' theme as it is known, albeit incorrectly. The text, from a poem by Schiller, is not an 'Ode to Joy' but to freedom. However, even the mighty Beethoven felt that was a sentiment best modified in the prevailing political atmosphere of 1824 and, curiously, 'Joy' it has remained in all but a very few performances to this day.

The Ninth runs for some seventy minutes, starting with an urgent and incisive first movement which sums up Beethoven's skill in exploiting his ideas: in its taut structure there is not one superfluous note. The galloping scherzo, with its prominent kettledrums is placed second, the sublime, gently undulating slow movement preceding the glorious finale. Opening with a blast from the orchestra, it quotes each of the preceding movements before abruptly dismissing them. 'Not these sounds,' intones the baritone soloist, and Beethoven concurs. The music takes flight as never before. It was to be, as succeeding generations of composers have discovered, a very hard act to follow.

Hector BERLIOZ (1803-69) France

Symphonie Fantastique, Op. 14

This most famous of French symphonies was first performed in Paris in 1830. The twenty-six year-old composer subtitled the work 'Five episodes in the life of an artist', although 'mind' would be a more appropriate term, given such vivid episodes as 'The March to the Scaffold' and 'Witches' Sabbath'. The underlying 'theme' is obsessive and unfulfilled love, represented by an *idée fixe* which insinuates each movement. Berlioz' trademark – absolute mastery of orchestration – is everywhere apparent in this colourful masterpiece of high Romanticism.

Georges BIZET (1838-75) France

Symphony in C

This charming, vivacious work, 'classical' in style and full of delicious melodies, was written when Bizet was just seventeen. However, he came to regard it as immature, suppressing its publication and it was not until the 1930s that the symphony was unearthed and given its first performance and the world was given another minor masterpiece.

Below: A characterful drawing of Johannes Brahms by Willy von Beckerath. Tchaikovsky, who took an ungenerous view of most of his fellow composers, once described him as 'giftless'.

Alexander BORODIN (1833-87) Russia

Symphony No. 2 in B minor

A *very* gifted amateur, Alexander Borodin was a chemistry teacher whose composing was confined to his leisure hours, hence his small, and in several instances incomplete output. Strongly influenced by elements of Slav and Oriental folk music, his work has a distinctly nationalist flavour, nowhere better heard than in this symphony, first performed in 1877, but not published until after his death. It is a captivating combination of the brutal, the boisterous and the benign and, as such, wholly characteristic of nineteenth-century Russian orchestral music.

Johannes BRAHMS (1833-97) Germany

Symphony No. 1 in C minor, Op. 68
(first performed Karlsruhe, 1876)
Symphony No. 2 in D, Op. 73
(first performed Vienna, 1877)
Symphony No. 3 in F, Op. 90
(first performed Vienna, 1883)
Symphony No. 4 in E minor, Op. 98
(first performed Meiningen, 1885)

Unlike his contemporaries Liszt and Wagner, Brahms was a conservative in his musical outlook. He rarely broke with tradition and in all four of his symphonies adhered to the 'classical' four-movement format, among other ground rules which others were eagerly breaking. Brahms revered Beethoven and was conscious that many saw him as the latter's logical heir. It almost certainly explains why it took him until his early forties to complete a first symphony (although earlier sketches were adapted as the D minor Piano Concerto of 1859).

Before the first performance, Brahms declared that his C minor symphony was 'long and not particularly amiable', a statement applauded by those who saw him as the champion of 'serious' music. In the event he was being a little too po-faced: while the

outer movements are indeed tough and sinewy, the two central ones are richly lyrical and extremely amiable. The symphony was immediately dubbed 'Beethoven's Tenth', by some as a compliment, but by Brahms' enemies as evidence of his unoriginality, especially given the apparent similarity between the main theme of the finale and the 'Joy' theme from Beethoven's Ninth.

In truth, although there is a melodic resemblance, temperamentally the music is worlds apart, the Brahms being distinctly earthbound in comparison. And, to be fair, Brahms openly acknowledged the similarity: 'any ass can see that', he is reputed to have said.

A second symphony followed within fourteen months of the first. Warm and genial throughout, it is in sharp contrast to the more rugged and rough-hewn elements of its predecessor: to many, it is Brahms's 'Pastoral', in substance if not in name. The Third Symphony is less easy to characterise, despite the descriptive three-note 'motto' which Brahms employs: the three notes, F-A/A flat-F were the initial letters of a youthful personal maxim *frei aber froh* ('free but happy').

The Third is also the most romantic of Brahms symphonies (his affection for the singer Hermine Spies was said to be an inspiration), reaching full flower in the third movement *poco allegretto*, one of the most disarmingly beautiful and poignant themes ever written and quite at odds with Brahms 'severe' image. Initially, the fourth movement threatens that mood, surging and stormy, only to develop an air of striking confidence. Yet it ends calmly and quietly as the F-A-F motif makes its presence felt again.

'Autumnal' is a description frequently applied to the wistful opening of the Fourth Symphony. It is not inappropriate, although the work is surely not the tragic utterance that many have concluded. The first movement is exceptionally song-like in character, the second hardly less lyrical, while the third is a rumbustious *allegro giocoso*, notable for its quite incongruous – for Brahms – interruptions on the triangle.

Appropriately, the symphony concludes with one of the composer's most cogent and finely-wrought symphonic statements, thirty-two variations on an eight-bar theme, or ground bass. This magnificent *passacaglia* fully sums up the depth and strength of Brahms's creative gifts.

Anton BRUCKNER (1824-96) **Austria**

If one includes an early work (now listed as Symphony No. 0), Bruckner wrote ten published symphonies, although the last, the Ninth, was incomplete at his death. A gauche and naïve personality, as well as a profoundly sincere one, he was very susceptible to criticism and his readiness to amend his scores in response to comments from all quarters is

Above: *Anton Bruckner (1824-96) at his Bösendorfer piano in Vienna about 1894. By this time he was ill and forgetful, but had been honoured by the Viennese and was working on his 9th Symphony.*

the reason why they continue to be produced to this day in widely differing editions. The trend now, though, in performance and recording, is to try to represent Bruckner's original thoughts, no matter how well intentioned the numerous changes made by his friends and colleagues.

Although conventional in plan, once heard Bruckner's symphonies are wholly distinctive: a scale and structure which, more than once, have provoked the description 'cathedrals of sound'; a fondness for declamatory fanfares and horn calls; vast sweeps of melody, and a harmonic language which owes much to Wagner, whom Bruckner worshipped second only to God.

It is easy to criticise Bruckner's symphonies on strictly compositional grounds: there is much repetition of phrase and awkward continuity, but against this must be set an often deeply moving spirituality and transcendental beauty.

Symphony No. 4 in E♭ *Romantic*

This is the only one of Bruckner's symphonies to acquire a nickname, if an inappropriate one: the music has little kinship with the tenets of nineteenth century Romanticism. Composed in 1874, Bruckner contrives an opening as mysterious as any. A theme on the horns glides over deep string *tremolandi* (a typical device of Bruckner) and from this the majestic first movement unfolds. The brooding stillness of the andante is in stark contrast to the bounding scherzo which the composer described as suggesting a hunt,

*César FRANCK
(1822-90)*

The only really exciting thing that ever happened to César Franck was during the revolution of 1848 when, in his own church of Notre-Dame de Lorette where he was organ accompanist, he anxiously awaited the arrival of his bride-to-be who was, had he but known, at that very moment and with the help of kindly insurgents, clambering over the barricades in her determination to reach him. She was from a theatrical family, which did little to endear her to Franck's father, a strict paterfamilias of Flemish stock who had reared his two sons to be musical prodigies, and who saw in the impending union a potential loss to the joint family income. Had he not scrimped and saved on their behalf, bringing them from Liége to Paris to give them more scope to develop their talents? But ungrateful César broke loose, made a home for himself and settled down to the routine of teaching and organ playing which comprised the rest of his career.

If you have not already done so, make a point of hearing the Symphony in D minor, the Sonata in A major, and the once enormously popular Symphonic Variations for piano and orchestra. There is no doubt that you will be much impressed, which is a good deal more than can be said for most of César Franck's contemporaries. R.H.

and there is no difficulty hearing that. In the finale, the dust settles and tranquility, very calmly and very deliberately, is restored.

Symphony No. 7 in E
(first performed Leipzig, 1884)

For some five decades after its composition, this remained the best-known of Bruckner's symphonies, largely through its epic slow movement. While working on this noble adagio, the composer learned of the death of his revered Wagner and in the mournful coda his grief can be plainly heard. By then he had already completed the first movement and the rustic scherzo, and went on to conclude the work with a dramatic and, ultimately, triumphant finale. He dedicated the work to Wagner's patron, King Ludwig II of Bavaria.

Symphony No. 8 in C minor
(first performed Vienna, 1892)

When, in 1887, Bruckner sat back after three years' work to assess his Eighth Symphony, he thought it his best work to date. Therefore, when the adverse comments of the conductor, Hermann Levi, a staunch champion of the Seventh Symphony, were relayed to him, the composer's confidence took a devastating blow. Revisions cost him three years – and his health (although for once they were worthwhile revisions). Levi was vindicated to a large extent when the Viennese audience, frequently Bruckner's most virulent critics, greeted the symphony – in essence a gigantic graduation from darkness into light – with unbridled enthusiasm.

Symphony No. 9 in D minor
(first performed Vienna, 1903)

Bruckner was working on his Ninth Symphony when he died. Anticipating that he would fail to complete the last movement, he suggested substituting his setting of the *Te Deum* in its stead, a juxtaposition which has proved unconvincing. However, like Schubert's *Unfinished*, the Ninth manages to sound 'complete' even if it is not.

After a typically expectant introduction, the main theme enters, as poignant and noble as anything in Bruckner. The succeeding scherzo manages to combine menace with a kind of eldritch playfulness, while the concluding adagio is an apt summation of Bruckner's work: meditative, reflective, a final vision of heaven.

Antonin DVOŘÁK (1841-1904) Czechoslovakia

Symphony No. 7 in D minor, Op. 70
(first performed London, 1885)
Symphony No. 8 in G, Op. 88
(first performed Prague, 1890)
Symphony No. 9 in E minor, Op. 95
From The New World
(first performed New York, 1893)

For some critics, the symphonies of Dvořák – especially the most popular of them, the Ninth – present irrefutable evidence of the decline of the genre, post-Beethoven. The listening public, however, has disagreed, resulting in the Ninth becoming one of the most performed and recorded of all symphonies. Hardly less agreeable are the rest of the mature symphonies, particularly the Seventh – the most 'classical' of the set – and the Eighth.

Only five of Dvořák's symphonies were published during the composer's lifetime, and with the delayed appearance of four, now rarely heard, earlier compositions, the original Nos 1-5 were renumbered as Nos 5-9.

Dvořák had an incomparable gift for melody. If flavoured with the folk idiom of his

Above: *Sir Edward Elgar, a portrait in oils by Talbot Hughes done at his home, Plas Gwyn, in Hereford in 1905. Watching the artist at work inspired Elgar to try his own hand at painting.*

native Bohemia, its appeal has proved to be universal: the last three symphonies were enthusiastically received at their first performances by audiences as diverse as Britons, Czechs and Americans. And it was Americans that were responsible, at least in part, for the most evergreen of his compositions, the *New World*.

Dvořák spent three successful and lucrative years in the United States as Director of the National Conservatory of Music. Ever since, there has been speculation about the effect that native American music had upon him: 'If I had not seen America, I should never have written my symphony . . . the way I did', wrote the composer, but the only apparent influence remains the famous (and much-abused) theme of the largo. It has the feel of a negro spiritual and a passing reference to 'Swing low, sweet chariot' is unmistakable.

Edward ELGAR (1857-1934) England

Symphony No. 1 in A♭ Op. 55
(first performed Manchester, 1908)
Symphony No. 2 in E♭ Op. 63
(first performed London, 1911)

Not only the first British symphonist of note, but the first British composer of true international stature to emerge for two centuries, since the seventeenth century's Henry Purcell, Elgar composed his two published symphonies in the short space of four years, between 1907 and 1911. A third symphony,

commissioned by the BBC, was left incomplete at his death.

The debt to the 'German symphony' – especially Brahms – is evident, but these are not the opulent anachronisms they are sometimes made out to be. Nor are they merely a swansong for the glorious sunset of the Edwardian age, even though the score of the second was dedicated to the memory of King Edward VII. Its elegaic larghetto is considerably more than a funeral lament for one man.

The First Symphony was immediately successful, receiving over one hundred performances in its first year, not only in Europe but in Australia and the United States as well. The valedictory Second – 'the passionate pilgrimage of a soul' as Elgar called it – took much longer to gain public affection, certainly until 1920 when it was memorably conducted for the first time by Adrian Boult.

César FRANCK (1822-90) Belgium

Symphony in D minor
(first performed Paris, 1889)

The Gallic symphony is one of music's rarities: after Berlioz, only Lalo and Saint-Saëns have augmented Franck's lonely masterpiece. Not that the D minor Symphony is noticeably French in character; indeed, in structure and scoring it is rooted in the Germanic tradition, apart from its use of harp and cor anglais (the instrument which gives the largo of Dvořák's *New World* its distinctive colour).

Consisting – unusually for the period – of just three movements, this discursive yet extremely coherent work can be regarded as the culminating triumph of Frank's uneven career.

Joseph HAYDN (1732-1809) Austria

Symphony No. 45 in F# minor,
Farewell (first performed 1772)
Symphony No. 88 in G
(first performed Paris, 1789)
Symphony No. 94 in G, *Surprise*
(first performed London, 1792)
Symphony No. 96 in D, *Miracle*
(first performed London, 1792)
Symphony No. 100 in G, *Military*
(first performed London, 1794)
Symphony No. 101 in D, *The Clock*
(first performed London, 1794)
Symphony No. 103 in E♭, *Drum-roll*
(first performed London, 1795)
Symphony No. 104 in D, *London*
(first performed London, 1795)

In his long career, Haydn composed one hundred and four symphonies, many for the Morzin and Esterházy families by whom he was employed as music director (with the latter for some thirty years). Another set of six symphonies (Nos 82-87) was composed

Franz Josef HAYDN
(1732-1809)

Second child of master-wheelwright Matthias Haydn, young Josef showed early musical talent, and at the age of eight was sent to Vienna to join the choir of St Stephen's. After his voice broke he was obliged to accept a succession of menial posts and later entered into a disastrous marriage. In 1761 he was engaged as vice-*Kapellmeister* in the Esterházy household, where he remained for thirty years. He had by this time many compositions to his credit, and despite burdensome administrative duties a stream of new works poured from his pen. Slowly his fame spread, and commissions started to arrive from many parts of Europe. When his court duties (but not his salary) ceased, at Salomon's invitation he made the first of two triumphant visits to England where he received a royal reception and a doctorate from Oxford University. Returning to Vienna, he bought a house and took in pupils, including Beethoven. During a final flowering of his genius he composed six great Masses and *The Creation*. Not long afterwards his health started to fail, and he died while French troops occupied Vienna. It is impossible to overstate the importance of Haydn's enormous output (104 symphonies, 20 operas, 13 Masses together with many cantatas and oratorios, and a vast number of works for solo instruments and chamber groups), or of his benign influence on many contemporaries and successors. R.H.

Above: *The New Philharmonia Orchestra (later the Philharmonic) in EMI's Abbey Road No. 1 studio under Otto Klemperer during recording sessions of Haydn's symphonies 88 to 104.*

for a series of concerts in Paris, but the finest and most famous date from 1790 onwards when, suddenly freed of his commitments, the composer accepted an offer from the violinist and impresario Salomon to come to London. Haydn composed twelve *London* symphonies for Salomon (Nos 93-104) of which six (see above) have been singled out as being of special interest.

However, one of the joys of exploring Haydn's large output is coming across the lesser-known masterpieces, gems such as No. 77 in B flat or No. 26 in D minor. A large number (including all but one listed here) have acquired nicknames, often apt, but occasionally highly tenuous.

Although Haydn did not 'invent' the symphony as is sometimes suggested, he certainly developed the form immeasurably, even under the constraint of providing music 'to order'. His music had to entertain , and humour is a regular component of his works, but that did not preclude the expression of deep feelings and strong emotions, or a degree of experiment. As the finest of his symphonies prove, he did much more than just prepare the way for Mozart and Beethoven.

The *Farewell*, No. 45, was a symphony with a purpose. Haydn's orchestra felt in need of a holiday and the composer allowed them to make their feelings plain by scoring the finale of this work so that one by one the players could blow out their candles, put down their instruments and leave the stage. Apparently the Esterházys took the hint!

Symphony No. 88 is typical of Haydn at his best: within a conventional framework there are memorable touches such as the use of trumpets and drums in the second movement, or the breathless brilliance of the concluding rondo. The 'surprise' of No. 94 is the sudden shattering by a drumstroke of the gentle progress of the andante, (interestingly, an afterthought). The *Miracle* of No. 96, however, is a misnomer: the miraculous escape of all beneath it when a chandelier fell to the ground occurred at a later London concert, not at the first performance of this symphony.

The *Military* Symphony was written for Haydn's second visit to London and it is from the slow movement that the nickname derives, the introduction of triangle, cymbals and bass drum embellishing the march rhythm with a parade-ground ambience. And it is again from the slow movement, with its 'tick-tock' theme, that No. 101 takes its name.

The source of No. 103's appellation is evident from the very first bars, but that of No. 104 could equally well be applied to any of the twelve written specifically for performance in the English capital.

Franz LISZT (1811-86) Hungary

A Faust Symphony, G108
Dante Symphony, G109

Though best known for his solo piano compositions, Liszt also wrote several significant orchestral compositions, including two 'programme' symphonies. Both take their inspiration from literature – the Faust Symphony from Goethe, and the other from Dante's Divine Comedy – and were completed in the period 1854-7.

In the former, a large work for soloist, orchestra and chorus, each of the three movements is given over to one of the main protagonists: the outer ones, depicting Faust and Mephistopheles are dark and fervent, while the radiant beauty of the central episode is perfect for the character of Gretchen, who in the drama saves Faust from damnation. Musically, the work is notable for an opening tune whose use of all twelve notes of the chromatic scale pre-empts the atonal theories of the Second Viennese School by several decades.

Written in the same style as the Faust Symphony, the Dante Symphony was finished in 1856 and is in two movements that correspond to the *Inferno* and *Pergatoria* of the Divine Comedy.

Witold LUTOSŁAWSKI (b. 1913) Poland

Symphony No. 3
(first performed Chicago, 1983)

The late emergence of Lutoslawski as a composer of considerable significance can be attributed to first the censorship imposed by the Nazis, and second to the stifling atmosphere in Poland immediately post-war, when the arts were essentially run from Moscow.

The Third Symphony was composed over a lengthy period to a commission from the Chicago Symphony Orchestra. This fascinating work, played in a single, thirty-minute span but in fact made up of two movements prefaced by an introduction and concluded with an epilogue and coda, is remarkable for its *ad lib* passages. Although the notes are specified in the score, timing and placing are left to the players, and to great effect. It is also a vividly colourful score, employing a variety of drums and other percussion and requiring a piano, but with four rather than just two hands to play it.

Gustav MAHLER (1860-1911) Austria

Symphony No. 1 in D
(first performed Budapest, 1889)
Symphony No. 2 in C minor, *Resurrection*
(first performed Berlin, 1895)
Symphony No. 3 in D minor
(first performed complete, 1902)
Symphony No. 4 in G
(first performed Munich, 1901)
Symphony No. 5 in C♯ minor
(first performed Cologne, 1904)
Symphony No. 6 in A minor
(first performed Essen, 1906)
Symphony No. 7 in E minor
(first performed Prague, 1908)
Symphony No. 8 in Eb
(first performed Munich, 1910)
Symphony No. 9 in D minor
(first performed Vienna, 1912)

The symphonies of Gustav Mahler span perhaps the most momentous transition in all music. While his adolescence coincided with the final flowering of late Romanticism, his later years witnessed the birth of a radicalism that was to undermine the centuries-old structure of music itself. In taking the traditional symphony to its expressive limits, and in so doing stretching the conventional tonal system to breaking point, Mahler effectively contributed to that demise.

First and foremost, though, the symphony for Mahler was the means to convey the panoply and full complexity of his ideas, and for this he needed large canvases. None of his symphonies lasts less than fifty minutes and five run for over eighty. All require large orchestras and four include voices, including the 'oratorio symphony' the Eighth which, at its first performance, was billed as the *Symphony of a Thousand*. Mahler disliked the

Above: *Gustav Mahler; the last picture of him taken on the boat bringing him back from America in 1911. He was already incurably ill and was going to visit a specialist in Paris; died in Vienna in May.*

term, but it was accurate in terms of the forces used.

Despite their immensity, a characteristic of the symphonies is their 'classical' clarity of texture. Like Berlioz, Mahler was a supreme orchestrator, part-product no doubt of his career as one of the leading conductors of the day. From much of his work, his place at the end of the line of great Viennese symphonists becomes evident, but so does the acknowledged inspiration of Austrian and German folk-poetry. Although he composed on an heroic scale, it was often to express a very simple, even childlike humanity.

The First Symphony, which draws noticeably on folk song, including a dirge-like reworking of *Frère Jacques*, was originally in five movements, each with a descriptive title.

Mahler quickly withdrew not only the titles, but also the second movement, called *Blumine (Flowers)*. A few conductors, however, elect to reinstate it.

In the Second Symphony, Mahler tackled no less a subject than life, death and the Day of Judgement, in a work of awesome power and ambition. There are few more stirring or more glorious passages in music than its concluding apocalyptic vision. Mahler also appended a programme to the Third Symphony, a paean for the joys of the natural world whose sixth movement – *What Love tells me* – is an adagio of the most sublime beauty. The altogether lighter Fourth Symphony grew out of the Third, music of disarming innocence, charm and skilful simplicity: the cloudless blue sky of paradise.

From the Fourth to the Fifth, the transition is brutal, the latter's stern fanfare akin to waking from a pleasant dream to face the cold dawn of reality. With the Fifth, best-known for its nostalgic and melancholy adagietto (theme music to Visconti's film *Death in Venice*), Mahler began a trio of purely instrumental symphonies. The Sixth was to be his bleakest and most objective vision, starkly fatalistic, while the Seventh emerged as his most oblique and bizarre, inhabiting strange sound worlds.

With the Eighth, he reintroduced voices; indeed, it is virtually an oratorio with complementary settings of the early Christian hymn, *Veni Creator Spiritus* and the closing scene from Goethe's *Faust*. By now confirmed as having a serious heart condition and also aware that for three great composers before him – Beethoven, Schubert and Bruckner – their Ninth Symphony was also their last, Mahler tried to trick fate by choosing to call his song cycle *Das Lied von der Erde (The Song of the Earth)* a 'symphony'. But it was not to be: the true Ninth, rightly the ultimate fulfillment of his orchestral style and a work to exhaust the emotions, was to be his last.

There is a 'Mahler Ten': the composer left enough sketches for several musicologists to attempt its complete orchestration, most convincingly the English scholar Deryck Cooke. His version has been both played in concert and recorded.

Felix MENDELSSOHN (1809-47) Germany

Symphony No. 3 in A minor, Op. 56
Scottish (first performed Leipzig, 1842)
Symphony No. 4 in A, Op. 90 *Italian*
(first performed London, 1833)
Symphony No. 5 in D, Op. 107
Reformation (first performed, 1832)

As a musical prodigy, Mendelssohn was every bit the equal of Mozart, evidenced by the set of twelve sparkling string symphonies composed between the ages of just twelve and fourteen. His five numbered symphonies, however, proved more troublesome, witness the incompatibility between numbering and

Artur SCHNABEL
(1882-1951)

Austrian pianist and composer who studied in Vienna after making his first public appearance at the age of eight. His rise to fame was slowly and methodically achieved, with a lasting reputation built on his authoritative interpretations of the major classics in the piano repertoire, especially works by Beethoven and Schubert. Fortunately, many of these interpretations were recorded, with the result that Schnabel's following is at least as great today as it was during his lifetime. He gave frequent recitals throughout the whole of Europe and the USA, but at the height of his powers he was exiled by the Nazis from both Germany and Austria. This brought to a end a distinguished teaching career in Berlin, although he was able to organise a highly successful series of summer courses in Italy, which attracted pianists from all over the world. By the outbreak of World War II Schnabel had sought refuge in the USA. After the war he returned to Europe to spend his last years in Switzerland. His compositions, in atonal style, include three symphonies, a piano concerto, and a number of string quartets, trios, sonatas and pieces for solo pianoforte. He edited the Beethoven piano sonatas and various works by Mozart and Brahms. R.H.

Above: *Felix Mendelssohn-Bartholdy (1809-47) painted by Eduard Magnus in 1845/6. Soon after this his health began to fail, with migraines and chills, but the exact cause of his early death is unknown.*

Olivier MESSIAEN (b. 1908) France

Turangalîla Symphony
(first performed Boston, 1949)

Messiaen, the most remarkable French composer of recent times, has always pursued a highly independent musical direction. The stimulus of his music has been love, both the spiritual – he is a fervent Catholic – and the physical, as well as the infinite variety of birdsong. Indeed, he has described this huge symphony (huge in both terms of length and scale) as a 'song of love, a hymn to joy', taking its title from Sanskrit: *turanga* is time 'which runs like a galloping horse' and gives the work its movement and rhythm;' *lîla* is 'play', but more the play of 'divine action on the cosmos . . . the play of life and death'. It is also 'love'.

As well as a full orchestra, Messiaen also gives prominent roles to piano and the early electronic instrument, the ondes Martenot. Coupled to a percussion section akin to the gamelan orchestras of Indonesia, the ten-movement symphony is, to say the least, exotic in its colouring. Four strong cyclic themes unite this sprawling tapestry, as powerful and erotic a celebration of sexual loves as Wagner's *Tristan*, a legend which Messiaen acknowledges as a strong motivation for the work.

Wolfgang Amadeus MOZART (1756-91)
Austria

Symphony No. 29 in A K201
(date of first performance unknown)
Symphony No. 31 in D K297, *Paris*
(first performed Paris, 1778)
Symphony No. 35 in D K385, *Haffner*
(first performed Vienna, 1783)
Symphony No. 36 in C K425, *Linz*
(first performed Linz, 1783)
Symphony No. 38 in D K504, *Prague*
(first performed Prague, 1787)
Symphony No. 39 in Eb K543
(date of first performance unknown)
Symphony No. 40 in G minor K550
(date of first performance unknown)
Symphony No. 41 in C K551, *Jupiter*
(date of first performance unknown)

Ludwig van BEETHOVEN
(1770-1827)

Beethoven's father, of Flemish stock, a minor court musician at Bonn and a drunkard, taught his son the rudiments of music partly hoping to exploit his natural gifts for financial gain. But after working for four years in the household of Count Waldstein, the young man was invited by Haydn, in 1792, to go to Vienna as his pupil. Beethoven's rough and uncouth manner made the relationship an uneasy one, but they held each other's work in high esteem. Beethoven's reputation as a brilliant improviser began to grow, and when his first works (three piano trios) were published in 1795 they were well received. Three years later Beethoven discovered that he was going deaf, and the rest of his life can be represented as an heroic struggle against his growing disability and the intractability of so much of his inspiration. 'I carry my ideas with me a long time', he once said, and his sketchbooks clearly show the titanic efforts involved in turning the first rough jottings into the finished masterpieces we know so well today. Beethoven occupies a pivotal position between the classicism of the eighteenth century and the spirit of the new Romantic age, which his music did so much to create. His unquenchable genius expanded and enhanced every musical form it touched, and left us with a legacy of masterworks quite without parallel in this or any other century. R.H.

performance of those listed above. Today, these three are the most performed of the five, especially the *Italian* and the *Scottish* which reflect, in mood and colour, Mendelssohn's love for these two very different landscapes. The *Italian*, as you would expect is full of gaiety and exuberance, and concludes with an exhilarating dance movement, a *saltarello*; the *Scottish* is more serene and, at times, darker in mood. The best known of its themes is the big, expansive tune of the coda, still regarded by some as an uncharacteristic misjudgement by the composer.

Composed for the tercentenary of the Diet of Augsburg (1530), the *Reformation*, with its infectiously happy scherzo and aristocratic slow movement, has been quite unjustly neglected.

Mozart composed his first symphony aged eight, and what can be regarded his first mature essay in the medium (although No. 25 displays striking touches of originality) ten years later. From the unexpected downward swoop of its opening, however, it is obvious that No. 29 is in a class of its own. The lively finale, too, has its touches of genius.

For Mozart, the symphony was not to be the profound personal statement that it was for Beethoven, at least not until the final triptych of 1788, Nos 39-41. He found more sublime expression in the piano concerto, and symphonies like the *Paris* the *Haffner* and the *Linz* are brilliant examples of his more extrovert skills. Horns and trumpets give a festive quality to the last of these, a work of astounding concentration, even by Mozart's standards.

His greatest achievements in the medium begin with the *Prague* Symphony of 1787. Mozart had arrived in the city to find it buzzing about his opera *Le Nozze di Figaro* and the audience was no less ecstatic when he presented this new symphony to them – a refreshing change from the indifference of Vienna. The circumstances surrounding the last three masterpieces, however, are less well documented. That they were composed in 1788 is not disputed, but the process occupied nearer three months than the six breathless weeks of legend (although even three months is wholly remarkable). It has been suggested that, as no dedicatee was given, Mozart wrote them purely for himself. If he did, it would be unusual: constantly impecunious, he composed very little that was not either commissioned or financed by subscription.

Least played of the three is the mellow K543 in the muted key of E flat; the G minor (Mozart's 'sadness' key) is a hauntingly beautiful work whose flowing opening theme will be immediately familiar (unfortunately, perhaps more because of its misuse). No. 41 did not acquire its nickname through the composer, but it is an undeniably apposite one for this magnificent symphony with its grandly imperious opening. It ends with a matchless contrapuntal *tour de force*, the dazzling interplay of a dozen themes that is not only one of the crowning glories of Mozart's music but of the entire eighteenth century.

Carl NIELSEN (1865-1931) Denmark

Symphony No. 1 in G minor, Op. 7
(first performed Copenhagen, 1894)
Symphony No. 2, Op. 16 *The Four Temperaments* (first performed Copenhagen, 1902)
Symphony No. 3, Op. 27 *Sinfonia espansiva*
(first performed Copenhagen, 1912)
Symphony No. 4, Op. 29 *Inextinguishable*
Symphony No. 5, Op. 50
(first performed Copenhgen, 1922)
Symphony No. 6, *Sinfonia semplice*

It is only relatively recently that Carl Nielsen has come to be recognised as one of the great symphonists of this century. Although revered in his native Denmark, for the rest of the world the 'Nordic symphony' meant Sibelius, and performances of Nielsen's work were few and far between.

Now, thanks to some fine recordings, we can appreciate Nielsen's distinctive 'voice' and chart his progress through these six symphonies, which contain his finest music. Certain 'fingerprints', certain patterns of expression are common to them all, as is an arresting melodic invention.

No revolutionary, Nielsen was nevertheless the first composer to break with convention by ending a symphony (his First) in a different

Above: *The great Russian composer Sergei Prokofiev, with Myra Mendelson in 1946. He had lived with her since 1940 though not divorced from his wife who was imprisoned on political charges that year.*

key from that which begins it. He gave four of his symphonies subtitles, that of No. 2 depicting four human character types: the impetuous, indolent, melancholy and cheerful in that order. It is the latter personality that triumphs in the Third, the *Sinfonia espansiva*, music of irresistible optimism and confidence with an idyllic 'pastoral' interlude of rare beauty. Composed during the horrors of the First World War, the Fourth is a passionate testament to the durability of the human spirit, although Nielsen never revealed if events on the battlefields had been a motivation. Similarly, he never adequately explained the bizarre role of the snare drum in his Fifth Symphony, where it has a prominent solo directed 'to be played as though intended at all costs to disrupt the flow of the music'. The Sixth stands apart from the rest, especially the 'heroic' Fourth and Fifth. After the first movement, it takes on a shadowy, ambiguous quality quite new for Nielsen.

Sergei PROKOFIEV (1891-1953) Russia

Symphony No. 1 in D, Op. 25 *Classical*
(first performed Leningrad, 1918)
Symphony No. 5 in B♭, Op. 100
(first performed Moscow, 1945)
Symphony No. 6 in E♭ minor, Op. 11
(first performed Leningrad, 1947)
Symphony No. 7 in C♯ minor, Op. 131
(first performed 1952)

There is an interesting symmetry to Prokofiev's symphonies. He begins with a sparkling

Above: *A portrait of composer-pianist Sergei Rachmaninov painted by K. Somon in 1925. He had left Russia after the 1917 revolution and was living in Switzerland, settling in the USA in 1935.*

and highly skilful pastiche of the 'classical' symphony, vaults to the opposite extreme with No. 2 (in the composer's own words, 'made of iron and steel') and continued this dense, rough-hewn toughness in the uneven Third and Fourth.

With the Fifth, he rediscovered nobility and idealism, and at precisely the right historical moment: with the end of World War II just four months away, it gained an emotional reception from a Moscow audience for whom it must have symbolized the hoped-for future. To embody 'the grandeur of the human spirit,' was Prokofiev's aim. The Fifth has claims to be the greatest of Prokofiev's symphonies – it is certainly the most popular, along with No. 1 – but those claims are strongly challenged by the uncompromising Sixth. Trenchant, often raw, it is by no means comfortable listening; rather, its directness challenges the listener.

If the Sixth pointed a new direction, Prokofiev did not pursue it: he came full circle and, in the Seventh, composed a symphony almost as genial and untroubled as his First.

Sergei RACHMANINOV (1873-1943) Russia

Symphony No. 1 in D minor, Op. 13
(first performed St Petersburg
[Leningrad], 1897)
Symphony No. 2 in E minor, Op. 27
Symphony No. 3 in A minor, Op. 44

Good tunes have always been an essential component of the Slavonic symphony and

Rachmaninov's music is full of them. Unashamedly romantic (sometimes coming perilously close to cloying sentimentality), his symphonies – like Tchaikovsky's – make a direct appeal to the emotions. Many respond to them equally emotionally, especially the supremely lyrical Second, the best known of the three.

Yet the first performance of Symphony No. 1 was a disaster. It was unsympathetically, even badly played and poorly received, to the extent that it shattered Rachmaninov's already fragile confidence. Rachmaninov withdrew the score, and it was subsequently lost altogether. We can only enjoy the work now thanks to the discovery of a set of orchestral parts at the Leningrad Conservatory in 1944.

It was 1906 before the composer again attempted a symphony and the result was not only longer than the First, but even richer in its melody. The clarinet solo in the poignant adagio remains one of the loveliest tunes ever written. By the time of the Third Symphony, 1935/6, Rachmaninov had settled in the United States, but his musical language remained the same: ardent lyricism, broad sweeps of melody and sumptuous orchestration, all within a strictly formal framework. For Rachmaninov, the twentieth century's revolution in music never happened, and there are many who are rather glad it didn't.

Camille SAINT-SAËNS (1835-1921) France

Symphony No. 3 in C minor, Op. 78 (Organ Symphony)
(first performed London, 1886)

This perenially popular work was composed to a commission from the Royal Philharmonic Society of London and dedicated to the memory of Franz Liszt, whose influence is apparent in the constant transformation of recurring themes. It takes its nickname from the inclusion of an organ, but no less original is the addition of a piano. The overlaying of the imperious organ chords of the final movement with glistening arpeggios on piano results in one of the most distinctive symphonic colourings in all music.

Franz SCHUBERT (1797-1828) Austria

Symphony No. 3 in D, D200
Symphony No. 4 in C minor, D417, Tragic
Symphony No. 5 in B♭, D485
Symphony No. 8 in B minor, D759,
Unfinished (first performed Vienna, 1865)
Symphony No. 9 in C, D944,
The Great C Major
(first performed Leipzig, 1839)

Despite composing five symphonies before his twentieth birthday, at least three of which are masterpieces to vie with anything Mozart composed during his adolescence, Schubert was unknown as a symphonist during his life-

Above: *Camille Saint-Saëns (1835-1921) was not a prolific composer and was remarkably adept at making the most of sometimes unpromising material. He dedicated his 3rd Symphony to Liszt.*

time and he had failed to make his mark in the world of opera. If he was acknowledged for anything outside his family, friends and the 'bohemian' circles in which he mixed, it was for his songs.

Haydn and Mozart, rather than Beethoven (whom Schubert revered from afar) are the models for the Third, Fourth and Fifth Symphonies. None could be called 'imposing', even No. 4 despite the composer's title, although it is the most dramatic of the three. The D Major No. 3 of 1815, on the other hand, is the most felicitous music imaginable, full of charm and sparkle. No less genial, but more classical and the most refined of these teenage works, the Fifth Symphony was composed a year later; it may also have been the only one of his symphonies Schubert ever heard performed, at a private concert in 1819.

No one knows why, three years later, Schubert failed to complete his Eighth Symphony, but it was not untypical of him. It tends to be forgotten that the preceding Seventh Symphony never progressed beyond the draft stage. But whatever else he may have put to one side, as far as the world is concerned, the *Unfinished* is Schubert's Symphony No. 8. Its surviving two movements, an allegro moderato and andante con moto, have a nobility and gravity worthy of Beethoven: this, if anything, would surely have been Schubert's *Tragic* symphony. It may be that his failure to finish the work had more to do with the difficulty of writing final movements to match the depth and intensity of the first two than any practical distraction.

Wolfgang Amadeus MOZART (1756-91)

The facts of Mozart's life are simply told. He was the son of Leopold Mozart, *Kapellmeister* to the Prince of Salzburg. At the age of three he was already playing the klavier; at five he started composing, and two years later he had mastered the violin. His elder sister Anna Maria was herself an accomplished musician, and Leopold took his gifted children on a series of strenuous tours to the great courts of Europe, where their talents were hailed with astonishment. Young Mozart met many leading musicians, some of whom became his teachers, and by the time he was twelve he had written numerous works, including two operas. In 1777 he went on tour accompanied by his mother, in place of Leopold, who was too ill to undertake the journey. She died while they were in Paris, and Mozart, no longer an infant prodigy, returned to Salzburg to the unsympathetic atmosphere of the archbishop's court. In 1781 he resigned, and a year later went to Vienna where he married Constanze Weber. His financial position remained uncertain during the last nine years of his life, so mysteriously cut short, but an unending stream of new works of all kinds poured from his pen during that time. Those are the facts. Of his genius, all that can be said was said some years later by Rossini, ' . . . Mozart is the only one.' Listen and give thanks. R.H.

Several attempts have been made to 'finish' the *Unfinished*. The concensus among musicologists is that one of the *entr'actes* from the incidental music to *Rosamunde* (discussed under orchestral compositions) fits the bill as a finale. It may even have been the original finale, urgently pressed into use elsewhere. This, together with a modern completion of the scherzo, gives a four-movement symphony which has been both performed and recorded.

Schubert finished his Ninth, longest and greatest symphony in the year of his death, whereupon – like that of the *Unfinished* – the score was shelved. It took eleven years and the earnest efforts of Robert Schumann and Felix Mendelssohn before this work, described by the former as being of 'heavenly length' (he meant it as a compliment) was heard. As well as being the glorious summation of Schubert's gifts, its importance as a transitional work can be appreciated, with foretastes not only of Schumann and Mendelssohn, but the expansive, and very 'Austrian' symphonies of Bruckner.

Robert SCHUMANN (1810-56) Germany

Symphony No. 1 in B♭, Op. 38 *Spring*
(first performed Leipzig, 1841)
Symphony No. 2 in C, Op. 61
(first performed Leipzig, 1846)
Symphony No. 3 in E♭, Op. 97 *Rhenish*
(first performed Dusseldorf, 1851)
Symphony No. 4 in D minor, Op. 120
(first performed Dusseldorf, 1853)

Surprisingly, for they are warmly Romantic and tuneful works, Schumann's symphonies have never attained the popularity, either in the concert hall or on record, of those of his great friend, Brahms. It is still suggested that Schumann never mastered the subtle art of orchestration, with the result that his textures can sound opaque and lacking in contrast and colour. Well-intentioned revisions of the orchestration of these symphonies have been undertaken, most notably by Gustav Mahler, but in the right hands Schumann's first thoughts remain wholly satisfying: there are more than sufficient compensations for any theoretical failings.

The First Symphony is a fine example of the symphonic unity Schumann was able to achieve with thematic links between all four movements. Although – in true Romantic tradition – poetry was the original stimulus for the work, Schumann eventually dispensed with the evocative titles given to each movement. Nevertheless, the nickname of *Spring* has stuck firmly and is not inappropriate for this vigorous, optimistic symphony.

Schumann next tackled a symphony in D minor, only to withdraw the work after its first performance in 1841. He did revise it, but not

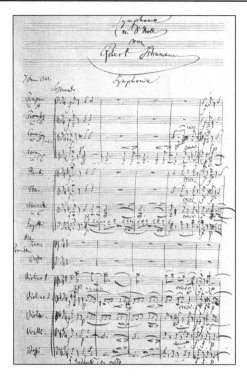

Above: *Manuscript of the opening bars of Schumann's Symphony No. 4 in D minor, written in 1841 and performed in Leipzig as No. 2 but revised and (as No. 4) first heard in Düsseldorf in 1852.*

until ten years had elapsed, with the result that this remarkable, exhilarating work then became his Fourth and last symphony. The four movements, again skilfully interrelated, are played without a break, a rich mixture of the assertive and the lyrical so typical of Schumann.

Between these works, he produced a published Second Symphony, notable for its

Below: *A portrait of Robert Schumann (1810-56) from the Museum of La Scala, Milan. He attempted to drown himself in the Rhine in 1854 but was rescued and spent the rest of his life in an asylum.*

ravishingly beautiful adagio espressivo, and then a Third, the *Rhenish*. Stimulated by the air and the scenery of the Rhineland, and by the warm reception he was accorded by the people of Düsseldorf upon his appointment in 1850 as City Music Director, Schumann's creative spark was revived. In the main, the Third radiates a brisk, cheery, open-air quality, sharpening the contrast with the lofty solemnity of the slow movement, apparently inspired by the atmosphere in Cologne Cathedral prior to the enthronement of a new archbishop.

Dmitri SHOSTAKOVICH (1906-75) Russia

Symphony No. 1 in F minor, Op. 10
(first performed Leningrad, 1926)
Symphony No. 4 in C minor, Op. 43
(first performed 1961)
Symphony No. 5 in D minor, Op. 47
(first performed Leningrad, 1937)
Symphony No. 6 in B minor, Op. 54
(first performed Moscow, 1939)
Symphony No. 7 in C, Op. 60 *Leningrad*
(first performed Kuibyshev, 1942)
Symphony No. 8 in C minor, Op. 65
(first performed Moscow, 1943)
Symphony No. 9 in E♭, Op. 70
(first performed Leningrad, 1945)
Symphony No. 10 in E minor, Op. 93
(first performed Leningrad, 1953)
Symphony No. 11 in G minor, Op. 103
The Year 1905 (first performed Moscow, 1957)
Symphony No. 13 in B♭ minor, Op. 113
Babi Yar (first performed Moscow, 1962)
Symphony No. 14, Op. 135
(first performed Leningrad, 1969)
Symphony No. 15 in A, Op. 141
(first performed Moscow, 1972)

The fifteen symphonies of Shostakovich point the differences, often apparently irreconcilable, between the public and the private faces of the Soviet Union's greatest composer. His First Symphony, a student work which displayed a notable mastery of the form as well as inspiration, was immediately acclaimed, not only in the Soviet Union but around the world. To the new Bolshevik government, Dmitri Shostakovich became an exploitable property and his next two symphonies, tough works entitled *To October* and *May Day*, did not disappoint.

The fall from grace came in 1936, with *Pravda's* notorious attack entitled 'Muddle instead of Music'. Though unsigned, the sentiments were self-evidently those of the tyrannical Soviet leader Josef Stalin and were echoed obediently by the music establishment. Prudently, Shostakovich withdrew the score of his Fourth Symphony, a darker, more questioning work than any of its predecessors, and turned to a Fifth which he subtitled 'A Soviet Artist's Reply to Just Criticism'. He did not elaborate upon whose or what criticism he considered just: it may have only been an acknowledgment of a need for musical maturity – the Fifth is more finely crafted than anything that came before – rather than political 'maturity'.

The Fifth was a success from the start (it remains his most popular symphony), yet Shostakovich had outwitted his critics. Superficially, the work is the unequivocal 'heroic' triumph they wanted to hear: at a deeper level, the triumph becomes hollow, the gestures empty and the confident declamations grotesque irony.

For his Sixth Symphony, the composer promised a magnificent tribute to Lenin (an idea he never did bring to fruition) but instead produced a work unusual in its three movement structure (slow, fast, faster) and, in the second and third of those, full of gaiety and good humour. The profound stillness of the opening largo, a glimpse of some unfathomable void, is among Shostakovich's most atmospheric writing.

From 1941, along with all the other citizens of Leningrad, the composer lived through the city's 900-day siege at the hands of the Nazi invaders. It inspired the Seventh Symphony, which in turn proved an inspiration not only for the Soviet people, but those of the west. Its message of resistance and hope was enthusiastically embraced everywhere the symphony was heard. Shostakovich's other 'war symphony', the Eighth, is much less defiant and musically much the finer work. Sorrow and suffering are all too evident here and, if anything, the middle movements portray horror and brutality even more chillingly than the famous 'invasion march' from the first movement of the *Leningrad*.

With the Ninth, Shostakovich again disappointed Stalin. The 'great leader' expected something at least along the lines of Beethoven's *Choral* not so much to celebrate the end of the war, but his achievement in ending it. What he got was a light and easy-going expression of relief, happiness and hope. Briefly, sunshine had broken through the cloud.

The years leading up to Stalin's death in 1953 were again difficult ones for Shostakovich and it was not until December of that year that his Tenth Symphony was premièred. It is arguably his greatest work and although its underlying motivation can only be guessed at, it surely bears painful, poignant witness to an era. The second movement, a violent, flailing musical onslaught, has been identified as a 'portrait' of Stalin.

For his Eleventh and Twelfth symphonies, Shostakovich returned to programmatic music – and propaganda. The former, depicting the bloody events of 1905 (the first 'Russian Revolution') is the better-constructed, more convincing of the two.

With the Thirteenth Symphony, new ground is broken in more than one respect. For the first time since the choral finale of the Second, voices are employed, and they are used to express the words of – at that time – one of the most controversial of Soviet poets, Yevgeni Yevtushenko. The symphony takes its name from Yevtushenko's *Babi Yar*, which recounts Nazi atrocities in the Ukraine, and points an accusing finger at anti-semitism in the Soviet Union.

Although the première was allowed, there was unease in high places and, despite some amendments by Yevtushenko, the work was effectively banned in the USSR for several years and only heard in the West through a pirated recording. Today, this powerful, uncompromising and chilling work can be heard both sides of the Iron Curtain.

If the Thirteenth can at least be categorised as a symphonic song cycle in the style of Mahler's *Das Lied von der Erde*, the Fourteenth Symphony seems to have few claims to such a description. It consists of settings of eleven poems by four poets to the accompaniment of a chamber orchestra and a battery of percussion. Death is the linking theme, Shostakovich having suffered two heart attacks by the time of its composition and acutely aware of his mortality. Perhaps his most profoundly philosophical work, it is certainly one of his greatest.

In his Fifteenth and final symphony, the composer returned to the traditional four-movement format and to purely instrumental forces, albeit with sparse textures and a delight in exotic instrumental timbres. It is Shostakovich at his strangest and most ambiguouus – why the quotations from Rossini (*William Tell*) and Wagner (*Die Walküre*), not to mention his own works? As well as posing riddles, it has humour and it hints at darker things, and in so doing reveals its essential 'Russianness'. Shostakovich kept us – and 'them' – guessing until the very end.

Below: *The world-weary face of Dmitri Shostakovich (1906-75) who spent his musical life in Russia riding the recurring criticism of 'bourgeois decadence' and 'intellectualism'.*

Muzio CLEMENTI
(1752-1832)

Prodigiously musical son of a musically inclined Roman silversmith, he was taken to England at fourteen to extend his studies, had a sensational London début as a pianist in 1770, and published the first three of his sixty piano sonatas in 1773. He spent most of the rest of his life in England, where he was variously engaged as pianist, conductor, teacher, composer, publisher, and piano manufacturer. But he made many lengthy European tours, during which he once engaged with Mozart in a test of skill at pianistic improvisation, etc, before the King of Prussia. A draw was declared, and Mozart complained that Clementi was a charlatan because he concentrated on mere technical showmanship, pioneering as he did the extensive use of thirds and octaves. On the other hand, Beethoven greatly admired some of his sonatas, which were the first to make a clear distinction between the requirements of harpsichord and piano, and were thus a pointer to the future. He also produced a collection of 100 studies called *Gradus ad Parnassum*, which became a standard guide to piano technique and had the honour of being parodied by Debussy in his *Children's Cornér*, where the first piece is called 'Dr Gradus ad Parnassum'. J.C.

Jean SIBELIUS (1865-1957) Finland

Symphony No. 1 in E minor, Op. 39
(first performed Helsinki, 1899)
Symphony No. 2 in D, Op. 43
(first performed Helsinki, 1902)
Symphony No. 3 in C, Op. 52
(first performed London, 1907)
Symphony No. 4 in A minor, Op. 63
(first performed Helsinki, 1911)
Symphony No. 5 in E♭, Op. 82
(first performed – original version Helsinki,
1915; revised, London 1921)
Symphony No. 6 in D minor, Op. 104
(first performed Helsinki, 1923)
Symphony No. 7 in C, Op. 105
(first performed Helsinki, 1924)

Sibelius was more than just geographically isolated from his European contemporaries. His music, too, developed along very different lines from that being composed by Mahler, Elgar or Richard Strauss. After two highly-charged, romantic symphonies whose richness and sweep of melody maintains their perennial popularity, he sought to refine and distill his orchestral writing. Compared to the luxuriant orchestrations of Strauss or Scriabin, the results were almost monochromatic, and this concentration of ideas reached its peak in the taut, concise Seventh Symphony.

The First and Second Symphonies display an obvious debt to Tchaikovsky, but by the Third Sibelius had developed a wholly and recognisably individual musical language, one characterised by its comparative sobriety and economy. However, this did not prevent him conjuring some fine melodies, especially in the Fifth, a work whose revision between first and subsequent performances occupied Sibelius for six years. The big horn tune of the final movement, which ends memorably with six unevenly spaced hammer blows, is quintessential Sibelius.

The composer once described the basic difference between his music and that of others as 'cocktails of all colours' compared to 'pure cold water', and this is nowhere more apparent than in the Fourth Symphony, considered by many to be Sibelius's greatest achievement. For some, it is an evocation of empty Arctic expanses; for others the bleak, brooding atmosphere is more psychological than geophysical. Certainly, the despair of the third movement is almost tangible and the climax of the symphony is one of the most original and disturbing in all music. Without question the Fourth is one of the peaks of symphonic composition this century.

The Seventh is eloquent testimony to what Sibelius sought from the symphonic medium: 'severity of form and the profound logic that creates an inner connection between all the motifs'. It also marked the end of his 'symphonic journey'. In the thirty-three years between its first performance and his death in 1957, he never returned to the form.

Igor STRAVINSKY (1882-1971) Russia

Symphony in C
(first performed Chicago, 1940)
Symphony in Three Movements
(first performed New York, 1946)

Three decades separate Stravinsky's E flat symphony, an apprentice work, and these two mature masterpieces. In that time, he had eschewed the opulent and colourful style of his teacher, Rimsky-Korsakov, and of Tchaikovsky for a neo-classicism which had both crystal clarity and a cutting edge. The C major work, composed for the 50th birthday of the Chicago Symphony Orchestra, is notable for the three-note motif which is the kernel of its first and third movement, and its richly contrapuntal slow movement.

Echoes of war characterise the Symphony in Three Movements, the urgency and aggression in sharp contrast to the repose of the central andante. A piano plays an important role in reinforcing the percussive and rhythmic elements of the work and the first movement, with its storming opening, is remarkable for being probably the first orchestral music to have no descriptive tempo indications, merely metronome marks to indicate the differing speeds.

Pyotr Ilyich TCHAIKOVSKY (1840-93) Russia

Symphony No. 1 in G minor, Op. 13
Winter Daydreams
(first performed Moscow, 1868)
Symphony No. 2 in C minor, Op. 17
Little Russian
(first performed Moscow, 1873)
Symphony No. 3 in D, Op. 29 *Polish*
(first performed 1875)

Below: *Igor Stravinsky, born in Russia, became a French citizen in 1934 but moved to the USA at the outbreak of war.*

Symphony No. 4 in F minor, Op. 36
(first performed Moscow, 1878)
Symphony No. 5 in E minor, Op. 64
(first performed St Petersburg
[now Leningrad], 1888)
Symphony No. 6 in B minor, Op. 74 *Pathétique* (first performed St Petersburg, 1893)

Tchaikovsky, a tormented soul if ever there was one, experienced more than his fair share of torment during the gestation of his First Symphony. He worked on it through most of 1866, despite being on the edge of a nervous breakdown. At first only individual movements were performed and, when the whole work did get a hearing, the composer went on to make cuts and revisions which delayed publication until 1874. The work, which owes something to Schumann and Mendelssohn both musically and in its use of descriptive titles, betrays none of the *angst* which overlaid its conception.

The Second Symphony, despite its finer craftsmanship, was also subjected to much revision. Here Tchaikovsky, never part of the 'nationalist' school, makes good use of the kind of delightful folk melodies beloved by its members (Borodin, Balakirev and so forth) and the work's exhilarating finale is based on a Ukranian folk song entitled *The Crane*. And it is from that area that the work gets its nickname, the Ukraine being rather condescendingly known as 'Little Russia'.

The title of the Third Symphony is slightly more tenuous: only the main theme of its finale is based on the rhythm of the polonaise, a Polish national dance.

With the Fourth, Tchaikovsky embarked on a trilogy of symphonies worthy to stand alongside any in the Austro-German tradition, in terms of form, development, weight and impact. In addition to those qualities, he could muster a unique gift for melody, harmony and orchestral colour, as well as a huge emotional range. He called the Fourth his 'fate' symphony, and announces the fate motif with an imposing brass fanfare at the very start of the symphony. A melancholy slow movement follows, then a delicious scherzo, the strings playing pizzicato throughout. The finale, with the 'fate' motif taking a prominent role, whirls between the hysterical and the merely frivolous before coming to an exuberant end.

A similar motif permeates all four movements of the Fifth Symphony, overall a finer work with less 'heart-on-the-sleeve' declamations. The elegant waltz of the third movement is one of Tchaikovsky's loveliest creations, while the finale has an imposing nobility.

Apart from the brash third movement, the mood of the Sixth, as its subtitle implies, is one of tragedy and pathos, although it escapes becoming 'pathetic' in the maudlin sense. What we hear in the last movement, the most starkly original music Tchaikovsky wrote, is not a tearful sentimentality but an

Above: *An earnest discussion by conductors Sir Adrian Boult and Sir Henry Wood passes over the head of composer Ralph Vaughan Williams prior to a performance of his music in the old Queen's Hall.*

aching, almost suicidal despair. Tchaikovsky was being excessively modest when he called the symphony 'a good piece': it belongs among the very greatest, and is his epitaph. With the *Pathétique*, he comes painfully to terms with fate.

Ralph VAUGHAN WILLIAMS (1872-1958) England

Symphony No. 2, *A London Symphony*
(first performed London, 1914)
Symphony No. 3, *A Pastoral Symphony*
(first performed London, 1922)
Symphony No. 4 in F minor
(first performed London, 1935)
Symphony No. 5 in D
(first performed London, 1943)
Symphony No. 6 in E minor
(first performed London, 1948)
Symphony No. 7, *Sinfonia Antartica*
(first performed Manchester, 1953)

In all, Vaughan Williams composed nine symphonies, a cycle which spans his entire creative life. Those generally acknowledged to be his best are listed above, though the other three have many qualities to recommend them, and the Ninth only just misses inclusion.

Both the Second and Third Symphonies are much more than evocative tone paintings. The former, powerfully atmospheric is no mere picture postcard impression of the city: there is colour, pageantry, gaiety, even a London fog and the chimes of Big Ben, but it explores other, deeper levels of expression, too. Similarly, the *Pastoral* is no bucolic romp. The fields which inspired its often haunting and poignant lyricism were those of

France, in the midst of World War I. Despite three slow movements and general quietude, the Third casts a spell which keeps it well clear of monotony.

'I don't know if I like it, but it's what I meant' was the composer's summing up of his Fourth Symphony, an often dissonant and brutally uncompromising work. In its refusal to pull punches, many see it as his finest, most 'European' symphony, but others cite the serene, quasi-mystical Fifth, with its radiant, glowing themes. At seventy-one, Vaughan Williams seemed to be looking towards heaven in the Fifth, but soon demonstrated it was not the glorious swansong some believed.

The Sixth Symphony, written between 1944 and 1947, mirrors uncertainty of the post-war world. It is a work of contrasting emotions: the ferocity of the first movement is interrupted by a lyrical central section that seems designed to offer comfort and reassurance. But the most original feature of the Sixth is its final movement – the Epilogue as the composer called it. In its eleven minutes length, this music never once rises above pianissimo, seemingly stalking some region of sunless desolation. It has been interpreted as the landscape of a post-nuclear holocaust, but Vaughan Williams gives the real clue with his quote from Shakespeare's *The Tempest*: 'We are such stuff as dreams are made on, and our little life is rounded with a sleep.'

The true landscape of cold desolation is to be found in the Seventh Symphony. Vaughan Williams had been asked to compose music for the film *Scott of the Antarctic* in 1947 and so absorbed was he by the story that two years later he reworked parts of this score into a large-scale symphony, the *Sinfonia Antartica*. Despite its literal use of effects such as a wind-machine, the work is much more than a musical equivalent of the film. The awesome fear, yet limitless fascination of nature has seldom been better conveyed.

William WALTON (1902-83) England

Symphony No. 1
(first performed [complete] London, 1935)

A boldly ambitious work of stunning vitality and invention, Walton's First occupies a special place in the canon of the English symphony. The composer had difficulty concluding the piece at first and allowed the performance of the first three movements alone just under a year before the première of the completed work. It had no effect on the enthusiastic acceptance of this brilliant début, although a Second Symphony failed to achieve the same stature.

Right: *Sir William Walton (1902-83) in the role of conductor. Walton spent the last years of his life away from the hurly-burly of the music scene on the island of Ischia, off Naples.*

Alexander BORODIN
(1833-87)

Illegitimate son of a Russian prince whose childhood talents encompassed both music and science, he opted for the latter, graduated in medicine at St Petersburg, studied at Heidelberg, and eventually became a senior lecturer in chemistry. But his musical interests persisted (he married a pianist), and a meeting with Balakirev in 1862 led to a serious study of composition. He stole what time he could from a busily chaotic life in science and teaching in order to compose, and became one of 'The Five' who collaborated in the cause of a truly Russian music. During visits to scientific congresses, etc, he made many musical contacts (Liszt was one helping admirer), and despite Tchaikovsky's remark that Borodin 'couldn't write a line without outside help', his limited output includes some splendid music. After eighteen years interrupted work on the opera *Prince Igor*, this had to be finished by Rimsky-Korsakov and Glazunov after his death. But it is acknowledged as a masterpiece, while his Second Symphony and Second String Quartet, and the tone-poem *In the Steppes of Central Asia*, give a place of honour to this genial and much-loved academic who once said that 'Science is my work and music is my fun'. J.C.

Coming from the Latin *concertare* (to contest, or rival), the first 'concertos' were indeed contests – amicable ones! – between groups of instruments. Out of these grew the *concerto grosso*, in which a small group of instruments played by the more proficient members of an orchestra would take prominent solo roles in a work. Corelli and Handel wrote groups of *concerti grossi* and Bach's Brandenburg Concertos qualify for this description.

Italian pre-eminence in the making and playing of the violin had led to the composition of many hundreds of *concerti* which were essentially display vehicles for the skills of the solo violinist. It was the beginning of the 'virtuoso concerto' and soon extended to other instruments, especially the harpsichord and later the fortepiano.

With Mozart, the fortepiano concerto went through an amazing transformation, becoming as great a means of expression as the symphony or the string quartet. Beethoven brought the 'heroic' style of concerto, as well as compounding the abilities required of the soloist. The nineteenth century saw the composition of increasingly large-scale and technically ambitious concertos, principally for piano and violin, and these works remain the soloist's staple fare.

The twentieth century has also produced its share of great concertos – by Bartók, Rachmaninov, Elgar, Prokofiev and Nielsen among others – and recent years have seen two fine violin concertos written for the American virtuoso Isaac Stern: one by Britain's Sir Peter Maxwell Davies, the other by Frenchman Henri Dutilleux. P.H.

Johann Sebastian BACH (1685-1750)
Germany

Harpsichord Concerto No. 1 in D minor, BWV1052
(first performed Leipzig, c. 1735)

It is thought that Bach was the first to compose concertos which gave a prominent solo role to a keyboard instrument – in his case, the harpsichord. Often, however, these concertos were adaptations and the D minor work was possibly based on an unknown violin concerto, probably as part of the music Bach provided for the Leipzig music society which he directed.

It is in the usual three movements, with the first and third also used as instrumental interludes from a church cantata (a wholly acceptable practice in Bach's time). A splendid piece, it amply displays Bach's dazzling mastery of a host of musical devices.

Concerto in D minor for two violins, BWV1043
(first performed Cöthen, 1717-23?)

The most famous of Bach's concertos (apart from the Brandenburgs), mainly thanks to its sublimely beautiful and loftily romantic slow movement. The soloists are treated as equals, each getting the opportunity for display, especially in the vigorous outer movements and, throughout, the interweaving of the violin lines never cease to delight.

Violin Concerto No. 1 in A minor, BWV1041
(first performed Cöthen, 1717-23?)
Violin Concerto No. 2 in E, BWV1042
(first performed Cöthen, 1717-23?)

Along with the Double Violin Concerto (above), these are the only violin concertos by Bach which survive in their original form, and are also products of his time at Cöthen. The influence of Vivaldi is apparent in their Italianate style, but the consummate use of counterpoint is pure Bach.

Béla BARTÓK (1881-1945) Hungary

Piano Concerto No. 1
(first performed Frankfurt-am-Main, 1927)
Piano Concerto No. 2
(first performed Frankfurt-am-Main, 1933)
Piano Concert No. 3
(first performed Philadelphia, 1946)

Like his fellow-countryman, Liszt, Bartók was a prodigiously gifted pianist who, harnessing this to his compositional genius, was able to open up new sound worlds for the instrument. In the main, he exploited its percussive possibilities rather than the lyrical, but – as the Third Piano Concerto shows – he also appreciated its more subtle, evanescent qualities.

Jagged, martial rhythms and a generally sour disposition have failed to endear the First Concerto to the listening public in all its sixty years' existence. As the composer intended, the Second Concerto is altogether more attractive, with its high-spirited, dancing outer movements. Two highly original features of the work are its orchestration – the full orchestra is used only for the last movement – and its central movement, a cleverly constructed 'scherzo within an adagio'.

Aggression and brilliance are absent from the Third Piano Concerto, a product of Bartók's American years and one of the last works he wrote. Lyrical, valedictory, this sublimely beautiful work is notable for, among other things, its extraordinary slow movement, marked adagio religioso by the composer. This tempo alludes to the chorale-like melody of its outer sections, while the central episode grows into one of Bartók's 'night musics', a hypnotic evocation of the colourful and delicate nocturnal sounds of nature. The whole movement is exquisitely scored.

Violin Concerto No. 2 in B minor
(first performed Amsterdam, 1939)

As far as the composer was concerned, this was his only violin concerto: what we now refer to as 'No. 1' is an early, two-movement work not published until after his death. Written to a commission from the virtuoso, and fellow-Hungarian, Zoltán Székely, Bartók managed to give his friend ample opportunity for display while not losing sight of the musical structure: first and third movements are closely related, while the slow movement is a rhapsodic set of variations. The world and its performers having got used to its difficulties, it now lays claim to parity with Beethoven and Brahms.

Below: *An 1870 painting by Toby Edward Rosenthal, imaginatively portraying Johann Sebastian Bach and his extensive family enjoying an evening with music occupying some degree of attention.*

Claudio ARRAU
(b. 1903)

Famous Chilean pianist. Studied with his mother who was an amateur pianist and showed such talent that he was sent on a government grant to study in Berlin, 1914-15. Performed throughout Europe before returning to Chile in 1921 to make his first professional appearance there. Toured the USA in 1924 and Russia 1929 and 1930. A comprehensive student of music, he achieved some remarkable firsts by playing the complete keyboard works of Bach in a series of twelve recitals in Berlin 1935-6, followed in 1936 by all the keyboard music of Mozart and, in 1938, by all the Beethoven piano sonatas and concertos. Settled in New York in 1941 and has continued to tour the world and record extensively until recent years. A universally admired pianist who plays with classical grace and precision yet always with great depth and understanding of the repertoire. P.G.

John FIELD
(1782-1837)

Now remembered primarily as originator of the pianistic *nocturne* – and then mainly because the form was taken up and further poeticised by Chopin – this Irish pianist-composer from a very musical family made his début in Dublin at nine. Moving to England, he played at the age of twelve to an audience including Haydn, who foresaw a big future for him. He became apprenticed to Clementi, whose pianos he demonstrated by extemporising on them at a London warehouse, and who took Field as an assistant on his Continental tours. This led to him settling in Russia in 1803, where he eventually became an important and fashionable teacher, while continuing to tour Europe as a virtuoso pianist. In the latter role he had a very polished but unaffected style, in contrast with the histrionic Liszt – who incidentally was a great admirer and later published an edition of Field's nocturnes with an enthusiastic introduction. Schumann was another enthusiast, especially for the piano concertos; but while the twenty nocturnes and seven concertos are joined by four sonatas, six rondos, and chamber and other works, little is heard of him these days. J.C.

Ludwig van BEETHOVEN (1770-1827)
Germany

Piano Concerto No. 1 in C, Op. 15
(first performed Vienna, 1795)
Piano Concerto No. 2 in B♭, Op. 19
(first performed Vienna, 1795)
Piano Concerto No. 3 in C minor, Op. 37
(first performed Vienna, 1803)
Piano Concerto No. 4 in G, Op. 58
(first performed Vienna, 1807)
Piano Concerto No. 5 in E♭, Op. 73,
Emperor (first performed Leipzig, 1810)

Beethoven inherited the piano concerto from Mozart and, like him, did not depart from the 'classical' three-movement form. The first two concertos (No. 1 was actually the second to be written: the later publication of 'No. 2' caused the transposition) are engaging, undemanding works that conclude with sprightly, cheerful rondos. As with the *Eroica* Symphony, it is with the third of the series that the style changes to something grander, more heroic and more ambitious. The

Below: *Ludwig van Beethoven (1770-1827) portrayed playing the violin. He was, as we might expect of the composer of one of the greatest of all violin concertos, a gifted exponent.*

vigorously assertive first movement is followed by a wistful second, while the bustling third is of sterner stuff than its predecessors.

The G Major is the most original of Beethoven's concertos. After an opening movement of poetic elegance and hushed intensity there follows an extraordinary dialogue between the 'aggressive' orchestra and the 'gentle' piano, with the latter eventually triumphant and suddenly bursting into the most jovial of rondos.

The composer and piano maker J. B. Cramer has been suggested as having given the Fifth its nickname. It is not inappropriate for this glittering work, the first of his concertos that Beethoven, due to encroaching deafness, was unable to première himself.

Violin Concerto in D, Op. 61
(first performed Vienna, 1806)

Beethoven's solitary concerto for violin was written for the Viennese virtuoso Franz Clement. Five soft beats on the kettledrum introduce a rhapsodic first movement. The rapturous larghetto, music of fragile beauty, leads into the rollicking finale.

Triple Concerto in C, Op. 56
(first performed Vienna, 1808)

This unusual work, which gives solo roles to the piano, violin and cello, is not without its flaws, but is hugely enjoyable. Two lively outer movements, the last in polonaise rhythm, frame a brief, reflective slow movement and, throughout, there are memorable moments for all three soloists.

Alban BERG (1885-1935) Austria

Violin Concerto
(first performed Barcelona, 1936)

This highly charged, deeply affecting work exemplifies Berg's close affinity with late Romanticism. It is dedicated 'To the memory of an Angel', the 'angel' being the teenage daughter of the architect Walter Gropius and Mahler's widow, Alma. Manon Gropius died of polio at eighteen, a tragedy given voice in the anguished opening to the second part of the concerto, while the final, consoling episode is notable for its apt use of Bach's noble chorale theme 'Es ist genug' ('It is enough').

Johannes BRAHMS (1833-97) Germany

Piano Concerto No. 1 in D minor, Op. 15
(first performed Hanover, 1859)
Piano Concerto No. 2 in B♭, Op. 83
(first performed Budapest, 1881)

These two large-scale, leonine concertos have enjoyed contrasting fortunes. The First, developed from ideas originally intended for a symphony, is intensely dramatic. After an imperious opening, the first movement is urgent and unrelenting. The storm abates for the meditative slow movement, which Brahms marked as a benediction, but returns in the pounding main theme of the finale.

The Second Concerto, unusually in four movements, has always been the more popular of the two, no doubt because of its more lyrical, more relaxed mood. It ends with an allegretto grazioso that takes its flavour from the high-spirited Hungarian gypsy music which Brahms loved, no doubt a more

Above: *The composer Johannes Brahms (1833-97) portrayed by Olga von Miller. His concerto repertoire included two piano concertos, a violin concerto and a double concerto for violin and cello.*

Above: *In this painting by Siemiradski of 1877, Chopin is playing in the drawing-room of Prince Anton Radziwill, no doubt performing some of his nocturnes, waltzes, polonaises and mazurkas.*

appealing conclusion than the unsettling agitation of the earlier work.

Violin Concerto in D, Op. 77
(first performed Leipzig, 1879)

Like Beethoven, Brahms composed only one Violin Concerto and, not surprisingly, it was dedicated to his longstanding friend and supporter, the virtuoso Joseph Joachim. No doubt Joachim's technique was equal to the great demands placed on the soloist in this grand and sinewy work. As with the Second Piano Concerto, there is an unmistakable Hungarian lilt to the bustling finale.

Double Concerto in A minor, Op. 102
(first performed Cologne, 1887)

With solo roles for violin and cello, this was Brahms's last orchestral composition. The soloists are given equal status, despite the violin's naturally greater penetration of the orchestral texture. It bears many typically Brahmsian hallmarks – the muscular, the lyrical, the reflective and, in the concluding vivace, the 'gypsy in his soul'!

Max BRUCH (1838-1920) Germany

Violin Concerto No. 1 in G minor, Op. 26
(first performed Koblenz, 1866)

The archetypal 'romantic concerto', this perenially popular work remains one of only two compositions for which Bruch is remembered (the other is his rhapsody for cello and orchestra, *Kol Nidrei*). The melancholy tune of the slow movement has proved irresistible to generations of listeners.

Frédéric CHOPIN (1810-49) Poland

Piano Concerto No. 1 in E minor, Op. 11
(first performed [public] Warsaw, 1830)
Piano Concerto No. 2 in F minor, Op. 21
(first performed Warsaw, 1830)

Both the Chopin concertos were written within the space of a year: the F minor was actually the first to be completed and performed, but was published after the E minor, hence its numbering. Predictably for a composer who wrote very little other than piano compositions, the orchestra plays mainly a supportive role in the concertos, especially the First, with its imposing opening, nocturne-like slow movement and dashing finale. Throughout, the orchestra provides a simple backcloth for the complex and richly melodic piano artistry, and the Warsaw première was Chopin's last concert in the Polish capital.

The F minor concerto has less overt rhetoric and display and the orchestral writing shows far more originality (although a debt is due to Chopin's contemporary Ignaz Mos-

cheles in the slow movement). Elements of folk dance enliven the finale, whose mood is set by the flamboyant, mazurka-like opening subject.

Antonin DVOŘÁK (1841-1904) Czechoslovakia

Cello Concerto in B minor, Op. 104
(first performed London, 1896)

Probably the best-known of all cello concertos, Dvořák composed this work during his sojourn in the United States. No other concertante work for the instrument (apart, perhaps, from the Elgar) so effectively exploits its warm, honeyed tone and rich, autumnal colours. The slow movement is particularly wistful, and makes reference to one of Dvořák's songs, one that was a favourite of his one-time love, Jozefina Kaunitzová. She eventually married the composer's brother, but there is little doubt that Dvořák retained a strong affection for his sister-in-law, and it was during the writing of this concerto that he learned she had been taken seriously ill. Jozefina later died and in the finale there is another echo of the tune she so loved.

It is but one of several memorable themes Dvořák introduced into this work, although the short but striking martial passage which punctuates the first movement, only to

Above: *Haydn (1732-1809) wrote a number of shapely keyboard concertos but put more individuality into his justly popular concertos for the cello and for the trumpet.*

vanish and never reappear, still sounds a structural misjudgement.

Edward ELGAR (1857-1934) **England**

Cello Concerto in E minor, Op. 85
(first performed London, 1919)
Violin Concerto in B minor, Op. 61 (first performed London, 1910)

Composed in the aftermath of World War I, the Cello Concerto was Elgar's final orchestral masterpiece. Unusually in four movements, the overall mood is set by the imploring voice of the cello at the very start of the work and by the immense sadness of the orchestral accompaniment which steals in a few bars later. The injection of a gruff, almost bumbling humour into the final allegro fails to dispel the prevailing sense of much lost and much regretted. The darker, more tragic hues of which the cello is capable are nowhere more eloquently employed.

Elgar's Violin Concerto was commissioned by the most prominent violinist of the era, Fritz Kreisler, although after the first few performances he seems to have lost enthusiasm for the work. However, this lyrical and impassioned work has gone on to become one of the great concertos in the soloist's canon.

George GERSHWIN (1898-1937) **USA**

Piano Concerto in F
(first performed New York, 1925)

Still the best-known of American concertos, Gershwin harnessed the formal three-movement layout to his own, highly individual musical language, itself derived from jazz,

blues and popular dance tunes. At times it is an uneasy partnership, but in the end Gershwin's mixture proves an agreeable one.

Edvard GRIEG (1843-1907) **Norway**

Piano Concerto in A minor
(first performed Copenhagen, 1869)

For a composer most at home with miniature forms – songs and short piano pieces – it is ironic that Grieg's solitary concerto has become his best-known work, along with the incidental music to Ibsen's *Peer Gynt* (discussed elsewhere). The A minor Concerto more than nods in the direction of Schumann's in the same key: Grieg's famous opening flourish is almost a 'romanticised' version of Schumann's more terse introduction.

The lyricism which tends to prevail in Grieg's music is evident throughout this work, whose qualities have managed to withstand decades of hackneyed and over-indulgent interpretation.

Franz Joseph HAYDN (1732-1809) **Austria**

Trumpet Concerto in E
(first performed Vienna, 1800)

Now the best-known work for trumpet and orchestra, Haydn's lively little concerto was largely neglected until this century. It was something of a milestone in the development of the instrument, being written for the soloist Anton Weidinger and the keyed trumpet he had developed, precursor of the modern valved trumpet.

Cello Concerto in C
(first performed [modern] Prague, 1962)
Cello Concerto in D
(first performed 1781?)

That Haydn had composed a C major Cello Concerto around 1765 had always been known, but it was not until 1961 that a set or parts for this presumed-lost score were uncovered in Prague. Unlike Mozart, Haydn wrote few concertos and his works contribute little to the development of the form, but both these compositions have their attractions, the tranquil slow movement of the C major, for example. A third cello concerto by Haydn remains lost.

Johann Nepomuk HUMMEL (1778-1837) **Bohemia**

Trumpet Concerto in E
(first performed Esterház, 1804)

Like Haydn's concerto (above), that of Hummel – best known as a piano virtuoso – was also written for Anton Weidinger. It is a dazzling work which must have fully exploited the talents of the dedicatee and his instru-

*Edvard GRIEG
(1843-1907)*

This gently good-humoured Scandinavian received his first musical tuition from his mother, a gifted pianist, and then went to the Leipzig Conservatoire, where he contracted a lung condition which plagued him for life. He moved between Oslo (then Christiania) and Copenhagen for a few years, became attracted by Norwegian folk idioms, married the singer Nina Hagerup in 1867, and promptly composed his famous Piano Concerto. This received high praise from Liszt, and by 1874 Grieg (who had been very active in promoting musical life in Oslo) was regarded highly enough to receive a government annuity. This gave him more freedom to compose, his immediate task being to produce music for a stage production of Ibsen's *Peer Gynt*. Finally settling in his native Bergen, life then became a busy round of composing, conducting and touring, the latter frequently as accompanist to his wife, who both inspired and performed many of the songs (over 120 in all) which are an important part of his output. *Peer Gynt* and the Piano Concerto have remained in the popular repertoire, while the various orchestral suites and sets of dances also have a continuing charm, as do Grieg's many piano works, including no less than ten books of Lyric Pieces. Not one to scale great symphonic heights, he was an unpretentious minor master who did what he did to perfection. J.C.

ment. However, the lack of acceptance of the keyed trumpet, for which the work was written, dismayed Hummel and he left the score unpublished. It was unearthed over 200 years later in the British Museum, and finally published in 1957.

Franz LISZT (1811-86) **Hungary**

Piano Concerto No. 1 in E♭
(first performed Weimar, 1857)
Piano Concerto No. 2 in A
(first performed Weimar, 1857)

Liszt's two piano concertos both originate from his time as music director of the grand-ducal court of Weimar. The visiting Berlioz conducted the first performance of No. 1, with the composer as soloist, while Liszt himself took the baton for the premiere of No. 2. Both are strongly Romantic works, even heroic, with an emphatically 'martial' flavour to both finales, and both are played without a break. It almost goes without saying, given Liszt's phenomenal talents, that the piano parts are difficult for the hands, if dazzling on the ear.

Felix MENDELSSOHN (1809-47) Germany

Violin Concerto in E minor, Op. 64
(first performed Leipzig, 1845)

Arguably the most poetically beautiful of all violin concertos, and certainly one of the most popular, the soloist for the first performance of Mendelssohn's concerto was Ferdinand David, leader of the composer's Leipzig orchestra. David gave Mendelssohn help with the technicalities of the solo writing (although the work doesn't tax the soloist in the same way as, say, Brahms's Op. 77), but the delicious themes of the elegant first movement and tender, song-like second are Mendelssohn at his most inspired.

Wolfgang Amadeus MOZART (1756-91) Austria

Mozart composed over thirty concertos which, by any standards, qualify for the epithet 'great' – if we take that to mean interesting, original ideas, skilfully and entertainingly developed, offering opportunities for both soloist and orchestra within the 'classical' framework. Yet for several of the piano concertos and one of the wind concertos, that description is hardly adequate.

It was for his own instrument – strictly speaking, the fortepiano, not our modern 'grand' – that Mozart reserved his most sublime expression in orchestral terms.

Bassoon Concerto in B♭, K191
(first performed 1774)
Flute Concerto No. 1 in G, K313
(first performed 1778)
Flute Concerto No. 2 in D/Oboe Concerto in C, K314
(first performed 1777/8)
Flute and Harp Concerto in C, K299
(first performed 1778)

Four engaging and leisurely works, well-crafted and of impeccable manners. Under-privileged bassoonists have been grateful for the K191 concerto since its inception: it was written specifically for the instrument rather than adapted from another concertante work: rare indeed. Mozart wrote the first of his flute concertos for the Dutch player and music patron, de Jean, in Mannheim in early 1778. De Jean's impatience for a second work almost certainly prompted the composer to transcribe an existing Oboe Concerto (written for the Salzburg oboist, Giuseppe Ferlen-

Above: *A romantic painting by Josef Danhauser portrays Franz Liszt at the piano playing to (l. to r.) the elder Dumas, Hugo, Sand, Paganini and Rossini with his mistress Marie d'Agoult at his feet.*

dis, in 1777) for flute, transposing it up a tone to D major. Ironically, the original oboe parts were then lost, only being rediscovered in the library of the Salzburg Mozarteum in 1920.

In fact, Mozart disliked the flute but, during his visit to Paris in 1778, was persuaded to write a third concerto for the instrument by the accomplished playing of the Comte de Guines, whose daughter's harp playing was no less 'magnifique', as the composer described it. Certainly, the accomplished young lady was given much to relish in the score's sparkling scales and arpeggios.

Clarinet Concerto in A, K622
(first performed Vienna, 1791)

Standing head and shoulders above the rest of Mozart's wind concertos is this late masterpiece, completed in the year of the composer's death for his friend, the virtuoso Anton Stadler. A deceptively effortless, radiant work, with a blissfully poetic slow movement, it has an interesting history. It

started life in 1789 for basset horn and in its final form was scored for what Stadler, a great exponent of the instrument, called a 'bass clarinet'. This instrument, however, was rapidly supplanted by the clarinet we know today and which offers three semitones less at the bottom of its range.

When finally published in 1801, Mozart's score was adapted for the newer instrument and it is only in the past few years, thanks to enterprising instrument makers who have copied the obsolete 'basset' clarinet (so-called to avoid confusion with the modern bass clarinet), that we have been able to hear the original sonorities of the work. And the gains have justified the effort, in what many clarinettists still regard as the finest concerto for the instrument, fully exploring its personality and never a mere display piece.

Horn Concerto No. 1 in D, K412
Horn Concerto No. 2 in E♭, K417
Horn Concerto No. 3 in E♭, K447
Horn Concerto No. 4 in E♭, K495
(first performed 1782-7)

All four of Mozart's Horn Concertos were written for the Salzburg player Ignaz Leitgeb, frequent butt of Mozart's humour as the comments on the manuscript scores prove. The First consists of just two outer movements,

*Felix MENDELSSOHN
(1809-47)*

Grandson of a Jewish philosopher, and son of a successful banker who added Bartholdy to the surname when he became a Protestant Christian, Felix Mendelssohn was taught the piano by his mother, and gave his first public recital when he was nine. At the age of twelve he met Goethe, and by the time he was seventeen he had composed twelve string symphonies, an opera and the overture to *A Midsummer Night's Dream*. At twenty he conducted the first performance of the *St Matthew Passion* since Bach's death, and then came to England where he gave the first performance of Beethoven's *Emperor* Concerto, and toured Scotland (*Hebrides*) before returning to Germany. This was the first of many visits, for he became a court favourite and both man and music were greatly admired throughout Britain. In 1846, a year before his early death through severe overwork and stress, he presented his oratorio *Elijah* in Birmingham. Mendelssohn was a man of many gifts: an accomplished painter and writer, as well as an outstanding pianist, organist and conductor. 'The Mozart of the nineteenth century' Schumann called him, and it is true that in much of his music we find romantic expression elegantly presented in classical form. For many years his work has been undervalued (possibly because he was too talented and his life was too easy?) but it is now being restored to its proper and deserved place in the repertoire. R.H.

Above: *The young Mozart, then aged seven, playing before the Prince de Conti on his visit to Paris in 1763. He was to write the finest corpus of concertos ever conceived by any composer.*

the middle one having been lost. For long, this work was thought to date from around 1782, but recent research indicates a date as late as 1791.

Whatever jokes Mozart may have had at Leitgeb's expense, the first of the completed concertos, K417, gives him many opportunities to impress, especially in the fanfares of the final movement. The Third Horn Concerto, K447, stands out from the rest not only because it is the longest of the four, but through the maturity of its harmonic vocabulary, most notably in the outer movements, and the sophistication of its scoring. While the central *romanza* may have its origins in the early 1780s, the rest hints at a later date.

There are no doubts about the origin of the last concerto, K495, which is clearly dated 1786, and its genial, witty style is wholly akin to its earlier predecessors. The lively 'hunting' finale is one of Mozart's best-known movements.

Violin Concerto No. 1 in B♭, K207
Violin Concerto No. 2 in D, K211
Violin Concerto No. 3 in G, K216
Violin Concerto No. 4 in D, K218
Violin Concerto No. 5 in A, K219
Sinfonia Concertante in E♭, K364

Mozart completed his five extant violin concertos in an astonishing burst of creativity between April and December 1775. The evident 'learning curve' between the first, K207 and the last, K219, is remarkable. In the B flat work, the Italian influence is apparent: there is no attempt to break with tradition and Mozart plays it safe. The Second Concerto is fresher, but it is the last three which capture the true Mozart spirit. We can only speculate what happened in the three months that elapsed between the composition of K216 and K218, but suddenly Mozart seems to have awoken to the true potential of the form, typ-

ified by the idyllic adagio of K216. The final concerto, K219 is notable for the Turkish flavour of its finale: the colourful music of Turkish military bands had a strong appeal for Austrians, and Mozart (among others) utilised it on three occasions.

Fine as these later concertos are, however, Mozart's greatest contribution to the violin (and viola) repertoire remains the Sinfonia Concertante K364 of 1779, a work of gleaming craftsmanship and ingenuity.

Piano Concerto No. 9 in E♭, K271,
Jeunehomme (first performed 1777)
Piano Concerto No. 10 for two pianos in E♭, K365 (first performed 1779)
Piano Concerto No. 11 in F, K413
(first performed 1782/3)
Piano Concerto No. 12 in A, K414
(first performed 1782/3)
Piano Concerto No. 13 in C, K415
(first performed 1782/3)
Piano Concerto No. 14 in E♭, K449
(first performed 1784)
Piano Concerto No. 15 in B♭, K450
(first performed 1784)
Piano Concerto No. 16 in D, K451
(first performed 1784)
Piano Concerto No. 17 in G, K453
(first performed 1784)
Piano Concerto No. 18 in B♭, K456
(first performed 1784)
Piano Concerto No. 19 in F, K459
(first performed 1784)
Piano Concerto No. 20 in D minor, K466
(first performed Vienna, 1785)
Piano Concerto No. 21 in C, K467
(first performed 1785)
Piano Concerto No. 22 in E♭, K482
(first performed 1785)
Piano Concerto No. 23 in A, K488
(first performed Vienna, 1786)
Piano Concerto No. 24 in C minor, K491
(first performed Vienna, 1786)
Piano Concerto No. 25 in C, K503
(first performed 1787)
Piano Concerto No. 26 in D, K537,
Coronation (first performed 1788)
Piano Concerto No. 27 in B♭, K595
(first performed Vienna, 1791)

The piano concertos, specifically numbers 14 to 27 which Mozart wrote in the last seven years of his life, represent the crowning glory of his orchestral music. The relationship, and the fusion between soloist and orchestra is perfectly judged, and the expressive potential of that relationship is explored to a degree attained by no other composer, not even Beethoven. Overall, these concertos are the most characteristic representation of Mozart's genius, always within the boundaries of form and taste, yet embracing an entire dramatic and poetic universe.

The leap from the early concertos of 1775-6 to the E flat K271 is startling in its new-found adventurousness. Written for a young French soloist, Mademoiselle Jeune-

Yehudi MENUHIN
(b. 1916)

One of the most gifted child prodigies of the present century, Menuhin had his first violin lesson at the age of four, first played in public when he was eight, and appeared at a concert in New York a year later. After a further year of study he went to Europe to work with Busch and Enesco, made his début in Paris, and then returned to New York to give a remarkable performance of the Beethoven violin concerto when he was still only eleven. In 1929 he performed this work together with the Brahms violin concerto and one by Bach in a single programme with the Berlin Philharmonic Orchestra under Bruno Walter in Berlin itself, and in Dresden and Paris. He also visited London, where he played to capacity audiences in the Royal Albert Hall. Three years later he made the celebrated recording of Elgar's violin concerto, with the composer conducting, at EMI's studios at Abbey Road, in London. Despite rumours of an early retirement his career progressed. Bartók wrote a solo violin sonata for him in 1942, and during the war years he gave many concerts for Allied troops. Shortly after 1945 he settled in England, and became artistic director of the Bath Festival from 1959 to 1969, appearing as conductor of his own chamber orchestra. R.H.

homme, the work has retained her surname as its nickname. More conventional is the two-piano concerto completed in 1779 for himself and his sister, Nannerl, destined to be Mozart's last completed concerto before leaving Salzburg.

Of the three concertos K413-15, all composed during 1782, the genial A major K414 has always been the most popular. The attractions of K413, however, if less overt, reward exploration. It is the most intimate of the three – not that Mozart could exactly 'commune privately with his muse': his concertos were all written for public performance and what satisfaction he might personally derive from them was secondary. With an orchestra that includes oboes, horns, bassoons, trumpets and drums, K415 requires larger forces than any of its predecessors, but is ultimately the least satisfying of this group.

The first of no less than twelve concertos composed between 1784 and 1786 is the comparatively underrated K449. A compact work, using an equally compact orchestra, it is elusive in its sometimes uneasy moods, and thematic links look ahead to the shadowy first movement of the C minor K491. With the lyrical K450 all is light, while K451 offers a clear-cut exuberance, though not without its moments of surprise.

The G major Concerto K453 is deservedly one of the most popular of this group from 1784, with the mellow radiance of its first movement and bitter-sweet tenderness of the second. The finale, a set of variations full of skittish good humour, points the relationship between Mozart's piano concertos and his operas: there are themes here that would be equally at home sung by Papageno in *The Magic Flute*.

Mozart intended most of his concertos for himself or for his pupils, but K456 is notable for being written for the blind Viennese virtuoso Maria Theresa Paradis for a concert in Paris. It is a work that, especially in its sensuous slow movement, reveals more with repeated listening.

Mozart completed the last of this quite astonishing sequence of concertos – six in under twelve months – in December 1784, and K459 is certainly the most robust and festive of all the concertos.

Yet his creative resources were undiminished: by February 1785 he was giving the première of the D minor Concerto K466, the first he placed in a minor key and, not surprisingly, a work of intense drama and passion, In many respects, this is a 'nineteenth century' concerto and an affinity with Beethoven, who wrote cadenzas for it, is readily apparent. A new year, and Mozart was again taking the piano concerto down new and exciting paths, a progress continued with K467 whose dreamy, languid andante has gained more recent fame from its use as the theme music to the film *Elvira Madigan*. In sharp contrast, Mozart concludes with one of his most exhilarating, bubbling rondos.

During the winter of 1785/6, three more concertos were finished, with the first, K482, notable for an andante of almost unrelieved sadness and deepest melancholy. This sublimely beautiful music is in sharp contrast to the grand and imposing opening movement and the disarmingly ingenuous finale. There is simplicity, too, in the allegro of the A major, K488, and once again the slow movement (marked 'adagio' in the autograph, not 'andante' as in the published editions) takes us to a different plane of expression. It is as if Mozart is placing two 'public' outer movements (K488 ends with the sunniest of prestos), around intensely inward, 'private' music. This slow movement is notable for

being in F sharp minor, a key which both Mozart and Beethoven used but once (the latter in the adagio of the *Hammerklavier* piano sonata). Its capacity to convey sadness and resignation is almost unequalled, and prompted Mozart to one of his most poetic utterances.

If, in these slow movements, Mozart made no concessions to his audience, the whole of the C minor Concerto K491 brooks no compromise. The dark, menacing tread of the opening must have shocked the Viennese, and this mood permeates even the 'quick march' of the finale. No wonder Mozart felt the need to follow this pessimistic work with the broad affirmation of the C major K503.

Benign and spacious, only in recent years has K503 emerged from the shadow of the two preceding masterpieces to be acknowledged for the fine work it is. The succeeding K537, however, is not up to the high standard of its companions, although its affability and brilliance were no doubt appropriate for the occasion which earned it its nickname: a coronation in 1790. Mozart completed his final piano concerto on 5 January 1791.

Niccolò PAGANINI (1782-1840) Italy

Violin Concerto No. 2 in B minor, Op. 7, *La Campanella*
(first performed Naples, 1826)

As one of the greatest virtuoso violinists of all time, it is to be expected that Paganini's two concertos for the instrument are very much showcases for the soloist's skill. However, both are also well-constructed works, if conservative in approach: the grand opening movement, lyrical adagio or andante, and brilliant finale. It is the latter that gives the Second Concerto, the finer of the two, its nickname, *La Campanella* or *The Bell*, for

Below: *An impression of Paganini playing one of his violin works before a fashionable audience. The wizardry that he displayed in his concertos and other works gave him a legendary reputation.*

which instrument Paganini duly included an obbligato role. Franz Liszt transcribed this rondo for piano as the fourth of his *Etudes d'exécution transcendante d'après Paganini* of 1838.

Francis POULENC (1899-1963) **France**

Organ Concerto in G minor
(first performed Paris, 1941)

Poulenc composed four concertos, among which this for organ, strings and kettledrums is easily the most popular. An ingenious work, it is played in one movement, although that is composed of a variety of moods and tempos. A solemn declamation on organ, nodding reverently in the direction of J.S. Bach, opens the work and returns to unify the whole work towards the end.

Sergei PROKOFIEV (1891-1953) **Russia**

Piano Concerto No. 1 in D♭, Op. 10
(first performed Moscow, 1912)
Piano Concerto No. 3 in C, Op. 26
(first performed Chicago, 1921)

The first of Prokofiev's five piano concertos was a student work. He was just twenty-one when he took the solo part at the Moscow première and, three years later, won the Rubinstein piano prize with a performance of the work. Played in one succinct movement, it is unified by an opening (and closing) theme that is mercurial and memorable. If there are hints of Rachmaninov, the fresh and original voice of Prokofiev is by far the more dominant with its mix of fantasy, romance and sharp-edged astringency.

The Third Concerto shares very much the same ingredients, with none of the 'iron and steel' that characterises some of Prokofiev's

Below: *The 20th-century French composer Francis Poulenc (1899-1963) wrote concertos for organ, harpsichord, piano and two pianos. His music was always adventurous, clever and often witty.*

other compositions of this period. The theme of the variation-form slow movement is a kind of gavotte-from-the-Steppes, while the finale is quite breathtaking in its dashing twists and turns.

Violin Concerto No. 1 in D, Op. 19
(first performed Paris, 1923)
Violin Concerto No. 2 in G minor, Op. 63
(first performed Madrid, 1935)

Any assumption that Prokofiev lacked the lyrical gifts of his countrymen Rachmaninov, Rimsky-Korsakov and Tchaikovsky is immediately dispelled by the haunting opening of the First Violin Concerto, a theme which becomes yet more magical as it returns at the end of the movement, now scored for solo flute and overlaid with delicate tracery by the violin. After a demonic scherzo, the richly lyrical mood returns for the finale.

More traditional in form and orchestration, the Second Concerto foreshadows the ballet *Romeo and Juliet*. An eloquent first movement is followed by a simple andante in 12/8 time and the whole rounded off with a rumbustious rondo imaginatively derived from a rustic dance theme.

Sergei RACHMANINOV (1873-1943) **Russia**

Piano Concerto No. 2 in C minor, Op. 18
(first performed Moscow, 1901)
Piano Concerto No. 3 in D minor, Op. 30
(first performed New York, 1909)
Piano Concerto No. 4 in G minor, Op. 40
(first performed Philadelphia, 1927)

With its sensuous, not to say sentimental themes, lush orchestration and glittering pianism, the Rachmaninov Second has become the quintessence of the romantic concerto, its popular appeal enhanced by its sympathetic use in the 1940s film drama *Brief Encounter*. In a similar rich vein is the Third Concerto, and hardly less popular, but the Fourth has struggled for acceptance ever since its lambasting at the hands of American critics after the première. Rachmaninov revised the work, the theme of whose slow movement bears a mischievous resemblance to *Three Blind Mice*, in 1941, but it remains something of an orphan among his works.

Maurice RAVEL (1875-1937) **France**

Piano Concerto in G
(first performed Paris, 1932)
Piano Concerto in D for the Left Hand
(first performed Vienna, 1931)

The apparently incongruous synthesis of Basque folk themes and the riper elements of jazz (Gershwin's influence can be readily felt) makes for a brilliant and entertaining work, with the simple tranquillity of the slow movement balancing the energy of the G major's

Sergei RACHMANINOV (1873-1943)

Of aristocratic family, Rachmaninov entered the St Petersburg Conservatory at the age of nine, and three years later went to the Moscow Conservatory to study the piano with Zverov and Siloti, and composition with Taneyev and Arensky. In 1891 he completed his first piano concerto and in the summer of the following year he wrote the *Prelude in C sharp minor*, the most celebrated of all his numerous piano compositions. His first opera, *Aleko*, was successfully presented at the Bolshoi Theatre in 1893, but his Symphony No. 1 failed under Glazunov in 1897 and was not performed again during the composer's lifetime. His first professional appearance abroad was in London in 1899, where he made a considerable impression as composer, pianist and conductor. But it was at this time he suffered a total loss of confidence and it was only after a course of hypnosis by a sympathetic amateur musician that he composed his most famous work, the Second Piano Concerto. The third concerto followed in 1909 during his first visit to the United States, where he settled eight years later to escape political unrest at home. His demanding concert schedule kept him away from his desk, but outstanding among his later works are the *Rhapsody on a theme of Paganini* (1934), Symphony No. 3 (1936) and *Symphonic Dances* (1940). R.H.

outer allegramente and diamond-like rondo.

The Left-Hand Concerto was one of a number of works written by major composers (Benjamin Britten and Richard Strauss were others) for the Austrian pianist Paul Wittgenstein whose right arm was amputated during World War I. It is a significantly darker, more impassioned work than its predecessor, a succession of ideas distilled into one sweeping movement.

Joaquín RODRIGO (b. 1901) **Spain**

Concierto d'Aranjuez
(first performed Barcelona, 1940)

The most popular of guitar concertos, largely through the stirring, impassioned nobility of its central adagio. Although not 'programmatic', the composer derived inspiration from Aranjuez, one-time home of the Spanish royal family and the concerto successfully depicts the colour and the flavour of the Bourbon reign there during the late eighteenth and early nineteenth centuries.

Camille SAINT-SAËNS (1835-1921) France

Piano Concerto No. 2 in G minor, Op. 22
Piano Concerto No. 4 in C minor, Op. 44

The Second and Fourth have become the most popular of the five piano concertos composed by Saint-Saëns (a concert pianist at the age of ten) between 1858 and 1896. The G minor is notable for opening with a broad andante sostenuto, followed in sharp contrast by a bouncing, genial scherzo and demonic helter-skelter presto based around a galloping triplet-motif.

Written to be played as one movement, the Fourth Concerto combines a sequence of themes within a framework of four tempos, divisible into two linked segments. Finely-crafted in terms of dialogues between soloist and orchestra, and demands placed on the soloist, this work rates as one of the composer's most inspired creations.

Robert SCHUMANN (1810-56) Germany

Piano Concerto in A minor, Op. 54
(first performed Dresden, 1845)

Clara Schumann, the composer's wife, was the soloist in the first performance of this work, a concerto whose qualities eluded publishers of the day who thought it difficult to understand. Now it is probably the best-loved and most performed of Schumann's orchestral works, classical in form but undeniably Romantic in feel.

Dmitri SHOSTAKOVICH (1906-75) Russia

Piano Concerto No. 1 in C, Op. 35
(first performed Leningrad, 1933)
Piano Concerto No. 2 in F, Op. 102
(first performed Moscow, 1957)
Cello Concerto No. 1 in E♭, Op. 107
(first performed Leningrad, 1959)
Violin Concerto No. 1 in A minor, Op. 99
(first performed Leningrad, 1955)

In total, Shostakovich composed six concertos: two for cello, and both dedicated to Mstislav Rostropovich; two for violin, again with a single performer in mind, this time the late David Oistrakh; and two for piano, extrovert works from early and late in his career.

The First Piano Concerto, a brilliantly-conceived four-movement work, is remarkable for its trumpet obbligato, while the no less lively Second was written for the composer's son, Maxim. The First Violin Concerto, its first movement – a nocturne – containing some

of Shostakovich's most intense music, was begun in 1947-8 but suppressed along with a number of other compositions in the wake of Zhdanov's artistic dictates.

The first of the Cello Concertos is a work in primary colours, direct and with nothing like the ambiguity of its successor, a work which even the dedicatee rarely plays.

Jean SIBELIUS (1865-1957) Finland

Violin Concerto in D minor, Op. 47
(first performed [original version] Helsinki, 1904)

Sibelius began his musical career as a violinist, and the formidable technical demands he makes of the soloist in his solitary concerto seem designed to sort the wheat from the chaff! The work was revised after its first performance and it is the latter version which is now played, with its radical opening – the soloist introducing both melody and rhythm against shimmering tremolando strings – plaintive slow movement and electrifying finale.

Richard STRAUSS (1864-1949) Germany

Horn Concerto No. 1 in E♭, Op. 11
(first performed Meiningen, 1885)
Horn Concerto No. 2 in E♭
(first performed Salzburg, 1943)

Strauss seems to have taken Mozart as his model for the First Horn Concerto, composed for Strauss senior who was principal horn in the Munich Court Orchestra. Unfortunately, the work – with its themes evolved from traditional hunting-horn fanfares –

Below: *Itzhak Perlman (b. 1945) has dazzlingly interpreted Sibelius's romantic Violin Concerto. One of the composer's early works, the imprint of Tchaikovsky is discernible throughout it.*

proved too difficult for his elderly father. Played as one movement, it is also unified by thematic cross-references, and it is noteworthy that on the autograph, Strauss specifies the *waldhorn*, the valveless, hand-stopped precursor of the modern instrument.

Numbered among Strauss's later masterpieces is the Second Horn Concerto, a more refined, more lucidly scored, and generally more 'classical' work than its predecessor. It was composed during the dark days of 1941 and, listening to it, it is impossible not to think of the composer endeavouring to recapture the qualities he saw in his beloved Mozart, and, which then were being destroyed all around him.

Igor STRAVINSKY (1882-1971) Russia

Violin Concerto in D
(first performed Berlin, 1931)

A fine example of Stravinsky's 'objective' neo-Classicism, this concerto was written for the American violinist, Samuel Dushkin. Evidence of its classical roots – although it is no mere pastiche, but a work of notable invention and technical difficulty – can be seen in the titles Stravinsky gave the four movements: an opening *toccata* and concluding *capriccio* enclose two exquisite *arias*.

Pyotr TCHAIKOVSKY (1840-93) Russia

Piano Concerto No. 1 in B♭ minor, Op. 23
(first performed Boston, 1875)
Violin Concerto in D, Op. 35
(first performed Vienna, 1881)

The popularity of these two concertos never seems to diminish, that for piano remaining probably the best-known of the genre. Yet it was rudely rejected by the Russian virtuoso Nikolai Rubinstein. Even the première was outside Russia, in Boston, Massachusetts. The massive introduction – if any 'introduction' can be as long as 106 bars – brings one of the two, big 'yearning' tunes (the other is in the finale) which have brought this work its fame (and notoriety!).

The genesis of Tchaikovsky's solitary Violin Concerto was also not without its problems: judged 'un-violinistic' by a leading virtuoso and 'stinking music' by one Viennese critic. However, its innate lyricism and the gaiety of its finale endeared it to the widest public and ensured its lasting success.

Antonio VIVALDI (c. 1678-1741) Italy

Violin Concertos, Op. 8 Nos 1-4,
The Four Seasons (first performed c. 1725)
Six Flute Concertos, Op. 10

The *Four Seasons* – the best-known and most recorded of all Baroque concertos – were largely unrecognised forty years ago, as was

Itzhak PERLMAN
(b. 1945)

Brilliant Israeli-American violinist, born in Tel Aviv. Afflicted with polio when he was four and has had to use crutches all his life, despite which he has led an unusually active career and remained an ebullient and cheerful character, becoming an internationally popular musical figure. He was discovered in Israel by Ed Sullivan who introduced him on his TV show in 1959, already a remarkably impressive violinist at fourteen. He stayed in New York and won a scholarship to the Juilliard School of Music and made his professional concert début in 1963. Taken under the wing of Isaac Stern, his career took off with an American tour in 1965-6 and a European tour 1966-7. His many concert appearances, working with compatriots such as Stern, Zukerman and Barenboim, and his fine recordings, have made him one of the top violinists of the day. He has shown a great catholicism of taste, playing not only classical music but also proving adept in the ragtime and jazz field, often in partnership with André Previn, and developing a successful TV personality. P.G.

Camille SAINT-SAËNS
(1835-1921)

Although Saint-Saëns came from a well-known Normandy family he was born in Paris, studied at the Conservatoire and was a private pupil of Gounod. He wrote his first symphony at the age of sixteen, but it was as an organist that he established his reputation, and for twenty years he held the coveted post of organist at the Madeleine. He was also a brilliant pianist: his own technical mastery may be judged from the five concertos he wrote for the instrument. He championed earlier French composers such as Rameau, and defended the Romantics – Liszt, Berlioz and Wagner – although in later life he turned against Wagner and attacked him for his 'Teutonizing influence on French music'. Of his three surviving symphonies (two were withdrawn at his own insistence) the 3rd (*Organ*) has become extremely popular in recent years. He wrote twelve operas, of which *Samson and Delilah* is the most frequently performed, and among the rest of his numerous works perhaps the best known are *The Carnival of Animals* and *Introduction* and *Rondo Capriccioso*. His music has invention, wit, gaiety and charm, qualities not calculated to endear him to the more sober-minded critics. R.H.

Below: *The Korean violinist Kyung-Wha Chung made a memorable recording of Tchaikovsky's Violin Concerto early in her career, interpreting its lyricism and gaiety quite superbly.*

Above: *Antonio Vivaldi spent his early career as a violinist. Ordained in 1703, he was known as the 'red-haired priest'. He wrote over 200 violin concertos and around 500 concertos altogether.*

most of Vivaldi's output of over 500 concertos, mostly for strings. They are but four of the concertos that make up a set of twelve which Vivaldi titled intriguingly *Il cimento dell'armonia e dell'invenzione (The trial between harmony and invention)* and dedicated to a Bohemian aristocrat, Count Wenzeslaus von Morzin. However, in terms of imagination and ambition their fame is merited, contrasting 'seasonal' effects being cleverly represented in the delightful interplay between violin and accompaniment.

Although the violin was the dominant instrument in Italian Baroque music, composers did not neglect wind instruments, especially as the numbers of proficient – and often well-off! – amateur players increased. Vivaldi's Amsterdam publisher probably encouraged the composition of these superb concertos for *flauto traversier* (transverse flute).

Carl Maria von WEBER (1786-1826)
Germany

Clarinet Concerto No. 1 in F minor,
Op. 73
(first performed, 1811)
Clarinet Concerto No. 2 in E♭,
Op. 74
(first performed 1811)

Just as the virtuosity of Anton Stadler inspired Mozart to compose his masterpiece for the clarinet, so Weber's two clarinet concertos owe their existence to a similarly distinguished player, in this case Heinrich Bärmann. The attractions of both works are to be found in Weber's extraordinarily delicious melodies, the song-like slow movements and brisk dance-rhythms of the faster sections, all skilfully wedded to strict classical form to produce music of pure delight.

Into this category come the Baroque dance suites of J.S. Bach, the divertimenti of Mozart, the descriptive 'programme' music of the nineteenth-century composers, the tone-poems and symphonic poems of Liszt, Richard Strauss, Sibelius and others. Space has precluded mention of the host of great overtures which rightly belong here and which are now frequently (and in some case, always) played separately from whatever opera or drama they were intended to introduce. The great overtures of Mozart, Beethoven, Berlioz, Mendelssohn, Rossini, Verdi and others deserve attention.

Some overtures – 'concert overtures' were written for specifically musical purposes – simply works to open concerts – and several of these are described in the text.

Omitted, though, are the orchestral excerpts which Wagner himself culled from his music dramas for concert performance. Many are favourites both on record and in the concert hall: the Prelude and *Liebestod* from *Tristan and Isolde*; the Overture and *Venusberg music* from *Tannhäuser*; the *Ride of the Valkyries* and Siegfried's *Funeral March*. Again space did not allow an analysis of these excerpts. P.H.

J.S. BACH (1685-1750) Germany

Brandenburg Concerto No. 1 in F, BWV1046
Brandenburg Concerto No. 2 in F, BWV1047
Brandenburg Concerto No. 3 in G, BWV 1048
Brandenburg Concerto No. 4 in G, BWV1049
Brandenburg Concerto No. 5 in D, BWV1050
Brandenburg Concerto No. 6 in B♭, BWV1051

These most famous of Bach's orchestral works date from his time at Cöthen and were intended for the orchestra of the Margrave of Brandenburg, an important nobleman whom Bach, it is thought, met on a visit to Berlin in 1719. We do not know if the Margrave's orchestra ever played these six concertos for varying groups of instrumental soloists, strings and continuo, but Bach certainly performed them at Cöthen, albeit in revised orchestrations if circumstances required.

Together, the Brandenburgs represent the highwater mark of the Baroque concerto, displaying an imagination and variety encountered nowhere else.

No. 1 gives prominent roles to horns, oboe and the *violino piccolo*, a small violin tuned a minor third higher than the usual instrument; it is also one of the two longest of the six. No. 2 is even more unusual, bringing together trumpet, recorder, oboe and violin (the trumpet of Bach's day would not have dominated its partners as the modern instrument would), while No. 3 requires just strings

Above: *The American composer Samuel Barber (1910-81) is best known for his often-played* Adagio for Strings *but has a wide-ranging list of compositions to his credit, including several operas.*

and continuo. It also poses a mystery: if Bach wrote a slow movement, what happened to it? If he did not, we can only assume the two E minor chords sandwiched between the vigorous outer allegros were intended only to indicate the required key of whatever the performers chose to insert.

Perhaps the most lyrical of the six is No. 4, with its solo roles for two recorders and violin: what a delightfully apt theme Bach gives the two wind soloists at the very start. At the opposite extreme is the robust, driving No. 5 – for flute and violin, as well, but virtually a harpsichord concerto, given the stunning first-movement cadenza.

No. 6 brings altogether different sonorities with its sextet of strings and continuo, which excludes violins but includes parts for two viola da gambas, sounding between the viola and the cello.

Orchestral Suite No. 1 in C, BWV1066
Orchestral Suite No. 2 in B minor, BWV1067
Orchestral Suite No. 3 in D, BWV1068
Orchestral Suite No. 4 in D, BWV1069

These four works will also be seen described as 'overtures', a consequence of the form having been originated by the French composer, Jean-Baptiste Lully: he called them *ouvertures* and set the pattern of an imposing, stately slow introduction (with a livelier interlude), followed by a sequence of movements set to dance rhythms. Bach exploited the format to the full in his four Suites, bending the 'rules' at will and to great effect.

Some of Bach's best-known music is to be found here – the badinerie of No. 3, the air (popularly, on a G string) of No. 3 among it. It now seems incredible that it was not until eighty-five years after the composer's death that these Suites were published.

Samuel BARBER (1910-81) USA

Adagio for Strings, Op. 11
(first performed New York, 1938)

It is curious that, of all his fine compositions, including an elegaic violin concerto, Barber remains best-remembered for this short (under ten minutes), poignant and solemn adagio, which began life as one of the movements of a string quartet but is now inescapably a 'national threnody' for Americans.

Béla BARTÓK (1881-1945) Hungary

Concerto for Orchestra
(first performed Boston, 1944)

Undoubtedly Bartók's most melodious and accessible work, as the name implies the *Concerto for Orchestra* is designed to give all the instrumental groups a chance to shine, very much in the manner of the eighteenth-century Italian concerto. Anyone who thinks Bartók a dour, spiky composer should listen to the noble *elegia*, or the sparkling finale, or the clever parody of the 'march' theme from Shostakovich's *Leningrad* Symphony which suddenly emerges within the 'Interrupted intermezzo'.

Music for strings, percussion and celesta
(first performed Basle, 1937)

One of the most original works of this century, not just in instrumentation but in its use of antiphonal effects, the *Music for strings, percussion and celesta* was written for the Basle Chamber Orchestra of the Swiss conductor, Paul Sacher. As well as the distinctive timbre of the celesta, the orchestration calls for piano and harp as well as kettledrums, snare drum, bass drum, cymbals, tam-tam and xylophone. The four movements alternate slow-fast-slow-fast, with the fugal first building to a searing climax, the third eerily hypnotic, and the second and fourth fiery, and with a Magyar flavour.

Arnold BAX (1883-1953) England

Tintagel

Despite a resurgence of interest in all of Bax's music in recent years (he composed seven symphonies and several other tone-poems), *Tintagel* remains his best-known work. Bax, an ardent lover of things Celtic, vividly evokes

Max BRUCH
(1838-1920)

A conventional, not to say reactionary, German composer whose long life, like that of Saint-Saëns, spans the period from Mendelssohn to Alban Berg, and whose musical style hardly developed at all during that time. However, his output includes far more than merely the familiar First Violin Concerto, and the set of variations for cello and orchestra *Kol Nidrei*, based on the Yom Kippur prayer. His choral music is still performed in his native land, and there are many other works, including two more violin concertos, that deserve far more attention than they now receive. Bruch was given a very thorough musical training and developed an enthusiasm for traditional Hebrew music (although he was not, himself, a Jew) and for folk songs, especially those of Scotland and Wales. He saw such music as a perennial source of fresh inspiration (e.g. the two *Scottish Fantasies*) and it is not inappropriate therefore that for a short period in his later years Vaughan Williams was a pupil, as was Respighi. Bruch's career, of which three years were spent in England, was as conventional as his music: he held many important posts within the German musical establishment and was awarded honorary degrees by the universities of Cambridge, Breslau and Berlin. R.H.

the atmosphere around this craggy part of the north Cornish coast, and the romantic legends associated with the ruined castle of Tintagel. That of Tristram and Iseult was not without parallels in his own, at that time, stormy life.

Alban BERG (1885-1935) Austria

Three Orchestral Pieces, Op. 6
(first performed [complete] Oldenburg, 1930)
Three Movements from the Lyric Suite
(first performed Berlin, 1929)

Of these two orchestral works by Berg, the Op. 6 is the earliest, despite its later performance date. These three movements for large symphony orchestra occupied him for over fifteen years, with final revisions in 1929. The influence of Mahler, and of Berg's mentor Schoenberg, is apparent, but this work succeeds through its highly individual use of variation and multiple polyphony. The first 'piece' is a prelude, followed by *Reigen* (round dance) with its bitter-sweet echoes of the Viennese waltz, and the work concludes with a march of barely disguised terror and ominous intent.

Berg's publisher suggested that he arrange three of the movements from his *Lyric Suite* (originally for string quartet) for string orchestra and the composer agreed, lifting the second, third and fourth movements: andante amoroso, allegro misterioso

Above: *The French composer Hector Berlioz (1803-69) is amusingly caricatured after a Viennese concert in 1846 as shattering his audience's senses with his vast arrays of instruments and effects.*

(with its 'trio estatico') and adagio appasionato. The *Lyric Suite* is notable for Berg's first use of the technique of composing – albeit freely – with twelve-note rows.

Hector BERLIOZ (1803-69) France

Harold in Italy, Op. 16
(first performed Paris, 1834)

A work which, given the composer's subtitle, could qualify equally as a symphony or concerto. Berlioz entitled this Byron-inspired work *Symphony for orchestra with viola solo*, and further motivation is also supposed to have come from the Italian virtuoso Niccolò Paganini who needed music to play on his newly acquired Stradivarius viola. However, the final result was apparently insufficient of a showpiece to satisfy him, although it is undoubtedly one of the finest of the (very few) concertante works for solo viola.

Leonard BERNSTEIN (b. 1918) USA

West Side Story: Symphonic Dances

As a composer, it is doubtful if Bernstein has

ever matched the sustained originality and unadulterated inspiration of what remains his best-known work, *West Side Story*. The brilliant and characteristic music for the set-piece dances has most successfully transferred to the concert hall.

Georges BIZET (1838-75) France

L'Arlésienne: suites
(first performed Paris, 1872)

Although Alphonse Daudet's play *L'Arlésienne* (*The Woman of Arles*) is seldom, if ever, performed, Bizet's colourful incidental music has thankfully survived to enliven, in its charming way, the concert repertory. Only one of the two suites was arranged by the composer; the second, which includes the vibrant *farandole*, was compiled after his death.

Johannes BRAHMS (1833-97) Germany

Academic Festival Overture, Op. 80
(first performed Breslau, 1881)
Tragic Overture, Op. 81
(first performed Vienna, 1880)
Variations on a Theme by Haydn
(St Anthony Variations), Op. 56a
(first performed Vienna, 1873)

Not without a little prompting, Brahms acknowledged the conferring of an honorary doctorate by the University of Breslau (now Wroclaw in Poland) with a short overture based on student songs, the most universally famous of which, *Gaudeamus igitur*, provides a suitably stirring coda to the piece.

He then used the concert overture again, this time to indulge his 'melancholy nature' as he described it. Though no expression of grief, it is nevertheless serious and, occasionally, severe music, expressing a stoic resignation in the face of life's darker side.

Brahms came across the 'St Anthony chorale' in the score for a suite for wind band thought at the time (1870) to have been written by Haydn (it is now thought to be the work of the ubiquitous 'anon.'). The theme so appealed to him, he based a finely worked set of nine variations around it and, as well as scoring the work for orchestra, produced a version for two pianos.

Benjamin BRITTEN (1913-76) England

Sinfonia da Requiem, Op. 20
(first performed New York, 1941)
Sea Interludes from Peter Grimes, Op. 33
(first performed [complete opera] London, 1945)
Variations on a theme of Purcell
(The Young Person's Guide
to the Orchestra), Op. 34
(first performed Liverpool, 1946)
Variations on a Theme of Frank Bridge, Op. 10
(first performed Salzburg, 1937)

In one respect, it is a very personal 'Requiem': Britten's parents had died in the years immediately preceding its composition in 1939-40. But there is also the global sentiment, expressed by Britten in the face of the inevitable. The three movements of the *Sinfonia da Requiem* take their titles from the Latin rite: *lacrymosa dies illa (day of tears); dies irae (day of wrath)*; and *requiem aeternam (eternal rest)*. Two slow movements enclose a scherzo of chilling power, and there can hardly be a more ominous, more doomladen opening in music than that which begins this disquieting work.

Ironically, it was composed to a commission from the Japanese government, although they rejected the result, finding the Christian symbolism insulting.

Peter Grimes was more than Britten's first great opera, it was a landmark in twentieth-century British music. To 'paint in' the East Anglian seascape for this potent drama of alienation, Britten composed four vivid *Sea Interludes*, which have become a concert piece in their own right. These four, supremely evocative pieces are titled: *Dawn, Sunday Morning, Moonlight* and *Storm*.

The *Young Person's Guide to the Orchestra* is much more than an educational piece, although it does the job of introducing the instruments extremely well (with or without narration). Britten's use of a theme from Henry Purcell's *Abdelazar, or The Moor's Revenge* is highly inventive and never fails to delight, and the concluding fugue has thrilling impact.

It was with another set of variations, this time on the theme of the second of three *Idylls* composed by his teacher, Frank Bridge, that Britten first came to wide public notice. One of the greatest works for string orchestra composed this century, it was completed in great haste to a commission from Boyd Neel. A pre-condition of Neel's string orchestra's appearance at the 1937 Salzburg Festival had been the première of a new work by an up and coming English composer. Britten did not disappoint them.

George BUTTERWORTH (1885-1916) England

A Shropshire Lad
(first performed Leeds, 1913)

Like many English composers, Butterworth was attracted to the poetry of Housman and had made many settings of the *Shropshire Lad* poems before developing the theme from one of them – 'Loveliest of trees, the cherry' – into this haunting rhapsody.

Such was the regard for the twenty-eight-year-old Butterworth that the première was

Above: *The elder statesman of American music Aaron Copland, born in 1900, has always had a split musical personality, writing lively Americana on one hand, austerely European music on the other.*

given by no less a conductor than Artur Nikisch. Sadly, Butterworth was denied the chance to develop his potential. Less than three years later, he was killed on the Somme.

Aaron COPLAND (b. 1900) USA

El Salón México
(first performed Mexico City, 1937)

Copland visited Mexico in 1932 and very effectively captured the spirit and atmosphere of a hot, colourful dance hall in this work. Brightly and richly coloured – Copland adds piano and a host of exotic percussion instruments to an already large orchestra – there is an authentic Mexican influence in the shape of three folk tunes, although Copland treats them very freely.

Claude DEBUSSY (1862-1918) France

La Mer: three symphonic sketches
(first performed Paris, 1905)

Debussy's largest orchestral work is also the closest he came to an orthodox symphony. Its three 'movements' translate as *'from dawn to midday on the sea'; 'games of the waves'*; and *'dialogue of the wind and the sea'*, and critics were divided after the first performance as to whether Debussy had succeeded in his intentions. While not as literal as some 'musical seascapes', its imagery and colour are never less than atmospheric and *La Mer* has gone on to become a significant

Above: *The French composer Claude Debussy (1862-1918) with his daughter Claude-Emma. The leading musical impressionist, he had a great influence on the course of modern music.*

landmark in twentieth-century orchestral composition.

Prélude à l'Après-midi d'un faune
(first performed Paris, 1894)

Taking his inspiration, and his title, from a poem by Mallarmé, Debussy here conjured some of his most sensuous, languorous and enchanting music. The flute – that symbol of the 'Arcadian ideal' – plays a major role.

Trois Images pour Orchestre: I. Gigues, II. Ibéria, III. Rondes de Printemps
(first performed 1908 (II), 1910 (III), 1913 (I))

As the performance dates suggest, this orchestral triptych was composed over a period (1908-12), with *Ibéria*, itself divided into three sections, the first to be completed. It has also remained the most popular of the *Images*, being frequently performed without its partners. For a composer who but once crossed the Pyrenees into Spain, it is a remarkable evocation of light, sound and colour, more so than *Gigues*, which represents England (most notably with a Northumbrian folk song). Two French folk songs add local colour to the May Day festivities of *Rondes de Printemps*.

Trois Nocturnes: I. Nuages, II. Fêtes, III. Sirènes
(first performed [complete] Paris, 1901)

It is not the nocturnes of Chopin that stand in the background, but those of the painter,

James Whistler: this is Debussy's 'study in grey'. But the music is far from monochrome, especially in *Fêtes*, with its fantastic imagery. On one side of this, Debussy captures the 'slow, solemn motion of the clouds', and, in *Sirènes*, the moonlit sea and – with the addition of women's voices – the Sirens of legend.

Frederick DELIUS (1862-1934) England

Brigg Fair
(first performed Liverpool, 1908)
On Hearing the First Cuckoo in Spring
(first performed Leipzig, 1913)
Summer Night on the River
(first performed 1911)

Delius discovered the Lincolnshire folk song *Brigg Fair* through his friend and fellow-composer, Percy Grainger. It inspired Delius to one of his best-loved compositions, perhaps the most 'English' of all his music in terms of colour: the oboe introducing the tune, for example.

It is a Norwegian folk song, one probably introduced to Delius by his teacher, Grieg, which characterises the exquisite miniature *On Hearing the First Cuckoo in Spring*. The unmistakable call of this normally little-loved bird is given to one of the two clarinets. The harmonies, however are pure Delius, and could only be Delius.

The evanescent qualities of Delius's music are nowhere better appreciated than in the wonderfully evocative *Summer Night on the River*. The palette is so subtle, the shading so delicate as to produce music that is both luminous and fragile.

Paul DUKAS (1865-1935) France

The Sorcerer's Apprentice
(first performed Paris, 1897)

A rigorously self-critical composer, Paul Dukas produced little and, before his death, destroyed much of that. His fame now rests on this entertaining and skilful scherzo, whose tale of the hapless apprentice and the magical broomstick has been nowhere better realised than in Walt Disney's 1940 cartoon film *Fantasia*.

Antonin DVOŘÁK (1841-1904) Czechoslovakia

Slavonic Dances, Op. 46 Nos 1-8, Op. 72 Nos 1-8
Serenade for Strings in E major, Op. 22
(first performed Prague, 1876)

Brahms, full of praise for Dvořák's music, introduced the Czech composer to his publishers, Simrock. They saw in Dvořák the ideal source of a set of Slavonic Dances to match the enormously successful Hungarian Dances of Brahms. Dvořák began work in

Richard STRAUSS (1864-1949)

Born in Munich, the son of the leading horn player in the Opera orchestra, Richard Strauss had music lessons from an early age, but followed a normal academic career until he reached university where, in 1883, he decided to devote himself entirely to music. He had by this time already written a number of works, including a symphony which had been publicly performed. A succession of conducting appointments followed, but it was the brilliant *Don Juan*, the second of several symphonic poems he composed between 1887 and 1899 (*Macbeth, Tod und Verklärung, Till Eulenspiegel, Also sprach Zarathustra, Don Quixote* and *Ein Heldenleben*), which brought him wide acclaim. In 1894 he married the soprano Pauline de Ahna, for whom he wrote many songs. His third opera, *Salome*, was completed in 1905, and in 1909 he began his long collaboration with the Austrian poet Hoffmannsthal with *Elektra*. Like his friend Mahler, Strauss was an uneven composer whose work ranges from the ridiculous *Symphonia Domestica* (1904) to the sublime closing pages of *Der Rosenkavalier* (1911) or of the much later *Capriccio* (1942) – music that goes to the deepest places in the human heart, in Bernard Levin's perceptive phrase. Another late work *4 Last Songs* (now, in fact, five) is also a product of the remarkable flowering of the composer's genius in his old age. R.H.

March 1878 and had the eight dances of Op. 46 ready in both piano duet and orchestral forms by August, but unlike Brahms, who took existing Magyar and gypsy folk melodies, all Dvořák's themes were his own, if allied to traditional Slavonic dance rhythms.

Given the success of Op. 46, the composer was not well treated by Simrock and, returning eight years later for a second set of dances, they encountered a Dvořák who could now command his worth. More wide-ranging in their moods, the Op. 72 dances are musically the better but have never quite attained the popularity of their predecessors.

With its freshness and fund of charming melodies, the String Serenade is among the sunniest, most carefree music ever written.

Edward ELGAR (1857-1934) England

Concert overture: Cockaigne (In London Town), Op. 40
(first performed London, 1901)
Variations on an Original Theme – Enigma, Op. 36
(first performed London, 1899)
Symphonic study: Falstaff, Op. 68
(first performed Leeds, 1913)
Introduction and allegro for string quartet and string orchestra, Op. 47
(first performed London 1905)
Serenade for Strings in E minor, Op. 20
(first performed [complete] Antwerp, 1896)
Concert overture: In the South (Alassio), Op. 50
(first performed London, 1904)
Pomp and Circumstance Marches Nos 1-5, Op. 39
(first performed 1901-30)

Elgar's reputation was established with the *Enigma Variations*. He never disclosed the theme upon which the work was based (*Auld Lang Syne* is often suggested), nor the identity of '***', subject of the *romanza* of Variation XIII. At least two ladies of Elgar's acquaintance have been nominated. The rest of the variations portray friends and associates, including the composer's wife and his music publisher, the latter the subject of the profoundly moving *Nimrod*.

Elgar was a master of orchestral textures and sonorities and these skills can be appreciated to the full in his two concert overtures, *Cockaigne*, a lively portrait of London, and the Italian-inspired *In the South*. The lyrical side of his character pervades the highly romantic *Serenade*, and the open-air exuberance and freshness of the *Introduction and allegro*, so redolent of the countryside of Elgar's native Worcestershire and the Welsh border, never fades.

Yet, what is perhaps Elgar's greatest orchestral work – outside the symphonies and concertos – has never attained the popularity of the above. Composed in four linked sections, and closely following Shakespeare's storyline, *Falstaff* follows the progress of the jovial knight, his rejection by Prince Hal, and his death. It is a superbly well crafted piece and far more than purely illustrative.

Elgar composed his *Pomp and Circumstance Marches* over a near-thirty year period: 1901-30. He had originally hoped to use the big tune of No. 1 in something more substantial and always regretted not making more of what has since become a quasi-alternative British national anthem. Elgar, however, was not responsible for, nor entirely approving of the jingoistic words later attached to the March. If not as well-known, the other marches are certainly no less attractive, with No. 4 perhaps the most regal of them all.

Manuel de FALLA (1876-1946) Spain

Symphonic Impressions: Nights in the Gardens of Spain
(first performed Madrid, 1916)

This work of three linked movements is far more subtle in its Iberian evocations than the title suggests. It is scored for orchestra with a glittering contribution from a solo piano, and much of the writing, especially in the first movement, inspired by the Alhambra in Grenada, is sensuous and magical. The music of Debussy is a perceptible influence. This stems from Falla's association with Debussy during his seven-year sojourn in Paris.

César FRANCK (1822-90) Belgium

Symphonic Variations for Piano and Orchestra (first performed 1885)

Taking his cue from Franz Liszt, Franck's neglected *Symphonic Variations* is based on the notion of thematic transformation. Here a somewhat grave, even lachrymose main theme undergoes a remarkable metamorphosis to emerge at the conclusion of the work as a jaunty dance.

George GERSHWIN (1898-1937) USA

Rhapsody in Blue
(first performed New York, 1924)
An American in Paris
(first performed New York, 1928)

The soaring clarinet which opens *Rhapsody in Blue* remains the best-known introduction in American music. It immediately and irreversibly set the mood for a work commissioned by bandleader Paul Whiteman and originally scored by the composer for 'jazz band and piano'. Sumptuous later orchestrations were made by the Whiteman band's orchestrator, Ferde Grofé. As recent recordings prove, playing the work as Gershwin conceived it changes its character quite forcibly, the 'jazz' version being more brash and raw-edged, and – many feel – preferable.

An American in Paris is also Gershwin at his brashest and breeziest, a vivid piece of impressionism, right down to honking car horns!

Edvard GRIEG (1843-1907) Norway

Peer Gynt: Suites Nos 1 and 2
(first performed [incidental music] Oslo, 1876)

The idea for incidental music to accompany *Peer Gynt* came from the playwright himself, Henrik Ibsen. Grieg's full score, which includes a number of vocal items, was later pared down by the composer to two concert suites. Their popularity now far outweighs that of the original play, thanks to Grieg's universally loved melodies, *Morning*, *In the Hall of the Mountain King*, and *Solveig's Song* being the most famous.

George Frideric HANDEL (1685-1759) Germany

Music for the Royal Fireworks
(first performed London, 1749)
Water Music: Suites Nos 1-3
(first performed London, 1717?)

Handel wrote this splendid music to accompany a fireworks display celebrating the Peace of Aix-la-Chapelle and, from the number of musicians specified, seemed determined that it should be heard above the pyrotechnics. It is not known whether strings were included in the original performance, but the composer certainly wrote parts for them. Some performances, however, still maintain the wind- and drums-only orchestration.

The no less celebrated *Water Music* is believed to have been composed for another

Left: *Composer Manuel de Falla (1876-1946) with the choreographer Leonide Massine (1896-1979) at the Fountain of Lions in the courtyard of the Alhambra at the time of* The Three Cornered Hat, *1919.*

Above: *The British composer Gustav Holst (1874-1934) portrayed by Bernard Munns. His* Planets *suite was his best-known composition and one of the few British works to be regularly played abroad.*

royal occasion: George I's trip down the Thames on 17 July 1717. The composer/conductor, Sir Hamilton Harty, arranged six of the pieces into a suite published in 1922 and, for many years, little else of the music was performed. More recently, though, the trend has been to play the *Water Music* in the three suites that Handel arranged it in and in the sequences he laid down. In the first, and longest suite, the horns are pre-eminent, in the second, trumpets, and in the third, flute and recorders; between them they contain some of Handel's best-known music, outside of *Messiah*.

Gustav HOLST (1874-1934) England

The Planets Suite, Op. 32
(first performed London, 1918)

Of all British music, Holst's *Planets* is undoubtedly the most famous of large-scale compositions, and deservedly so, for it is a masterpiece of imagination and musical craftsmanship. It was first conducted by Sir Adrian Boult, who then went on to make several recordings of the work in a relationship lasting five decades, but has also entered the repertoire of a galaxy of other star conductors.

Essentially, Holst produced strikingly original 'portraits' of the character traits associated with seven of the planets in our solar system (Earth was excluded, and Pluto yet to be discovered). Like Elgar, Holst suffered from having one of his 'big tunes' – the central theme of *Jupiter* – adapted for a patriotic hymn, but nothing could detract from the enduring qualities of this work, which starts thunderously with *Mars* and ends hauntingly with the receding voices of *Neptune*, the mystic.

Leoš JANÁČEK (1854-1928)
Czechoslovakia

Sinfonietta
(first performed Prague, 1926)
Rhapsody for Orchestra: Taras Bulba

Both these compositions are products of Janáček's astonishingly prolific last years. *Taras Bulba*, a stirring three-part work based on Gogol's tale of the Ukranian Cossack partisan who leads his people against the Polish invaders, dates from 1915 to 1918.

The *Sinfonietta* had its genesis in a request for fanfares to accompany a gymnastic festival. The resulting 'blaze of brass' became the opening and closing statements of this masterly five-movement 'divertimento', which displays Janáček's gifts to the full. It also provides a treat for brass players, requiring no less than nine trumpets, two bass trumpets and two tenor tubas.

Zoltán KODÁLY (1882-1967) Hungary

Háry János: suite
(first performed [complete opera]
Budapest, 1926)

Although the opera from which it is taken is now virtually unheard, the amusing and attractive orchestral suite taken from it has become by far Kodály's best-known work. The fanciful exploits of the soldier, Háry János, inspire the composer to some delightful effects and the whole work is 'goulash-flavoured' with the distinctive timbre of the cimbalon, a kind of Hungarian dulcimer.

Edouard LALO (1823-92) France

Symphonie espagnole for violin
and orchestra
(first performed Paris, 1875)

Strictly speaking, the work for which Lalo is now remembered is a concerto for violin, the soloist being given many opportunities for brilliant display. However, Lalo – who was of Spanish descent – composed the work in five movements and chose to call it a 'Spanish Symphony' although it hardly conforms to symphonic notions. Wherever it is categorised, it remains ravishing music.

Franz LISZT (1811-86) Hungary

Les Préludes: symphonic poem
(first performed Weimar, 1854)
Hungarian Rhapsody No. 2

Whether Liszt 'invented' the symphonic poem is debatable, but he certainly exploited the form as no one before him. A current disaffection with Liszt's orchestral works has left *Les Préludes* as the most played of them today. As with most such Romantic works, there is a literary inspiration behind the

*Ottorino RESPIGHI
(1879-1936)*

Italian composer, conductor, performer and teacher who studied violin and composition first in Bologna, and then studied under Rimsky-Korsakov in St Petersburg, and Max Bruch in Berlin. He was also much influenced by the music of Richard Strauss. Although his reputation rests on a comparatively small output, few twentieth century composers can match Respighi's sumptuous and colourful use of the orchestra. He was also a very considerable musical scholar in his own right. Early in his career he produced editions of Monteverdi and Vitali, and later composed three popular orchestral suites based on Italian and French lute music. His arrangement of Rossini's music for the Diaghilev ballet, *La Boutique Fantasque*, is another well-deserved favourite, and the symphonic poems *The Pines of Rome, The Fountains of Rome, The Birds, Roman Festivals* and *Brazilian Impressions* are frequently performed. After the production of his opera *Semirâma* he was, in 1913, appointed teacher of composition at the Conservatorio di Santa Cecilia in Rome, where he settled permanently. He was elected a member of the Italian Academy in 1932. Respighi once said that the 'Italian genius is for melody and clarity': two qualities that are to be found in abundance in his own music. R.H.

music: Lamartine's poem which suggests that life is merely a 'prelude' to what follows.

Originally for piano solo, Liszt later transcribed his twenty Hungarian Rhapsodies for orchestra. With rhythms and melodies taken from Magyar gypsy music, these colourful showpieces have never lost their appeal, the exuberant No. 2 remaining the most popular.

Felix MENDELSSOHN (1809-47) Germany

A Midsummer Night's Dream:
incidental music
(first performed [overture] Stettin, 1827;
[complete] Potsdam, 1843)

The precocious Mendelssohn was just seventeen when he wrote the brilliant overture to *A Midsummer Night's Dream*, originally for

Sergei PROKOVIEV (1891-1953) Russia

Lieutenant Kijé: symphonic suite, Op. 60
(first performed [concert suite] Paris, 1937)

The tale of Kijé, the 'clerical error' soldier that had to be 'invented' to keep the Tsar happy, was made the subject of a Soviet film in the thirties. Prokofiev provided suitably entertaining and witty accompanying music, later making a five-movement suite from it.

Peter and the Wolf

Like Britten's *Young Person's Guide to the Orchestra*, Prokofiev's children's fable is designed as an entertaining way of introducing the instruments of the orchestra, and contains some of his most agreeable and popular tunes.

Sergei RACHMANINOV (1873-1943) Russia

Rhapsody on a theme of Paganini, Op. 43
(first performed Philadelphia, 1934)
The Isle of the Dead, Op. 29
Symphonic Dances, Op. 45

The three Symphonic Dances – a deceptively innocuous title – were Rachmaninov's last major orchestral composition, and arguably his greatest. More dances of death than life – the gaiety hollow, the waltz spectral – Rachmaninov's familiar 'motif' of the *dies irae (day of wrath)* plainchant plays a key role, as it does in so many of his other major orchestral works. *The Isle of the Dead*, inspired by a painting of the Venetian island cemetery of San Michele, is one of them, and the popular *Paganini Variations* another.

Rachmaninov was by no means the only composer to have been inspired by the last of Niccolò Paganini's twenty-four caprices for violin. His variations fall roughly into the three sections of a concerto, fast-slow-fast, with the emotional heart of the work the famous and romantic eighteenth variation.

Maurice RAVEL (1875-1937) France

Boléro
(first performed Paris, 1928)
Pavane pour une infante défunte
(first performed [orchestal version] 1910)
Rapsodie Espagnole
(first performed 1908)
Le Tombeau de Couperin
(first performed 1920)
La Valse: choreographic poem
(first performed Paris, 1920)

Essentially a lengthy study in crescendo, Ravel's tongue-in-cheek description of his *Boléro* was 'a piece for orchestra without music'! Written to a commission from the dancer, Ida Rubinstein, it grows from the softest drum taps to a full orchestral barrage.

piano duet. Seventeen years later, King Frederick William IV of Prussia commissioned further incidental music for a production of the play at his court theatre and it spurred Mendelssohn to some of his most delightful music, much more than is included in the familiar concert suite. As well as the overture, the suite includes a superb example of the composer's affinity for the scherzo, a limpid, angelic nocturne and, of course, the all-too-familiar wedding march.

Overture: The Hebrides (Fingal's Cave), Op. 26
(first performed London, 1832)

A boat trip around the Scottish Hebrides, including the Isle of Staffa and its famous cave, was the overwhelming inspiration for this effective, but typically unexaggerated 'seascape in music'. It is a wonderful example of Mendelssohn's art (the subtitle, however, was his publishers' idea).

Wolfgang Amadeus MOZART (1756-91) Austria

Serenade for Strings in G major
(Eine Kleine Nachtmusik), K525
(first performed 1787)
Serenata Notturna, K239
(first performed 1776)

Mozart's serenades and divertimentos were written as pure entertainment, 'background' music for functions and festivities, and the evergreen *Eine kleine Nachtmusik* was no exception to this. As played today, though, the work is incomplete: the autograph shows the first minuet and trio to have been torn out early in the work's existence for reasons we shall probably never know. The *Serenata Notturna*, distinguished by its unusually prominent role for kettledrums, is another 'fun' work, probably written for the Salzburg carnival of 1776.

Above: *Ben Shahn painting of* Peter and the Wolf, *the work by Sergei Prokofiev which has become well-known and well-liked by both children and adults since first performed in 1936.*

Modest MUSSORGSKY (1839-81) Russia

Pictures at an Exhibition
(first performed [orchestration by Ravel] Paris, 1920)

Mussorgsky composed his tribute to his late artist friend, Viktor Hartmann in 1874, but only for solo piano. Orchestrations were made later, of which that by Maurice Ravel is far and away the most popular. Whatever the qualities of the orchestrated version, however, the piano version is no poor substitute. In many ways, it has the more impact, conveying just how imaginative and persuasive Mussorgsky was in his treatment of the divers, often grotesque subjects of the paintings themselves.

Night on Bare Mountain: tone-poem

Mussorgsky's startling boldness was sometimes too much for his fellow-composers and mentors, which is why the version of this piece most played today – a very free reworking of the original music by Rimsky-Korsakov – seems positively demure alongside the unbridled excitement of the fiery original. Mussorgsky composed this in 1866, titling the work *St John's Night on Bare Mountain*, that being midsummer eve, and the name that of a mountain near Kiev in the Ukraine.

Following criticism from his teacher Balakirev, Mussorgsky revised the piece, even to the extent of adding a respectable ending to this satanic music with the solemn ring of the matins bell. It was this revised version which Rimsky-Korsakov took and tamed yet further. Hearing the original is, therefore, quite a revelation.

The *Pavane* began life as a piano piece in 1899. Apparently, Ravel had in his mind the kind of Spanish princess *(infanta)* that Velazquez might have painted, and the kind of graceful dance the little girl may have performed. In its orchestral version, with prominent role for horn, the *Pavane* retains its melancholy charm.

Ravel's first major orchestral work was the colourful and intoxicating *Rapsodie Espagnole*, a romanticised vision of Spain, but nevertheless a very skilful one, as the Spanish composer Manuel de Falla confirmed. Brilliantly orchestrated, with magical textures and sonorities, the colours, sounds and perfumes are almost tangible.

Le Tombeau de Couperin is much more than a pastiche of the dance music of eighteenth-century France, and of one of its finest composers, François Couperin. The work was begun as a six-part piano suite in 1914 but not finished until 1917, after Ravel had been invalided out of the French army. Now its movements also became memorials to six of his friends killed during the war. When Ravel orchestrated the suite, with his usual impeccable taste and lucidity,' he omitted two of the movements, retaining the *Prélude, Forlane, Menuet,* and *Rigaudon.*

Ravel's skill at 'stylising' musical forms is nowhere better heard in what he himself described as an 'apotheosis of the Viennese waltz'. The elegant dance is transformed into an ecstatic, whirling frenzy, seemingly – and surprisingly, for so urbane a character as Ravel – uncontrollable. Suddenly, both dance and dancers are extinguished, exhausted.

Ottorino RESPIGHI (1879-1936) Italy

The Fountains of Rome: symphonic poem
The Pines of Rome: symphonic poem

Dating from 1916 and 1926 respectively, these two works remain the best known from Respighi's considerable output. Displaying a matchless mastery of the orchestral palette, he conjures romantic impressions of, first, four of Rome's historic fountains and the different atmospheres surrounding them, and second, the city as might be witnessed by its pine trees: children playing at the Villa Borghese, the catacombs, night on the Janiculum Hill, and the legions marching in triumph along the Appian Way. Hardly a trick is missed in music of unalloyed pleasure.

Nicolai RIMSKY-KORSAKOV (1844-1908) Russia

Scheherazade: symphonic suite, Op. 35
(first performed St Petersburg [Leningrad], 1888)

A fascination with colours and sounds was something Rimsky-Korsakov shared with several other nineteenth-century Russian composers. For him, it came to fruition in this opulent and richly melodic suite based upon *1001 Tales of the Arabian Nights.* Two themes dominate: an aggressive, impatient one representing the Sultan, and a radiantly beautiful violin solo which, throughout, becomes the persuasive voice of Scheherazade, and which – in the *Tales* – finally spares her life through its enchanting story-telling.

Capriccio Espagnol, Op. 34
(first performed 1887)

This scintillating five-movement suite was first intended as a 'Fantasy on Spanish Themes for violin and orchestra', hence the major role still played by the solo violin in the final score. It may be picture-postcard Spain, but Rimsky-Korsakov's feel for melody and colour lifts the work above the banal.

Camille SAINT-SAËNS (1835-1921) France

Carnival of the Animals
(first performed Paris, 1922)
Danse Macabre, Op. 40
(first performed Paris, 1875)

Although audiences never fail to respond to the light-hearted humour of what the composer described as a 'grand zoological fantasy', Saint-Saëns regarded it as a piece of private fun. Until the first full performance shortly after the composer's death, only the famous solo for cello and two pianos, *The Swan*, had been heard in public.

The imagery of *Danse Macabre* is unmistakable: the figure of death plays a merry dance on his violin, while the xylophone – its first use in a concert work – rattles out its skeletal accompaniment.

Arnold SCHOENBERG (1874-1951) Austria

Five Pieces for Orchestra, Op. 16
(first performed London, 1912)
Verklärte Nacht
(first performed [string sextet version] Vienna, 1902)

One of the seminal orchestral works of this century, Schoenberg's *Five Pieces* was one of the very first applications of atonal composition in the orchestral sphere. Schoenberg appended titles to each of the pieces, one very descriptive *(Colours: summer morning by a lake)*, the others less tangible, including the curious *Obligatory recitative*. The composer reduced the outsize orchestration – purely for practical reasons – in 1949.

Ten years before the first performance of *Five Pieces* came the première of the most influential of Schoenberg's early compositions. Originally scored for string sextet, *Verklärte Nacht* is searingly emotional music loosely based on Richard Dehmel's poem of confession and forgiveness. Wagner and

Manuel de FALLA
(1876-1946)

Although his mother taught him piano when young, it was not until he was seventeen that attendance at a concert made him resolve to become a composer. But progress was still slow, with only two unsuccessful *zarzuelas* to show before he met the musicologist Felipe Pedrell in his mid-twenties. Pedrell's enthusiasm for a Spanish musical revival inspired Falla, who set about absorbing folk influences. At twenty-eight he was awarded a prize for his short opera *La vida breve*, and in that same year won a piano competition. In 1907 he visited Paris for a one-week trip, but stayed for seven years, becoming a friend of Debussy, Dukas and Ravel, from whom he learnt much about modern orchestral usage. His *Four Spanish Pieces* for piano appeared in 1908, and he then worked on *Nights in the Gardens of Spain*, an impressionistic work for piano and orchestra. This was completed after his return home, as also was his ballet *Love the Magician.* Then in 1919 Diaghilev's production of *The Three Cornered Hat* finally established his fame. All these (and various other pieces) have a strikingly colourful Andalusian feel, but in the 1920s Falla drew on cooler Spanish influences, and also went through a neo-classical phase, as in his Harpsichord Concerto for small ensemble. His last years were spent in self-imposed exile. J.C.

Tristan loom large in the background, a connection made more evident in Schoenberg's sumptuous version for string orchestra.

Franz SCHUBERT (1797-1828) Austria

Rosamunde: incidental music
(first performed Vienna, 1823)

It is said that Schubert composed the music to Helmina von Chézy's romantic drama in just five days. The play lasted just two performances, never to resurface; Schubert's score, however, has proved immortal. The items for chorus and soprano soloist – the *Chorus of the Spirits* and *Chorus of the Shepherds* among them – employ some of his most meltingly beautiful melodies.

Alexander SCRIABIN (1872-1915) Russia

The Poem of Ecstasy, Op. 54
(first performed New York, 1908)

This extraordinary work, by a no less extraordinary composer, began life as a symphony, a musical interpretation of the composer's own visionary *Poem of Ecstasy*. A vast orchestra is called for, with a large brass contingent and assorted percussion, as well as the usual forces and, throughout the heady score, Scriabin goes to great lengths to convey the sound he seeks. The opening, for example, is marked 'with languid desire'.

Jean SIBELIUS (1865-1957) Finland

Karelia Suite, Op. 11
(first performed Helsinki, 1893)
The Swan of Tuonela, Op. 22, No. 2
(first performed Helsinki, 1896)
Finlandia: tone-poem, Op. 26
(first performed Helsinki, 1900)
Valse Triste, Op. 44
(first performed Helsinki, 1904)
Tapiola: tone-poem, Op. 112
(first performed New York, 1926)

The landscape and the legends of Sibelius's homeland dominate all but one of these orchestral works. Incidental music to accompany a series of tableaux produced by Helsinki students was the genesis of the *Karelia Suite*, while the growing nationalist movement in Finland (the country was under Tsarist Russian rule) found its anthem in the rousing *Finlandia* of 1899. The *Swan of Tuonela* is the second of four *Legends* inspired by Finland's folk epic, the *Kalevala*. On the black waters which surround Finland's 'land of the dead' glides a lonely swan, represented orchestrally by some wonderful solo writing for cor anglais. Sibelius's scene painting is nowhere more effective.

The equally melancholy *Valse Triste* is derived from music which Sibelius wrote to accompany a play by his brother-in-law, entitled *Kuolema*: death waltzes with a dying woman before claiming her life.

An altogether larger conception than any of the other works here, however, is *Tapiola*, which was destined to be Sibelius's last major published composition. Again, the *Kalevala* supplies the inspiration: Tapio is the god of the forest, and Tapiola his domain, its brooding darkness and mystery magically conveyed in the composer's wholly individual orchestral style.

Bedřich SMETANA (1824-84) Czechoslovakia

Má Vlast: symphonic poems

Smetana expressed his own nationalistic feelings, and those of his countrymen (at that time under Austro-Hungarian rule) in a series of six descriptive symphonic poems collectively known as *Má Vlast (My Fatherland)*. Of these, *Vltava* (the river on which Prague is built) has become far and away the best known since its first performance in that city in 1875.

Johann STRAUSS (1825-99) Austria

The Blue Danube, Op. 314
(first performed Vienna, 1867)

Although correct, 'waltz' seems an inadequate description for what is a superbly constructed tone-poem, a tapestry of lilting tunes brilliantly woven together. It is a sad fact that this most famous of the Strauss waltzes is seldom performed as he originally intended – with a chorus supporting the orchestra.

Richard STRAUSS (1864-1949) Germany

Ein Alpensinfonie, Op. 64
(first performed Berlin, 1915)
Also sprach Zarathustra: symphonic poem, Op. 30
(first performed Frankfurt-am-Main, 1896)
Don Juan: symphonic poem, Op. 20
(first performed Weimar, 1889)
Don Quixote, Op. 35

Above: *The great 'Waltz King' Johann Strauss II, composer of the immortal* Blue Danube *and* Die Fledermaus *in his country retreat in Ischl where he often entertained Brahms and other friends.*

Ein Heldenleben: symphonic poem, Op. 40
(first performed Frankfurt-am-Main, 1899)
Metamorphosen for 23 solo strings
(first performed Zurich, 1946)
Till Eulenspiegels lustige streiche: symphonic poem, Op. 28
(first performed Cologne, 1895)
Tod und Verklärung: symphonic poem, Op. 24
(first performed Eisenach, 1890)

Richard Strauss's greatest contributions to the orchestral repertoire remain his symphonic poems. He sprang to fame with the first of them, *Don Juan*, a – for the time – risqué portrait of the fabled seducer that immediately revealed not only a gifted originator but a fluent and confident orchestrator. He followed this with the more philosophical *Tod und Verklärung (Death and Transfiguration)*, expressing the triumph of the human spirit over the pain of death. *Till Eulenspiegels lustige streiche (Till Eulenspiegel's Merry Pranks)* is in a much lighter vein. Till is a character from German folklore, an itinerant prankster and rogue whose exploits Strauss piquantly relates, including his final apprehension by the law.

The following year came the première of the Nietzsche-influenced *Also sprach Zarathustra (Thus Spake Zarathustra)* whose 'dawn of mankind' opening is most widely known for its use in Kubrick's film, *2001*. Like mankind, the work then evolves towards the Nietzschean ideal of the 'superman', although from the exquisitely funny dance that Strauss gives him it is hard to believe he took the concept that seriously.

Cervantes' literary masterpiece was the inspiration for *Don Quixote*, which gives a concertante role to the cello, but the 'hero' of the next major symphonic poem was the composer himself: thanks to Strauss's innate musicality, *Ein Heldenleben (A Hero's Life)* stops short of bombast and banality. Its six linked parts recount the hero's battles with his enemies (presumably the critics), his peaceful deeds and his love-life.

From his villa at Garmisch, Strauss could see the mountainscape he so vividly depicts in the *Alpensinfonie*, with its 137-strong orchestra. But thirty years on, a very different Germany presented itself to the eighty-year-old composer and he conveyed his feelings eloquently and movingly in *Metamorphosen*, completed in the last days of the war in 1945; it is one of his very greatest works.

Pyotr TCHAIKOVSKY (1840-93) Russia

Capriccio Italien, Op. 45
(first performed 1880)
Overture – 1812, Op. 49
(first performed Moscow, 1882)
Romeo and Juliet: fantasy overture
(first performed Moscow, 1870)
Serenade for Strings in C major, Op. 48

The composer Mily Balakirev not only suggested the Shakespearean tragedy as a likely musical subject, but was responsible for some of the revisions Tchaikovsky made after *Romeo and Juliet*'s indifferent reception in 1870. Indeed, he continued to amend the score until the final version of this popular work was republished in 1881.

A year earlier had seen the first performance of his *Capriccio Italien*, a frothy confection of Italian popular dances and songs that become sheer delight in Tchaikovsky's skilled hands. However, that most famous of orchestral showpieces, *1812*, was a commission for which he had less than overwhelming enthusiasm. Historically, the piece is a nonsense: Napoleon's army was defeated by cold and starvation, not by Russian cannons.

Far closer to his heart was the carefree *Serenade for Strings*, with its charming waltz and first-movement 'homage' to the composer Tchaikovsky admired the most, Mozart.

Michael TIPPETT (b. 1905) **England**

Concerto for Double String Orchestra
(first performed London, 1940)

It was this 'neo-Baroque' composition which first drew international attention to Tippett's music. Like the traditional Baroque concerto, it demands two instrumental groups, here of equal size and weight. Tippett plays these groups off against each other quite brilliantly, with often exuberant results: an ideal starting-point in exploring the music of this important British composer.

Ralph VAUGHAN WILLIAMS (1872-1958) **England**

Fantasia on a Theme of Thomas Tallis
(first performed Gloucester, 1910)
Flos Campi
(first performed London, 1925)
The Lark Ascending
(first performed London, 1921)
The Wasps: overture
(first performed Cambridge, 1909)

Vaughan Williams was delighted when asked to provide incidental music for Cambridge University's 1909 production of Aristophanes's *The Wasps*. He produced an entertaining score, from which the overture has become a popular concert item in its own right. Far greater, though, was the work he conducted for the first time in Gloucester Cathedral the following year. While working on *The English Hymnal*, Vaughan Williams came across nine tunes by the Tudor composer, Thomas Tallis. So taken was he by one of them, he adopted it as the basis of a free 'fantasia' for strings: two string orchestras and a string quartet. It is music of both majesty and mysticism, moving from rapt meditation to soaring intensity, his first work to become well known.

Soaring through the open air, rather than a cathedral vault, the *The Lark Ascending* gives wing to the solo violin. But this is no mere pastoral rumination: there is vitality as well as rhapsodic contemplation, and a down-to-earth folk song quality to the orchestral writing. It is the solo viola which has the spotlight in the enigmatic *Flos Campi*, some of the most sensuous and quasi-erotic music Vaughan Williams ever wrote, taking its inspiration from the Biblical *Song of Solomon*.

Richard WAGNER (1813-83) **Germany**

Siegfried Idyll
(first performed Lucerne, 1870)

A surprise birthday present for the composer's wife, Cosima Wagner, was a performance of this sumptuous work for small string orchestra. Wagner had been working on the music drama *Siegfried* at the time, and there are thematic links between the *Idyll* and this third of the *Ring* operas. Interestingly, however, the original title was taken from the Wagners' Swiss villa – the *Tribschen Idyll*.

William WALTON (1902-83) **England**

Façade: suites for orchestra
(first performed [first suite] London, 1926: [second suite] New York, 1938)

First devised as a suitably witty accompaniment to the somewhat eccentric poetry of Edith Sitwell, Walton later made two orchestral suites from the original score for small ensemble. This delightful, often jazzy and tongue-in-cheek music went on to become among Walton's most popular. P.H.

Below: *Richard Wagner (1813-83) with his wife Cosima and his father-in-law Franz Liszt in his work-room at the Villa Wahnfried in Bayreuth, painted by W. Beckmann in 1880.*

*Percy GRAINGER
(1882-1961)*

Born in Melbourne, travelled in Europe, studied with Busoni, a collector of British folk songs (he spent 1900-15 in England), admired and befriended by Delius and Grieg, this eccentric musician – who described himself as a sort of musical democrat – finally settled in the USA. In early days he was a concert pianist and became a noted protagonist of Grieg's Piano Concerto, and by all accounts he was a lively stimulant to others, a sort of constant breath of Australian fresh air. But his fame rests primarily on his orchestral adaptations of traditional tunes, pieces such as the popular *Mock Morris, Molly on the Shore, Shepherd's Hey* and *Handel in the Strand*. There are also a number of choral settings, while the edited folk-song transcriptions encompass some fifty items. His choral arrangement of *Shallow Brown* was greatly admired by Britten, and his edition of *Brigg Fair* prompted Delius to produce his own orchestral rhapsody on the same theme. Any reader who saw the great Ken Russell film about Delius will remember Percy Grainger rushing back and forth through the house to throw a ball over the roof and then catch it on the other side. That was the happy-go-lucky, open-air Grainger, and there's a lot of that free, direct atmosphere in his music. J.C.

Dancing has been part of music probably since the first notes were played, but the ballet has its origins in fifteenth and sixteenth century France. The *ballet de cour* (court ballet) developed from the medieval masquerades, mixtures of both vocal and dance music. The first *ballet de cour* was probably staged towards the end of the sixteenth century, after which the form divided into the *opera-ballet* and the non-vocal *ballet pantomime*.

Dance was an integral part of French and Italian Baroque opera, but the large-scale ballet, of which the works of Tchaikovsky, Stravinsky and Prokofiev are perhaps the best known, was very much a nineteenth-century innovation. The Russian influence on ballet has been considerable, not just in the music of the composers above, but in the work of the remarkable impresario Serge Diaghilev and his Ballets Russes which inspired a host of great compositions in the first two decades of the twentieth century. P.H.

Adolphe ADAM (1803-56) France

GISELLE
(first performed Paris, 1841)

The multi-talented Adam (he took on roles as theatre-owner, critic and teacher as well as composing and conducting) wrote twelve ballets of which only *Giselle*, one of the first in the grand romantic style, is performed today. Based on a folk tale of jilted love, its melodies can also be enjoyed through an orchestral suite derived from the score.

Above: *Costume for one the Furies designed for the Capiola ballet* Les Noces de Pélée et Thétis. *The first performance of the ballet was in Paris.*

Below: *The Paris Opéra maintained a large ballet company and demanded that its composers wrote ballets into their operas to keep it employed. L'Opéra moved to the Rue Lepeletier in 1822 and into a glorious period of its history with works by Rossini, Donizetti, Weber, Meyerbeer and French opéra-comique.*

Béla BARTÓK (1881-1945) Hungary

THE MIRACULOUS MANDARIN, Op. 19
(first performed Cologne, 1925)

The composer described this work as a 'pantomine in one act', but it hardly qualifies as children's entertainment. Bartók came across the story in a literary magazine in 1917, and wrote the ballet based on it over the ensuing two years. Three pimps use a young girl to lure unsuspecting 'clients' into their clutches. The last of three visitors is a strange mandarin (Bartók uses the quasi-Chinese pentatonic scale, and a combination of trombones and tuba to depict him) who enchants the girl and then defies attempts to kill him until his lust has been sated.

Ludwig van BEETHOVEN (1770-1827) Germany

THE CREATURES OF PROMETHEUS, Op. 43
(first performed Vienna, 1801)

The story of the fire-stealing demi-god who brings two statues to life, and then fills them with knowledge and creativity was Beethoven's first work for the stage. The whole score is rarely played today (apart from the overture) but significantly the dance tune from the finale of the ballet provided Beethoven with the theme for the last movement of his *Eroica* Symphony.

Arthur BLISS (1891-1975) England

CHECKMATE
(first performed Paris, 1937)

The game of chess, with its opportunities for pageant and symbolism, inspired Bliss to one of his finest scores, written for the Royal Ballet's first visit to Paris in 1937.

Frédéric CHOPIN (1810-49) Poland

LES SYLPHIDES
(first performed St. Petersburg, 1907)

Orchestrations – not by Chopin – of seven of his well-known piano pieces (three waltzes, two mazurkas, a prelude and a nocturne) were combined to produce this ballet score, whose first production featured choreography by Fokin.

Aaron COPLAND (b. 1900) USA

APPALACHIAN SPRING
(first performed Washington, 1944)
RODEO
(first performed New York, 1942)

Along with a third ballet, *Billy the Kid*, these scores are Copland at his most American,

Above: *Scene from* Giselle, *one of the best-known of the great 19th-century ballets, first performed in 1841 and still considered the very essence of the romantic ballet movement.*

Below: Les Sylphides, *first performed at the Maryinsky Theatre, St Petersburg, 1907, with Pavlova in the leading role, has a score of orchestrated Chopin piano pieces and choreography by Fokine.*

Maurice RAVEL
(1875-1937)

French composer, of Basque descent on his mother's side, whose family moved to Paris when he was three months old. He entered the Conservatoire in 1889 to study the piano with Bériot and composition with Gabriel Fauré. From his earliest works, composed in the late teens, his maturity of style and use of unorthodox harmonies were regarded with suspicion by the academics of the day, and he was repeatedly denied the highest award in the Prix de Rome. The last occasion was in 1905, when his elimination at the preliminary stage caused such an uproar that the director of the Conservatoire was forced to resign. By this time the *Pavane pour une infante défunte*, his *Jeux d'eau*, the orchestral song cycle *Shéhérezade*, and the string quartet had all been published. In 1911 the comic one-act opera *L'Heure espagnole* was coolly received, but a year later his brilliant scores for the ballet *Daphnis et Chloé*, commissioned by Diaghilev, were given their first performance. He saw military service as an auxiliary in the 1914-18 war, but was invalided out in 1917, the year of *Le Tombeau de Couperin*. *La Valse* followed together with his marvellous orchestration of Mussorgsky's *Pictures at an Exhibition*. Among his later works are the opera *L'Enfant et les sortilèges* and, of course, the inescapable *Bolero*, a piece for orchestra without music, as he himself described it. R.H.

commanding the musical idioms of his country as few others have done. Love among cowboys and cowgirls is the subject of *Rodeo* whose popular symphonic suite includes *Buckaroo Holiday* and *Hoe-down*.

Two years later, Copland followed *Rodeo* with his 'ballet for Martha' – Martha Graham and her dance company. *Appalachian Spring* is set during a wedding within the plain-dealing Shaker community of the Appalachian Mountains. It is wonderful music, effective both with or without dance, and notable for its skilful adaptation of the old Shaker hymn, *Simple Gifts* in a brilliant series of variations. The original score was for just thirteen instruments, but in 1945, with some minor cuts, Copland made an arrangement for symphony orchestra.

Claude DEBUSSY (1862-1918) **France**

JEUX
(first performed Paris, 1913)

Debussy's *poème dansé* is one of his most important works, despite the unlikely subject of a tennis match and the hunt for a lost ball. Musically the score is remarkable for the interaction and development of its no less than twenty-three thematic motifs.

Jeux (*Games*) was commissioned by Serge Diaghilev for his Ballets Russes, and the original idea – which, despite its apparent innocence has, according to Debussy, 'something sinister in the darkening shadows' – came from Diaghilev's star performer, Nijinsky.

Léo DELIBES (1836-91) **France**

COPPÉLIA
(first performed Paris, 1870)
SYLVIA
(first performed Paris, 1876)

Subtitled *The Girl with Enamel Eyes*, Delibes best-loved ballet, a sequence of lovely melodies often performed as a concert suite, was first produced with choreography by Louis Mérante. *Coppélia* tells the story of a youth who falls in love with a lifesize doll (and of the reaction of his very alive girlfriend).

Mérante also provided the choreography for the lesser-known *Sylvia, ou La Nymphe de Diane*, with its scenario by Jules Barbier and Baron de Reinach.

George BALANCHINE
(1904-83)

George Balanchine, one of the most influential of all dancers and choreographers, was born in St Petersburg and in 1914 entered the Imperial Ballet Academy, from which he graduated seven years later. His early work as a choreographer was severely criticised for its unorthodoxy, but while he was touring Germany with his own small dance company in 1924, he auditioned for Diaghilev who immediately offered him a post in Ballets Russes. A year later Balanchine became chief choreographer of the company, and began a lifelong friendship with Stravinsky. After the death of Diaghilev in 1929, Balanchine took on a number of short-term assignments, but in 1934 he accepted Kirstein's invitation to go to the USA to establish the School of American Ballet. From his best students he created American Ballet, which made its New York début in 1935 and became the resident company of the Met for the next three years, staging a memorable Stravinsky Festival in 1937. In the mid-1940s Balanchine helped to set up the company which later became the New York City Ballet, and it is as artistic director of that highly successful company that he became one of the most powerful exponents of neo-classicism, linking American ballet with the European tradition yet constantly reaching out towards exciting new frontiers. R.H.

Manuel de FALLA (1876-1946) **Spain**

EL SOMBRERO DE TRES PICOS (The Three Cornered Hat)
(first performed London, 1919)
EL AMOR BRUJO (Love the Magician)
(first performed Madrid, 1915)

Falla's two great ballets, both full of colourful and exciting music, have Spanish scenarios and an unmistakably Iberian flavour derived from the ethnic *cante jondo* of Andalusia. The first, *El Amor brujo*, which includes the dazzling *Ritual Fire Dance* in a tale of ghostly enchantment and female wiles, was requested by one of the great flamenco dancers of the day, Pastora Imperio.

In 1916, Diaghilev persuaded Falla to turn what had been planned as a pantomime into a ballet. This jocular tale of the lecherous local official – his badge of office is the *sombrero de tres picos* – who gets his come-uppance at the hands of the quick-witted miller, after attempting to seduce the latter's wife, was premièred, surprisingly, at the Alhambra Theatre, London, with decor by Pablo Picasso.

Alexander GLAZUNOV (1865-1936) **Russia**

THE SEASONS
(first performed St Petersburg [Leningrad], 1900)

An important figure in Russian musical life at the time, Glazunov is now largely remembered for this ballet score, which fully displays his lyrical and melodic gifts. It was first produced with choreography by the incomparable Marius Petipa.

Ferdinand HÉROLD (1791-1833) **France**

LA FILLE MAL GARDÉE
(first performed Paris, 1828)

One of several ballets written by Hérold, *La Fille Mal Gardée* is best-known today in the frequently performed version by John Lanchbery, itself a commission from Sir Frederick Ashton. However, the original mixture of folk tunes and popular songs telling a tale of unrequited love pre-dates Hérold.

Aram KHACHATURIAN (1903-78) **Russia**

GAYANEH
(first performed Molotov, 1942)

For his ballet scores *Gayaneh* and *Spartacus*, Khachaturian drew heavily on the folk music of his fellow Armenians. Whatever the deficiencies of his storylines (one set on a collective farm, the other during a gladiators' rebellion in ancient Rome), the music works happily alone thanks to its blend of fiery exuberance and sweeping romance.

Darius MILHAUD (1892-1974) **France**

LA CRÉATION DU MONDE
(first performed Paris, 1923)

Milhaud was nothing if not an eclectic and his exposure to jazz idioms during the early twenties bore fruit in this ballet for the Ballet Suedois. Using just seventeen players, the score adapts the jazz and blues elements that

Léo DELIBES
(1836-91)

Left: La Fille Mal Gardée *was originally seen in 1779, then re-scored by Ferdinand Hérold in 1828. Re-arranged by John Lanchbery, the Royal Ballet production of 1960 put it firmly in the repertoire.*

Above: *Prokofiev's ballet* Romeo and Juliet *was first produced in Brno in 1938, then in Leningrad in 1940 at the Kirov Theatre. It has become one of the modern classics of ballet.*

Delibes started his musical career as a choirboy at the Madeleine and other churches in Paris, and entered the Conservatoire where he studied the piano, harmony and advanced composition under a number of teachers, one of whom was Adolphe Adam, composer of the ballet music for *Giselle*. Through his influence Delibes was invited to join the Théâtre Lyrique as accompanist in 1853, and was offered the post of organist at Saint Pierre de Chaillot. He wrote several short comic operas and a number of operettas, some of which were very successful, and at the same time fulfilled his church obligations by composing choruses for male voices as well as for children, and a Mass. With his appointment as accompanist at the Paris Opéra in 1863 new horizons were opened up for him, and he revealed such a gift for melody that he was entrusted with the setting of an entire ballet, *Coppelia* (1870), which was followed six years later by the larger-scale, mythological ballet, *Sylvia*. He also wrote three operas for the Opéra Comique, of which the best known is *Lakmé* (1883). Other popular works include the incidental music for *Le Roi s'amuse* and his song 'Les filles de Cadiz'. One of his pupils, the violinist Fritz Kreisler, described Delibes as 'a gay blade, flighty and irresponsible'. R.H.

delighted Milhaud in Harlem to an African tribal creation myth, and the result is unexpectedly restrained but strikingly effective.

Jacques OFFENBACH (1819-80) Germany

GAÎTÉ PARISIENNE
(arranged Rosenthal)
(first performed Monte Carlo, 1938)

In 1938, the French director and composer Manuel Rosenthal assembled an affectionate pot-pourri of some of the finest music from seven of Offenbach's operettas. The nine items make for a ballet suite of high spirits and lively humour and include the raucous *Cancan* (from *Orpheus in the Underworld*) and the *Barcarolle* from *Tales of Hoffman*.

Serge PROKOFIEV (1891-1953) Russia

CINDERELLA, Op. 87
(first performed Moscow, 1945)
ROMEO AND JULIET, Op. 36
(first performed Brno, 1938)

Prokofiev's two substantial scores remain among the finest and most enduring ballet music written this century. *Romeo* is closest to the great ballets of Tchaikovsky with its set-piece dances: music wholly appropriate to the story, consistently inspired and brilliantly executed. *Cinderella* is hardly less fine and both ballets can be sampled through the orchestral suites which Prokofiev made from the full scores, and can be seen as the pivot of modern ballet.

Maurive RAVEL (1875-1937) France

MA MÈRE L'OYE (Mother Goose)
(first performed Paris, 1915)
DAPHNIS ET CHLOÉ
(first performed Paris, 1912)

Taking his inspiration from nursery tales by Perrault, Ravel completed his *Mother Goose* suite for piano duet in 1908. Some years later

Below: *Prokofiev's ballet version of the age-old* Cinderella *story was first seen at the Bolshoi Theatre in 1945. A superbly witty score has all the well-known Prokofiev characteristics.*

he scored this charming, delicate work as a ballet, to a scenario by Louis Laloy. An altogether more ambitious work is *Daphnis et Chloé*, which stems from the story by the Greek writer, Longus, but is more akin to the idealized version of arcadian Greece beloved of eighteenth-century French landscape painters.

Ravel calls for a large orchestra and chorus to evoke the moods and scenes of his imagination, and also prepared two concert suites from the score (the second of which is the most frequently played). *Daphnis et Chloé* was another inspired commission by Diaghilev for his Ballets Russes.

Igor STRAVINSKY (1882-1971) **Russia**

AGON
(first performed Los Angeles, 1957)
APOLLO
(Apollon Musagète)
(first performed Washington DC, 1927)
JEU DE CARTES
(first performed New York, 1937)
L'OISEAU DE FEU (The Firebird)
(first performed Paris, 1910)
ORPHEUS
(first performed New York, 1948)
PÉTROUCHKA
(first performed Paris, 1911)
LE SACRE DU PRINTEMPS (The Rite of Spring)
(first performed Paris, 1913)

A list of works that confirms Stravinsky as the leading ballet composer of this century; what they do not reveal are the extraordinary changes in his music that these works document, from the incandescence and colour of the 'Russian' ballets to the cool translucency of *Apollo* or the cut-glass objectivity of *Agon*.

His first ballet was to Diaghilev's requirement for one based on the legend of the *Zhar-Ptitsa*, the magical bird with wings of flame. Ironically, Stravinsky took considerable persuasion to take on the commission which brought him international acclaim from its very first performance. The music, vivid, exciting, exotic, owes much to his teacher, Rimsky-Korsakov.

Diaghilev was anxious to repeat the success of *The Firebird* and, hearing that Stravinsky was working on a concertante piano work depicting a puppet that comes to life, urged the composer to turn this idea into a ballet. *Pétrouchka* is a bolder, more elemental work than its predecessor, vigorous and dramatic as befits its bizarre, ever disquieting scenario. However, it did not prepare the Paris audience for what was to follow: the first performance of *Le Sacre du Printemps* remains the most sensational in musical history. More importantly, it was a watershed in music. For some, 'modern music' was born that evening in 1913 with this ballet of unprecedented rhythmic primitivism and unashamed savagery.

Above: *The ballet* Daphnis and Chloé *was first given by Diaghilev's Ballets Russes at the Théâtre du Châtelet in Paris in 1912. Score by Ravel, choreography by Fokine, with Karsavina and Nijinsky.*

Below: Pétrouchka, *or* Petrushka, *had the same birthright, venue and personnel as* Daphnis and Chloé *(above) except that its wonderfully virile score came from the up-and-coming Stravinsky in 1911.*

Serge DIAGHILEV
(1872-1929)

One of the most celebrated of all impresarios, Russian-born Diaghilev started his career by reading law at St Petersburg (1890-97), but developed an early taste for journalism and art criticism. As a result, he was invited to become artistic adviser to the Maryinsky Theatre in 1899. In 1908 he went to Paris to supervise a series of Russian music concerts, including a production of *Boris Godunov*, in which Chaliapin sang the title role. The following year he made a sensational return to Paris presenting a season of Russian ballet with Nijinsky as the star dancer, choreography by Fokine and sets and costumes by Bakst and Benois. A permanent company, Ballets Russes, was formed, which Diaghilev directed through many financial and artistic hazards until his death. New works were commissioned from many avant-garde composers such as Ravel, Stravinsky, Strauss and Debussy. Diaghilev also attracted leading artists of the day, including Picasso, and he was able to hand-pick dancers and choreographers especially from Russia, where there was no escape from the strictly classical ballet tradition. His artistic success was so phenomenal that he was able to set his own terms, and his revolutionary influence not only on the development of ballet, but also on many other art forms during the early years of the twentieth century, was of the greatest possible significance and importance. R.H.

Stravinsky claimed that the idea for this pagan ritual came to him in a dream: it is certainly rooted in the soil of old Russia.

By the time of *Apollo* fifteen years later, Stravinsky had left Europe for America, and the darkly elemental for neo-classical purity. Scored for strings only, it was his first American commission.

The idea for a ballet based upon a card game came to Stravinsky – himself an avid poker-player – in the twenties and a commission from Balanchine's newly established American ballet in 1936 gave him the chance to bring *Jeu de Cartes* to fruition. Like *Apollo* of twenty years earlier, *Orpheus* is again based on a myth of classical Greece, but there the similarities end. His music is now tauter and sharper, more sinewy, as befits the action which, the composer said 'was worked out from Ovid and a classical dictionary'.

Agon from 1957 has no 'plot': if anything it is a 'contest' between the twelve participating dancers ('agon' is Greek for contest) and has strong associations with the formal dances of the Baroque (Stravinsky was motivated by a seventeenth-century French ballet manual he had been studying). Instrumentally, it presents some spicy textures, the quartet for harp, mandolin, violin and cello being perhaps the most ear-catching.

Pyotr TCHAIKOVSKY (1840-93) Russia

THE NUTCRACKER
(first performed St Petersburg
[Leningrad]), 1892)
THE SLEEPING BEAUTY
(first performed St Petersburg, 1890)
SWAN LAKE
(first performed Moscow, 1877)

These three famous ballets include some of Tchaikovsky's best-loved music: his gifts were uniquely suited to the medium, which he inherited from France and Delibes, as well as his native Russia.

The Nutcracker is based on a children's tale by E.T.A. Hoffmann and the popular concert suite accounts for a small proportion of the total score. That said, it does of course contain a host of Tchaikovsky's most sparkling melodies. However, he thought it much inferior to the ballet based on the traditional story of *The Sleeping Beauty*: listening to the waltz from this, his opinion becomes understandable. Equally fine, not only in terms of inspiration, but in the enormous care that Tchaikovsky took in every aspect of the ballet, is the bitter-sweet *Swan Lake*: music of sumptuous elegance and superb craftsmanship.

Right: *The* Nutcracker *ballet (1892) with music by Tchaikovsky was first seen in St Petersburg. A loosely constructed work with much of its focus on the final divertissement, it has undergone many adaptations over the years.*

Above: *Tchaikovsky's* Sleeping Beauty *had its première at the Maryinsky Theatre in Moscow in 1890. A peak of pre-revolutionary Russian culture, it has remained one of the great classics.*

Ralph VAUGHAN WILLIAMS (1872-1958) England

JOB – a masque for dancing
(first performed [concert] Norwich, 1930)

When shown sketches for a ballet based on illustrations from William Blake's *Book of Job*, Vaughan Williams insisted that the work be titled a 'masque' and be danced in the style of Blake's time. That agreed, he went on to produce one of his vivid and powerful scores. Each of its nine scenes has a biblical preface. The music is among Vaughan Williams's most varied, encompassing the serenely noble, the pragmatically English, swooning hypocrisy (superbly conveyed by the saxophone), radiant beauty and utter terror: the revelation of Satan on the throne of God is one of the great dramatic moments in music. P.H.

*Igor STRAVINSKY
(1882-1971)*

With each passing year, Igor Stravinsky is more clearly seen as the key figure in twentieth-century music. His father was principal bass with the Imperial Opera in St Petersburg. He studied law before taking up music, becoming a pupil of Rimsky-Korsakov's. Two early orchestral pieces, *Fireworks* and *Scherzo fantastique* were heard by Diaghilev, who promptly invited him to write a ballet, originally entrusted to Liadov, on the legend of *The Firebird*. When the ballet was first produced during the 1910 Paris season Stravinsky became world-famous overnight, and was hailed as leader of the modern movement. A year later *Petrushka* appeared, followed in 1913 by *The Rite of Spring*, the notorious first performance of which, under Pierre Monteux, created riots in the Champs Elysées Theatre. After the confiscation of his property during the Bolshevik Revolution he formed a small touring company for whom he wrote *The Soldier's Tale*. Another Diaghilev commission, *Pulcinella*, based on the music of Pergolesi, followed in 1920. He abandoned his native Russia to live in France, which marked a further stage in his musical development, as did his final decision to settle in the USA in 1939. In his latter years Stravinsky wrote short, sparse works, often religious in feeling, and in contrast to his earlier, opulent style. He died in 1971, having left instructions in his will that he should be buried in Venice, near the grave of Diaghilev, with whom he had worked so much. R.H.

PART TWO

THE OPERA

Below: *The Royal Opera production of Cavalleria Rusticana in 1976, with Placido Domingo as Turiddu.*

During the second half of the sixteenth century a number of musicians and poets met together in the houses of two Florentine nobles, Giovanni de Bardi and Jacopi Corsi. They were nicknamed the 'camerata' because of the room in which they met, and they were interested in reviving the old Greek tragedies and performing them as nearly as possible to the original style. They knew that the choruses had been sung or intoned, but they had no idea of the type of music which the Greeks had employed. Their first experiments were naturally very tentative, but they were assisted by various composers, including Jacopo Peri who wrote the music for *Dafne* in 1597, and this is generally acknowledged to have been the first opera. Unfortunately the music has not survived but three years later Peri and his fellow composer Caccini both wrote settings of the poet Rinuccini's *Euridice* and Peri's score has been preserved. When the work was first given in Florence in 1600 it created a sensation.

At this time there were no opera houses and only the rich and privileged were able to hear these early works in the homes of the nobility. Fortunately, a musical genius in the person of Claudio Monteverdi appeared and his first opera *La Favola d'Orfeo* was soon followed by masterpieces like his *Il Ritorno d'Ulisse in Patria* in 1641 and *L'Incoronazione di Poppea* in 1642. Meanwhile, the first opera house – Il Teatro San Cassiano – had been opened in Venice in 1637

The very first operas contained a great deal of recitative, and the airs were comparatively simple, but gradually the music developed into a series of elaborate display pieces for the greatest singers of the day.

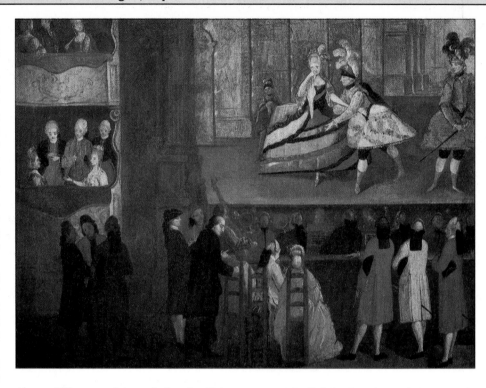

Above: `L'Opera seria' – painting by Pietro Longhi depicting an early performance at La Scala, Milan, which opened in 1778 with Salieri's *Europa Riconosciuta.*

Meanwhile, the craze for opera had spread to other western European countries, and in England Henry Purcell had written a masterpiece with his *Dido and Aeneas* which was first performed in 1689 or 1690.

In Italy two different types of opera had emerged – the *opera seria* where the plot was generally taken from classical subjects of the past, and the lighthearted *opera buffa* which was originally introduced as an intermezzo to provide comic relief to the *opera seria*. Probably the greatest of these intermezzi is Pergolesi's *La Serva padrona* which was introduced into his *opera seria, Il Prigionier superbo*.

By the beginning of the eighteenth century, Italian opera really dominated Western Europe and it was already hidebound by certain conventions. The advancement of the plot was usually confined to the recitatives of which there were two main kinds – the *recitativo secco* which was accompanied by a single instrument like the harpsichord or the cello, and the more elaborate *recitativo stromentato* which introduced a group of instruments. The arias had already been subdivided into many different categories like the Aria di Bravura, the Aria Cantabile, the Aria d'Imitazione and many more examples, and they were usually tailor-made for the talents of individual singers.

Leading composers in Italy included Stradella (1639-82), Vivaldi (1675-1741) and above all Alessandro Scarlatti (1660-1725). It was the latter who really established the operatic conventions which lasted for almost a century. Meanwhile, in France, Jean Baptiste Lully (1632-87) was the leading composer and he wrote in a rather simpler style, since the French singers of the day were generally less accomplished than their Italian counterparts in the art of elaborate *coloratura*. In England the German, Handel, and the Italian, Bononcini, were rivals for a time, but Handel who wrote in the Italian manner finally emerged triumphant.

The only English opera composer of any importance to emerge during the eighteenth century was Thomas Augustine Arne. He wrote in the highly artificial manner which would have delighted the singing teachers of his day, and a good example of his over-

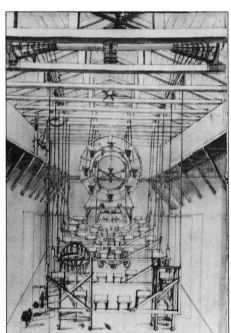

Above: *Plan of the stage mechanics behind the elaborate scene (right) for Legrenzi's* Germanico sul Reno *in Venice in 1675. It shows how elaborate such devices could be even at this early stage.*

Above: *Scene from* Germanico sul Reno *by Giovanni Legrenzi (1626-90) produced in 1675; one of seventeen operas he wrote between 1664 and 1684, nearly all produced in Venice.*

Above: *Portrait of the celebrated prima donna Maria Malibran (1808-36) whose death after a riding accident ended a brilliant career in Europe and the USA.*

decorated style is 'The soldier tir'd of war's alarms' from his opera *Artaxerxes*. This has been superbly recorded by Joan Sutherland in her album *The Art of the Prima Donna* which is available as an LP album, or on cassette or compact disc. It makes exciting singing but illustrates that by this time opera had become a mere vehicle for the vocal display of the great singers of the day.

A reaction to the excesses of the Italian school came with the works of Christoph Willibald Gluck (1714-87) who originally wrote in the conventional over-decorated manner, but he became dissatisfied with the tyranny exercised by the virtuoso singers of the day, particularly the castrati, and, finally, in his preface to his *Alceste* he stated his aims very clearly. These were to adopt a simpler vocal style with the words becoming more important and with the excesses of decoration being avoided.

Gluck's reforms were not, however, generally adopted, and it was left to Mozart to point the way towards a greater freedom of expression and to establish three distinct types of opera. *Opera seria* was always set to the plots of classical antiquity. The arias were highly stylised and often of great technical difficulty while the language was always Italian. Two typical works by Mozart in this genre are *Idomeneo* and *La Clemenza di Tito*. *Opera buffa* was also generally set to

Right: *Cartoon, attributed to Hogarth, of the opera stars Senesino, Cuzzoni and Berendstadt seen in Handel's* Flavio *(1725). The liberties they took with scores infuriated the composers.*

Italian texts but there was much greater freedom in every way and the plots were usually concerned with contemporary life. The three greatest of Mozart's works in this category are *Così fan tutte*, *Don Giovanni* and *Le Nozze di Figaro*.

Finally, there was the *Singspiel* which was written in the vernacular, and included spoken dialogue, and it has been described as a kind of musical pantomime. Mozart's outstanding contributions in this form were *Die Entführung aus dem Serail* and finally *Die Zauberflöte*. These works of Mozart are the earliest which are still in the repertoire of almost all opera houses. The works by Monteverdi, Handel, Haydn and other earlier composers are revived from time to time, but it was left to the genius of Mozart to provide the foundation of the modern repertoire.

By the beginning of the nineteenth century the influence of Italian opera started to weaken and many countries began to establish their own national traditions.

In Germany the works of Weber – *Der Freischütz*, *Oberon* and *Euryanthe* – marked the beginnings of the German operatic tradition. In France, Rousseau proved an important influence but the works of Spontini and Cherubini for a time marked a return to the Italian influence and it was left to Hérold, Auber and above all Meyerbeer to establish a flourishing French school. Russia also emerged as a power in the operatic firmament with the works of Glinka, who is generally acknowledged as the father of Russian opera. England produced little of consequence during the first half of the nineteenth century. There were some pleasant ballad operas by composers like Balfe, Wallace and Benedict, but the influence of the great Italian masters was still paramount.

It is now better to deal individually with the various national schools, and in Italy the dominant figure in the 1820s and 1830s was undoubtedly Rossini. Although he is now remembered mainly for his comic operas like *Il Barbiere di Siviglia*, he was equally cele-

Claudio MONTEVERDI
(1567-1643)

A chorister of Cremona Cathedral and pupil of Ingegneri, Claudio Monteverdi published his first work, some sacred madrigals, at the age of sixteen, before entering the service of the Duke of Mantua as a viol player and singer. In 1595 he accompanied the Duke on a military campaign in Hungary and, four years later, a political mission to Flanders where he met a number of French musicians. His musical development was also influenced by the operas of the Camerata in Florence. In 1607 he produced his first opera, *La Favola d'Orfeo*, a work which broke completely fresh ground and is of the utmost significance in the history of opera. Other important works followed during his time at the court of Mantua, but in 1613 Monteverdi was unanimously elected *maestro di capella* at St Mark's in Venice, an appointment that carried great prestige and gave him, for the first time, financial security. Here he remained for the rest of his life, producing a great harvest of liturgical and secular music which, with its richness and variety of melody and harmonic invention, has a special appeal to the modern listener. As Michael Kennedy has pointed out, Monteverdi's place in the history of Renaissance music can be justly compared with that of Shakespeare's in the history of literature. R.H.

brated during his lifetime for his works based on serious and tragic themes, like *Semiramide, La Donna del Lago* and *Otello*. All these works demanded singers of very great technical proficiency and they are seldom revived because of the tremendous difficulty shown in the vocal writing. He simplified his style for his last and possibly his greatest work, *Guillaume Tell*, which was written for the Paris Opéra. His two immediate successors were Bellini and Donizetti and they represent the highwater mark of the *bel canto* school with such works as *Lucia di Lammermoor, L'Elisir d'amore, Norma, La Sonnambula* and *I Puritani*. Before the middle of the century the influence of Verdi was already felt, and he virtually dominated the Italian operatic scene until 1893, when his final masterpiece *Falstaff* was first produced. Three years before this the first of the true verismo operas, *Cavalleria Rusticana*, appeared, and its composer Mascagni broke entirely new ground by writing an opera where stark realism was brought to the operatic stage. This was followed closely by Leoncavallo's *I Pagliacci* and verismo reached its climax in the works of Puccini. Other composers who followed the same tradition include Catalani, Cilea, Giordano and Zandonai.

No one of the stature of Puccini has emerged since his death in 1924, but the works of composers like Montemezzi, Wolf-Ferrari, Refice and Dallapiccola have all achieved a limited success.

In Germany the beginning of the nineteenth century provided two supreme examples of the *Singspiel*. The first was Beethoven's *Fidelio* which had its première in 1805. The other was Weber's *Der Freischütz*, and this and other works of Weber made a great impression on Richard Wagner. His first operas are only occasionally revived, but *Der Fliegende Holländer* was an immediate success. It was still fairly conventional with its set arias and recitatives, and the same applies to *Tannhäuser* and *Lohengrin*, but already Wagner's idea of music drama was

beginning to appear. The orchestra was playing a more important part and the principal of the *Leitmotiv* – a short musical passage associated with a particular character – was appearing in his works. His great masterpiece *Der Ring des Nibelungen* was written over a period of years and was first given as a complete operatic cycle at Bayreuth in 1876. It initially received a good deal of hostile criticism but was soon acknowledged as a work of genius. It effectively changed the course of German serious opera and influenced subsequent composers like Humperdinck (*Hansel und Gretel*) and Richard Strauss (*Der Rosenkavalier*), and to a lesser extent the younger generation of German composers

Below: *Poster for* L'Africaine *by Giacomo Meyerbeer (1791-1864), his last opera and one of sumptuous splendour, first performed at the Paris Opéra in 1865.*

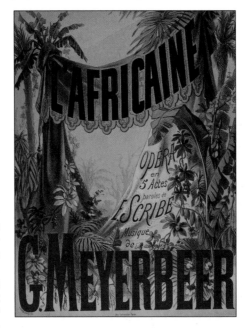

Below: *Scene from ENO production of Shostakovich's* Lady Macbeth of Mtsensk, *which caused a political uproar when it was first produced in Leningrad in 1934.*

including Alban Berg, Paul Hindemith and Kurt Weill. Meanwhile German comic opera continued along more conventional lines with the works of Lortzing, Nicolai, Von Flotow, Von Suppé, Cornelius and Johann Strauss II.

In France the works of Meyerbeer established a tradition of grand opera which lasted to the end of the century. *Les Huguenots, Le Prophète* and *L'Africaine* demanded singers of the highest quality and productions of sumptuous splendour. Other important figures were Halévy, Berlioz, Thomas, Gounod, Saint-Saëns, Bizet and Massenet. Many of their works like Berlioz's *La Damnation de Faust* and *Les Troyens*, Gounod's *Faust* and *Roméo et Juliette*, Saint-Saëns' *Samson et Dalila*, Bizet's *Carmen* and *Les Pêcheurs de Perles* and Massenet's *Manon* and *Werther* are still in the current repertoire of most major opera houses.

Opéra-comique, while being much lighter in style, still demanded singers trained in the best traditions of bel canto. Among the most successful composers were Boïeldieu, Auber, Adam, Offenbach, and Delibes.

Later, with the influence of impressionism in all the arts, an entirely new school developed. The greatest influence was Debussy with his masterpiece *Pelléas et Mélisande*, and he was succeeded by Ravel, Milhaud and Poulenc among others. In these works the orchestral accompaniment is of much greater importance while clarity of diction and vocal colouring play a much larger part.

Up to the end of the eighteenth century, Italian opera had dominated the Russian scene, but with the works of Glinka a national school emerged. His operas still show the influence of the West and particularly of Italy but he founded a native school which came to fruition with acknowledged masterpieces by Borodin (*Prince Igor*), Mussorgsky (*Boris Godunov*), Tchaikovsky (*Eugene Onegin* and *Pique Dame*) and Rimsky-Korsakov (*Sadko* and *Le Coq d'Or*). Their more recent successors are Stravinsky (*Le Rossignol* and *The Rake's Progress*), Prokofiev (*The Love of Three Oranges* and *War and Peace*) and Shostakovitch (*Lady Macbeth of Mtsensk*).

Czech opera developed its individuality during the second half of the nineteenth century with the works of Smetana, whose *Bartered Bride* and *Dalibor* are best known. Dvořák wrote a number of operas, many of which are seldom performed, but his *The Jacobin* and above all *Russalka* are delightful works which are still regularly heard. Leos Janáček's operas are very popular in Czechoslovakia and some of them have earned international recognition, *Jenufa, The Cunning Little Vixen* and *Katya Kabanovà* being particularly well known. More recently, the operas of Bohuslav Martinů, *Julietta* and *The Greek Passion* have taken their place in the international repertoire.

English opera in the nineteenth century was originally limited to ballad works like

Above: *Scene from the English National Opera 1985 production of Tippett's* The Midsummer Marriage, *with Helen Field and John Treleaven. The opera was first performed at Covent Garden in 1955.*

Below: *Scene from the 1986 Sadler's Wells revival of the popular one-act Christmas opera* Amahl and the Night Visitors *by Gian Carlo Menotti (b.1911), first seen on NBC, New York television in 1951.*

Henry PURCELL
(1659-95)

Thomas Purcell was a gentleman of the Chapel Royal so it was not difficult to find a place there for his son, Henry, as soon as he showed musical ability. After his voice broke he joined John Blow's composition class, and from 1676 onwards a number of works appeared over his name including an elegy on the death of Matthew Locke. In 1679 he succeeded Blow as organist of Westminster Abbey, and began the series of odes and 'welcome songs' which formed an important part of his total output. In 1682 he became an organist of the Chapel Royal, and the following year saw the publication of the first of his printed compositions, the twelve sonatas for two violins and bass, very much in the Italian style. In 1685 he wrote the anthem *My Heart is Inditing* for the coronation of James II; and in 1689 *Dido and Aeneas*, the only perfect English opera ever written according to Gustav Holst, was performed at a girls' school in Chelsea. Then followed a great outpouring of songs, theatre music, festival odes and instrumental music, characterised by a freshness of invention, a sense of drama and an immediacy that makes his music so appealing to the modern listener. With Purcell's death at the age of thirty-six the voice of English music was silenced for nearly 200 years: his contemporaries recognised him for the genius he was, as we do today. R.H.

Maritana (Wallace) and *The Bohemian Girl* (Balfe). Later, Sullivan's only attempt at grand opera – *Ivanhoe* – had an initial success but was soon dropped from the repertoire. Subsequently composers, including Delius, Vaughan Williams, Ethel Smythe and Rutland Boughton all wrote works which have barely survived, but more recently William Walton with his *Troilus and Cressida*, Michael Tippett with *The Midsummer Marriage, King Priam* and *The Knot Garden* and above all Benjamin Britten have brought a revival in our native opera. Britten's *Peter Grimes* is now acknowledged as a work of genius and as a landmark in British opera, and many of his subsequent works are extremely popular.

American opera developed its own identity comparatively recently. Gershwin's *Porgy and Bess* is now acknowledged as a masterpiece in the jazz idiom, and more recently the Italian-born Gian Carlo Menotti has had great success with works like *The Medium, The Telephone* and *Amahl and the Night Visitors*.

A passing mention of operas of other nationalities must include the Spaniard Manuel de Falla's *La vida Breve*, the Hungarian Béla Bartók's *Duke Bluebeard's Castle* and the Polish composers Moniuski and Penderecki who wrote *Halka* and *The Devils of Loudon* respectively.

In conclusion, it may be said that in the seventeenth and eighteenth centuries the singer was all important, and the emphasis was on agility and beauty of tone, rather than sheer power. At the beginning of the nineteenth century the same tradition persisted for a time, but gradually tastes changed as audiences demanded voices of extraordinary range and greater volume. It was not until the arrival of Duprez, who was in his prime in the 1830s, that a tenor attempted a high C from the chest. This excited audiences but dismayed lovers of the old school. Rossini referred to Duprez's high C as 'like the squawk of a capon when its throat is being cut'. Gradually the old insistence on a fine legato line was being replaced by the more forceful ringing tones of the new generation of singers. These were admirably suited to the works of the verismo composers. Still later, a declamatory style was necessary for works like Richard Strauss's *Salome* and *Elektra*, and even more for Berg's *Lulu*, while the orchestra became more and more important. J.F.

The operatic repertoire is immensely rich and varied and there is something in it to suit everyone, ranging from the weighty drama of the Wagnerian epics to the light frivolities of French *opéra-comique* and operetta. Puccini and Mozart may seem to be opposites in the world of operatic creation but they both tap the same spirit and are touched with the same magic. In the following pages the background of our 'Top 60' choice of operas (see page 90) is examined and explained.

Ludwig van BEETHOVEN (1770-1827)

FIDELIO
(1805)

Beethoven laboured long and lovingly over *Fidelio*. The first version in three acts was given its première at the Theater an der Wien on 20 November 1805, and it was a failure. No doubt the fact that the French were occupying Vienna, which the Emperor and his court had abandoned, was partly responsible, but the work also had certain defects which Beethoven quickly recognised. A new version in two acts came out a year later but a quarrel with Baron von Braun, the theatre's manager, led to its withdrawal. After further revisions, it was given on 23 May 1814 at the Theater am Kärntnerthor and this time was an immediate success. Beethoven liked the libretto with its high moral values and wrote some of his finest music for it. The plot, with Leonora disguised as a man, Fidelio, and with Marzelline being unaware of the disguise, may be difficult to accept, but the music is so wonderful that one can overlook any weakness in the libretto. The second act with Florestan's great solo is an inspired piece and the trumpet call which announces the arrival of the Minister of State is one of the most thrilling in all opera. Equally fine is Leonora's great scene beginning 'Abscheulicher!'.

Vincenzo BELLINI (1801-35)

LA SONNAMBULA
(1831)

The opera was first produced in Milan on 6 March 1831 at the Teatro Carcano with Pasta and Rubini in the principal roles. It is very much a prima donna opera with some exquisite melodies for the soprano. It was a great favourite with Patti and with Tetrazzini, and more recently Callas and Sutherland have both shone as the sleepwalker Amina. There is a scene which can be hilarious if not carefully handled where Amina, still asleep, crosses a rickety bridge over a stream, and the bridge collapses almost immediately after Amina has safely made the crossing. When a singer of the embonpoint of a Tetrazzini is involved, it obviously calls for considerable ingenuity on the part of the property designers! However, nothing can efface the beauty of the music and especially of the wonderful aria 'Ah non credea mirarti' with its Chopin-like cantilena.

NORMA
(1831)

Norma had its première at La Scala, Milan, on 26 December 1831, only ten months after *La Sonnambula*. It is the greatest and most demanding of Bellini's operas and requires an artist of supreme ability to do justice to the title role. The two greatest exponents within living memory were undoubtedly Rosa Ponselle and Maria Callas. It demands a singer who can spin out a fine legato line for the great aria 'Casta Diva' and who can cope with the *coloratura* of the cabaletta 'Ah bello a me ritorna'. It also requires an artist who can instil dramatic fire into the wonderful recitatives and who can dominate the stage with her presence. Callas possessed all these qualities, as those of us who had the privilege of hearing her will never forget.

Hector BERLIOZ (1803-69)

LA DAMNATION DE FAUST
(1846)

Berlioz called the work a 'légende dramatique' and had no thought of its being staged. It was first given at the Opéra Comique in 1846 in concert form with the composer himself conducting. It was not until 1893 that it was staged in an adaptation by Raoul Gunsberg at the Opéra in Monte Carlo with a fabulous cast including Rose

Above: *Cover (by Fraipont) for a publication of the 'légende dramatique' La Damnation de Faust by Hector Berlioz (1803-69), first heard in Paris in 1846.*

Caron, Jean de Reszke and Maurice Renaud. It is a notoriously difficult work to produce convincingly but it has been frequently performed since its stage première in 1893. The score is full of beauty, and among the many wonderful solos are the 'Air des Roses', a sensuously insidious song for Mephistopheles and the romance for Marguérite, 'D'amour l'ardente flamme'.

Georges BIZET (1838-75)

LES PÊCHEURS DE PERLES
(1863)

The opera has always been popular in France, just as the lovely melodies have always appealed to great singers. Bizet wrote the opera following the established conventions of the day, and there is little sign of any ability to portray character in music, which he certainly showed in *Carmen*. There have been occasional revivals in London: it was given for Tetrazzini in 1908 at Covent Garden, and Sir Thomas Beecham included it in his season of 1920, while recently it has been given in an English translation by the English National Opera. The wonderful duet 'Au fond du temple saint' has been a favourite item with nearly all the great tenors of the past, including Caruso, Gigli and Björling and, more recently, Nicolai Gedda.

CARMEN
(1875)

The original short story by Prosper Merimée is a classic of French literature and provided an ideal libretto for Bizet. He was able at last to write an opera which satisfied his dramatic instincts, and he flew in the face of convention in many ways. The music is strikingly original, and the heroine or anti-heroine, Carmen, is a woman of loose morals and the role is written for a mezzo-soprano! This outraged many opera lovers. Convention demanded a soprano heroine, whose virtue was unquestioned, and who had at least one major showpiece to sing! The work was not an absolute failure, but the critics slated it mercilessly. Nevertheless there were forty-eight performances at the Opéra Comique in the first season, which hardly suggests a box office débâcle. Bizet, however, died after the thirty-fifth performance, and never received the worldwide acclaim his opera later achieved. The most widely know aria is the 'Toreador song', although it is not representative of the work as a whole.

Arrigo BOITO (1842-1918)

MEFISTOFELE
(1868)

Boito was a poet and a composer. He wrote the libretti for Verdi's *Otello* and *Falstaff* and for Ponchielli's *La Gioconda*, and also com-

Above: *Scene from an ENO production of Carmen, Bizet's ever-popular opéra-comique, which got off to a slow start before earning its deserved acclaim.*

posed several operas himself, of which *Mefistofele* is the best know. It has had a chequered career but contains some inspired music. The Prologue, for example, is superb in every way, and there are beautiful arias for Marguerite, Faust and Mefistofele. The work was revived at La Scala, Milan, in 1901 with Caruso and Chaliapin in the two main roles and with Toscanini conducting. With artists of this stature it was an immense success. Faust's final aria, in which he is finally at peace with the world, is one of the great moments.

Alexander BORODIN (1833-87)

PRINCE IGOR
(1890)

Borodin was a scientist who wrote music as a hobby, and numbered certain well-known Russian composers among his friends. Extremely gifted, he spent twenty years on the music of *Prince Igor*. When he died he left enough material for his friends to complete the work, and this is precisely what Glazunov and Rimsky-Korsakov did. It contains some wonderful music, including the celebrated Polovtsian Dances which have a richly coloured savagery about them. (One of the themes has been popularised as 'Stranger in Paradise'.) The work is difficult to produce, and so far no definite solution has been forthcoming, but in its original form it is very lengthy and so usually heavily cut. One of the most beautiful of all tenor arias is Vladimir's wonderful cavatina which contrasts with Galitzby's roistering 'I hate a dreary life'.

Luigi CHERUBINI (1760-1842)

MÉDÉE
(1797)

Cherubini, now a somewhat neglected figure, was thought of by Beethoven as, after himself, the greatest living composer. Spent most of his life in Paris, becoming director of the Conservatoire in 1822 and wrote thirty operas, sixteen in Italian and fourteen in French. Most of them suffer from poor libretti. *Médée*, produced in Paris in 1797, is now his only work that is regularly heard. The title role of Medea is said to be one of the most exacting in the operatic repertoire and Cherubini was accused of going beyond what could properly be asked of a singer. It was such musical and dramatic demands that made it a favourite role of the great Maria Callas who first sang it in Florence in 1953. She clearly identified herself with the powerful emotions of the part and Medea's obsessive love for Jason. The aria 'Ah che forse la miei di' is one of its most passionate moments.

Claude DEBUSSY (1862-1918)

PELLÉAS ET MÉLISANDE
(1902)

Maurice Maeterlinck, the author of the original play, at first approved of Debussy writing an opera based on his work, but when Debussy insisted that the Scotswoman Mary Garden should create the role of Mélisande in preference to his wife, he was furious. The opera is in a world of its own – a place of shadows and twilight – and Debussy felt that Mary Garden's slightly strange French accent helped to create the ethereal atmosphere of this unique opera. So in a world of its own, it

Christoph Willibald GLUCK (1714-87)

One of Gluck's endearing characteristics is that he appears not to have shown any signs of musical precocity. Indeed, apart from the fact that he was born in Bohemia, and was of humble origin, very little is known about his early years. At the age of eighteen he was a student in Prague where he learned singing, the violin and cello. In 1736 he moved to Vienna to take up a post as chamber musician in the court of a minor prince, and a year later he went to Italy, where he became a pupil of Sammartini. It was in Milan that he wrote the first of his many operas. As his reputation grew he travelled widely throughout Europe until, in 1754, the Empress Maria Theresa appointed him opera *Kapellmeister* to the court theatre in Vienna, where he was required to compose in the more sprightly French style rather than in the ornate Italian tradition. Gluck made two important contributions to the development of opera as an art form. First, he gave the drama priority over the singers. And secondly he achieved his sublime effects not by technical mastery (indeed, he was less well equipped in this regard than many of his contemporaries) but by the purity and simplicity of his melodic line, as exemplified especially by two of his greatest works, *Orfeo ed Euridice* (Vienna 1762) and *Alceste* (Vienna 1767, Paris 1776) R.H.

has had no apparent influence on subsequent composers. The music and French text are inseparably bound up; an attempt to give it in translation or to update it would be fatal.

Gaetano DONIZETTI (1797-1848)

L'ELISIR D'AMORE
(1832)

L'Elisir d'amore was the first of Donizetti's comic operas to achieve international recognition. After its very successful première in Milan, it reached London within four years and New York two years after that. The reasons for its success are obvious. The score is full of sparkling melodies and the libretto, if not highly original, is very well constructed. There is a superb *buffo* aria for the quack, Dr

Dulcamara – 'Udite, udite, o rustici!' – in which he extols the virtues of his elixir, which he claims is a cure-all. There is also the wonderful aria for tenor, 'Una furtiva lagrima', which always brings the house down when it is well sung. Caruso, Gigli, Di Stefano, Schipa and Pavarotti are just a few of the tenors who have revelled in the role.

LUCIA DI LAMMERMOOR
(1835)

Based on Sir Walter Scott's novel *The Bride of Lammermoor* and freely adapted by the librettist Cammarano, it is generally held to be Donizetti's greatest tragic opera, and is the only one of his serious works constantly in the current repertoire of the great opera houses. Recently many of his almost forgotten works have been revived, but *Lucia* has always been popular. One of the highwater marks of the bel canto age, it was left to Maria Callas and Joan Sutherland to make one realise that it is much more than an opera for 'canary fanciers'. The famous mad scene is a superb example of its kind, and when well sung can sound highly dramatic. The great Sextet is a masterpiece of concerted writing, matched only by the equally famous Quartet from *Rigoletto*.

LA FAVORITE
(1840)

The opera was first produced in Paris in French, and although later it was frequently performed in an Italian translation, recent revivals have almost all been in the original language. Like all Donizetti operas it abounds in lovely melodies. The plot is unusual with the heroine a mezzo-soprano who is the mistress of Alfonso XI, king of Castile. The opera is much beloved by celebrated tenors who have the necessary range to sing the famous aria 'Ange si pure', perhaps better known in its Italian translation as 'Spirto gentil'. It climaxes with a high C and requires a beautiful legato line and wonderful control of breathing.

DON PASQUALE
(1843)

Undoubtedly Donizetti's comic masterpiece. The plot is fairly typical, with the old guardian, Don Pasquale, wanting to marry his young ward Norina, a sprightly young widow. Norina is in love with Pasquale's nephew, Ernesto, who sings a magical serenade in the last act. Naturally, being a comedy, everything works out well in the end but not without a good deal of scheming on the part of Norina and her friend, Dr Malatesta. However, early in the opera Norina takes charge in no uncertain manner, and in her aria 'Qual guardo il cavaliere' she shows that she knows precisely where she is going and who's going with her!

Above: *Sidney Poitier as Porgy (and Dorothy Dandridge as Bess) singing 'Bess, you is my woman now' in the Goldwyn film version of Gershwin's* Porgy and Bess, *directed by Otto Preminger in 1959.*

George GERSHWIN (1898-1937)

PORGY AND BESS
(1935)

Porgy and Bess had a successful first production in Boston in 1935, but it really hit the headlines when a company including Leontyne Price and William Warfield took it to Europe in 1952, going to Berlin, Vienna and finishing up at the Stoll Theatre, London, where it had a highly successful season running until February 1953. A splendid opera in the jazz idiom, when given in English it *must*, by the terms of George Gershwin's will, be given with an all black cast. It finally achieved the accolade of performance at the Metropolitan Opera, New York, in 1985, and was also a great hit at Glyndebourne in 1986. Clara's lullaby 'Summertime' has proved universally popular as a soprano solo.

Umberto GIORDANO (1867-1948)

ANDREA CHÉNIER
(1896)

This opera is based loosely upon the life of the poet André Chénier at the time of the French Revolution. It has its dull moments, but there are also some magnificent opportunities for a tenor with the necessary qualities to do it justice. The first Chénier was Giuseppe Borgatti who was a *tenore robusto* and much admired

for his singing of Wagnerian roles. He later became a famous teacher, and among his pupils was Heddle Nash. Among the famous tenors who have sung the role are Tamagno, Caruso, Gigli, Lauri Volpi and Del Monaco. It is very much a work of the *verismo* school, and although uneven it is highly dramatic and very effective in the theatre. The most famous aria is the wonderful 'Improvviso' in which Chénier is challenged by Madeleine de Coigny to improvise a poem.

Mikhail Ivanovich GLINKA (1804-57)

IVAN SUSANIN
(1836)

Ivan Susanin was the original title, but the opera is more commonly known as *A Life for the Tsar*. It was first performed in Moscow and St Petersburg in 1836 and after that opened every season until 1917. The title was changed at the instigation of the Imperial Court to *A Life for the Tsar* but after the Revolution it reverted to its original title. Glinka is always regarded as the father of Russian music and the score, while showing some Italian influence, is very definitely coloured by the use of Russian folk music.

Christoph Willibald GLUCK (1714-87)

ORFEO ED EURIDICE
(1762)

Of the operas that have a regular place in the current repertoire, *Orfeo* is one of the earliest. It was the first one in which Gluck fully carried out his reforms, with orchestrally accompanied recitatives and a simplification of the vocal line, avoiding the excesses of contemporary Italian opera with its frequent bravura passages to satisfy the demands of virtuoso singers. The great aria 'Che farò senza Euridice' is the most famous in the score. Kathleen Ferrier sang the role of Orfeo for the last time at Covent Garden in 1953, when she was desperately ill.

Charles GOUNOD (1818-93)

FAUST
(1859)

Faust was once regarded as the 'opera singer's grammar'. The most popular opera in the world, it was given every season at Covent Garden from 1863 to 1911! Often performed in Germany as *Margarethe*, it was dismissed by certain critics as being unworthy of Goethe's *Faust*. Certainly it looks at the Faust legend through rose coloured glasses! Mephistopheles is a genial devil – not to be taken too seriously – but at the same time the score is packed with the most beautiful melodies, and provided it is given a traditional production and not 'interpreted' by an over clever producer, it can still be effective.

*Georges BIZET
(1838-75)*

Bizet's father was a singing teacher and a minor composer, his mother was a talented pianist and herself came from a musical family. So young Georges was destined for a musical career, and at the age of nine was sent to the Paris Conservatoire where he achieved considerable academic success and came under the influence of Gounod. His piano technique drew praise from both Liszt and Berlioz. In 1853 he entered the composition class of Halévy, whose daughter he married some years later. In 1855 he wrote his Symphony in C major, when he was just seventeen, a work which although full of invention and spontaneity did not receive its first performance until eighty years later in 1935. In 1857 he won the Grand Prix de Rome and during his stay in that city he composed an *opéra bouffe* and a choral symphony. On his return to Paris he wrote *The Pearl Fishers* (1863), *The Fair Maid of Perth* and a third opera, *Djamileh* (1867), none of which was well received. In fact he scored much more success with his orchestral works such as the incidental music to *L'Arlésienne* (1872), the *Petite Suite* and *Jeux d'enfants* (1873). Even his great operatic masterpiece *Carmen* failed when it was first presented in Paris in 1875. Bitterly disappointed, Bizet succumbed to a throat infection and died at the tragically early age of thirty-seven. R.H.

Engelbert HUMPERDINCK (1854-1921)

HÄNSEL UND GRETEL
(1893)

Poor Humperdinck! First of all his name was appropriated by a pop singer, and producers have recently decided that his work must be rationalised and brought up to date! The whole charm of the opera lies in its escape from reality. There are many enchanting moments in the score. The famous 'Dance Duet', the father's song and the 'Evening hymn' take us into another world. The music is influenced by Wagner, which is not surprising since Humperdinck assisted Wagner in the preparation of *Parsifal*, but it also has an enchantment all its own.

Ruggiero LEONCAVALLO (1858-1919)

I PAGLIACCI
(1892)

Leoncavallo wrote a masterpiece in *I Pagliacci* which, with Mascagni's *Cavalleria Rusticana*, formed the very foundations of the *verismo* movement. He never repeated this early success and it is with *I Pagliacci* alone that he is assured of a place in musical history. The great aria *'Vesti la giubba'* is certainly one of the most famous of all show pieces for tenor.

The plot is based on a newspaper account of a murder in a company of travelling players and finishes with Canio, the clown, saying (not singing) *'la commedia è finita'* (the comedy is ended). 'Cav' and 'Pag', as they are affectionately known among opera lovers, make an ideal double bill.

Above: *Scene from the ENO production of the well-loved opera* Hänsel und Gretel *by Engelbert Humperdinck (1854-1921). It was hailed by Richard Strauss as 'a masterpiece of the first rank'.*

Pietro MASCAGNI (1863-1945)

CAVALLERIA RUSTICANA
(1890)

Cavalleria Rusticana is usually considered to be the first *verismo* opera and was written by Mascagni for a competition organized by the music publishers Sonzogno. It won first prize and was soon popular on both sides of the Atlantic. The plot is based on a story by Verga, and as a play it was popularized by the great actress Eleanora Duse. Musically it contains moments of great passion, with some quieter moments of great beauty. The Prelude, a serenade for the tenor, is sung behind the curtain, and this was just one of the unusual touches which made *Cavalleria* so popular. Two of the most famous pieces are Santuzza's *'Voi lo sapete o Mamma'*, where Santuzza tells Mamma Lucia how she was seduced by Turiddu (Mamma Lucia's son), and the 'Easter hymn' with its lovely soaring soprano line over a splendid choral background.

Wolfgang Amadeus MOZART (1756-91)

DIE ENTFÜHRUNG AUS DEM SERAIL
(1782)

Mozart wrote three types of opera – *opera seria, opera buffa* and *Singspiel*. The last was always comic in character with spoken dialogue and *Die Entführung* is a superlative example of this kind. Despite its comic element it has music of the very greatest beauty and difficulty, and requires first-class singers to do it justice. Osmin, the bass is the steward of the harem and his first aria *'Wer ein Liebchen hat gefunden'* ('When a maiden takes your fancy') is a masterpiece. There are parts for two sopranos and two tenors, and the leading soprano, Constanze, has one of the most taxing arias even Mozart ever wrote, ranging from B below the stave to D'''.

LE NOZZE DI FIGARO
(1786)

The plot is based on Beaumarchais' *Le Mariage de Figaro* and is a sequel to *Le Barbier de Séville* which Rossini set to music.

Above: *Mozart's* The Marriage of Figaro *produced at Covent Garden in 1987 with Karita Mattila as Susanna and Stella Kleindienst as Cherubino.*

The score is one of the greatest masterpieces of *opera buffa* and is from beginning to end a continuous flow of wonderful melodies. Characterisation is wonderfully expressed too in musical terms, with the jaunty and confident figure of Figaro very much to the fore. In contrast Mozart has given some of the most moving operatic music he ever wrote to the disillusioned Countess. Her 'Dove sono i bei momenti' in which she sadly wonders what has happened to her marriage to the philandering count is heartrending.

Another wonderful aria is Figaro's 'Non più andrai' where he sends the page Cherubino packing into the army. Mozart must have been very fond of the aria, for he quotes it in his next *opera buffa*, *Don Giovanni*.

DON GIOVANNI
(1787)

Don Giovanni is a complete contrast to *Le Nozze di Figaro*. The opera is centred entirely around the Don and his attempts to seduce every woman in the cast. There is no time for sentiment – all is unbridled lust and eroticism. Despite this, Mozart wrote some of his finest music for the work, and there is also a delightful character study of a young woman, Zerlina, who knows all the answers and has them all beaten when it comes to psychology. She twists her betrothed, Masetto, round her little finger in an aria of surpassing beauty, 'Batti, batti, o bel Masetto'.

Don Giovanni and his cowardly servant Leporello are splendidly characterised in their music, but Don Ottavio remains a cardboard figure despite his two lovely arias. The work was first given in Prague, and Mozart was feted wherever he went in the Czech capital. It is again full of splendid music but although highly dramatic it seldom moves one in the same way as *Le Nozze di Figaro*.

COSÌ FAN TUTTE
(1790)

Da Ponte was in cynical mood when he wrote the libretto for this opera. It is all great fun and certainly the most superficial and conventional of Mozart's great *opere buffe*. It was written only a year before the composer died, and he wrote music of surpassing beauty for the work. The arias and concerted numbers are masterpieces in the Baroque style. Only two characters have red blood flowing through their veins – Despina and Don Alfonso. The two lovers and their ladies are cardboard characters. Needless to say they have wonderful music to sing, such as Ferrando's 'Un'aura amorosa'.

DIE ZAUBERFLÖTE
(1791)

For his last stage work Mozart decided upon a *Singspiel* with an absurd plot and with Masonic undercurrents. The libretto is a sort of glorified pantomime, but so superb is Mozart's music that the work is a permanent monument to the composer's genius. Compton MacKenzie compared the two arias of Sarastro the High Priest to the great speeches of Prospero in Shakespeare's *The Tempest*; to Bernard Shaw they were the only music worthy of proceeding from the mouth of God. Papageno's music is much lighter but equally wonderful, and the role is a gift for any baritone worth his salt. All the characters have splendid arias to sing, while the Queen of the Night has two of the most difficult of all *coloratura* arias, both rising to F'''. Perhaps for sheer beauty one might single out Pamina's 'Ach, ich fühl's' or Tamino's 'Dies Bildniss ist bezaubernd schön'.

Modest MUSSORGSKY (1839-81)

BORIS GODUNOV
(1874)

The opera had stormy origins: it was originally rejected by the Committee of the Imperial Theatres, and after some revision by Mussorgsky a second version was offered. This too was rejected and only in 1874 was the entire opera finally given at the Maryinsky Theatre, St Petersburg. The orchestration, which was considered crude, was revised by Rimsky-Korsakov and this is the form in which it is now most commonly heard. Undoubtedly a masterpiece, when the title role is sung by a Chaliapin or a Christoff it can be an overwhelming theatrical experience. The famous Clock scene is particularly fine.

Jacques OFFENBACH (1819-80)

LES CONTES D'HOFFMANN
(1881)

Having achieved fame (and a fluctuating fortune) through his sparkling witty and tuneful operettas (thereby more or less founding a

Below: *Scene from the opera* Boris Godunov *by Modest Mussorgsky (1839-81) in a performance at the Bolshoi Theatre in Moscow in 1987 with Evgeny Nesterenko as Boris.*

new genre of popular musical theatre entertainment), Offenbach in the mode of the comedian wanting to play Hamlet spent his last years trying to write a 'grand' opera. Already a very sick man, he began work on it in 1878 and started by finding an excellent piece of music tucked away in an unsuccessful operetta, which became the famous 'Barcarolle'.

There were other demands on his attention but he continued to work on the opera through 1879, writing to the Director of the Opéra Comique, 'Hurry up and stage my opera. I haven't much time left and my only wish is to attend the opening night.' Alas, the wish was never fulfilled. In September 1880 he was able to attend some of the rehearsals, but he died at the beginning of October. The work was staged in 1881, much hacked about by well-intentioned producers and editors, with Adèle Isaacs in the three principal female roles. It ran for 100 initial performances, and today, often produced nearer to the way that Offenbach intended it, is an accepted masterpiece of the operatic repertoire. It is neither better nor worse than his best operettas and certainly contains much (as in the famous 'Doll Song') that is in the typical Offenbach vein.

Amilcare PONCHIELLI (1834-86)

LA GIOCONDA
(1876)

It is impossible to think of Ponchielli as but a one work composer. He did write several other operas and ballets but his reputation now rests solely on *La Gioconda* which survives as an effective and sturdy music drama much enhanced in reputation by the sparkling ballet interlude, 'The Dance of the Hours'. His other claim to fame is that he was Puccini's teacher.

First produced at La Scala, Milan, in April 1876 with a libretto by the accomplished Arrigo Boito (with whom Ponchielli had a stormy partnership), *La Gioconda* was an immediate triumph, conducted brilliantly. The popular tenor Gayarré was the first to encore the favourite 'Cielo e mar'.

Giacomo PUCCINI (1858-1924)

MANON LESCAUT
(1893)

Manon Lescaut was Puccini's first real success when it was given its première at the Teatro Regio, Turin, in 1893. Massenet's *Manon* was already an established favourite and it was a bold stroke of Puccini's to write a work on the same story. Actually the two operas are quite different. Massenet wrote a more refined and less starkly realistic work, while Puccini emphasised the grim, sordid side, particularly in the third act, where the characterisation is superb. There is the germ

of verismo here combined with moments of great lyrical beauty, as in Manon's second act 'In quelle trine morbide'. The audience in Turin on the first night acclaimed a new genius. Puccini had fifty curtain calls.

LA BOHÈME
(1896)

After Verdi, Puccini was to prove himself the greatest master of Italian opera, extending its golden age into the twentieth century. He was a master of the musical theatre though he did not immediately enjoy success. This came with *Manon Lescaut* in 1893. His masterpiece, *La Bohème*, was first performed in Turin in 1896, a clever as well as effective work with its four acts corresponding to the four movements of a symphony, and full of his finest melodies.

The opera was first produced under the direction of Toscanini. Initially it had little success, but after a third production in Palermo it was recognised as a masterpiece. The opera has a memorable beginning as Mimi responds to 'Che gelida manina' with the justifiably famous aria 'Mi chiamano Mimi'.

TOSCA
(1900)

La Bohème had established Puccini's world popularity, and another opera by the same composer was eagerly awaited. *Tosca* was first given in Rome at the Costanzi Theatre on 14 January 1900 and it was an immediate success. It is certainly more bloodthirsty and sadistic than the composer's earlier works, but Tosca's prayer 'Vissi d'arte, vissi d'amore' is a great moment.

The last act is a masterpiece of atmospheric colouring and contains some of the

Below: *Probably the most popular opera of all time, judging by performances and recordings, Puccini's* La Bohème *here has Placido Domingo in the role of Rodolfo.*

Jules MASSENET
(1842-1912)

French composer, whose background and career followed the conventions of the day. His father, an iron-master until ill-health forced him to move to Paris, invented a steam-hammer. His mother helped to augment the family income by giving piano lessons, and taught her own four children, all of whom were musically gifted. At the age of eleven, Massenet was sufficiently advanced to enter the Conservatoire without difficulty and as a senior student he took up composition with Ambroise Thomas, who was to achieve fame with his opera *Mignon* (1866). Massenet's first professional engagement was playing the triangle at the Théâtre Lyrique, but he gained a number of prizes of which the most important was the Prix de Rome in 1863. On his return to Paris he was obliged to do hack-work to survive, but success came in 1872 with a comic opera *Don César de Bazan*. From that time on his position in French musical life was assured. He was astute enough to work within his own limitations and to give his public exactly what they wanted – rich, voluptuous melodies, undemanding harmonies and easy-to-follow story lines. 'Once you've heard *Manon*, you've heard Massenet', said one unkind critic of his best-known opera. But that kind of comment diminishes neither the man nor his music, which has given much pleasure to a lot of people. R.H.

THE TOP SIXTY OPERAS

1 **LA BOHÈME** *(1896) [Puccini]*
2 **TOSCA** *(1900) [Puccini]*
3 **I PAGLIACCI** *(1892) [Leoncavallo]*
4 **CAVALLERIA RUSTICANA** *(1890) [Mascagni]*
5 **MADAMA BUTTERFLY** *(1904) [Puccini]*
6 **LA TRAVIATA** *(1853) [Verdi]*
7 **AIDA** *(1871) [Verdi]*
8 **CARMEN** *(1875) [Bizet]*
9 **RIGOLETTO** *(1851) [Verdi]*
10 **IL BARBIERE DI SIVIGLIA** *(1816) [Rossini]*
11 **LE NOZZE DI FIGARO** *(1786) [Mozart]*
12 **COSÌ FAN TUTTE** *(1790) [Mozart]*
13 **DON GIOVANNI** *(1787) [Mozart]*
14 **IL TROVATORE** *(1853) [Verdi]*
15 **LUCIA DI LAMMERMOOR** *(1835) [Donizetti]*
16 **UN BALLO IN MASCHERA** *(1859) [Verdi]*
17 **FIDELIO** *(1805) [Beethoven]*
18 **ORFEO ED EURIDICE** *(1762) [Gluck]*
19 **DIDO AND AENEAS** *(1689) [Purcell]*
20 **FAUST** *(1859) [Gounod]*
21 **BORIS GODUNOV** *(1874) [Mussorgsky]*

22 **OTELLO** *(1887) [Verdi]*
23 **DER FLIEGENDE HOLLÄNDER** *(1843) [Wagner]*
24 **DIE ZAUBERFLÖTE** *(1791) [Mozart]*
25 **DER ROSENKAVALIER** *(1911) [Strauss]*
26 **TANNHÄUSER** *(1845) [Wagner]*
27 **THE BARTERED BRIDE** *(1866) [Smetana]*
28 **HÄNSEL UND GRETEL** *(1893) [Humperdinck]*
29 **LA FORZA DEL DESTINO** *(1862) [Verdi]*
30 **NORMA** *(1831) [Bellini]*
31 **L'ELISIR D'AMORE** *(1832) [Donizetti]*
32 **DON PASQUALE** *(1843) [Donizetti]*
33 **DIE ENTFÜHRUNG AUS DEM SERAIL** *(1782) [Mozart]*
34 **TURANDOT** *(1926) [Puccini]*
35 **DIE MEISTERSINGER VON NÜRNBERG** *(1868) [Wagner]*
36 **FALSTAFF** *(1893) [Verdi]*
37 **TRISTAN UND ISOLDE** *(1865) [Wagner]*
38 **PELLÉAS ET MÉLISANDE** *(1902) [Debussy]*
39 **LA GIOCONDA** *(1876) [Ponchielli]*

40 **DIE WALKÜRE** *(1877) [Wagner]*
41 **DER FREISCHÜTZ** *(1821) [Weber]*
42 **LOHENGRIN** *(1850) [Wagner]*
43 **LA DAMNATION DE FAUST** *(1846) [Berlioz]*
44 **MEFISTOFELE** *(1868) [Boito]*
45 **LES CONTES D'HOFFMANN** *(1881) [Offenbach]*
46 **ANDREA CHÉNIER** *(1896) [Giordano]*
47 **SALOME** *(1905) [Strauss]*
48 **DAS RHEINGOLD** *(1869) [Wagner]*
49 **EUGENE ONEGIN** *(1879) [Tchaikovsky]*
50 **PORGY AND BESS** *(1935) [Gershwin]*
51 **ARIADNE AUF NAXOS** *(1916) [Strauss]*
52 **SIEGFRIED** *(1876) [Wagner]*
53 **LA FAVORITE** *(1840) [Donizetti]*
54 **MANON LESCAUT** *(1893) [Puccini]*
55 **PARSIFAL** *(1882) [Wagner]*
56 **LES PÊCHEURS DE PERLES** *(1863) [Bizet]*
57 **LA SONNAMBULA** *(1831) [Bellini]*
58 **MÉDÉE** *(1797) [Cherubini]*
59 **IVAN SUSANIN** *(1836) [Glinka]*
60 **PRINCE IGOR** *(1890) [Borodin]*

(With the exception of nos. 53, 59 and 60, which, at the time of listing, are available only on LP, all the above operas are available on both LP and CD.)

The above listing does not pretend to be 100% scientifically accurate, but it does give a fair view of the comparative popularity of most of the world's great operas. The assessment was arrived at through calculations based on the number of LP issues of each opera balanced with the number of productions of each work in selected years at Covent Garden, London, and the Metropolitan Opera, New York. The list has been confined to full-length operas with the obvious exception of *Cavalleria Rusticana* and *I Pagliacci* which come so high in the rating that they could hardly be ignored; but, as aficionados will note, we have excluded other popular works that are not long enough to provide a complete production on their own.

Most opera enthusiasts may find that the list does not exactly fit in with their own preferences. Many works that are not there are very popular by name because of a memorable overture or an oft-sung aria. A work like *Porgy and Bess*, judged by its individual songs, is obviously higher in public esteem than the list suggests, but nevertheless its small number of complete recordings and performances puts it statistically at No. 50 – which perhaps says more about statistics than it does about music.

Just to add a few more favourite names, the next twenty or so in the list would have been: *I Puritani; Lulu; Louise; Adriana Lecouvreur; Manon; Werther; Idomeneo; Die lustigen Weiber von Windsor; Gotterdämmerung; Wozzeck; Lakmé; La vida breve; Martha; L'Incoronazione di Poppea; La Fanciulla del West; Mignon; Guillaume Tell; Peter Grimes; Russalka; Jenufa; Les Huguenots; Les Troyens; Don Carlos; La Fille du Régiment* . . . but even that by no means exhausts the list of possible candidates. For example, most of the Britten operas are handicapped by only having one recording and being English. The ratings should at least provide good fuel for operatic argument.

(Grateful thanks go to Decca Classics for the loan of the Puccini and Wagner Compact Discs shown above.) P.G.

most evocative music Puccini ever wrote. The curtain rises with the dawn, as a shepherd sings, and this is followed by the sound of bells from innumerable churches in Rome. Finally the theme of Cavaradossi's great aria emerges. Some purists have objected to the Grand Guignol atmosphere of *Tosca* and Joseph Kerman, author of *Opera Drama*, called it a 'shabby little shocker' but it is still immensely popular and, when sung by artists like Callas and Gobbi, utterly compelling.

MADAMA BUTTERFLY
(1904)

When it was first produced in Milan in February 1904, *Madama Butterfly* was hissed off the stage. Much of this was due to organised agitation from rival factions curiously supported by the Milan opera-goers who may have felt that Puccini had deserted them for too long. There was little wrong with the opera or a first rate cast; but it was immediately withdrawn and the scores removed from the shops. Puccini did a thorough revision and when it was re-staged in Brescia three months later it was rapturously received. The opera benefitted from the changes, so its delay was all to the good, and such arias as 'Un bel di vedremo' could now offer their legacy of enchantment.

TURANDOT
(1926)

Puccini was already dying of throat cancer when he wrote his last and unfinished opera. He had completed the first two acts and had written the third act as far as Liu's funeral music. He had also sketched twenty-three pages of the final love duet which was intended to be the climax of the work. His friend and fellow composer Alfano finished the score, using Puccini's notes and at the first performance at La Scala, Milan, in 1926, Toscanini stopped the orchestra at the point where Puccini had left the opera unfinished and, turning to the audience, said, 'At this

Above: *Placido Domingo in the leading tenor role of Calaf in Puccini's* Turandot *in a performance at the Royal Opera House, Covent Garden in 1984.*

point the maestro laid down his pen.' The original Turandot was the soprano Rosa Raisa, but the title role will always be associated with Dame Eva Turner whom Alfano described as 'the perfect Turandot'. Puccini had Caruso in mind when he started to write the music for Calaf, but the great tenor died in 1921 and the favourite aria 'Nessun dorma' was first sung by Miguel Fleta.

Henry PURCELL (1659-95)

DIDO AND AENEAS
(1689/1690)

Certainly the first great operatic work written by a British composer. The first performance was given at Mr Josias Priest's Boarding School for Girls in Chelsea in either late 1689 or early 1690, and it is in three short acts. Purcell shows a great gift for dramatic writing throughout the work, culminating in the superb lament 'When I am laid in earth', one of the noblest songs in operatic literature. One of the outstanding productions took place at the Mermaid Theatre in London in 1951, with the great Kirsten Flagstad in the role of Dido.

Giacchino ROSSINI (1792-1868)

IL BARBIERE DI SIVIGLIA
(1816)

The young Rossini, moderately successful, but still waiting for his big hit, must have been truly depressed by the initial failure of his masterpiece, *The Barber of Seville*, yet another example of a now world-famous opera being whistled and booed off the stage by an ungrateful Italian audience. Although Rossini had taken care to ask permission of the ageing Paisiello, whose version of the

Giacomo MEYERBEER
(1791-1864)

Son of Herr Beer, a wealthy Jewish Banker in Berlin who, after a legacy from a rich relation named Meyer, changed the family name accordingly. Giacomo (Jakob) showed great promise as a pianist and it was assumed that he was destined for a brilliant concert career. However, he also showed much talent for composition. After two operas and an oratorio he produced a comic opera, which failed miserably in Vienna. His early works show the influence of Italian opera, especially those of Rossini, but Weber and others urged him to return to the German tradition. However, the turning-point in his development came in 1826 when he visited Paris. He made the city his home and, putting composition to one side, absorbed as much as he could of French character and culture. Eventually *Robert Le Diable* (1831) was produced, and proved an overwhelming success. Lavish staging, brilliant and innovative orchestration, strong melodies and powerful drama were the hallmarks of the new Meyerbeer, that found even more forceful expression in his next opera *Les Huguenots*, first performed in 1836. Other successes and honours followed. Meyerbeer used his considerable wealth to create spectacular productions and to pay for innumerable rehearsals of his work. He constantly corrected, polished and revised and, as a result, quite failed to enjoy the success and fame his music brought to him. R.H.

same story some twenty-five years earlier was still a popular favourite, the poaching was still held against him when his new setting was first heard in Rome in 1816. A disastrous first night even found the audience drowning out Figaro's famous opening song, and only the catchy 'Una voce poco fa' managed to find any favour with the critical listeners.

Strangely, the opera was equally badly received in Paris, and it was only a revival of Paisiello's work, which now seemed a bit out-dated, that made people realise the worth of Rossini's piece which gradually earned the affection that it is now automatically accorded. Figaro's 'Largo al factotum' is probably the most famous 'patter song' in all opera.

Bedřich SMETANA (1824-84)

THE BARTERED BRIDE
(1866)

The Bartered Bride has become a national institution in Czechoslovakia and is universally considered to be a model of nationalist folk opera. In his other operas Smetana was much less Bohemian in outlook and was criticised for it. It was unlikely, however, that anyone could resist the positive élan of the famous Overture.

The themes for the sparkling Overture are all taken from Act 3, where, outside the village inn, a circus troupe perform the famous 'Dance of the comedians'. If the opera is best remembered for its delightful orchestral interludes it is also rich in vocal items such as the Act 1 duet.

Richard STRAUSS (1864-1949)

SALOME
(1905)

The libretto of the opera was based on Oscar Wilde's famous play in a German translation. First performed in Dresden with Marie Wittich in the title role and Carl Burrian as Herod, it prompted Arnold Bax to write of 'A horrifying Herod slobbering with lust and apparently decomposing before our very eyes.' New York, too, was outraged when the opera was given at the Metropolitan Opera House in 1907: it was withdrawn after a dress rehearsal and one performance. A resolution of the Board of Directors stated that *Salome* was 'objectionable and detrimental to the best interests of the Metropolitan Opera House'. Times have changed: nowadays the role of Salome is considered one of Strauss's finest characterisations and many will remember Ljuba Welitsch's interpretation of the role which she first sang under Strauss's direction

Below: *Grace Bumbry in a production of the initially shocking* Salome *by Richard Strauss (1864-1949) at the Royal Opera House, Covent Garden, in 1978.*

in Vienna in 1944. Strauss's demands upon the singers are tremendous and the orchestral writing is superb. There is an amusing story that during the first rehearsals Strauss called out to the orchestra 'Louder, louder, I can still hear the singers!'.

DER ROSENKAVALIER
(1911)

Surely Strauss's masterpiece. It has often been said that he had a permanent love affair with the soprano voice and his writing for the two sopranos and the mezzo-soprano reaches inspired heights in the 'Presentation of the silver rose' and the final trio and duet. For many years Lotte Lehmann laid claim to the role of the Marschallin, while Richard Mayr, the bass was equally famous for his portrayal of the Marschallin's boorish cousin Baron Ochs. The part of the young Octavian is written for a mezzo-soprano and this is one of the last and most famous of all 'breeches' roles.

ARIADNE AUF NAXOS
(1912)

Originally written to follow a performance of Molière's *Le Bourgeois Gentilhomme*, with incidental music for the play written by Strauss, it was revised in 1916 and this is the current version. Instead of Molière's play we are given a prelude in which the Bourgeois Gentilhomme says that an opera company and a troupe performing a *commedia dell'arte* have both been engaged, and will have to play simultaneously. The result is a delightful comedy and it also contains one of the most daunting *coloratura* arias ever written, sung by Zerbinetta.

Pyotr Ilyich TCHAIKOVSKY (1840-93)

EUGENE ONEGIN
(1879)

The libretto is by Shilovsky, based on a Pushkin poem. The opera was given a student performance in Moscow in 1879, but the first

Above: *The opera* Eugene Onegin *by Tchaikovsky (first performed in 1879) in a typically spectacular production at the Kirov Opera in 1987.*

professional one was at the Bolshoi in 1881, since when it has been generally acknowledged as one of the great masterpieces of Russian opera. Tchaikovsky shows his great ability in this work to delineate in musical terms the various characters. He is said to have written Tatiana's great letter scene first, and then to have composed the rest of the opera. Onegin's aria in which he coldly rejects Tatiana's overtures, Lensky's love song, and above all the famous letter scene are among the classics of Russian opera.

Giuseppe VERDI (1813-1901)

RIGOLETTO
(1851)

Rigoletto was written in fifty-one days and is a *tour de force* of musical creation. In it Verdi introduces a form new to Italian opera – the dramatic monologue for baritone. Rigoletto's first big outburst 'Pari siamo' marks a tremendous step forward in the composer's development. The conventions of the earlier operas are put aside and the whole work is a masterpiece, and remains a great popular favourite. The story, based on Hugo's *Le Roi s'amuse*, is set in the sixteenth century but is a typical nineteenth-century melodrama, and is really an aristocratic relative of 'Maria Martin in the Red Barn'. When first produced in England a critic wrote that the opera was 'devoid of melody apart from a vulgar little song for the Duke [obviously 'La donna è mobile'] and a pallid little air for soprano based on the key of E Major'. The work is of course full of the most beautiful melodies while being at the same time intensely dramatic. The celebrated Quartet 'Bella figlia dell'amore' is one of the supreme masterpieces of Italian opera.

Above: *A Royal Opera House production of Verdi's* Rigoletto. *Originally titled* La Maledizione, *it was first seen in Venice in 1851.*

IL TROVATORE
(1853)

The opera was produced in Rome on 19 January 1853 and was rapturously received. The critic of the *Gazzetta* wrote 'Last night *Il Trovatore* was produced in a theatre over-flowing with people . . . The music trans-ported us to heaven, and of a truth, how could it be otherwise, because this is, without exaggeration, heavenly music.' In a way it is a retrograde step after *Rigoletto*, with a return to the older and more conventional arias. The plot is difficult to follow, but the constant flow of melody and the enormous rhythmic drive of certain passages have ensured its enduring popularity. One duet in particular – the 'Miserere' – has become one of the most famous of all the operatic 'war horses'.

LA TRAVIATA
(1853)

Incredible as it may now seem, *La Traviata* was an absolute failure when it was first pro-duced in Venice on 6 March 1853. Verdi's re-action was calm: he wrote '*La Traviata* last night was a fiasco. Is the fault mine or the singers? Time will tell.' Of course, he had written another masterpiece but apparently the artists who sang at the première were not very distinguished, and the subject, dealing with the life of a courtesan, would have horri-fied the more straight-laced members of the audience. Also it was given in contemporary costume, an unheard of innovation. The Pre-ludes to Act I and III were generally admired, and are indeed beautifully scored and writ-ten, and these were applauded. Violetta's great aria 'Ah fors è lui' is one of the most popular of all famous *coloratura* showpieces and was a favourite of many singers.

UN BALLO IN MASCHERA
(1859)

Verdi had had trouble with censorship before, but nothing compared to the trouble he had before *Un Ballo in Maschera* could be pro-duced. Originally the opera was to be called *Gustavo III* and dealt with an historical fact – the assassination of Gustavus III, the king of Sweden, in 1792. The opera was originally to have been staged in Naples in the spring of 1858. Eventually, after Verdi had changed the plot to avoid mentioning the assassination of a monarch, and had moved the scene from Sweden to Boston, Massachusetts, the opera was passed for performance, but not in Naples. The first performance was in Rome in 1859. It was well received and critics were quick to notice the more imaginative orches-tration, and the increased use of big ensem-bles. Also, the role of Oscar, the page, gives us a glimpse of humour which was to come to fruition in the composer's *Falstaff*. There are many wonderful solo passages also, includ-ing the great baritone aria 'Eri tu che mac-chiavi'.

LA FORZA DEL DESTINO
(1862)

Verdi's reputation was now universal, and he was commissioned to write an opera for St Petersburg. With no difficulties with the cen-sors the opera was produced at the Court Theatre in St Petersburg in November 1862. *La Forza del Destino* was well received but without any real show of enthusiasm, and no doubt the extremely gloomy plot had some-thing to do with this. There are some lighter moments in the work, however, for Preziosilla and the character of Fra Melitone bring well-timed comic relief, while there is also much wonderful concerted music and the orches-tration goes another step forward. Among the best loved numbers is the well-known duet for tenor and baritone 'Solenne in quest'ora'.

Giuseppe VERDI
(1813-1901)

A grocer in Busseto spotted Verdi's potential at an early age and offered to pay his fees at Milan Conservatory, who turned him down on account of his poor piano playing. So he studied privately in Milan for two years before returning to Busseto, throwing himself into the musical life of the local community and marrying the grocer's daughter. One of his early operas was successfully performed at La Scala, but between 1838 and 1840 he lost his wife and two children. Grief-stricken, he vowed never to compose again. But he was persuaded to write *Nabucco* (1842) and its overnight success marked the true beginning of his career. For from that point on an astonishing succession of works followed, among them *Ernani, Giovanna d'Arco, Attila, Macbeth, Luisa Miller, Il Trovatore, La Traviata, Rigoletto, La Forza del destino, Don Carlos* and *Aida*, which he wrote in 1871. Not only had Verdi grown in musical stature to become one of the greatest of all operatic composers, but he was hailed as a national hero as well, a symbol of the new, united Italy. In 1874 he completed the great *Requiem* in memory of the poet Manzoni, and five years later his publisher, Ricordi, suggested that he should write an opera on Shakespeare's *Othello*, with Boito as his collaborator. *Otello*, and its successor, *Falstaff*, which he completed in his eightieth year, represent the very pinnacle of Verdi's colossal achievement. R.H.

AIDA
(1871)

Aida was commissioned by the Khedive of Egypt, Ismail Pasha, and was intended for the opening of the new Italian Theatre. However, owing to many difficulties it was delayed, and was actually given there a year later than in-tended, on 24 December 1871. Despite its being a huge success, Verdi was not entirely happy. The work again shows an advance on his previous operas with added attention to the orchestral writing, and some critics accused him of being influenced by Wagner. This was quite unjustified, and hurt Verdi deeply. It is essentially Italian in spirit and style. In a way it is the very epitome of grand

opera with the emphasis very much on the 'grand'. It is said that Benjamin Britten studied *Aida*, considering it the best of its kind, when he was working on *Peter Grimes*. Verdi was a little unkind to the tenor! His big solo 'Celeste Aida' comes within minutes of the curtain being raised, before he has had a chance to warm up. In the bad old days, when it was quite usual for fashionable society to arrive late and cause a disturbance getting to their seats, it was said that the only way to hear 'Celeste Aida' in comfort was by listening to gramophone records!

OTELLO
(1887)

Verdi was in his seventies when he wrote *Otello* and, apart from his great *Requiem*, he had written nothing of consequence since *Aida* sixteen years earlier. He adored Shakespeare and, with the help of Boito, who wrote the libretto, he was determined to do justice to the great dramatist and poet. Once again enormous strides are shown in his attention to orchestral detail and to his handling of the chorus. The inclusion of the 'Ave Maria' for Desdemona was an inspiration. It would not have been effective in the play, but in the opera it provides a moment of calm before the storm of the final scene. The original Otello was the trumpet-voiced Tamagno, and the great actor-singer Maurel was the Iago. They both made recordings from the work, and these are of the greatest historical interest. Toscanini, too, was a cellist in the orchestra at the première. One of the great moments is the death of Otello – 'Niun mi tema se anco armato mi vede' ('Do not fear me if you see me still armed').

FALSTAFF
(1893)

Six years after *Otello*, when he was in his eightieth year, Verdi wrote his final opera, and again he chose Shakespeare. The music is incredibly fresh and youthful, and there is no trace of the early Verdi with his powerful but often crude rhythms used for dramatic

Above: *The spectacular* Aida, *first staged in Cairo in 1871, has tempted many to large-scale and even outdoor performances; this one took place at the Verona arena in 1984.*

effect. Here all is lightness and delicacy. The whole work is a miracle of comic invention, and the final *'Tutto nel mondo è burla'* ('All the world's a stage') was Verdi's supreme farewell to the art he had served so well.

Richard WAGNER (1813-83)

DER FLIEGENDE HOLLÄNDER
(1843)

This is the earliest of Wagner's works to retain its position in the current operatic repertoire. The composer came to London in 1839 to avoid his creditors and the sea journey was sufficiently rough to inspire the writing of *Der Fliegende Holländer*, the first work to show the true genius of Wagner. He was still bound by certain operatic conventions: Senta's famous 'Ballad' is in the traditional form of a slow opening section followed by an exciting allegro. Here, too, for the first time we meet Wagner's obsessive theme of redemption through love. Weber's influence is still to be found in certain passages, but there is also much which is highly original, and Wagner's ability to express character by purely musical means is already present.

TANNHÄUSER
(1845)

When Wagner met Rossini in Paris, Wagner explained how he wished to develop his musical theories. Rossini replied courteously that what Wagner suggested would be the death knell of melody! How wrong he was, for *Tannhäuser* has some of the most wonderful melodies, an outstanding example being Wolfram's moving and beautiful song to the evening star *'O du mein holder Abendstern'*. There is also a superb overture, some magnificent choral writing, while another great moment is Elizabeth's 'Prayer'.

LOHENGRIN
(1850)

Wagner had to wait eleven years after the first performance before he ever heard the opera. It was first produced in Weimar at the Court Theatre, conducted by Liszt. It was in fact Liszt's championship that made the production possible, and it is a tribute to him that he was able to recognise the genius of Wagner, so early in his career. *Lohengrin* is really the last of the 'singers' operas' that Wagner wrote. There are still formal arias although they are more freely constructed than in his earlier works. The writing for strings is particularly beautiful and also highly original, the 'Bridal chorus' being universally known and loved.

TRISTAN UND ISOLDE
(1865)

From 1848 to 1853 Wagner wrote no music of any consequence. He was thinking of future works and probably writing the libretto for *Tristan* and also pondering deeply about his future musical dramas. His meeting with Mathilde Wesendonk and their subsequent friendship provided the inspiration he needed. Their feelings were probably purely platonic, but they inspired and refreshed him so that he wrote the music of *Tristan und Isolde* between 1857 and 1859. He had to wait until 1865, however, before he could obtain a production. This was in Munich and the conductor Hans von Bülow. For the first time Wagner breaks away entirely from all the previously accepted conventions of opera, and the work shows a tremendous advance on anything he had previously written. The final *'Liebestod'* is only one of the many magical passages.

DIE MEISTERSINGER
(1868)

Die Meistersinger is the only one of Wagner's works which contains an element of comedy. It would be wrong to call it a comic opera, because much of it is full of warm humanity without in any way being comic! In fact, only the character of Beckmesser supplies any obvious comedy, and the humour is generally rather ponderous and certainly the weakest part of this great work. It is great in more senses than one, for it lasts at least five hours with the customary intervals! Much more important than the comic element is the message which Wagner is anxious to give – that music must grow and develop through the ages, and not be hidebound by any ridiculous and outdated conventions. He set himself a tremendous challenge in the work. Walther's 'Prize song' had to be the triumphant culminations of all that had gone before, and Wagner did not fail – it certainly is! At its best it is the thrilling climax of a great and noble work.

DER RING DES NIBELUNGEN
(1869-76)

Wagner became fascinated with the old German legends of the Nibelungen while he was living in Zurich in the 1840s. He began to write a prose version of the stories and later re-wrote these in more poetic form for the four works which make up the cycle known as *Der Ring des Nibelungen*. By the end of 1856 he had written the music for *Das Rheingold* and *Die Walküre* and shortly afterwards he wrote the first act of *Siegfried*. Then he stopped work on the cycle and only resumed in 1869.

DAS RHEINGOLD
(1869)

Wagner had to wait thirteen years for a production of *Das Rheingold*, which took place in Munich under the conductor Wüllner. The *Leitmotiv* is heard throughout the entire cycle, and Wagner's mastery in incorporating these into the overall musical structure is superb. One of the most telling moments in *Rheingold* is when Wotan and Loge descend to Niebelheim, where the Nibelung dwarfs can be heard hammering out the gold. The theme of the Rhinemaidens is also unforgettable.

DIE WALKÜRE
(1870)

A year after *Das Rheingold*, *Die Walküre* was produced in Munich on the 26 June 1870. We are introduced to the children of Wotan, Siegmund and Sieglinde and their love duet in the first act is superb. Sieglinde's reply to Siegmund's 'Liebeslied' is wonderful, and other great moments are Brünnhilde's 'Battle cry' and the 'Ride of the Valkyries', while in the last act the Magic Fire Music is a superb example of Wagner's mastery of orchestral colour. The work originally had a very mixed reception: the Munich newspapers made much of Wagner's affair with Cosima von Bülow, and his patron, King Ludwig, refused to see him until he had regularised his union with Cosima!

SIEGFRIED
(1876)

Wagner restarted work on the *Ring* cycle in 1869, and *Siegfried* was completed, probably in 1873, although Wagner had deliberately kept its completion secret, as he did not want a repetition of the troubles in Munich, where King Ludwig would no doubt have expected the première to take place. Instead, he kept it until the first festival in Bayreuth was held in

Right: A Welsh National Opera performance of Wagner's Siegfried *with Jeffrey Lawton taking the leading role in 1986.*

1876, and *Siegfried* was given there for the first time on 16 August. The 'Forging song' is one of the many exciting passages in the score, but the most thrilling of all is the moment where Brünnhilde is awakened by the young hero.

PARSIFAL
(1882)

Wagner called *Parsifal* his *Weltabschieds-werk* (literally work of farewell to the world), and it contains some of the most sublime music he ever wrote. It reveals the complexity of Wagner's own nature, a mixture of religious belief, sexuality and mysticism. He had, according to his friend Nietzsche, been converted to Christianity, but at the same time he was indulging in a brief love affair with a young Frenchwoman, Judith Gautier! Parsifal reflects Wagner's feelings and beliefs of that time and the music is at once deeply devotional and highly sensual. He saw the opera as a sort of religious rite and did not want it to be performed outside Bayreuth; but even by 1903 his wishes had been ignored and it was performed at the Metropolitan Opera, New York. Since then it has been given in most of the great opera houses.

Carl Maria von WEBER (1786-1826)

DER FREISCHÜTZ
(1821)

Der Freischütz is a *Singspiel* and one of the greatest of them all. Weber wrote it at a time when the interest in the supernatural was being expressed in painting, literature and music. Schubert's setting of 'Der Erlkönig' is just one example of this. Wagner worshipped at the shrine of Weber. The *Wolf's Glen scene* is a superb essay in expressing the uncanny in dramatic and musical terms. There are few if any arias in German operatic literature more beautiful than Agathe's 'Leise, leise'.

Vincenzo BELLINI
(1801-35)

Born in Catania, Sicily, the son of an organist, Bellini also had the good fortune of attracting the attention of a benefactor in his early years. A local nobleman paid for his musical training in Naples, and his first work, *Adelson e Salvini* (1825), appeared while he was still at the academy. The manager of La Scala, Milan, happened to be in the audience, and he promptly commissioned the young composer to write an opera for the San Carlo. The result was *Bianca e Gernando* (1826) which pleased the Neapolitan public and produced a further commission, this time for La Scala itself, *Il Pirata* (1827). This put Bellini firmly on the map in Italy and elsewhere. His simple expressive melodies were most favourably compared with the florid style of Rossini, and his great soprano roles in *La Somnambula, Norma* and *I Puritani* are more than enough to guarantee him a permanent place in the operatic repertoire. It was widely believed in Italy that he was haunted by the ghost of a jilted lover, in the shape of a white dove, and that when he finished his tenth opera the bird would alight on the score, give ten sighs and disappear. All nonsense, of course. *I Puritani* was Bellini's eleventh opera; he died of a mysterious illness shortly after its first performance, at the age of thirty-four. R.H.

At one stage of operatic history there was much ill-feeling between singers and composers because of the star performer's inclination to alter, amend and add to the score (often with totally unsuitable songs designed to show off their vocal prowess). Composers like Verdi insisted on their music being given it due respect; since when the great opera singers today set out to respect and glorify the composer's vision. Biographical entries follow of a selected number of cherished opera singers.

Janet BAKER (b. 1933)

The possessor of one of the most beautiful mezzo-soprano voices of the day, she is equally at home in opera, oratorio and song recitals. While still at the height of her powers she decided to retire from opera in 1982, but she has left behind indelible memories of her operatic performances. Among her greatest triumphs have been Dido in *Les Troyens* (Berlioz), Dorabella in *Così fan tutte* (Mozart) Diana in *La Calista* (Cavalli) and Penelope in *Il Ritorno d'Ulisse in Patria* (Monteverdi). To all of these she has brought her innate musicianship, her acting ability, her technical mastery of a well-schooled voice and her warm and engaging personality. Although no longer appearing in opera, she is still active as a concert and oratorio singer of unusually wide repertoire.

Mattia BATTISTINI (1856-1928)

Still remembered as the supreme exponent of bel canto among operatic baritones. He made his début in Rome at the age of twenty-two and from 1902 until 1924 he was a prolific recorder. He retained his powers almost undiminished throughout his life and gave two outstanding recitals in London as late as 1924, when he was sixty-eight. He was known in his native land as 'La Gloria d'Italia' and has become a legend among opera connoisseurs. Fortunately EMI have released a superb album entitled *Mattia Battistini – King of Baritones* and this includes all his published discs as well as several released for the first time (EMI EX 2907903 – 7 discs).

Teresa BERGANZA (b. 1935)

The Spanish mezzo-soprano made her début in 1957. Her voice which is not a particularly large one, is warm and luscious and she excels in the *coloratura* roles of Rossini's comic operas, her success in which has been world wide. Her charming personality and lovely voice have made her equally successful in concert work, particularly in Spanish songs. She has made a number of recordings which show her as a more technically perfect singer than her great predecessor, Conchita Supervia, but the latter was unique in her ability to convey on disc a sense of impish humour.

Above: *Teresa Berganza started her career in the* zarzuela *world, then became known as a fine interpreter of many roles in the operas of Rossini. Here she is seen as Rosina in* The Barber of Seville.

Carlo BERGONZI (b. 1924)

Originally made his début as a baritone in 1948. However, he soon found that his voice was developing an impressive upper range, and after retiring for further study he made his début as a tenor in *Andrea Chénier* (Giordano) in 1951. He rapidly became in great demand for the exceptional refinement of his style with which he has always used his fine tenor voice. He excels in the more lyrical roles in the Verdi operas, and also in the verismo repertoire. His scrupulous artistry and avoidance of all exaggeration have earned him a place among the greatest tenors of his generation.

Jussi BJÖRLING (1911-60)

Came from a family of singers and while still in his teens was a member of the Björling Male Quartet. He made his début in 1930 as a solo artist, and the lovely unforced lyrical quality of his voice soon earned him international recognition. He was for long one of the favourite tenors at the Metropolitan Opera House, New York, and his occasional appearances at Covent Garden were always eagerly awaited. His Rodolfo (*La Bohème*) his Cavaradossi (*Tosca*) and his Des Grieux (*Manon*) were unsurpassed by any of his contemporaries and his voice retained a youthful freshness throughout his career. His acting ability was limited, but his pleasing stage presence and the sheer beauty of his voice made him a great favourite wherever he sang.

Montserrat CABALLÉ (b. 1933)

Made an early début in 1957 and sang for several years without causing any great interest, until one night in 1965 when she sang the title role in *Lucrezia Borgia* (Donizetti) in a concert performance in the Carnegie Hall, New York. She created a sensation and was immediately catapulted to stardom. Her voice is a pure lyric soprano of lovely quality and her command of it is superb. She can produce a ravishing pianissimo on a high note and then dazzle you with intricate scale passages sung with amazing rapidity and effortless ease. Her singing of 'Nel cor piu non mi sento' is a supreme example of her art. She has recorded it with the variations originally sung by the legendary Catalani as shown in Henry Pleasants' book *The Great Singers* (Macmillan). Her acting is her weakness, being generally confined to a few gestures suggesting a 'traffic cop' on duty, but her gracious personality and above all her exquisite vocalisation are sufficient to compensate for any dramatic limitations.

Maria CALLAS (1923-77)

Made an early début as Santuzza at the age of fifteen but her real career started when she was singing in Trieste at the end of World War II. Even before her first appearance at the Arena in Verona in *La Gioconda*, stories had begun to circulate of an extraordinary soprano who could sing the major Wagnerian roles and then give a virtuoso performance of a great bel canto part like *Norma*. Her voice at this period was a thrilling soprano of great range and power, but her early essays into the dramatic Wagnerian roles took an inevitable toll. The very highest notes were there, but they always revealed a wide vibrato and this remained a flaw in an otherwise superb tech-

Below: *Maria Callas was supreme in all her leading soprano roles. She rediscovered the role of Medea, which she sang at Covent Garden in 1959.*

nique. Before she slimmed so drastically, however, the voice was an exceptional instrument and her *coloratura* in such a purely display piece as the 'Bell song' from *Lakmé* is staggering. Her acting was always impressive, but particularly after her working with Visconti she became the greatest singing actress of her day, and it was she who showed the way to sing the bel canto roles with overwhelming dramatic intensity. She rehearsed meticulously so that every gesture coincided with and emphasised the musical phrase, giving the illusion of complete spontaneity. Towards the end of her career her vocal resources were much impaired, but so great was her artistry that as late as 1964, when she sang *Tosca* at Covent Garden, she achieved one of the most brilliant triumphs of her career. She was undoubtedly the greatest singing actress of the first half of this century.

Emma CALVÉ (1858-1942)

A Marchesi pupil who possessed a voice of extraordinary range. She created the part of Suzel in Mascagni's *L'Amico Fritz* but her most famous role was Carmen and her lower register had the depth and resonance of a contralto, while she could also sing *coloratura* soprano roles like Ophélie in *Hamlet* (Thomas). No doubt her Carmen would seem mild today, compared with some recent artists, but it was considered crude and oversexy in its day. Bernard Shaw wrote after attending a performance, 'Nothing would induce me to go again. To me it was the desecration of a great talent.' Even today, when opera-goers think of *Carmen* the name of Calvé crops up continually. She left a number of recordings which reveal a voice of great purity but they reveal little evidence of the dramatic talent which she undoubtedly possessed.

José CARRERAS (b. 1946)

Carreras saw the film *The Great Caruso* when a small boy. So thrilled was he by the voice of Mario Lanza, who played Caruso, that he determined to study music and if possible to sing as a tenor. When his voice broke, it was soon clear that he would become a singer of exceptional quality and he made his début in 1970 in the tiny role of Flavio in Bellini's *Norma*. Fortunately for him Montserrat Caballé was singing the title role, for she was deeply impressed by the young beginner and gave him every possible encouragement. His lovely voice, handsome appearance and dramatic ability soon brought him to the forefront and his performances at Covent Garden in such roles as Rodolfo (*La Bohème*) and Cavaradossi (*Tosca*) established him as a firm favourite. Recently he has added rather heavier parts to his repertoire, but it is in the purely lyrical roles that he has achieved his greatest triumphs.

Above: *Enrico Caruso was the first great opera star to make an impact on the gramophone age. His recording of* 'Vesti la giubba' *sold over 1 million copies.*

Enrico CARUSO (1873-1921)

Caruso worked hard to achieve the success he eventually enjoyed. His voice was essentially a lyric tenor and at the commencement of his career he was nicknamed *il tenore svento* (the breathy tenor) by his fellow students. Originally, his voice was of limited range and it was only after some years that he was able to reach his famous high C with any security. By the time he was twenty-five, however, he must have improved tremendously, because he was chosen by Giordano to create the tenor lead in the composer's *Fedora*, opposite the celebrated soprano Gemma Bellincioni. His success was instantaneous and shortly after this he made his début at La Scala, Milan, with Toscanini conducting. Later in the season *L'Elisir d'amore* was given

Gaetano DONIZETTI
(1797-1848)

Faced with parental opposition to a musical career, Donizetti, who was born in Bergamo, joined the Austrian army so that he could compose in his spare time. After the success of his sixth opera, *Zoraide di Granata* (Rome 1822), he obtained his discharge. The first of his operas to win acclaim outside Italy was *Anna Bolena* (Milan 1830), which was followed by *L'Elisir d'amore* (Milan 1832) and probably his finest work, *Lucia di Lammermoor* (Naples 1835). Unlike Bellini, Donizetti was an amiable man, not given to envy and very modest about his own achievement. But Verdi, among others, acknowledged his debt to Donizetti's skill in dramatic construction, and recent revivals of some of his lesser-known works have shown them to be of considerable interest and merit. Towards the end of his career, cut short by syphilitic disorders, he said 'My heyday is over: I am more than happy to cede my place to people of talent.' He worked at great speed, producing seventy-five operas and many other works, including twelve string quartets, some orchestral pieces and church music, in just over twenty years. When asked by Sir Charles Hallé if he believed that Rossini had written *The Barber of Seville* in a fortnight, Donizetti replied, 'Oh, I expect so: but then he has always been such a lazy fellow!' R.H.

and here Caruso achieved a triumph. Toscanini remarked after the first performance, 'If this young Neapolitan continues to sing like this, he will have the whole world talking about him.' At this stage Caruso's voice was of incomparable beauty and his technique was outstanding. Gradually, however, he undertook heavier roles, and his Canio in *I Pagliacci* was sung with overwhelming intensity. His dramatic temperament undoubtedly caused him to overtax his voice and in 1908 he had an operation to remove a nodule from his vocal chords. After this, the voice, while still unrivalled by any of his contemporaries, became darker and more voluminous. His recordings of this period show clearly that the former effortless ease of his singing had disappeared and, although he continued to sing until the year before his death at the early age of forty-eight, the strain he had put on his voice produced a gradual deterioration in his performance. But he remained supreme to the end and his place in operatic history is secure.

Feodor CHALIAPIN (1873-1938)

Born in the same year as Caruso and, like the great tenor, the Russian bass had a brilliant career, singing well into his sixties with undiminished success. He was a towering figure of a man and was undoubtedly the greatest singing actor of his day. His performances of Boito's *Mefistofele*, in which he sang the title role at La Scala in 1902, with Caruso as Faust, set the seal on his international fame, and he was soon in demand in all the world's great operatic theatres. The voice was a fine quality bass baritone, with an extended upper register, capable of tremendous power but also able to produce a lovely *mezza voce*. In later years he was unrivalled in the leading roles in *Boris Godunov* and *Prince Igor*, and all subsequent performers have been judged against the standards he set. He was an equally successful recitalist and left many excellent recordings which give some insight into his unquestioned genius.

Boris CHRISTOFF (b. 1914)

Studied with the great Italian baritone Riccardo Stracciari and made an early début in Rome in 1946 as Colline in *La Bohème*. It soon became clear that his forte was in the great roles from Russian opera inevitably

Below: *Boris Christoff, the great Bulgarian bass, sang in a choir in Sofia during his early days and made his operatic début in Rome in 1946. A superb actor and singer.*

associated with Chaliapin. The greatest compliment that could be paid him was to say that he was easily the finest of the celebrated Russian's successors. Although now a veteran he still sings occasionally. In his prime his bass baritone voice was of beautiful quality, while he was a splendid actor with a dominating stage personality.

Victoria de LOS ANGELES (b. 1923)

Made her professional début in 1945 in Barcelona at the Teatro Liceo as the Countess in *Le Nozze di Figaro* (Mozart), and after winning a number of vocal competitions she came to London to sing for the BBC. She made a great impression and returned the following year to make her début in 1950 at Covent Garden as Mimi in *La Bohème*. Soon recognised as a soprano of outstanding qualities, she was acclaimed at all the great operatic centres. Her voice is one of outstanding beauty, particularly full and warm in the mezzo-soprano range, and it has made her ideal for roles such as Cio Cio San (*Madama Butterfly*), Marguerite (*Faust*), Eva (*Lohengrin*) and Manon in Massenet's opera of that name. She has always been a delightful recitalist, particularly in songs of her native Spain. Although now a veteran, she returned as recently as 1987 to give a recital in London.

Fernando de LUCIA (1860-1925)

A great exponent of the art of bel canto. He was possibly the last of a line of tenors able to do full justice to the *coloratura* passages of such roles as Count Almaviva in Rossini's *Il Barbiere di Siviglia*. He recorded from 1903 onwards but by this time his voice was not a high one although he used it with incomparable artistry, and was unequalled in roles which demanded a *tenore di grazia*. He also sang more dramatic roles and won praise for his Canio in *Pagliacci*, but he was criticised for a very noticeable vibrato when he sang this heavier music, and this made him less successful in England, although he was particularly idolised in Italy. He created the part of Fritz, the wealthy young landowner, in Mascagni's *L'Amico Fritz* and upon his retirement became a celebrated teacher.

Mario del MONACO (1915-82)

Made his début at Pesaro in 1939 and soon attracted attention with his magnificent tenor voice and his handsome appearance. His voice was a genuine *tenore robusto* and he was at his best in the more heroic roles of such operas as *Otello* and *Andrea Chénier*. He was not the most artistic of singers and seldom attempted to sing at anything less than forte, but he was a fine actor and was immensely popular in Italy and for a time at the Metropolitan Opera, New York. His finest role was Otello.

Above: *Jean de Reszke, with his equally famous brother Edouard, was a key member of the Paris, Metropolitan and Covent Garden companies during the 1890s.*

Jean de RESZKE (1850-1925)

The most celebrated tenor of his generation. He sang for some time as a baritone, but his brother Edouard, a bass, was convinced that Jean was really a tenor and persuaded him to study in Paris with the famous teacher Sbriglia, who also taught Nordica and Plançon. He made his début as a tenor in 1879 but made little immediate impression and sang in concerts for the next five years. He then appeared at the Paris Opéra in the première of Massenet's *Hérodiade*. His success was immediate and from then on he was generally acknowledged as the leading tenor of his generation. He was strikingly handsome, tall and aristocratic in bearing, with a beautiful voice which he used with consummate artistry. He made his Covent Garden début in 1888 as Vasco da Gama in *L'Africaine* (Meyerbeer) and was unchallenged in roles like Romeo, Faust, and in most of the later Wagnerian works, being equally successful as Lohengrin, Siegfried, Walther and Tristan. His voice was not a particularly high one but in his prime he easily reached a ringing B natural and the quality was warm, sympathetic and resonant. His last role was Canio (*I Pagliacci*) at the Paris Opéra in December 1902, after which he retired and taught many famous artists including Bidú Sayǎo, Louise Edvina and Maggie Teyte.

Emmy DESTINN (1878-1930)

A Czech soprano who is still remembered as probably the finest of all exponents of the role of Cio Cio San in Puccini's *Madama Butterfly*. She made her début as Santuzza in

Berlin in 1898 and was the first artist to sing Senta in Wagner's *Der Fliegende Holländer* at Bayreuth in 1901. She had a lyrico-dramatic soprano of great power and beauty of tone while her voice was rock steady even in the most melting of pianissimi. She was also a fine actress, particularly in dramatic roles. Herman Klein considered her to be the legitimate successor of the great Thérèse Tietjens and she was chosen by Puccini and Toscanini to create the role of Minnie in the composer's *La Fanciulla del West* opposite Caruso. She has always been known in Czechoslovakia as Ema Destinnova and at the time of writing these notes the Supraphon Company are reissuing her entire recorded repertoire in five LP albums, to perpetuate the memory of the greatest of all Czech singers.

Giuseppe di STEFANO (b. 1921)

Still sings occasionally, but his great days were in the 1950s when his tenor voice was considered to be the most beautiful of the time. It was warm, superbly controlled and of extended range, while his *mezza voce* was a joy to hear. By the 1960s, although he was still singing regularly, the voice had lost much of its unique charm, but he will always be remembered for his wonderful series of recordings, many of them made with Maria Callas, including a splendid *I Puritani* (Bellini) and an equally fine *Lucia di Lammermoor*. He sang with Callas on her final concert tour, but although the artistry was still there, neither singer was able to revive the great days of the past.

Ghena DIMITROVA (b. 1940)

Made a sensational début in London at the Barbican Centre in a concert performance of *La Gioconda* (Ponchielli) and since then she has confirmed her position as one of the greatest dramatic sopranos of her time. The voice is large and brilliantly sustained throughout its range, although occasional harshness occurs on the very highest notes when sung forte. Among recent successes have been her highly acclaimed Turandot at La Scala, Milan, and her Abigaille in Verdi's *Nabucco*. A press notice of the latter performance stated: 'Her voice is huge and beautifully schooled – chromatic scales and arpeggios are perfectly placed and her dynamic control is complete, up to a pianissimo top C.'

Placido DOMINGO (b. 1941)

Combines beauty of voice with dramatic ability and unusual musicianship, and these qualities, added to his fine appearance, have made him one of the very greatest tenors of the day. He is basically a lyric tenor but is able to sing the more heroic roles superbly. As a young man he sang as a baritone in his parents' zarzuela company in Mexico, and later made his début as a tenor in 1961. Since then he has gradually added the most testing of tenor roles including the name part in Verdi's *Otello*. His Dick Johnson in a Covent Garden revival of Puccini's *La Fanciulla del West* was a great personal triumph, and even today after more than a quarter of a century on the operatic stage, he can still give a performance of great lyrical beauty in some of the lighter tenor roles.

Dietrich FISCHER-DIESKAU (b. 1925)

The most versatile of baritones. His voice is possibly less sensuously beautiful than some of his Italian contemporaries, but his fine vocal technique allied to his dramatic ability and his musical intelligence have placed him at the very top of his profession. Equally fine as an operatic artist and as a lieder singer, he has given innumerable memorable recitals; his recorded output has been phenomenal. A criticism of his singing of Italian opera has been that the quality of voice has made him sound rather unidiomatic, but he is certainly to be counted among the great singers of our day.

Kirsten FLAGSTAD (1895-1962)

Probably the greatest dramatic soprano of this century. She started early, singing operetta, then moved into the lighter operatic repertoire and finally developed into a superb Wagnerian singer. She was almost on the point of retiring when she was given the opportunity to sing at Bayreuth in minor roles where she was offered the part of Sieglinde in *Die Walküre*. Her career took off and within a year she was singing the same role at the Metropolitan Opera, New York, and shortly afterwards added Brünnhilde and Kundry to her repertoire. Frida Leider was reaching the end of her great career, and

Below: *Placido Domingo starred in the film of* Otello *with Katia Ricciarelli as well as playing the role on stage at Covent Garden in 1987 and elsewhere.*

*Gioacchino ROSSINI
(1792-1868)*

Despite Donizetti's strictures Rossini was another very fast worker, but one who concentrated virtually the whole of his formidable output into the first half of his career. He was the only child of Giuseppe Rossini, the town trumpeter of Lugo and inspector of slaughter-houses, and a talented singer. After early lessons in singing and the harpsichord he entered the Bologna Academy in 1806 to study counterpoint and the cello. Among his student pieces were an opera and a cantata, which attracted some attention. He was then commissioned by the manager of the San Moisé theatre in Venice to write a comic opera, *La cambiale di matrimonio* (1810), the first of many such assignments in Venice, at La Scala in Milan and in Naples where, in 1814, he was appointed music director of both opera houses. *Otello* belongs to this period as does *The Barber of Seville*. In 1822 Rossini married Isabella Colbran, a celebrated soprano, and went to Vienna where he visited Beethoven. In 1824 he moved to Paris and wrote three operas for the Théâtre Italien, one of which was *William Tell* (1829). After that, nothing, apart from a *Stabat Mater* (1842), the *Petite Messe Solenelle* (1864) and some trifles, the 'sins of old age'. In 1855, with his second wife, he settled in Paris, to become a focal point of artistic society and a renowned gourmand. R.H.

Above: *Kirsten Flagstad was on the verge of retiring in 1933 when she was engaged to sing minor roles at Bayreuth, going on to help a postwar Wagner revival.*

Flagstad inherited her mantle as the greatest Wagnerian soprano of her day. Her voice was wonderfully even throughout its wide range and her tone was truly golden, always suggesting vast reserves of power. Her possible weakness was a lack of the inner fire which Leider had possessed but the sheer volume and flawless legato were unique. She was very successful as Leonora in Beethoven's *Fidelio* and made a memorable Dido in Purcell's *Dido and Aeneas* at the Mermaid Theatre just before she retired.

Amelita GALLI-CURCI (1882-1963)

Born in Milan and made an early début in 1906 at Trani in Italy. She was almost entirely self taught, and was discovered by Mascagni, a friend of the family. She was studying to make a career as a solo pianist, but when Mascagni heard her sing he persuaded her to give up the piano and to concentrate on her voice. After serving an apprenticeship in the smaller Italian houses, she went to South America in 1910 and returned in 1912. Later the same year she came back to Milan and sang in *Lucia di Lammermoor* at the Dal Verme theatre, having been turned down by the management of La Scala. She resolved never to sing at this famous house after such a rebuff, and really made her great career in America. She sang at the Colón, Buenos Aires, in 1915, receiving rave notices, and from 1916 onwards she was engaged at the Chicago Civic Opera, where she was an immediate favourite. She made her first records at this time and they became, with those of Caruso, the best sellers of the day. Her voice was one of haunting beauty – Geraldine Farrar likened it to the velvet at the heart of a pansy – and her *coloratura* technique, while

not as dazzling as Tetrazzini's, was impeccable. She was later accused of occasionally singing off key, but this probably started when she developed goitre which eventually ended her career. In her prime, however, she was a unique artist singing with ease up to an E in alt., while her phrasing had an individual charm. She undoubtedly possessed an incomparably lovely voice and her best recordings particularly of arias by Bellini and Donizetti are historical treasures.

Nicolai GHIAUROV (b. 1929)

Like his senior fellow countryman Boris Christoff, is Bulgarian and has achieved notable successes in Russian opera and also in Verdi roles. His voice is slightly lighter in quality than Christoff's and he uses it in the best bel canto tradition. He is a fine actor with a dominating stage personality. His Mephistopheles in both Berlioz's *Damnation de Faust* and in Gounod's *Faust* have been particularly brilliant and he has been a notable King Philip in Verdi's *Don Carlos*.

Beniamino GIGLI (1890-1957)

After Caruso, the most celebrated tenor of the century. His beautiful voice was warm and full in the lower register and his upper notes were produced with an ease and a brilliance unequalled by any of his contemporaries while his *mezza voce* and piano singing were perfectly controlled. He was inclined to over sentimentalise in certain of his roles and he made little attempt to act, but after the

Below: *Beniamino Gigli had a voice that has been called the most beautiful of the century; he was still singing superbly at the age of sixty.*

death of Caruso he became the most popular tenor in the world. He never forced his voice and as a result he was still singing beautifully into his sixties; indeed, he gave recitals until shortly before his death at the age of sixty-seven.

Tito GOBBI (1913-84)

Possessed a fine baritone voice which he used with consummate artistry. He made his début in Rome in 1938 but the war interfered with his early career and his real fame started from his appearances after 1945. He was a superb actor and had the ability to colour his voice to suit each role he sang. His *Falstaff*, for example, sounded fat and unctuous while his Scarpia (*Tosca*) was the very embodiment of evil. His performances in this latter role with Callas as Tosca at Covent Garden in 1964 have become part of operatic history. In his later years his master classes and his operatic productions were equally successful. His two books *Tito Gobbi: My Life* and *Tito Gobbi on his World of Italian Opera* make fascinating reading.

Edita GRUBEROVÁ (b. 1946)

Has been hailed as one of the finest *coloratura* sopranos of the day. She has a voice of extended range and can sing the most difficult bravura passages with commendable accuracy, while her appearance and her charming stage manner have added greatly to her overall performance. Her recordings are possibly a little disappointing with the voice sounding a little strained at the extreme top, but her singing of *Lucia di Lammermoor* (Donizetti) with Alfredo Kraus and Renato Bruson in the other principal roles and her Gilda in *Rigoletto* with Neil Shicoff and Renato Bruson, have received considerable critical acclaim.

Marilyn HORNE (b. 1934)

Sang for Dorothy Dandridge in the film *Carmen Jones* and since then she has become one of the most versatile and popular mezzo-sopranos in the world. Her *coloratura* technique is unbelievably brilliant and in the dramatic operas of Rossini with their elaborate *fioriture* she has been unrivalled in her day. She has been equally successful as Marie in *Wozzeck* (Berg) at San Francisco in 1960, and in 1972 added the role of *Carmen* to her many triumphs. Her voice is warm and brilliant with an astonishing range encompassing the lowest notes of a true contralto and the upper notes of a soprano.

Hans HOTTER (b. 1909)

Has been hailed as the greatest bass-baritone since the war. He started his apprenticeship with the Hamburg opera as early as 1934, but it was in the period immediately following

World War II that he achieved supremacy in parts like Wotan. He was hailed as the successor of the great Friedrich Schorr and his acting and superb voice brought him world-wide fame. He created the roles of the Kommandant in Richard Strauss's *Friedenstag* and also that of Olivier in the same composer's *Capriccio*. He was somewhat past his prime when he recorded the role of Wotan in *Die Walküre* in Georg Solti's *Ring*, but his interpretation and his authority remained unequalled. In the 1960s he produced many of the Wagnerian operas, including a complete *Der Ring des Nibelungen* at Covent Garden and has also given a number of lieder recitals.

Gwyneth JONES (b. 1936)

Started life as a mezzo-soprano but soon found her true métier as a dramatic soprano. At her best she is one of the most exciting artists performing today, combining a beautiful appearance with a voice of thrilling power. She joined the Royal Opera at Covent Garden and sang Vienna, Bayreuth, Munich and Milan. Recently she made a triumphant return to Covent Garden in the title role of *Turandot*, in which part she was coached by Dame Eva Turner, and fortunately her voice had retained much of its former steadiness.

Kiri Te KANAWA (b. 1944)

Has one of the most beautiful soprano voices now before the public. She first hit the headlines following her performances as the

Below: *Kiri Te Kanawa, from New Zealand, has become one of the best-known names in contemporary opera with a controlled voice of great power and beauty.*

Above: *Gwyneth Jones combines good looks with a richly powerful voice that makes her one of the most exciting of contemporary sopranos.*

Countess in Mozart's *Le Nozze di Figaro* at Covent Garden in 1971 and at Glyndebourne in 1973, and she followed this with an outstanding Desdemona in Verdi's *Otello* at Covent Garden and at the Metropolitan Opera, New York, in 1974. Above all, it is her glorious singing which has made her a star, her voice being as effective in the recording studio as on stage.

Alfredo KRAUS (b. 1927)

Certainly one of the most stylish singers in the world today. He has a voice of good quality with an extended range reaching easily top C sharp or even D and his technique enables him to phrase with an intelligence and an elegance almost unparalleled among his contemporaries. Now in the veteran stage, his voice has become drier in timbre but he still sings with all the finesse of his best days. His refined style makes him a particularly fine singer in the Bellini and Donizetti roles and also in such parts as the Duke in Verdi's *Rigoletto*.

Selma KURZ (1874-1933)

A pupil of Mathilde Marchesi and one of the stars of the Vienna State Opera during the Mahler régime. She possessed a very beautiful soprano voice particularly suited to the great *coloratura* operatic roles, but she also sang lyrico-dramatic parts like Elsa in *Lohengrin* and Sieglinde in *Die Walküre*. She was famous for her exquisite trill which she could hold for an extraordinary length of time, and she was also a woman of great personal beauty. She made an early début as a mezzo in 1895 in Hamburg but soon turned to soprano roles. She sang at Covent Garden

Ruggiero LEONCAVALLO
(1857-1919)

The son of a Neapolitan magistrate, Leoncavallo's musical career seems dogged throughout by misfortune and ill-luck. He began his musical studies with the piano and then went on to the Conservatorio to learn harmony and composition. He was awarded a 'Maestro' diploma at the age of eighteen and set to work on a remarkable project, an opera based on the drama by Alfred de Vigny which tells the tragic story of Chatterton. When the work was ready for production, the impresario walked off with the funds leaving the young composer virtually penniless. He scraped a living giving lessons and playing at café-concerts, travelling extensively throughout Europe. On his return to Italy he approached the publishers Ricordi with a vast three-part scenario dealing with the history of the Renaissance, of which he had already written the first section, *I Medici*. Ricordi accepted the project but did nothing with it, and in despair Leoncavallo went to a rival house three years later, for whom he wrote the one work which has made his name famous all over the world, *I Pagliacci*. It was a success he was never able to repeat. Even *La Bohème* (Venice 1897), while it was more favourably received than many of his other works, was completely overshadowed by Puccini's opera of the same name, which had opened a few weeks earlier, also in Venice. R.H.

from 1904 to 1907 but was then absent until 1924, when she was past her prime.

Lotte LEHMANN (1888-1976)

One of the great stars of the Vienna State Opera from 1914 until 1938, and her performance of the role of the Marschallin in Richard Strauss's *Der Rosenkavalier* has always been considered the ideal interpretation. She possessed a lyric soprano voice of great beauty and warmth and her singing was always full of feminine charm. Richard Strauss was a great admirer of her talents, and she created the roles of the Composer in *Ariadne auf Naxos* and the Dyer's wife in *Die Frau ohne Schatten*. An artist whose talent completely eclipsed her technical limitations – her breathing was always noisy, for example – her tender and affectionate approach to all she did made her a unique artist.

Frida LEIDER (1888-1975)

The greatest Wagnerian dramatic soprano of the years immediately following World War I. She made her début in 1915, but the war confined her performances to German opera houses. She came to Covent Garden in 1924 and sang there every year until 1938 and was generally acknowledged as the supreme Brünnhilde and Isolde of her generation. Her voice was rich and of lovely quality and her technique enabled her to sing many Verdi and Mozart roles with equal distinction. In addition to her lovely voice, she was a fine dramatic actress and was a more exciting singer than the vocally superb Kirsten Flagstad, upon whom her mantle descended.

Jenny LIND (1820-87)

Possibly the most famous of all the pupils of the great teacher Manuel García II. She made a début in 1838 but her voice failed and eventually she went to Garcia for advice. He agreed to train her, stipulating that she should first have a complete rest, and she made her second début in 1844 in *Norma* in Berlin. She was immediately hailed as a superstar and when she eventually appeared in England the 'Jenny Lind Fever' reached unheard of heights. She sang for a few more years on the stage before giving up her operatic work on religious grounds. Nicknamed the 'Swedish Nightingale', she continued to sing in concert for a few more years after which she taught for a time at the Royal College of Music.

John McCORMACK (1884-1945)

Won a gold medal in a Dublin singing competition when only twenty. After studying in Italy with Sabatini he sang in opera for a few years, making his début at Covent Garden as Turiddu in *Cavalleria Rusticana* (Mascagni) in 1907. His sympathetic and highly individual tenor voice won critical applause and his performances as Don Ottavio in Mozart's *Don Giovanni* were highly praised, but his lack of acting ability prompted him to leave the stage, and thereafter his operatic performances, particularly after 1913, took second place to his concert career. His lyric tenor voice was produced with an easy virtuosity which enabled him to spin out a marvellous pianissimo while his breathing control was phenomenal. His recordings of 'Il mio tesoro' (*Don Giovanni*) and 'O sleep why dost thou leave me?' (*Semele*) demonstrate this to perfection. His versatility was amazing and although inimitable in the lighter Irish ballads he was a wonderful lieder singer and a fine interpreter of many English art songs by Vaughan Williams, Elgar, Bax and others.

Above: *Giovanni Martinelli started his career in 1910 and sung until 1965. Here seen in an early part in* The Jewels of the Madonna *by Wolf-Ferrari in 1912.*

Above: *Famous picture of Nellie Melba as Nedda and Fernando De Lucia as Canio in Leoncavallo's* I Pagliacci *at Covent Garden in 1893.*

Eva MARTON (b. 1948)

Has recently come to the fore as one of the leading dramatic sopranos of the day. Her singing in the title role in Puccini's *Turandot* at Covent Garden in 1987 brought her considerable critical acclaim. Her voice is a warm and powerful soprano and she sings with great dramatic conviction. She has made her name as Tosca, Desdemona, Elsa in *Lohengrin* and Leonore in *Fidelio*. She is also noted for her work as an oratorio and lieder singer.

Giovanni MARTINELLI (1885-1969)

Had a distinguished career which was remarkable for its longevity. He made his début in Milan in 1910 and then was chosen by Puccini to be the first European Dick Johnson in *La Fanciulla del West* in 1911. He was very successful at Covent Garden in 1912 and 1913, before going to America to become a great favourite at the Metropolitan Opera, New York, from 1913 to 1946. His final stage appearance was as the Emperor in *Turandot* at the age of eighty. His voice had not the golden warmth of Caruso, but he was superior to the latter in his ability to suggest nobility of character, and his exceptional upper range enabled him to become the finest Arnoldo (*Guillaume Tell*) since Tamagno. His Otello was sung with an intensity and a dignity which made up for any lack of power in the big dramatic moments.

Nellie MELBA (1861-1931)

The most famous of all the pupils of Mathilde Marchesi. She was born in Melbourne, the daughter of a wealthy business man of Scottish extraction. She first studied singing in Australia and sang at a few concerts with some success, before coming to Europe. As plain Helen Armstrong (*née* Mitchell) she was advised by Mathilde Marchesi to change her name to Nellie Melba, and she made her début under that name in Brussels in 1887 at the Théâtre de la Monnaie as Gilda in *Rigoletto*. A year later she made her Covent Garden début as Lucia in Donizetti's *Lucia di Lammermoor*. She was successful, but her real fame started from her singing of the role of Juliette in Gounod's *Roméo et Juliette* in 1889. She had a voice of exceptional purity and wide range and her execution was quite brilliant. She became the ruling queen of Covent Garden and retained most of her powers until her retirement in 1926. Her acting was elementary and some opera lovers found her rather cold, but in her prime she was considered to be head and shoulders above most of her contemporaries. Mary Garden, no admirer of Melba as a person, wrote in her memoirs, 'The way Melba sang that high C [in *La Bohème*] was the strangest and weirdest thing I have ever experienced in my life. The note came floating over the auditorium at Covent Garden; it left Melba's throat, it left Melba's body, it left everything, and came over like a star and passed us by in our box and went out into the infinite. I have never heard anything like it in my life. Not from any other singer. It just rolled over the hall of Covent Garden. My God, how beautiful it was!' That says it all.

Lauritz MELCHIOR (1890-1973)

Almost certainly the greatest *heldentenor* of this century. He sang as a baritone for a short time, mostly in his native Denmark, but soon made his début as a tenor in Copenhagen in 1918, and quickly made a name for himself. He came to Covent Garden for the first time in 1924 and then established himself as the principal Wagnerian tenor at the Metropolitan Opera, New York, singing there regularly until 1950. His voice, untiring in the heroic roles of the Wagnerian music dramas, was thrilling in the sheer volume and ringing quality of his upper range. He added the role of Otello to his repertoire and although he sang it well the rather un-Italian quality of his voice prevented him being a complete success. Undoubtedly his forte was Wagner, and Frida Leider wrote of him, 'To me, he was always the perfect Tristan . . . and the greatest *heldentenor* of his time.'

Sherrill MILNES (b. 1935)

The legitimate descendant of a long line of celebrated American baritones, including Lawrence Tibbett, Leonard Warren and Robert Merrill. He is the possessor of a fine quality high baritone voice which he uses with great skill. He is particularly known for

Above: *The fine American baritone Sherrill Milnes made his début at the Metropolitan Opera, New York, in 1965. Here, singing in a TV production of* Rigoletto *in 1975.*

his singing in the Verdi operas, but he is a versatile performer and a fine actor. He made his début at the Metropolitan Opera, New York, in 1965 as Valentine in *Faust* and his first appearance at Covent Garden came six years later as Renato in Verdi's *Un Ballo in Maschera*. He is widely known for his many recordings which do full justice to his voice.

Birgit NILSSON (b. 1918)

The immediate and legitimate successor to Kirsten Flagstad. She made her début in Stockholm in 1946 as Agathe in *Der Freischütz* (Weber) and was at Glyndebourne to sing the role of Electra in Mozart's *Idomeneo* in 1951, but she really came to fame following her appearances in Munich in 1954-5, when she sang Brünnhilde and Salome during the season. This was the year of Flagstad's retirement and it left Nilsson unrivalled in the great Wagnerian dramatic soprano roles. Where Flagstad's voice was truly golden, Nilsson's was like a silver clarion, both powerful and untiring. It was rather cold in quality and made her an almost ideal Turandot, while her acting was statuesque rather than intense. She has now retired but so far no one of equal status has emerged.

Adelina PATTI (1843-1919)

For years the undisputed Queen of Song. Her parents were opera singers and legend has it that she was literally almost born on the stage: her mother was singing in *Norma* the night before she gave birth, and she was born in the green room of the opera house in Madrid. Shortly afterwards her parents went to America and the little girl made her concert début at the age of seven, singing 'Ah non giunge' and 'Una voce poco fa' to the amazement of the audience. She made her official stage début at the age of sixteen in New York in *Lucia di Lammermoor* and then sang Amina in Bellini's *La Sonnambula* at Covent Garden two years later. She was immediately hailed as the successor to the great Giulia Grisi, and she sang for twenty-five successive seasons at Covent Garden. Her voice was initially a high soprano with a range reaching to F''' and it was of the loveliest possible quality, limpid, full and brilliant. She was not a great musician but her phrasing and style were matchless, and although she had a charming appearance she was only a passable actress. In her later years the voice darkened, and by the time she recorded in 1905-6 she was virtually a mezzo-soprano. Her last appearance was at the age of seventy-one, when she sang 'Voi che sapete' at the Albert Hall in a concert in aid of charities for World War I.

Right: *Adelina Patti sang for twenty-five consecutive seasons at Covent Garden in all the major Italian roles and as Marguerite in Gounod's* Faust.

Pietro MASCAGNI (1863-1945)

The other half of the *Cav* and *Pag* partnership, *Cav*, of course, being an abbreviation of *Cavalleria Rusticana* (1890), the one work on which Mascagni's reputation entirely rests. His father, a baker, wanted him to become a lawyer, so young Pietro had to pursue his musical studies in great secret. But eventually he was discovered, and had it not been for a well-disposed uncle, music's loss might well have been the law's gain. He flourished in his new environment and started to compose in earnest. His father became reconciled to having a musician in the family so that when the uncle died, Mascagni, then aged eighteen, returned home on cordial terms. He then wrote a setting of Schiller's *Ode to Joy* which so impressed a wealthy local amateur musician that he offered to pay Mascagni's fees at the Milan Conservatory. But he found the discipline of formal study intolerable, and embarked on a precarious career with travelling opera companies. Eventually he married and settled down near Foggia as an impecunious music teacher. He submitted his one-act opera in a competition, winning first prize. When it was performed in Rome the audience went wild with enthusiasm, and Mascagni suddenly found himself famous. Sadly, despite many other attempts, it was his only triumph. *Cav* and *Pag* are indeed well matched. R.H.

Above: *Luciano Pavarotti has been one of the top tenors since his débuts at Covent Garden, Glyndebourne and La Scala, Milan, in the mid-sixties. Here he is seen in Verdi's* Aida *at Covent Garden in 1984.*

Luciano PAVAROTTI (b. 1935)

Worked for two years as a school teacher before becoming a professional singer. He made his début in 1961 as Rodolfo in *La Bohème* in Emilio Reggio and had a meteoric rise to fame. He was already at Covent Garden in 1963, at Glyndebourne in 1964 and at La Scala, Milan, in 1966. Since then he has been at the very top of his profession. His voice is large, of good quality and of extended range. Thus the role of Arturo in Bellini's *I Puritani* holds no terrors for him, while he is capable of the most beautiful *mezza voce* as well. In addition to his operatic work he has been overwhelmingly successful as a concert singer where his pleasant personality always endears him to his audiences. Recently he has become rather mannered – the large silk handkerchief and the frequent mopping of the brow are an unnecessary adjunct to a singer of his distinction!

Aureliano PERTILE (1885-1952)

Idolised in Italy, and was reputed to be Toscanini's favourite tenor. The voice was large but not particularly beautiful, and it was the dramatic intensity of his singing which made such an impact in the opera house. He was a very intelligent man and reigned as *primo tenore* at La Scala from 1921 to 1937. His earlier records contain some lovely lyrical singing but by the time he recorded for *La Voce del Padrone* in the late twenties his style had become highly dramatic and at times explosive. At his best, however, he was certainly one of the greatest tenors of the inter-war years, added to which he had a dynamic stage personality.

Ezio PINZA (1892-1957)

Sang briefly in 1914, but World War I intervened and he made his real début in Rome in 1921. That same year he appeared at La Scala and was soon recognised as the greatest Italian bass-baritone of his generation. His voice was of beautiful quality, resonant, warm and powerful, while he was a fine actor with a commanding stage presence. He was capable of singing roles usually associated with a true baritone, being a notable *Don Giovanni* at Salzburg from 1934 to 1937. At the end of his operatic career he turned to light opera, and was the star of the original production of *South Pacific*.

Rosa PONSELLE (1897-1981)

Sang in cinemas and vaudeville for a time with her sister Carmela Ponselle. Caruso recommended her to the Metropolitan Opera, New York, and she made her début there as Leonora in Verdi's *La Forza del Destino* opposite Caruso on 15 November 1918. Her success was immediate. Her voice was a true dramatic soprano which was absolutely even throughout its entire range, and she was able to sing the dramatic *coloratura* roles like *Norma* with a virtuosity that astonished her hearers. She sang at the Metropolitan Opera from 1918 to 1937 and retired while still at the height of her powers. She came to Covent Garden for three seasons, beginning in 1929, and also sang at the Maggio Musicale in Florence in 1933, but her main career was in America. Her recordings give us some idea

Below: *Famous American soprano Rosa Ponselle in her first appearance as Violetta in Verdi's* La Traviata *at Covent Garden in 1930.*

of the richness and exciting qualities which made her one of the greatest singers of the century.

Hermann PREY (b. 1929)

Hermann Prey made his stage début in 1952 at the Wiesbaden State Theatre, and he went to Hamburg as the leading baritone at the Hamburg State Opera in 1953. From then onwards he has had a distinguished international career singing in all the great opera houses of the world. His voice is a true baritone of fine quality and one which he uses with great intelligence. He is equally distinguished as a lieder singer, where his immaculate control and firm legato combined with a strong feeling for words have made him an outstanding interpreter.

Leontyne PRICE (b. 1927)

Has been at the top of her profession since 1952 when she took part in a two-year tour of *Porgy and Bess*. She made her Covent Garden début in 1958 as *Aida*, and since then has sung at all the great operatic centres. Her voice is a wonderfully even creamy toned dramatic soprano while she is an actress of more than average ability. She is considered by many connoisseurs to be the finest Aida of her day, and excels in the later Verdi operas, including *La Forza del Destino* and *Il Trovatore*. She also made a notable success as Donna Anna in Mozart's *Don Giovanni* at Salzburg in 1960.

Below: *Leontyne Price, the American soprano, is considered by many to be one of the great Aidas of this century; here seen singing the role in San Francisco.*

*Carl Maria von WEBER
(1786-1826)*

Titta RUFFO (1877-1953)

Possessed the largest and probably the most beautiful baritone voice of his day. He made his début as the Herald in *Lohengrin* in Rome in 1898, but it was above all in the great Verdi baritone roles that he was unsurpassed, while his Figaro in Rossini's *Il Barbiere di Siviglia* was unequalled for its sheer vocal splendour. Giuseppe de Luca said of him 'Quella non era una voce, ell'era un miracolo' ('that was not a voice, it was a miracle') and added that even in 1951 Ruffo could still sing a ringing top A flat. He was also a tall and distinguished figure with a dominating stage personality.

Tito SCHIPA (1888-1965)

One of the great operatic stylists. His voice was not large, and was probably less beautiful than some of his contemporaries, but he was an acknowledged master of his art. His phrasing, vocal colouring, restraint and superb diction combined to make him a supreme artist. As Gigli so rightly said, 'When Schipa sang, we all had to bow down to his greatness.' He made his début in 1911 as Alfredo in Verdi's *La Traviata* in Vercelli, and first sang at La Scala in 1915. His last appearance there was in 1950, after which he still continued to sing in the provinces for a few years.

Friedrich SCHORR (1888-1953)

Friedrich Schorr possessed one of the loveliest baritone voices of his day. Although he will always be remembered as the finest Wotan, Sachs and Dutchman of the inter-war years, he was also equally at home in lieder and in oratorio. He was the legitimate successor to the great Anton Van Rooy, and surpassed him technically, especially with his superb *mezza voce* singing. He clearly showed that it was possible to *sing* Wagner with a true legato rather than to declaim him with the explosive attack used by other lesser artists of his day.

Above: *Both sides of the great German soprano Elisabeth Schwarzkopf are reflected in one of her great roles as the Marschallin in Richard Strauss's* Der Rosenkavalier. *She was also a wonderful interpreter of the operetta repertoire.*

Elisabeth SCHWARZKOPF (b. 1915)

Made an early début in Berlin in 1938 and for some years followed in the footsteps of her teacher, Maria Ivogün, singing *coloratura* roles. After 1947 she decided to concentrate on the lyric soprano repertoire and sang in all the principal operatic centres. She was particularly famous for her singing of the operas of Mozart and Richard Strauss. She possessed a lovely silvery soprano which she used with great skill and she was also a woman of great beauty. Towards the end of her career she sang less in opera and concentrated on lieder. She finally became a little mannered in some of her interpretations, but lovers of fine, intelligent, stylish singing will never cease to be grateful for the classic recordings of opera and lieder that she made, most of them fortunately still available. She is now holding a number of master classes.

Renata SCOTTO (b. 1934)

Made her début at the Teatro Nazionale in Milan in 1953 and for some time sang *coloratura* roles with great success, on one occasion replacing an ailing Callas for the final performance of *La Sonnambula* in Edinburgh in 1957. She is now singing mainly lyric roles, and is one of the most intelligent artists before the public, phrasing with wonderful subtlety and showing deep involvement in all she does. In recent years her voice has become unpleasantly hard when she sings forte at the extreme top of her range, but this is more evident in her recordings than in her live performances. At her best she is still one of the finest lyric sopranos before the public.

Weber's father was a none too successful and much-travelled impresario, so from earliest childhood his son was very much at home in the theatre world. For a short time he was a pupil of Michael Haydn's, and by the time he was fourteen he had already written a mass, an opera and several pieces for the piano. In 1803 he went to Vienna to study with Vogler. A variety of posts followed, not all of them musical, and on one occasion he was thrown into prison on a false charge of embezzlement. He eventually rejoined Vogel in Darmstadt and, with Meyerbeer, took lessons from him once more. Here Weber wrote his first successful opera *Abu Hassan*. He went to Munich in 1811, was appointed director of the Prague Opera in 1813 and then Court *Kapellmeister* at Dresden in 1817. Four years later *Der Freischütz* was presented in Berlin, where it was hailed as a great masterpiece. *Euryanthe* followed in Vienna in 1823, by which time Weber was suffering acutely from tuberculosis. However, he accepted a commission from Covent Garden to write a new opera, *Oberon*. Seven weeks after conducting the first performance in 1826, he died in London. It can be said of Weber that he was the founder of German opera, and that Wagner was his true heir. R.H.

Ebe STIGNANI (1903-74)

The possessor of a superb voice of lovely warm quality and unusual power, Ebe Stignani was generally acknowledged as the greatest Italian mezzo-soprano of her generation. She made an early début in Naples in 1925 and then appeared later the same year at La Scala, Milan, where she remained unrivalled until her retirement in 1957. The compass of her voice was extraordinary, ranging from the contralto F to C''' and enabling her to sing certain dramatic soprano roles. She acted superbly with her voice and despite a rather ordinary figure she made her commanding presence felt on the stage. Her Adalgisa to Callas's Norma in the Covent Garden *Norma* of 1952 made operatic history. den production of *Norma* of 1952 made operatic history.

Conchita SUPERVIA (1895-1936)

Both unique and incomparable. She sang while still a girl in Buenos Aires at the age of fifteen and was Octavian in the Rome première of *Der Rosenkavalier* a year later. These early performances probably overtaxed her voice and may have had something to do with the vibrato which was present in her later years, but she was a wonderful singer of the great *coloratura* mezzo roles in the Rossini comic operas. Her brilliant singing of the Rossini roulades, her sense of fun and her striking appearance made her quite inimitable. She first sang the Rossini operas in Turin in 1925, and really it was she who restored them to the repertoire, in the same way that Callas re-introduced some almost forgotten works of Bellini and Donizetti. Supervia's tragic death in childbirth in 1936 robbed the world of a beloved artist who has never been entirely replaced, for she had a magnetism all her own.

Joan SUTHERLAND (b. 1926)

Almost certainly the greatest Australian singer since Melba. She came to England and sang lyric roles at Covent Garden from 1952 onwards and added Gilda in *Rigoletto* a little later, but it was her triumphant appearance in *Lucia di Lammermoor* at Covent Garden in 1959 which amazed and delighted her audience and firmly established her as the greatest dramatic *coloratura* of the day after the decline of Callas. She blazed a trail around the world, earning extravagant praise from the critics, and was named 'La Stupenda' by the Milanese, after her début at La Scala. Her voice is of beautiful quality,

Below: *Joan Sutherland, the greatest Australian opera singer since the days of Melba, proved herself supreme in the LP era in the great* bel canto *roles. Here she is seen in* Lucrezia Borgia *at Covent Garden in 1980.*

powerful and brilliant beyond measure in the most difficult *coloratura* passages, while her trill is quite exceptional. Now in her early sixties but still singing magnificently, she wisely limits her appearances.

Francesco TAMAGNO (1850-1905)

Possessed a robust tenor voice of almost limitless power and he had an exceptionally high range, which made him ideal in parts like Arnoldo in Rossini's *Guillaume Tell*. He was chosen by Verdi to create the name part in the composer's *Otello*, and sang the role many times in all the great opera houses. He recorded in 1902 and the primitive recordings give some idea of the huge voice and powerful declamation of this legendary tenor.

Left: *The Austrian tenor Richard Tauber switched successfully from grand opera to operetta during a turbulent career in Dresden, Vienna and London.*

Richard TAUBER (1892-1948)

Really had two careers, as a fine opera singer and as an unrivalled singer in operetta. He sang for some years, principally in the German and Austrian opera houses, and following his début at Chemnitz in 1911 he became a great favourite particularly in Mozart and Puccini roles. He turned more and more to lighter music in his later years, and his beautiful voice and unique charm made him an inimitable operetta singer. He settled in England after 1938 and frequently toured with his own light opera company, showing that he had lost none of his ability to sing the classical repertoire. A year before he died he sang a superb Don Ottavio in Mozart's *Don Giovanni* at Covent Garden, a performance which is now legendary.

Renata TEBALDI (b. 1922)

After Callas, the finest soprano specialising in the Italian repertoire in the period immediately following World War II. Her greatest successes were in the works of Verdi and Puccini, and her lovely voice, which she used with great artistry, combined power with a warmth and a purity which had few rivals. She was not the great actress that Callas was, but she made a dignified and compelling figure on the stage. Her Cio Cio San (*Madama Butterfly*) was hailed as the greatest since the days of Emmy Destinn and her Desdemona in Verdi's *Otello* was also supremely beautiful.

Luisa TETRAZZINI (1871-1940)

A miraculous *coloratura* soprano. She had few lessons, her teacher saying 'I have no need to place your voice, God has done that.' After an early début in 1890 she spent a number of years singing in Italy, South America and Russia. She had considerable success in San Francisco in 1904, and set her sights on Covent Garden where Melba was all powerful. Eventually she made an unheralded appearance during the then unfashionable autumn season at Covent Garden in 1907 as Violetta in *La Traviata* and her success was sensational. Melba may have been caught napping but once Tetrazzini had sung here, there was nothing she could do! Tetrazzini's voice was amazing in the upper ranges rising easily to the F''' and her scale passages and staccato were brilliant beyond description, while her legato singing was beautifully controlled. She made little attempt to act and her ample figure, which increased year by year, eventually caused her to give up operatic performances after about 1914. She still sang in concerts for some years and returned to England for a farewell tour as late as 1931.

Above: *The finest English exponent and, considered by some, the finest of all portrayers of Turandot, was the Oldham-born soprano Eva Turner.*

Eva TURNER (b. 1892)

A living legend. Born in Oldham she was brought up in Bristol and joined the Carl Rosa Opera Company in 1916, singing for a year in the chorus. She was soon given small parts and later became the prima donna of the company. She was heard by Maestro Panizza in London in 1924 and he was so impressed that he invited her to go to Italy to audition for Toscanini for La Scala. Toscanini's comments were terse and to the point: 'Beautiful voice, good figure, fine pronunciation.' She was immediately engaged and made her début at La Scala in 1924 as Freia in *Das Rheingold*, her great career as an international artist followed. Her voice was a huge dramatic soprano, brilliant and tireless above the stave, and she will always be remembered as an unrivalled Turandot. She was also a superb Aida and was a wonderful Amelia in Verdi's *Un Ballo in Maschera*; she was equally fine in the leading Wagnerian roles, in particular Brünnhilde and Isolde. In her mid-nineties, she is still active, devoting much time to encouraging young artists.

Jon VICKERS (b. 1926)

One of the finest singing actors to emerge since the end of World War II. His voice is not a remarkably beautiful one, but it is large and he uses it to great dramatic effect, colouring it admirably. His career has been world wide since his début in 1956, and his first major success was his Aeneas in Berlioz's *Les Troyens*, since when he has become famous for his singing of the heroic roles in Verdi and for his Wagnerian interpretations. His voice has darkened over the years, and he is now a veteran, but he will be remembered particularly for his Florestan in Beethoven's *Fidelio*, which has had no peer in recent years.

Galina VISHNEVSKAYA (b. 1926)

Now past her prime, but when she first left Russia in the 1960s and sang in London and New York, she was immediately recognised as a lyric soprano of outstanding quality, with a rather dated style of acting, but with a superb voice and a commanding presence. Her most famous role is probably Tatiana in Tchaikovsky's *Pique Dame*.

Frederica von STADE (b. 1945)

Made her début in 1970 as one of the genii in Mozart's *Die Zauberflöte* at the Metropolitan Opera, New York. She stayed there for three years and then was engaged for Glyndebourne to sing Cherubino in *Le Nozze di Figaro* in 1973. From then onwards her career was assured. She has a beautiful quality high mezzo-soprano voice, beautifully trained and capable of singing the Rossini *coloratura* roles with consummate artistry. Her beautiful appearance and her voice are her strongest points, but although her acting is at times secondary, she moves easily on the stage and has a charming personality.

Right: *Frederica von Stade with Yvonne Minton in the Covent Garden production of* La Donna del Lago *in 1985.*

Giacomo PUCCINI
(1858-1924)

Entered the Milan Conservatoire in 1880 and studied under Bazzini and Ponchielli. His first opera, *Le Ville*, was entered for a competition where it was beaten by Mascagni's *Cavalleria Rusticana* but was eventually produced in 1884 and was so admired that it led to a commission for the unsuccessful *Edgar*. The first major success came when *Manon Lescaut* was produced in Turin in 1893. Puccini went on to become the most famous opera composer of the day; in Italian opera history he is rated second only to Verdi. His sure theatrical touch, his open sentiment and melodrama, above all his sweeping tunes ensure the immortality of such works as *La Bohème* (1896); *Tosca* (1900); *Madama Butterfly* (1904); *La Fanciulla del West* (1910); *La Rondine* (1917); *Suor Angelica* (1918); *Gianni Schicchi* (1918); *Turandot* (1926). P.G.

In the late nineteenth century it was usually the singers who were virtual dictators, and the conductors were with few exceptions mere accompanists. The man who more than any other changed all this was Arturo Toscanini (1867-1957). He had been a cellist in the première of Verdi's *Otello* at La Scala, Milan, in 1887, when he was barely twenty, and a year earlier when he was playing in an orchestra in Rio de Janeiro, he was suddenly called upon to replace a conductor who had failed. He stepped in at a moment's notice, conducted *Aida* from memory and scored an immediate triumph. Both Verdi and Puccini appreciated his great gifts and he was the conductor for the world premières of *I Pagliacci*, *La Bohème*, *La Fanciulla del West* and finally *Turandot*. He had an uncanny ability to identify himself completely with the original inspiration of the composer, and a personal magnetism which enabled him to inspire the artists under his direction. Towards the end of his life he tended to become rather ruthless in his demands and was inclined to drive the artists without allowing them the necessary freedom to express any individuality. However, he will always be remembered as the greatest operatic conductor of this century.

A more genial figure, but a truly great conductor was Tullio Serafin (1878-1968) who devoted his whole life to conducting opera and to coaching singers, among them Rosa Ponselle, Tito Gobbi, Maria Callas, and Joan Sutherland. He first conducted at Covent Garden in 1907, then two years later, in 1909, he was at La Scala, Milan. He was at the Metropolitan Opera from 1924 to 1934 after which he had a truly international career. He was the conductor at Covent Garden on that historical night in 1959 when Joan Sutherland made her first appearance in the title role of Donizetti's *Lucia di Lammermoor*, and also conducted many world premières, including Gruenberg's *Emperor Jones* and Taylor's *Peter Ibbotson* at the Metropolitan Opera, New York.

Gustav Mahler (1860-1911) was probably more celebrated during his lifetime as an opera conductor rather than as a composer. He was the virtual music dictator at the Vienna State Opera from 1897 to 1907 and during his engagement there he made it into one of the supreme opera houses of the world, gathering together a brilliant team of singers including Selma Kurz, Anna Bahr-Mildenburg, Leo Slezak and Richard Mayr. It was he who first used the phrase 'Tradition ist Schlamperei' ('Tradition is slovenliness') and he obtained the most wonderful ensembles in the world during his régime in Vienna.

In England it was Sir Thomas Beecham (1879-1961) who dedicated his genius, his personal fortune and his enthusiasm to the cause of opera. After conducting a small touring company in the early years of the century, he was responsible for a season at Covent Garden in February and March 1910

which included the first English performances of Richard Strauss's *Elektra* and *Salome* together with the world premières of Ethel Smyth's *The Wreckers* and Delius's *A Village Romeo and Juliet*. In 1913 he conducted the first English performance of *Der Rosenkavalier* at Covent Garden and also introduced a season of Russian opera at Drury Lane, bringing over Chaliapin and other famous artists. After the war he spent more time in the concert hall, but he will always be remembered as one of the great opera conductors and fortunately we have his recording of *La Bohème* with Victoria de Los Angeles and Jussi Björling among the artists as a permanent memorial to his genius.

Karl Böhm (1894-1981) earned a great reputation as an operatic conductor, not only in his native Austria, but also in Italy, Germany, England and America. He was for long closely associated with Salzburg and Bayreuth and was particularly celebrated for his conducting of operas by Wagner, Mozart, and Richard Strauss. He gave the world premières of Strauss's *Die Schweigsame Frau* and *Daphne* at Dresden, and conducted some seasons at the Metropolitan Opera, New York.

In Italy, Victor de Sabata (1892-1967) was usually considered second only to Toscanini. He conducted the world première of Ravel's *L'Enfant et les sortilèges* and was musical director at La Scala, Milan, for many years, staying there from 1929 to 1953. He was especially famous for his Wagner and Verdi, and came over with the Scala Company to Covent Garden in 1950, where his *Otello* and *Falstaff* were singled out for special praise.

Another Italian conductor who will always be remembered with gratitude for his help in the revival of some of Rossini's operas was Vittorio Gui (1885-1975). He was responsible also for the founding of the Maggio Musicale in Florence and worked at La Scala, Milan, with Toscanini. He was well known and extremely popular at Glyndebourne from 1952 onwards, where his scintillating con-

Above: *Carlo Maria Giulini, conductor in the great Italian tradition who limits his performances and recordings to the works he really admires and understands, and never fails to enhance them.*

ducting of Rossini's *Cenerentola* was an immense success.

We can lay the blame fairly and squarely on the shoulders of certain producers for the fact that Carlo Maria Guilini (b. 1914) has almost given up conducting opera, for he disapproved of many of their so-called improvements. He was responsible for some of the legendary operatic performances in collaboration with Visconti at La Scala, Milan, with Maria Callas as prima donna, and he also worked with Zeffirelli, while older operagoers still remember a magical *Falstaff* at Covent Garden in 1961 with the producer and musical director presenting a masterpiece.

Wilhelm Furtwängler (1886-1954) was a superb Wagnerian conductor who worked at Bayreuth for a number of seasons, beginning in 1931. He was at Covent Garden in 1935 when he conducted *Tristan* and he returned there in 1937 and 1938 for performances of *Der Ring des Nibelungen*. His highly individual interpretations were not to everyone's liking and the famous Ernest Newman could not accept his reading of the Wagner operas. His recording of *Tristan*, however, with Flagstad as a noble Isolde, is one of the classics of the gramophone and has earned him a place in musical history.

Herbert von Karajan (b. 1908) will no doubt be treated more fully elsewhere in this book, but his contribution to opera is too great for him to be omitted in this short section. He is a perfectionist, and is capable of inspiring singers to excel themselves under his baton. Recently he has been criticised for sometimes choosing singers for roles which are not always suited to their vocal capabilities, but at his best he has been responsible for some magical performances.

Erich Kleiber (1890-1956) had a rather

Above: *Riccardo Chailly, one of the leading opera specialists of the younger generation who has conducted at La Scala, Chicago and the New York Met. and produced many fine recordings.*

Richard WAGNER
(1813-83)

Richard Wagner dominated the musical world of his time in a way which few composers had done before him, and none since. The man himself was a paradox. On the one hand he was a vain and unscrupulous poseur, with more than a hint of cruelty in his character. On the other, he was capable of acts of spontaneous generosity and kindness to his family and friends. He came from a theatrical background, received a good classical education at Dresden and the Thomasschule in Leipzig, where Bach had once taught, and then turned his attention to composition. True to his own precepts, he wrote all his own libretti and supervised every aspect of the production of his mammoth works. His powerful genius not only forged a totally new theory of music drama, in which he strove to achieve a union of all the arts, but also secured the means by which his lifework could be presented in an ideal setting, a theatre at Bayreuth built specially for the purpose. He was an author and poet, as well as a composer-conductor, deeply read in German myth and legend, the main sources of his inspiration and material. He represents the ultimate expression of German romanticism, and among his many great masterpieces the *Ring* cycle must be regarded as one of the most outstanding achievements of creative human endeavour. R.H.

troubled career, but there is no doubt about his genius as a conductor. He was able to obtain exactly what he wanted from every member of the orchestra and the players respected and loved him. He was *Generalmusikdirektor* of the Berlin State Opera from 1923 to 1933, but resigned when the Nazi government banned the first performance of Hindemith's *Mathis der Maler*, and went to Argentina. He became guest conductor at many of the world's leading opera houses, including the Colón, Buenos Aires, and eventually became an Argentinian national. He was at Covent Garden from 1950 to 1953 and helped greatly in re-establishing opera there after World War II. His son Carlos is an equally fine conductor of opera.

Georg Solti (b. 1912) worked with Toscanini in 1938 in Salzburg, but being Jewish he was forced to leave Austria and settled for a time in Switzerland. After World War II he conducted with great success in Munich and Frankfurt and was then appointed Music Director of Covent Garden in 1961, where he remained for ten years. His interpretations were often controversial but there was never any doubt about his ability to generate excitement in his performances. His Wagnerian work was particularly outstanding and he was certainly responsible for raising the standard of performance at Covent Garden to a high level during his régime.

Many other gifted conductors have worked most successfully in opera in addition to their concert performances; and among those who will always be remembered are Claudio Abbado (b. 1933), John Barbirolli (1899-1970), Leonard Bernstein (b. 1918), Leo Blech (1871-1958), Fritz Busch (1890-1951), Colin Davis (b. 1927), Clemens Kraus (1893-1954), John Pritchard (b. 1921),

Charles Mackerras (b. 1925), Bruno Walter (1876-1962) and, latterly, Guiseppe Sinopoli (b. 1946). J.F.

Among those who will be particularly remembered as opera specialists are Lamberto Gardelli (b. 1915), an Italian who spent much of his conducting career in Scandinavia, working in Stockholm (1946-55) and in Copenhagen (1955-61). In 1973 he was appointed musical director of the Royal Opera in Copenhagen and his name has become familiar on opera recordings, most recently with the Hungarian State Opera. Francesco Molinari-Pradelli (b. 1911) is another Italian steeped in opera tradition. In 1946 he conducted at La Scala, in 1951 at Covent Garden, then at San Carlo, Naples. From 1957 he was conducting opera in San Francisco and Los Angeles. Particularly known for his Wagner and Puccini. Of an older generation of Italians, Antonino Votto (b. 1896) worked as assistant to Toscanini in Milan, later becoming the regular conductor there and frequently working with Maria Callas with whom he recorded such operas as *La Sonnambula* and *La Gioconda*. He also conducted in Buenos Aires, at Covent Garden and in Chicago. Notable amongst the French opera specialists is Georges Prêtre (b. 1924), conductor at the Opéra Comique from 1955 and at the Paris Opéra from 1959. Appeared at the Met. in 1964 and has worked in London, Milan, Vienna and Salzburg, his name associated with many fine French opera recordings. The Australian Richard Bonynge (b. 1930) has mainly been associated with his wife Joan Sutherland and with her has made many classic recordings of Italian and French opera, particularly noteworthy for his valuable revival of the lesser-known products of the French *opéra-comique* and operetta tradition. Was appointed musical director of the Australian Opera in Sydney in 1976. The Italian tradition still runs strong in the works of Riccardo Muti (b. 1941) who was appointed principal conductor of the Teatro Communale in Florence in 1970 and became known

through his work at various festivals and through a steady output of EMI recordings of the standard opera repertoire. Riccardo Chailly (b. 1953) was appointed assistant conductor at La Scala, Milan, in 1972 and in 1974 conducted *Madama Butterfly* in Chicago. Made his début at the Met. in 1982 with *Les Contes d'Hoffmann*. In America the name of Thomas Schippers (1930-77) rated highly in opera, conducting first performances of Menotti, with the New York City Opera from 1955 and the same year appearing at La Scala, Milan, and at the Metropolitan Opera, New York, where he was to direct many memorable productions before he succumbed to lung cancer. A worthy successor at the Met. as conductor and planner has been the brilliant James Levine (b. 1943), also notably heard in Salzburg and Bayreuth.

Every opera-goer – indeed, probably every opera singer – has his or her favourite opera house. This section looks briefly at some of the best-known and loved, from Barcelona to Vienna. Invidious though it may be, it is inevitable that Italy, arguably the home of opera (Venice was the world's first popular opera house to open), should be represented by five entries – Milan, Florence, Naples, Rome and Venice.

Barcelona

EL GRAN TEATRO LICEO

Barcelona, rather than Madrid, is the musical centre of Spain. Opera was first given there in 1708, but the celebrated Gran Teatro Liceo was not built until 1847. The cost was met by private subscriptions and by subsidies from the leading industrialists, and the theatre was opened with great splendour on 4 April 1847. It suffered the fate of so many theatres of the time, being gutted by fire and reduced to ruins in 1861, and the present house which is elaborately decorated in the Isabelline style was opened on 20 April 1862. Many great singers of Victorian times performed there and more recently Victoria de los Angeles, Montserrat Caballé and José Carreras have been great favourites. The season usually lasts from late November till early March. (Seating capacity 3,000.)

Bayreuth

DAS FESTSPIELHAUS

There was already a large opera house in Bayreuth when Wagner first visited the town, but he did not consider it suitable for his plans. With the help of Ludwig of Bavaria, land was purchased nearby and the present Festspielhaus was started in 1872. It was completed four years later in 1876 and the first *Ring cycle* was given there in the same year beginning on 13 August. The theatre, which is architecturally comparatively severe in appearance, has superb acoustics with a sunken orchestral pit. The original productions had elaborate scenery and effects, but the tendency in recent times has been to simplify the stageing and rely more on symbolism rather than attempts at realism. The season is a short one, lasting only about five weeks in late July and August. (Seating capacity 1,800.)

Brussels

LE THÉÂTRE DE LA MONNAIE

The first theatre on the site of the present opera house was opened in 1700, on the site of an earlier mint, hence the name. The existing theatre dates from 1856 and occupies a commanding position in the Place de la Monnaie. A number of well-known operas have had their premières here, including Massenet's *Hérodiade*. Among the many famous singers who chose La Monnaie for their operatic débuts were Rose Caron, Emma Calvé and Nellie Melba. (Seating capacity 1,700.)

East Berlin

DIE DEUTSCHE STAATSOPER

Berlin was comparatively late in building an important opera house. The first one was opened in 1742, but before that performances were given in the reign of Frederick III as early as 1688, in the private Court Theatre. During World War II the city was ravaged by fire and the Deutsche Staatsoper on the Unter den Linden was reduced to rubble. After the war, the theatre was rebuilt and opened in 1955, using the plans of the original theatre which had first opened in 1914. Before World War II the musical directors included Leo Blech, Erich Kleiber, Wilhelm Furtwängler and Herbert von Karajan, and among the list of singers were Maria Ivogün, Frida Leider, Tiana Lemnitz, Peter Anders, Heinrich Schlusnus, Helge Roswaenge and Franz Völker. (Seating capacity 1,500.)

West Berlin

DIE DEUTSCHE OPER

The Deutsche Opernhaus on the Bismarck Strasse was opened in 1912 and destroyed by bombing in 1944. After the war it re-opened for a time in the Theater des Westens, but eventually moved back to the rebuilt theatre on the Bismarck Strasse in 1961. Among the music directors since the war has been Lorin Maazel, and well-known singers have included Elisabeth Grümmer, Dietrich Fischer-Dieskau and Ernst Häflinger. The opera houses in both sectors have also engaged numerous internationally famous singers as guest artists, but the unfortunate division of the city has caused problems to both theatres. (Seating capacity 2,300.)

Florence

IL TEATRO COMMUNALE

Florence was the birthplace of opera as we know it, and in the seventeenth century the Teatro della Pergola was built. It still stands but is only used now for special occasions. In 1862 a larger and more modern theatre, the Politeama Fiorentino Vittorio Emanuele, was opened. Florence has its fair share of fine weather, but it still seems incurably optimistic to have built a theatre without a roof, but this in fact is what happened. The theatre was burnt down in 1863 and was rebuilt, still minus a roof, in 1864, and it was only in 1883 that the building was fully covered over. It was renamed the Teatro Communale in 1932 and was modernised in 1959 and re-opened in 1961. Florence is a treasure house of beautiful buildings, but the Communale is not one of them, although it is now one of Italy's most important opera houses. (Seating capacity 2,000.)

Leningrad

THE KIROV THEATRE

Originally called the Maryinsky, the Kirov Theatre was first opened in 1860. It is a beautiful building of the greatest historical importance. Almost all the premières of operas by Russian composers of the second half of the nineteenth century took place here, and it was only after the revolution that the operatic centre of Russia moved from Leningrad to Moscow. After the revolution the theatre was renamed the State Academical Theatre of Opera and Ballet, but this longwinded name was soon changed to the Kirov, after Sergei Kirov, head of the Leningrad Communist Party in the 1920s. It alternates between performances of opera and ballet. The company is renowned for its lavish traditional productions – no questionable updatings here! Many famous Russian singers including the Figners, Chaliapin and Sobinov were for years the star attractions. (Seating capacity 1,625.)

Below: *The Royal Opera House at Covent Garden, London, has been a world opera centre for 130 years and almost every famous singer has appeared on its stage.*

Benjamin BRITTEN
(1913-76)

Celebrated English composer, conductor and pianist whose remarkable gifts were recognised in childhood, and on whom his teacher, Frank Bridge, had a most profound influence. Studied unhappily at the Royal College of Music 1930-33 and after publishing a number of remarkable early works, including the *Sinfonietta*, joined the Post Office Film Unit. *Variations on a theme of Frank Bridge* followed in 1937, and in 1939 Britten and his friend, the tenor Peter Pears, went to the United States where they stayed for three years, during which time the Violin concerto and *Sinfonia da Requiem* were first performed in Carnegie Hall under Sir John Barbirolli. Not long after his return to England, Britten achieved international stature overnight with the production, at Sadlers Wells, of his second opera, *Peter Grimes*, in June 1945. This was followed a year later by the much-performed *Young Person's Guide to the Orchestra*. He settled in Aldeburgh, where he founded the renowned Festival in 1948 in which he frequently appeared, either as conductor or soloist, and composed music of all kinds, including song settings, chamber and instrumental music, choral works and several more operas. Britten was much admired by musicians all over the world including the Soviet Union, where Shostakovich dedicated his Fourteenth Symphony to him. R.H.

London

COVENT GARDEN

Covent Garden was so named because the first theatre was built upon the site of an old convent garden. Originally it was used for many types of theatrical entertainment, having opened in 1732 with Congreve's *The Way of the World*. The first theatre was burnt down on 19 September 1808. A year later it was rebuilt and among the first of the many operatic premières to be held there was Weber's *Oberon*, in 1826. The opera was enthusiastically received and Weber, who conducted, was given a standing ovation. For good measure the evening closed with a farce called *The Scape Goat* and on another occasion Shakespeare's *Othello* was performed, followed by a production of *The Barber of Seville* with music by *Paisiello, Rossini* and *Bishop*. In 1847 the theatre was renamed The Royal Italian Opera and from then on performances were confined to grand opera, always in Italian. The theatre burnt down again in 1856 and the third theatre, which is basically the one still in use, opened with Meyerbeer's *Les Huguenots* on 15 May 1858. It was again called the Royal Italian Opera and all performances were in Italian. The first performance of *Lohengrin* in England was given at the theatre on 8 May 1875, but of course *still* in Italian, with Albani, Nicolini and Maurel in the principal roles! It was only when the word 'Italian' was dropped and the opera house became simply the Royal Opera in 1892 that works were performed in their original language. During the hundred and thirty years of its existence Covent Garden has become one of the great centres of opera in the world, and almost all of the greatest singers have appeared on its boards, including Adelina Patti, Nellie Melba, Enrico Caruso, Feodor Chaliapin, Luisa Tetrazzini and, in more recent times, Maria Callas, Joan Sutherland, Placido Domingo and Luciano Pavarotti. Due for extensive alterations in 1993. (Seating capacity 2,117.)

Above: *One of the most famous opera houses in the world, La Scala, scene of the first performance of operas by Verdi, Bellini, Donizetti, Puccini and others.*

Milan

IL TEATRO ALLA SCALA

Although there has been opera in Milan from the early eighteenth century, it was only gradually that the city attained its pre-eminence in the operatic world, so that today it is the ambition of every aspiring young opera singer to appear at La Scala. The first theatre was built in 1778 and it survived almost unchanged until it was virtually destroyed by bombing in 1943. It became the most celebrated opera house in the world, and the list of important premières held there is almost endless, including Rossini's *La Gazza Ladra*, Bellini's *Norma*, Donizetti's *Lucrezia Borgia*, Verdi's *Otello* and *Falstaff* and Puccini's *Madama Butterfly* and *Turandot*. The great conductor Toscanini was musical director from 1898 to 1903, then again from 1906 to 1908 and finally from 1921 to 1929. These were some of the most glorious periods in the history of the theatre. After the bombing in 1943 it was rebuilt and opened in May 1946, in very much the same style as the original theatre, with its walls decorated in cream, gold and maroon. The lovely interior is in marked contrast to the rather drab exterior. The productions at La Scala have long been renowned for their lavish settings, and in recent years the Visconti presentations of *La Traviata, La Vestale* and *La Sonnambula* all starring Maria Callas have become legendary. The season lasts from Christmas until spring. (Seating capacity 3,600.)

Moscow

THE BOLSHOI THEATRE

The first Bolshoi Theatre was opened in Moscow in 1825, and it was burnt down in 1853 and re-opened in 1856. Until the Revolution the Maryinsky Theatre in Leningrad (formerly St Petersburg) was probably the most important centre of operatic life in Russia, and almost all the operas of Tchaikovsky and his contemporaries had their premières there. After the revolution the cultural focal point moved to Moscow. In 1917 changes were made in the general administration and the Bolshoi was re-opened on 8 April 1918 and now divides its time equally between ballet and opera. From 1964 the company has toured, visiting La Scala, Milan, and other leading centres and among recent artists who have sung at the Bolshoi are Dolukhanova, Kozlovsky, Lemshev, Petrov, Reizen and Vishnevskaya. Almost all performances are given in Russian, and their spectacular productions of the great Russian master-pieces are traditional and highly authoritative. (Seating capacity 2,000.)

Munich

DAS HOF UND NATIONALTHEATER

Opera reached Munich in 1653 and a hundred years later the Rezidenztheater was opened. Here Mozart's *La Finta Giardiniera* and *Idomeneo* had their first performances. In 1818 the magnificent Nationaltheater was opened. It had a short life, however, being burnt down only five years later. The citizens were determined to rebuild it, and a penny was added to the beer tax to provide the necessary funds! It was re-opened in 1825 and soon became one of the most important opera houses in the world. The premières of *Tristan und Isolde, Die Meistersinger, Das Rheingold* and *Die Walküre* all took place here and much later it was chosen by Richard Strauss for the first performance of his *Capriccio* in 1942. The theatre was destroyed by bombing in 1943 and was rebuilt and re-opened in 1963 with a performance of *Die Meistersinger* on 23 November. Musical directors have included Von Bülow, Mottl, Walter, Krauss and Solti. Apart from the strong Wagnerian tradition the Nationaltheater has been particularly associated with the works of Richard Strauss who was himself *Kapellmeister* there from 1886 to 1889 and again from 1894 to 1898. From 1919 onwards there were summer festivals of the Strauss operas and the composer himself frequently conducted his own works. The theatre was originally modelled on the classical lines of the Paris Odéon, and today it has been superbly rebuilt. Almost every German singer of repute has been proud to sing on its boards.

Naples

IL TEATRO SAN CARLO

The first Teatro San Carlo was opened on 4 November 1737, and after various alterations and additions it was finally burnt down in February 1816. The second theatre, which has survived, underwent alterations in 1844 and 1929, and was damaged in an air raid in 1943, but mercifully the damage was slight and it was possible to continue performances. During the occupation by the Allied troops it was under the administration of the British forces and opera became so popular with the armies that, as a result, the whole San Carlo company were invited to Covent Garden in 1946, where they gave a highly successful season. In his book *Great Opera Houses*, Spike Hughes describes the interior as 'perhaps the most spectacularly beautiful of all opera houses, combining the majesty of La Scala with the decorative radiance of La Fenice with a nobility and beauty of design and decoration of its own'. The Teatro San

Above: *The Bolshoi, Moscow, has been the home of Russian opera since 1825. It has become increasingly international in outlook since the Revolution.*

Below: *The Lincoln Center in New York has been the home of the New York City Opera Company since 1965; very much the cradle of modern American opera.*

Carlo has been the scene of quite a number of operatic premières which have included Rossini's *Mose, Armida* and *La Donna del Lago*, Donizetti's *Lucia di Lammermoor* and Verdi's *Attila* and *Luisa Miller*. (Seating capacity 3,500.)

New York

THE METROPOLITAN OPERA

The old Metropolitan Opera House opened on 22 October 1883 with a performance of Gounod's *Faust*, but before that seasons of opera had been given at the Academy of Music. By 1892 one of the finest companies of singers ever assembled were on the roster of the 'Met', including Jean and Edouard de Reszké, Lilli Lehmann, Ernestine Schumann-Heink, Sembrich, Ternina and Maurel. In 1908, Toscanini was appointed chief conductor and the greatest singers in the world were attracted by the high salaries offered to them. Caruso had previously arrived in 1903 and remained there until his final illness in

1920 and among other famous artists who graced the boards at the old Met were Ruffo, Tetrazzini, Melba, Eames, Destinn, Scotti, De Luca, Martinelli and Gigli – in fact almost every singer of note in the first three decades of the century. The opera house has consistently retained its high standard, but it was eventually considered necessary to leave the old theatre and build a new one at the Lincoln Center. The new Met opened on 16 September 1966 with a performance of Samuel Barber's *Anthony and Cleopatra*. Since then it has reinforced its position among the world's great opera houses. (Seating capacity 3,800.)

Monte Carlo

L'OPÉRA DE MONTE CARLO

This small but beautifully proportioned theatre was built by Charles Garnier, who had already become famous as the architect of the Paris Opéra. The theatre, still the private property of the Prince of Monaco, is decorated in gold, crimson and cream, with a large stage, and many important works have had their premières here, including Massenet's *Jongleur de Notre Dame* and Puccini's *La Rondine*, while the list of great singers who have appeared there is equally impressive, including such historic figures as Patti, Tomagno, Melba, Jean de Reszke, Calvé and Caruso. (Seating capacity 600.)

Paris

L'ACADÉMIE DE MUSIQUE

The first operas were given in Paris in 1645, and the first Académie de Musique was opened in 1671. The present building, usually known as 'L'Opéra' or 'Le Palais Garnier' was finally opened in 1875. The richly ornate interior, designed by Charles Garnier, has been the subject of much criticism. Spike Hughes wrote of it, 'Inside – and this is where the Opéra has it over the interior-less Albert Memorial – the building is decorated with the same abandoned *fantaisie* and orgiastic delight in banal extravagance for its own sake. Only more so.' It is certainly impressive! The theatre had a period of glory during the directorship of Pedro Gailhard between 1885 and 1906, after which it lost its position as one of the leading opera houses. Recently it has regained its importance under the direction of Rolf Liebermann who came to Paris from Hamburg in 1972. (Seating capacity 2,600.)

Prague

THE NATIONAL THEATRE

Italian opera was first heard in Prague as early as 1627, but the National Theatre was not built until 1881. Before this opera was performed at the Tyl Theatre which opened its doors in 1783, and it was there that the world première of Mozart's *Don Giovanni* took place. The National Theatre now shares the production of operas in Prague with the equally fine Smetana Theatre. (Seating capacity 1,598.)

Rome

IL TEATRO DELL'OPERA

There have been opera houses in Rome since 1695 but the leading theatre is the Teatro dell'Opera which was opened in 1880 as the *Costanzi*. Later it became the Teatro Reale dell'Opera but when Italy became a republic the word 'Reale' (royal) was naturally omitted. The interior of the opera house is rather unusual and the arabesque arches give it what Spike Hughes called 'a period pseudo Moorish look'. A number of important premières have taken place in the theatre including *L'Amico Fritz* (Mascagni), *Tosca* (Puccini), and *Giulietta e Romeo* (Zandonai). It was largely rebuilt in 1926 and 1927 and

continued to give performances during World War II. It is now among the leading Italian opera houses, although for some years after the war its importance declined, and it has never been considered in the same light as La Scala (Milan), the San Carlo (Naples) or La Fenice (Venice). (Seating capacity 2,200.)

Sydney

THE OPERA HOUSE

This highly original building was designed by the Dane Joern Utzon and it is, to say the least, very unconventional in appearance, with its exterior roof structure resembling sails billowing in the wind. Catering for much more than opera, it also houses theatre, drama theatre, cinema and concert hall. Although completed in 1954, the first operatic performance was Prokofiev's *War and Peace* conducted by Edwin Downes and produced by Sam Wanamaker. (Seating capacity 1,500.)

Venice

IL TEATRO LA FENICE

The first public opera house in the world was opened in Venice in 1637 and was called *Il Teatro San Cassiano*, and since then the city has always been one of the major centres of operatic activity. The most famous of its theatres, *La Fenice* was opened on 16 May 1792, but was destroyed by fire in 1836. It was the scene of many world premières, including Rossini's *Tancredi, L'Italiana in Algieri* and *Semiramide* and Bellini's *I Capuletti ed i Montecchi* and *Beatrice di Tenda*. The second theatre, built to the original plan, was opened on 26 December 1837, and among many other Verdi operas which had their premières there were *Ernani, Rigoletto* and *La Traviata*. The winter season usually lasts about two months. (Seating capacity 1,500.)

Vienna

DIE STAATSOPER

As in so many of Europe's capital cities, opera came quite early to Vienna. The centre of the city was rebuilt in 1857, and a new opera house, originally called Die Oper am Ring, was built as part of the original plan. It opened with *Don Giovanni* in 1869, and after a time of fluctuating fortunes it reached its period of pre-eminence under the direction of Gustav Mahler between 1897 and 1907. The most successful of Mahler's successors was probably Franz Schalk who was director from 1918 to 1929, and among the famous singers attached to the company were Schumann, Lehmann, Nemeth, Jeritza, Kurz, Tauber, Piccaver and Slezak. After the Anschluss in

**Leoš JANÁČEK
(1854-1928)**

Of humble beginnings and making a long, slow start via teaching and conducting, this post-romantic Czech composer straddles the nineteenth and twentieth centuries in both chronological and musical senses. To some degree continuing the nationalist tradition of Smetana and Dvořák, he is known primarily for his operas, of which the first real success was *Jenufa*. Produced in 1904 but not seen in Prague until 1916, when Janáček was over sixty, this distinctly lyrical work is widely regarded as his masterpiece. But as time went on his style toughened, becoming more bleak and chromatically assertive, as in *The Makropoulos Affair* of 1926. The subjects of his operas generally assert strong humanistic values (if sometimes allegorically), but he was always greatly concerned to capture or echo the essence of speech, which links his music very closely to the Czech language while at the same time explaining some of its thrusting, exclamatory idiom. Sometimes there are striking harmonic juxtapositions, with a late-romantic glow suddenly giving way to strong blasts of cool modern air, as in *Katya Kabanova*. But there is a great mass of music beyond the ten operas, in various genres, two popular items being the orchestral *Taras Bulba* and the vocal *Glagolitic Mass*. J.C.

1938 many of the artists left and things became very unsettled, the theatre finally closing in September 1944 on the orders of Gœring. The building was destroyed by bombing in March 1945, and the re-built theatre was finally re-opened on 5 November 1955, with a performance of *Fidelio*. In 1956 Herbert von Karajan became musical director and among the leading singers were Gueden, Jurinac, Dermota, Seefried, Schwarzkopf, Lipp, Hotter, Kunz and Patzak. Another period of great artistic achievement followed, and in recent years the Staatsoper has shared its interests almost equally between the German and Italian repertoire and the company has exchanged visits and productions with La Scala, Milan. In no other city is the opera house such a focal centre. (Seating capacity 2,200.)

PART THREE

THE COMPOSER

Below: *Sir Michael Tippett is the best-known and most highly rated composer working in England today.*

How does a composer write music? This question is often asked by people who have little technical knowledge of it. They feel that there is a kind of mystery involved that cannot be reached by a layman however hard he tries. They may know that as a man Beethoven was as fallible as ourselves and had many personal problems, and yet his creation of music seems to put him into a superhuman category which ordinary mortals cannot hope to understand.

Of course, Beethoven was a genius. Even so, the ability to create is not reserved to a few supremely gifted souls such as he. The word 'compose' only means 'arrange', or 'put together'. Every time we write a letter or a diary entry we arrange our thoughts in a permanent form. Describing an event to a friend, we create a picture of it for his imagination. We don't call ourselves authors, but in a small way that is what we are. Similarly if we arrange flowers in a vase, we do the same thing as a painter preparing to paint a still life – in other words, create a subject that's pleasant to look at. True, we don't then paint it as he does and so produce a finished work of art, but we could if we attended an art class and learned to use brush and colour.

Thus part of creativity is simply the exercise of a craft that can be learned, as we learn to write, and not a kind of divine gift reserved to a few. It is also accessible at all levels of skill. Indeed, there are basically only two differences between our absentmindedly humming a tune and Beethoven writing a symphony. One is that we forget our tune while the composer preserves his music in a written and playable form; the other is of course

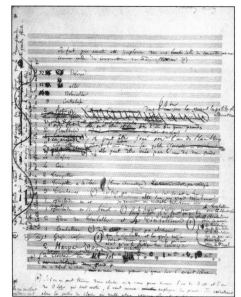

Above: *Some of the initial thoughts of composer Hector Berlioz about to embark on the full score of his well-known* Symphonie fantastique *written in 1830.*

that Beethoven's thought is vastly more complex and interesting, not only because of his genius but also because he has been thoroughly trained in the craft and 'language' of music.

And is music such a mystery? Musicians train in this craft without attaching any mystique to it. J.S. Bach learned music as a boy simply because he came from a family whose 'trade' was music and learning that trade began within the family. In turn, Bach himself had three sons who became well-known com-

posers. In the same way, the fathers of both Mozart and Beethoven were professional musicians, and so was Mozart's son, Franz Xaver. The great musicians were simply the most adept among thousands who practised the art without any talk of inspiration or genius. Another thing is that in the past composing was not thought of as something separate from the rest of music-making. Playing instruments, singing, teaching and writing music were all just skills to be learned. The three geniuses we have mentioned did all these things at one time or another, and each of them was famous as a performer. Indeed, they were all celebrated for improvising – sitting at a keyboard and creating music spontaneously for the delight of those around.

They could do this because highly trained musicians have music as a kind of language in which they naturally express themselves. To take a parallel with words, imagine that you could stand up and delight people with a poem or story produced on the spot. Such a talent is by no means unusual in some cultures, and in the Middle East you can still find people gathered around storytellers in a market-place. Today we think of a real author as one who writes down his poem, story or play, thus giving it a permanent readable form; and similarly a composer is one who writes down his musical work so that others may play or sing it. The processes of improvisa-

Below: *Richard Wagner (1813-83) seeking inspiration. A painting of the composer at home in the Villa Wahnfried by Gemaelde von Schweninsky.*

tion and composition are basically the same, ie finding a sequence of musical ideas that add up to a satisfying whole.

Undoubtedly part of the mystique about composition lies in the nature of the writing-down process which we call musical notation. This is a kind of 'script' that has grown up over a thousand years. Musicians are as familiar with it as they are with words, but to others a complex musical score means no more than a book in Chinese characters would to most Westerners. Yet the principles of notation are pretty simple. For example, as the notes of a melody rise and fall, they move up and down on the lines and spaces of the five-line system called a stave. Rhythm is indicated by using notes in a different format to show their relative duration; for example, a note with a little hook on its stem (a quaver) will be half the length of one with no hook (a crotchet). There are ways to indicate speed, levels of volume (dynamics), the kind of articulation and tone required and so on. Obviously there is more to notation than this; but it is a language that can be learned, and the composer uses it in such a precise way that a performer or performers can reproduce his music with accuracy. Amazingly, a work for full orchestra and/or chorus such as Bach's *Mass in B minor* or a Mahler symphony can be contained in a 'book' no larger than a paperback.

Notation can be approached in three ways, of rising levels of difficulty. The easiest is to follow a musical score with the eyes as the piece is performed. The next level involves reading and performing simultaneously: easiest for a singer with only one note to read at a time and no need to find it on an instrument, hardest for a keyboard player with up to ten notes at a time for his ten fingers. Hardest of all is the composer's task: to turn the sounds he imagines or reproduces on an instrument such as the piano into a set of instructions for a performer or performers who have only his score for guidance. To learn this skill involves both talent and train-

Above: *Benjamin Britten (1913-76), the foremost British composer of opera in the 20th century at work in his home in Aldeburgh.*

ing; but it can be learned in the end.

However, that is of course not the whole story, and we must now face the daunting concept of inspiration itself. This is the point that puzzles many people most. How does the composer actually *think* of his beautiful melodies, thrilling rhythms, fascinating textures? How does he join ideas together so that they form a satisfying whole? Well, one might argue that a composer makes music naturally, just as birds sing. Perhaps this is evading the issue. But the answer to such a question can never be purely rational. No one can 'explain' beauty in music, any more than we can 'explain' love, or the glory of a sunset, or the freshness of a rose newly in bloom. (A psychologist or a botanist can tell us only facts, not the essentials.) But there are still some useful things to be said. You may see the Taj Mahal by moonlight and be enraptured, and leave it at that: probably that was what the architect (and the emperor who built it in memory of his wife) intended. Nevertheless the architect originally had to devise his plans and choose his materials, creating a framework for what we see only as a finished artefact. Beethoven may have intended us simply to revel in the sounds of his *Pastoral* Symphony, perhaps imagining the idyllic countryside he depicts; indeed, he once said of his music, 'it came from the heart; may it go straight to the heart'. Yet as its creator he had to invent melodies and link them with others that varied the mood; he had to choose the instrumentation so that his orchestra would make sounds evoking a gentle stream, or birdsong, or a storm; he must have thought of contrasts and balances of keys, rhythmic patterns, textures, speeds, dynamics and so on. Music has been called 'architecture in sound', and here Beethoven was of necessity a craftsman as well as an

Michael TIPPETT
(b. 1905)

An erudite English composer of deep social concerns and wide-ranging literary and psychological interests. He tends to use his music as a medium for expressing feelings about the condition of humanity, or for exploring problems of conflict, reconciliation and spiritual growth. His output includes string quartets, piano sonatas, songs, concertos, symphonies and operas, but he is probably best known for the *Concerto for Double String Orchestra*, the oratorio *A Child of Our Time* (a pacifist protest against Nazi tyranny) – these both include the 'blues' harmony of negro spirituals – and the operas *A Midsummer Marriage* and *The Knot Garden*. Sir Michael (he was knighted in 1966) writes his own librettos, and brings a Jungian turn of mind to bear on his characters, who are either mythological or tend to become entangled with myth, in situations loaded with metaphor. His music, which can be tough, includes a powerful lyrical element, while he is inclined to balance the starker side of his compositions, with quotations from popular idioms (the 'blues' in particular and from earlier composers. His 1977 opera *The Ice-Break* plunged into all manner of social and political problems, while his vast ten-movement *The Mask of Time* (1984) depicts the evolution of life on earth, ponders the meaning of existence and the problems posed by man's destructive drives, looks at our growing mastery of the world, and offers some tentative hopes for the future. J.C.

inspired genius. As Benjamin Britten once said, where the one role overlaps with the other is impossible to say.

Finally, a few comments by composers themselves. 'My imagination plays on me as if I were a keyboard' (Haydn). 'You will ask where my ideas come from – I can't say for certain' (Beethoven). 'There's no real creation without hard work . . . [inspiration] is a present' (Brahms). 'The sound of the sea, the curve of the horizon, the wind in the leaves, the cry of a bird . . . issues forth to express itself in the language of music' (Debussy). 'All the inspiration I ever needed was a phonecall from a producer' (Cole Porter). 'About a third of our songs are pure slog' (Paul McCartney). C.H.

Music can do, and be, many things. Consequently it has been described in a variety of ways: the integration of sound and silence, the expression of a human soul, mathematics for the soul, aural architecture, tone painting and so on. The Viennese critic Eduard Hanslick declared simply that 'music means itself'.

Composers too have had different approaches to their art. Very often the titles they choose for their works make this clear at once. Naming a piece 'Prelude in C minor' suggests a different intention than calling it, say, 'Sleigh Ride'. In the one case, we are invited to take the music on its own terms and are only told its key and, since a prelude is usually short, its likely length. In the other, we are presumably expected to link the sounds we hear with all that the title suggests: brisk motion in the open air, a snow-clad scene, a bracing and probably cheerful mood, and perhaps the sound of sleigh bells.

Broadly speaking, the first kind of piece belongs in the category we call abstract or absolute music, whereas the second is programme or pictorial music. Historians often state, or imply, that abstract music belongs principally to the Baroque period, the eighteenth century in which Bach and his contemporaries composed their preludes, fugues, concertos and so on, while programme music belongs to the Romantic era in which Berlioz created his *Fantastic* Symphony with its story of a lover's opium dream and Dukas painted the exciting adventures of *The Sorcerer's Apprentice* let loose among his master's magic books.

But the truth is not so simple, and both kinds of music are found in all periods. The Baroque era produced the first operas, and here the drama itself often meant that the music had to be programmatic, for example depicting birdsong, an earthquake or a storm at sea. (However, we usually reserve the term 'programme music' for works not relying on sung words to convey their meaning.) Vivaldi's *The Four Seasons* concertos for violin belong to this same period and describe in music the pastoral sonnets attached to each of them. And while it is true that early in the nineteenth century Beethoven's *Pastoral* Symphony evokes the Austrian countryside with shepherds, streams, birds and a thunderstorm, as his movement titles tell us, the symphonies he wrote immediately before and after it (Nos 5 and 7) paint no such pictures. A 'programmatic' element in music is often subtle, or minimal: Schumann called one piano piece simply *Why?* and said of his *Spring* Symphony that it was not intended 'to describe or paint anything definite, but I think the season did much to shape the particular form it took'. Elgar wrote much programme music, such as his Shakespearean 'symphonic study' *Falstaff*, but he also stated that it was 'a lower form of art than absolute music'. To complicate the issue further, we may recall a remark of Richard Strauss, him-

Leonard BERNSTEIN
(b. 1918)

A fine conductor and pianist, his talents in these directions have tended, throughout his career to divert his efforts away from composing. Nonetheless he has a respectable output of symphonies and other orchestral works, with his *Chichester Psalms* now a popular classic in the choral field. As a composer he has, like Sullivan and others, experienced a further division of loyalties between the serious world of music and the world of entertainment. Many would consider that it is in the latter field that his greatest talents lie; in works like *Fancy Free, On the Town, Candide*, and especially the highly successful *West Side Story* (1957) which is one of the great classics of the American musical theatre. The only regret is that he has not been able to repeat the success of this work; while so much time has been used in continuing to build an international reputation as a conductor. Bernstein himself has never been certain how best to divide his musical genius. P.G.

Above: *Mozart's autograph score of his Piano Concerto in C minor, K491, composed in Vienna in March, 1786. The first two pages of the 3rd Movt.* allegretto.

Left: *Mozart's autograph score of* 'Das veilchen' ('The Violet'), K476, *a setting of words by Goethe written in Vienna in 1785.*

Right: *Mozart's autograph score of one of Cherubino's arias from* The Marriage of Figaro *which was first performed in Vienna in 1786.*

self a master composer of programme music: 'There's no such thing as abstract music; there's good music and bad. If it's good, it means something, and then it's programme music.'

Perhaps that's going too far, for we can still distinguish between abstract and programme music, just as composers themselves have usually done. And today we value them equally: Bach's *Art of Fugue* and Debussy's *La Mer* have wholly different aims but are both masterpieces. C.H.

The word 'classical' as applied to music is both indispensable and vague. Historians use it to mean the period from about 1750 to 1830, the time of Mozart and Beethoven. Others use it for anything which is not 'popular', in other words what is sometimes for want of a better name (but dully) called 'serious music'. Others again use it for anything that isn't at all recent, and probably still refer to Debussy, who died as long ago as 1918, as 'modern'!

This third kind of usage is common. And if this section is called Classical versus Modern it is because very often the people who think along these lines also use these terms to distinguish what kind of music they like and what kind they do not. Almost always their liking is for the 'classical' style and their aversion is towards so-called modernists. Admittedly, there is an exception to this general rule among the many teenagers who would say they liked only 'modern' music – in other words the pop and rock that is made by contemporaries for immediate consumption – but then they hardly realise that there is any other kind of music or, if they do, regard it as a sort of museum culture without any contemporary relevance.

For both the conservative music-lover and the teenager with no interest in the past, this is an unfortunate division of music according to the labels that they attach to it. Most experienced music-lovers feel that we should try to keep an open mind in our responses, and certainly make these on the basis of what we hear rather than the music's date of composition or any other fact about it. Today those of us who live in the more affluent countries have an enormous amount of music that is easily and cheaply accessible via recordings, radio and video at a very high level of performance and reproduction. What a pity if we close our minds and ears in advance to much that might give us great pleasure and even, to use a phrase of the art historian Bernard Berenson which Benjamin Britten once quoted approvingly, 'enhance our lives'.

In fact there is something in common between the basic conservatisms both of the older listener reluctant to hear something

Above: *The young Mozart with his father Leopold and sister. A watercolour by Carmontelle painted in Paris 1763/4. This, one of three versions, is from the Musée Carnavalet, Paris.*

Right: *An example of the friendly association of the two worlds of music, as the popular singer Frank Sinatra lights the cigar of the renowned pianist Artur Rubinstein.*

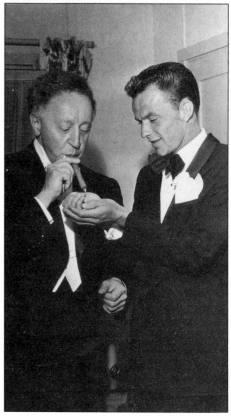

George Bernard SHAW
(1856-1950)

Celebrated Irish playwright who earns his place in any musical reference book. He was a close friend of Elgar, who dedicated the *Severn Suite* to him. His play *Arms and the Man* was taken by Oscar Straus as the basis for the popular operetta *The Chocolate Soldier* in 1894, and more than sixty years later his *Pygmalion* inspired the fabulously successful musical *My Fair Lady*. But most importantly, at the outset of his career, from 1888 to 1894, Shaw wrote brilliant critical columns for the London periodicals *The Star* and *The World* under the pseudonym (until 1890) 'Corno di Bassetto', reprinted many years later as part of the collected edition of his works. Some of his opinions were idiosyncratic to say the least: he once described Schubert's C major Symphony as an 'exasperatingly brainless composition'. But his characteristic prose style and incisive wit could not have presented a sharper contrast to the dull, turgid work of so many of his contemporaries. He was well-informed, made no secret of his prejudices and regarded those who gave less than their best in public performance as his personal enemies. He was an early champion of Wagner's music, and one of the first critics to attempt a political interpretation of the *Ring*. A reference to his musical writings is a sure source of pleasure as well as enlightenment. R.H.

Above: *Two great violinists, Stephane Grappelli from the jazz world and Sir Yehudi Menuhin from the classical world, always enjoyed recording together.*

Below: *Both in classical and popular musical spheres, technology is playing an increasing part. Songwriter Paul McCartney supervises a Wings recording.*

Ralph VAUGHAN WILLIAMS (1872-1958)

A burly Englishman whose creative life spanned an astonishing seventy composing years, from a piano trio at sixteen until death halted work on a three-act opera at eighty-six. Symphonies, concertos, songs, suites, fantasias, operas, rhapsodies, oratorios, quartets, theatre and film music, liturgical works, masques, cantatas and organ pieces all poured from him, as did active participation in English musical life, from teaching composition to editing hymns, from conducting choirs to collecting folk songs. The latter was crucial to RVW's own musical style, which consciously abjured the nineteenth-century German influence that had dominated British music up to and including Elgar. He looked back to Tudor roots and to the surviving folk idioms, and evolved from these a music as unmistakeably English as Dvořák's and Bartók's are Czech and Hungarian. Yet his style is absolutely personal, not in the least 'quainte Olde England', indeed often imbued with a sweeping, visionary quality which seems to encompass yet transcend all influences. His rugged, individual stamp shows, whether it be via the easy tunefulness of *The Wasps* or the ecstatic intensity of the *Tallis Fantasia*, the Fourth Symphony's harshness or the Third's idyllic pastoralism, the lumbering fun of the Tuba Concerto or the icy grandeur of *Sinfonia Antarctica*, the quiet summer haze of *Lark Ascending* or Satan's menacing jabs of sound in *Job*. He is certainly a composer to be reckoned with. J.C.

new and the younger one uninterested in the old. Psychologists seem to agree that we learn our overall responses most willingly and lastingly in the formative years of childhood and young adulthood. The person of forty or more who would gladly pay *not* to hear Black Sabbath playing heavy metal rock music, or for that matter a concert of music by Pierre Boulez, may in part merely be reflecting a generation gap that is just as apparent in music as it is elsewhere. The effort of making what must seem like a radical cultural re-orientation is far too great for someone whose own youthful musical experiences may be linked to school or church choirs, brass bands, or symphony concerts. He or she has

formed musical likes and dislikes at precisely the same stage of development as has been reached today by the teenager belting rock music into his head through earphones. Similarly, a teenager may ask why he should bother listening to Mozart's *Alleluia* or Gounod's *Ave Maria* simply because his teacher thinks he should or even because they are his grandmother's favourite songs.

Yet there is no real need of conflict. The generation gap is not insurmountable. A whole family can together enjoy a Christmas pantomime, or a football match, or a public occasion such as a royal wedding. An elderly person may laugh along with a young one at the latest TV situation comedy. Everything we

enjoy in music, including our oldest favourites, was new – even 'modern' – to us once. But we do not have to be slaves to time and fashion (who dresses in the style of thirty or forty years ago?) either by clinging to *or* by repudiating the past. With a little effort we can open our minds and hearts to different kinds of music: liking one kind doesn't push out another. That is not to say that every piece and style will be equally rewarding. Of course not: some we will reasonably dislike. But there is good and bad music of many kinds, classical and modern, and we should be willing to listen and widen our tastes, remembering that the greatest effort can bring the greatest reward. C.H.

Twenty years ago, we would have been safe in saying that most references to 'music' meant Western music and nothing beyond: even dictionaries of music largely ignored non-Western styles. Today our horizons are wider, as instant worldwide communication makes the music of all countries accessible.

But the term 'Western' was useful. By it we could understand a culture – musical and otherwise – that derived from the customs, languages and learning of a continent which had inherited philosophy from the Greeks and laws (as well as roads and languages) from the Romans, and which was also to some extent united by Christianity. This culture varied according to place but was always identifiable. It had spread outwards to North America with the Pilgrim Fathers and others, to the southern part of Africa, to Australasia and so on; but wherever it might now be found geographically it was still recognisably of the West.

Yet as so often happens, the facts of the matter prove on closer examination to be less simple. Tracing the origins of what we call Western civilization back beyond Greece and Rome takes us to such places as Mesopotamia (now Iraq) in South-West Asia and Egypt in North Africa. The Jewish faith into which Christianity was born had its roots in such places as these. It also seems that one

of the first Greek music theorists, Pythagoras, studied in both of them. Even our shared Indo-European languages, which include not only European tongues as different as Welsh and Russian but also Indian ones such as Hindi, are now recognised as belonging to a vast family with Sanskrit and Hittite among its oldest members.

Of course this does not mean that these languages are mutually comprehensible; but scholars see countless common features and even words – thus the Russian word *dom* for 'house' is related to our 'domestic'. The situation is rather similar in music. Even the words for some instruments remind us of this: compare the Indian sitar, the Greek *kithara* and the German zither with our 'guitar', all plucked string instruments, or the Arabic *al 'ūd* with our 'lute'.

But deep down links are less obvious than immediate differences. An Indian *rāga* played by sitar and tablā (drum) is evidently miles away in its style and the nature of its appeal from a Beethoven symphony or Chopin nocturne, and it does not take a scholar to tell us that a Tibetan wedding hymn would sound distinctly out of place at a wedding in Glasgow or Paris.

Yet the links between East and West in music are worth remembering. Like any other scientific laws, the basic principles of acoustics apply to all music. As Pythagoras stated over two thousand years ago, the notes obtained by dividing a vibrating string (or pipe) into half its length (which gives the octave), a third, a quarter and so on give a 'harmonic series' of ascending notes spelling out the major chord, with the fundamental starting note as its 'keynote' or chief resting place. Though Indian, Chinese and Western

Below: *A wall-painting, dating from around 1400 BC, which portrays musicians and dancers from Thebes playing and performing in the manner of the times.*

Left: *The best-known Indian musician in the West, through his many concert and television appearances, is Ravi Shankar, skilled player of the sitar.*

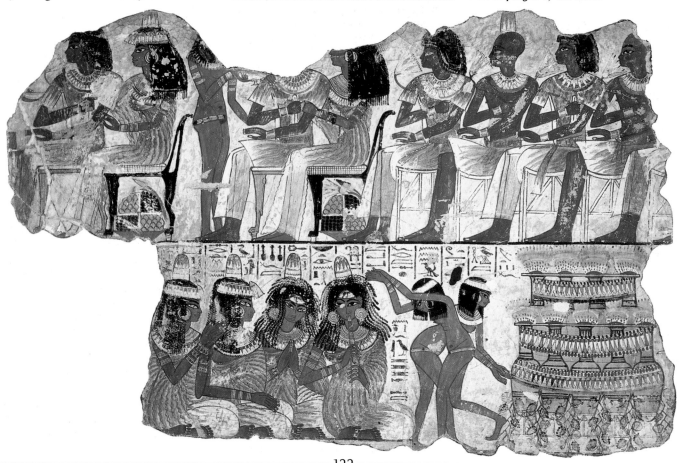

scales may differ in their division of the octave, the octave and the idea of a keynote are common to both: indeed the Indian sitar has a keynote 'drone' built into it just like the Scottish bagpipe. The second interval of the harmonic series is a fifth, and the Chinese found that a sequence of notes a fifth apart – say C, G, D, A, E – placed together within an octave gave the five-note (pentatonic) scale which is the basis of their music: C, D, E, G and A. And because this applies everywhere, we find exactly this same 'Chinese' scale as the basis of many Scottish folksongs such as 'Coming through the rye' and 'Over the sea to Skye'. The British historian Dr Charles Burney noted this as long ago as 1789 when he wrote: 'The Chinese scale, take it which way we will, is certainly very Scottish.'

So much for resemblances. But one fundamental difference between much Eastern music and our Western variety lies in its form or structure. This is perhaps best explained by saying that whereas a Western piece normally goes through contrasting events or themes in a kind of planned sequence, an Eastern one may be a continuous though evolving meditation on one single musical idea. The one kind of music is narrative, the other contemplative – or if you like, dynamic as opposed to static. Beyond this, the Eastern musician improvises instead of playing from a set score provided by a composer. Each Indian rāga has its basic style of melody and rhythm, but the sitar player will treat it in his own way; it will not be written down, and every 'performance' will be a different treatment, a new exploration from the same starting point. It is clear therefore that this music can only be for one main performer, perhaps with a supporting ('following') instrument or instruments: the big forces of a Western symphony orchestra or chorus are impossible when the music proceeds according to the free and spontaneous invention of a single musician. The nearest parallel to this in Western music is the way in which a jazz musician can improvise a solo while his colleagues follow him, but even here there is usually prior agreement about the sequence of harmonies.

One notable exception to the Eastern practice of improvisation is found in the *gamelan* orchestras of South-East Asia, notably Bali and Java in Indonesia. Here groups of musicians directed by a drummer play music that has been pre-composed and carefully memorised. The most prominent instruments are metallophones or gong-chimes (tuned percussion): their music is dazzling, hypnotic and, once heard, unforgettable. Instrumental ensembles are found also in other countries such as Thailand, Vietnam and Malaysia. They can feature in theatre shows, courtly ceremonies, dances or religious rituals.

In much of this music, particularly in the more popular kinds, there may be a role for the human voice. The ranges for men and

Above: *Rejoicings at the birth of Salim, son of the Mughal Emperor Akbar at Fathpur Sikri in 1569. Original drawing by Kesu Kalan (c.1590), painted by Dharmdas.*

Below: *A highlight of Burmese village life is the touring puppet show given in the open air to the accompaniment of gongs, drums and cymbals.*

Olivier MESSIAEN
(b. 1908)

French composer, organist and influential teacher who combines his deep Catholic faith with a passionate interest in birdsong and a fascination with folk music, exotic instruments, Hindu rhythms and oriental percussion, all of which play important parts in his music. Apart from a period as a prisoner in World War II (when he composed *Quartet for the End of Time*, his only important chamber work), Messiaen has spent most of his life in Paris, teaching and playing the organ, and producing a series of idiosyncratic and often very lengthy compositions which serve his religion and express his feelings about love and nature. His works include orchestral, vocal, organ and piano music, and employ complex rhythmic patterns, polytonality, rare sonorities, odd chordal progressions, and frequently very slow tempi, which can create difficulties for unaccustomed listeners. He is most well known for the massive *Turangalîla* Symphony of 1948, which augments the traditional orchestra with a vast array of percussion, four keyboard instruments, and an electronic device known as the Ondes Martenot. The latter also appears in his *Three Small Liturgies of the Divine Presence*, which caused a sensation in 1945 with its celesta, vibraphone, maracas, Chinese cymbals, gong, piano, strings and a unison soprano choir. His organ music is notable for a radical use of contrasted registrations, while his religious works tend to be accompanied by didactic essays explaining how theology and musical structure are interlinked. J.C.

women in Eastern countries are much the same as in the West, but the style of singing – tone quality, vibration or fluctuating pitch, types of ornamentation and so on – usually differs widely from what we regard as normal. But Westerners too have very widely differing styles. Compare, for instance, an American country singer with an Italian tenor or an English cathedral choirboy – and a little perseverance can convince us that an unfamiliar vocal style is right for the special kind of music to which it is allied. Here as elsewhere, a little open-minded familiarity will often bring respect, understanding, appreciation and finally, hopefully, affection for different kinds of music. C.H.

The British composer Vaughan Williams declared that 'the art of music above all other arts is the expression of the soul of a nation'. Certainly his own music can suggest a peaceful English landscape or the bustle of early twentieth-century London, just as the rugged grandeur of Sibelius seems to belong to Finland and the warm sensuality of Falla to Spain. We know too that each country's folksongs have characteristics derived from its language, and since a composer's style may reflect his 'folk' background a national flavour may be strong even in his symphonies and other concert works. The Czech composer Janáček believed that all music grew from 'the melody and rhythm of spoken language'.

Yet this is not the whole story. A lullaby or a march will always remain recognisable as such, for such pieces convey basic moods and rhythms common to us all and so easily cross national boundaries. So do musicians themselves, as the term 'wandering minstrel' reminds us, and they can adapt to new lands and cultures. Handel, a German by birth, wrote Italian operas before writing that most English of sacred works, *Messiah*. Beethoven and Brahms were German but chose to live in the Austrian capital Vienna, as the Pole Chopin [p.163] settled in Paris and the Hungarian Liszt [p.177] in Weimar and then Rome. Rachmaninov [p.59], Schoenberg [p.207], Bartók [p.157] and Stravinsky [p.77] all left Europe to live in the United States.

Many of the origins of what we call classical music can be traced back to one single supra-national source. The Christian Church had its centre in Rome and an ordered musical style that a medieval pilgrim could hear wherever he went. This was plainchant, unison singing used for psalms and some other parts of a service. On the other hand, every country had its own kind of folk songs and dances provided by minstrels ranging from humble entertainers to courtly French troubadours and German *Minnesinger*.

Little by little both church and secular music (whether of court or countryside) became more elaborate, as Europe moved into the intellectual flourishing that became known as the Rennaissance. Musicians went wherever their work called them: thus in the fifteenth century the Englishman John Dunstable worked in France while the Frenchmen Guillaume Dufay and Josquin Desprez were in Italy. Their style was still acceptable everywhere. But with the Reformation in the sixteenth century, the situation changed. Differing musical aims arose in church music because the Protestant spirit of Northern Europe required a plainer kind of worship. In Britain, Byrd contributed to both kinds of sacred music with success, his music to English texts showing a fresh national spirit that existed also in politics.

The new styles themselves spread everywhere that men and ideas could go, and sometimes by means of printed scores.

Above: *Painting 'Flute Concerto at Sans Souci' by Adolf von Menzel. C.P.E. Bach is at the harpsichord accompanying amateur flautist Frederick the Great.*

English composers such as Byrd and Morley learned the vocal madrigal style from Italy, just as Purcell later learned that of the instrumental sonata, but they made them their own. Italy was a major source of secular music, as it had been of sacred, as the very words sonata, concerto and opera (all Italian) remind us; and yet Purcell's *Dido and Aeneas*, written for a London girls' school in 1689, is English in feeling, and not just because of its English libretto. By the start of the Baroque era around 1600, it seems that each country had found its own musical voice, whatever the forms and media used.

GERMANY AND AUSTRIA

In 1700, Bach and Handel reached the age of fifteen. It is for his instrumental works, Passions and church cantatas that Bach is renowned, while Handel excelled as a composer of opera and oratorio.

Bach [p.183] was one of a family of musicians and soon learned to play the organ, harpsichord, clavichord and violin. He served court and church employers, and his music covers every field except opera. His cantatas written for the Lutheran church service amount to about two hundred, and he also contributed greatly to the organ repertory. His '48' Preludes and Fugues for harpsichord or clavichord demonstrate the equal temperament system of keyboard tuning that made all twenty-four major and minor keys available. His keyboard suites, incorporating dances of his time such as the allemande, minuet, sarabande and gigue, are models of their kind, as are his concertos. Two late ensemble works are his *Musical Offering* and *Art of Fugue*: here we may

salute a master of polyphony and structure.

As we have already noted, Handel's [p.185] career developed on different lines. At nineteen he composed an Italian opera for the theatre at Hamburg, and he followed this with operatic successes in Italy. When approaching thirty, he settled in England (1712) and became a successful composer of Italian opera. He also composed instrumental suites, orchestral *concerti grossi* and the ceremonial *Water Music* and *Fireworks Music*. Eventually he turned from opera to oratorio, and when *Messiah* was first heard in 1742 it was hailed as a masterpiece.

If Bach and Handel differently represent the rich yet formal Baroque style, a change to yet others is summed up in the work of Telemann and Bach's son C.P.E. Bach. Telemann [p.17] wrote forty-four Passion settings to Bach's three, as well as forty operas and much else. But his humour, fantasy and charm brings us into the lighter world of Rococo style which gradually displaced Baroque dignities: he could be entertaining and charming as in his *Music for the Table* and his cantatas on the seasons, country life and a 'sweet-singing canary'. C.P.E. Bach, on the other hand, extended the language that he inherited from his father towards a more subjective and dramatic kind of expression which was to lead to Romanticism. This 'storm and stress' style is exemplified in his sonatas and symphonies, and he also moved away from polyphony towards a 'melody plus harmony' layout. He was a progressive who strongly influenced his successors Haydn and Mozart; Haydn said that he owed him all he knew. But the truest inheritor of his style was Beethoven, whose work was to change the course of European music by the nature of its emotional content.

The year 1750 is a turning point in the story of German-Austrian music. J.S. Bach died, and an Austrian musician of eighteen called Haydn [p.43] was just beginning to

Johann STRAUSS
(1825-99)

Son of the famous Johann Strauss (1804-49) who, with Josef Lanner (1801-43), set the popular Viennese waltz on its way, Johann II was not encouraged to follow in the family footsteps, but eventually he did, took over the family orchestra and earned himself the title of 'The Waltz King' with such immortal works as 'The Blue Danube', 'Tales from the Vienna Woods', 'Voices of Spring', 'Wine, Women and Song', 'Vienna Blood' and 'Roses from the South'. Besides these there were dance works in every form, sparkling polkas, lively marches and galops, quadrilles, all from a prolific and continually inspired pen that brought him world fame and a demand for his conducting services all over the globe. Such music was destined to add its sparkle to the world of operetta and, following the inspiration of Offenbach's works which had become very popular in Vienna, Strauss, after several attempts, produced perhaps the greatest of all Viennese operettas, *Die Fledermaus*, in 1874, followed by the almost equally fine *Der Zigeunerbaron* in 1885. P.G.

make his way in the world. He fully used what he learned from C.P.E. Bach in the burgeoning forms of the sonata, string quartet and symphony. In fact he is often called the 'father of the symphony', for his works in this form – over one hundred – gave it a permanent stature. He also wrote operas to Italian and German words for the theatre at Eszterház where he served a noble family for thirty years, and much sacred music, crowning his long career with the two oratorios *The Creation* and *The Seasons*.

Mozart [p.47] was born a generation after Haydn and also composed much for the Catholic Church; but later in life his chief spiritual interest was in Freemasonry, reflected in the symbolism of his opera *The Magic Flute*. Despite the age difference, these two composers were friends. Haydn called Mozart 'the greatest composer I know, either personally or by repute', and he is certainly a supreme example of natural musical genius. Although he died at thirty-five, he used all the forms and media of his time with

Above: *A portrait of Ludwig van Beethoven (born 1770, died 1827) at work on his* Missa solemnis *from a painting by Josef Stieler in 1819.*

no lapses of craftsmanship and few of inspiration: even the works he composed for glass harmonica and a mechanical organ in a clock are masterpieces. He called his six string quartets dedicated to Haydn 'the fruits of long and laborious endeavour', but they have a typically Mozartean art that conceals art. The last three of his forty-one symphonies and his *Requiem* are among other major works. A fine keyboard player, he composed piano sonatas and other solo pieces as well as a series of piano concertos that set a model for the kind of structured dialogue, elegant and dramatic by turns, that has since been an accepted model. His operas are to both German texts (e.g. *The Seraglio* and *The Magic Flute*) and Italian (*The Marriage of Figaro* and *Don Giovanni*). Here we feel his sympathy with a wide range of characters (not

even the philandering Don Giovanni is hateful) and recognise his genius for writing for the human voice, whether in a solo aria or in ensemble.

Mozart was successful in music but not in his life, which ended in anxieties, poverty and the overwork which probably killed him. Yet normally a musician's life during the eighteenth century was fairly assured, for both the church and the nobility needed his art, the one for worship and the other for ceremonial or entertainment. Bach and Haydn were employed in this way; but Mozart seems to have been quite unable to secure a steady and adequate income. However, Beethoven [p.45], the greatest figure of the next generation, succeeded where Mozart had failed by assuring for himself the support of wealthy patrons who would provide him with lodging and funds and subsidise the publication of his music without ever seeking to assume the employer's role that he would have repudiated. He was a contemporary and supporter of the social changes symbolised by the French Revolution, and his music takes us into the nineteenth century by virtue of its intense vitality and force of personality. Here, we feel, is no longer the universal message sought by the devout Bach but the direct and purposeful expression of one proud man's view of the world. His music has many different facets which all self-evidently belong to the one creative spirit, symbolised by such achievements as the *Moonlight* and *Appassionata* Sonatas for piano, the heroic rescue opera *Fidelio*, the profound last string quartets, the choral *Missa solemnis* and the symphonies culminating in the *Choral* Ninth. Beethoven was a difficult person even in his youth – Goethe called him 'undomesticated' – and he became even more isolated from his fellow human beings by deafness. But 'God has never deserted me', he wrote in the *Missa solemnis* score, and his message to humanity, as the finale of the Ninth Symphony has it, was 'Be embraced, ye millions'. He told a friend that there was 'no higher mission than to come closer than others to the Divine and to spread the divine rays among men'.

Schubert [p.187] was born a generation after Beethoven, but only outlived him by a year. This Viennese schoolmaster's son wrote nine symphonies, over six hundred songs, church music, chamber and piano music and much else. But it is perhaps above all for his later symphonies, chamber works such as the *Trout* Quintet and C major String Quartet, and his melodious yet deeply expressive songs that he is best remembered and loved. There was a warm, even sentimental, side to

Below: Schubert enjoying party games with a group of friends at Atzenburg. Aquarelle by Leopold Kupelweiser (1796-1862) painted in 1821.

this artist that endears his music to many; yet there are also darker shadows, as in the *Death and the Maiden* String Quartet and the *Unfinished* Symphony – not his last, incidentally, that being the 'Great' C major. Schubert also wrote operas, but they await revival.

After these two men, German-Austrian music went in two main ways, and it is a tribute to Beethoven's genius that the followers of both thought that they were following in his footsteps. A broadly conservative school of thought represented by Mendelssohn and Brahms saw the sonata and symphony as forms still valid and alive, but a New German School with Wagner as its figurehead took Beethoven's programmatic *Pastoral* Symphony and the *Choral* Ninth to point towards music dramas.

But before this, German opera became fully established with the work of Weber [p.105]. His *Der Freischütz* (1821) set the tone with a story set among ordinary village people and having a mixture of love interest, hunting, a shooting competition and the supernatural. This was far removed from older operatic plots and more to the taste of nineteenth-century audiences. His later operas *Euryanthe* and *Oberon* also touch on the magical and in this respect Wagner owed him much.

Mendelssohn [p.57] was a child prodigy with much ability and charm. Few composers save Mozart can match his youthful achievement in, for example, his String Octet and *A Midsummer Night's Dream* Overture, both written before he was eighteen. He went on to write five symphonies, the piano *Songs without Words*, the oratorio *Elijah* (for Birmingham) and much else. His *Hebrides* Overture and *Scottish* Symphony remind us of his lik-

Below: Portrait of the composer Felix Mendelssohn-Bartholdy (1809-47) at the age of twelve in the childish garb he was soon to abandon as he became famous.

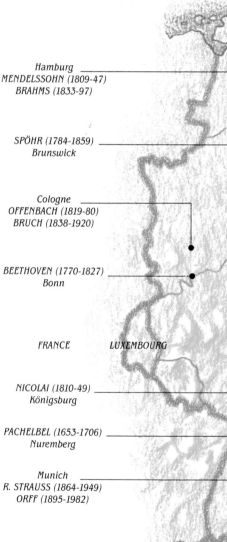

Hamburg
MENDELSSOHN (1809-47)
BRAHMS (1833-97)

SPÖHR (1784-1859)
Brunswick

Cologne
OFFENBACH (1819-80)
BRUCH (1838-1920)

BEETHOVEN (1770-1827)
Bonn

FRANCE   LUXEMBOURG

NICOLAI (1810-49)
Königsburg

PACHELBEL (1653-1706)
Nuremberg

Munich
R. STRAUSS (1864-1949)
ORFF (1895-1982)

Geneva
BLOCH (1880-1959)
MARTIN (1890-1974)

SWITZERLAND

ing for Britain, an affection that was warmly reciprocated. He also revived Bach's music and directed a Conservatory at Leipzig. The craftsmanship and geniality of his music always give pleasure, though it may be that in comparison with some other composers there is also a certain blandness.

Schumann [p.189] admired Mendelssohn but was a less stable character. His marriage to the pianist Clara Wieck was bitterly opposed by her father, and though it was happy his career was less successful; finally he attempted suicide and died in an institution. His early music is all for piano, and in it he aimed to express his varied emotional experiences. There is an attractive element of fantasy and occasional eccentricity in his music that is lacking in the more sober Mendelssohn. Such piano works as his *Carnival, Scenes from Childhood* and *Fantasy* bubble over with feeling. As a song composer too he wrote with great imagination and sympathy for his text. He founded a music journal in which he saluted the talents of, among others, the young Brahms and Chopin. He left four symphonies, much chamber music, an opera called *Genoveva* and a fine Piano Concerto.

Below: *Outline map of Germany and Austria showing the birthplaces of famous composers within the present boundaries of those countries.*

Antonin DVOŘÁK (1841-1904)

Greatest of the Czech composers, he brought to fruition the nationalism pioneered by Smetana, combining a natural feel for pastoral idioms, a Schubert-like gift of melody, and remarkable powers of musical organisation. Son of an innkeeper-cum-butcher, by 1866 he was an orchestral viola player and had already composed several chamber works, two symphonies, a Mass, a cello concerto, and a set of love songs. He received an Austrian prize for his third symphony in 1874, then again for some duets, which led him to meet Brahms, for whose friendship and help Dvořák remained for ever grateful. He was soon a huge success, receiving particularly strong support in England, and later in America during an extremely productive three-year stay which gave rise to the *New World* Symphony, the great B minor Cello Concerto, and the *American* String Quartet. Some of his naïve geniality seems to underlie the music, much of which remains as popular as ever, whether it be the later symphonies or the *Dumky trio*, a few of the fifteen string quartets or the colourful *Carnival Overture*, his *Slavonic Rhapsodies* or the *Serenade for Strings*, or even *Rusalka*, an opera with great child-appeal. J.C.

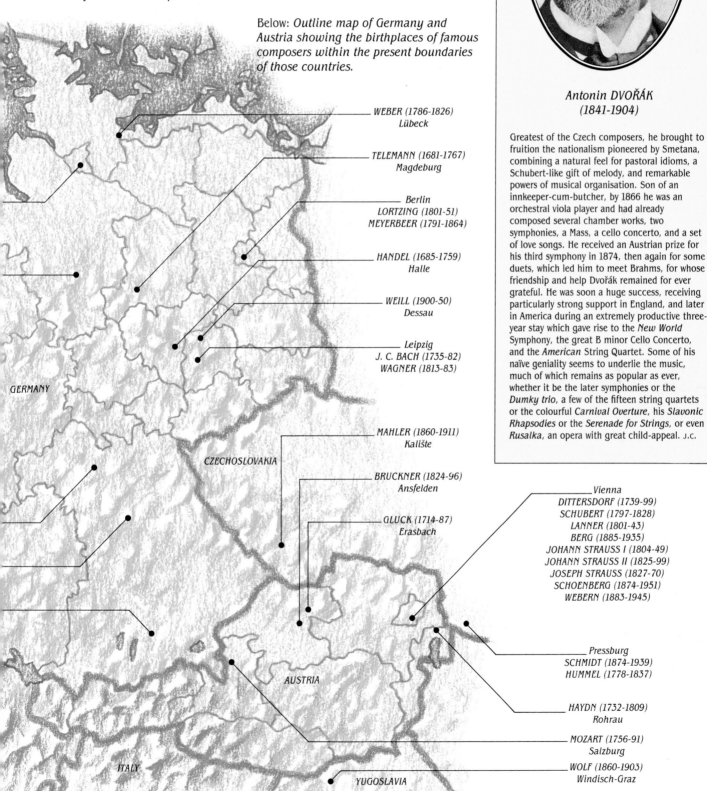

WEBER (1786-1826)
Lübeck

TELEMANN (1681-1767)
Magdeburg

Berlin
LORTZING (1801-51)
MEYERBEER (1791-1864)

HANDEL (1685-1759)
Halle

WEILL (1900-50)
Dessau

Leipzig
J. C. BACH (1735-82)
WAGNER (1813-83)

GERMANY

MAHLER (1860-1911)
Kalište

CZECHOSLOVAKIA

BRUCKNER (1824-96)
Ansfelden

GLUCK (1714-87)
Erasbach

Vienna
DITTERSDORF (1739-99)
SCHUBERT (1797-1828)
LANNER (1801-43)
BERG (1885-1935)
JOHANN STRAUSS I (1804-49)
JOHANN STRAUSS II (1825-99)
JOSEPH STRAUSS (1827-70)
SCHOENBERG (1874-1951)
WEBERN (1883-1945)

AUSTRIA

Pressburg
SCHMIDT (1874-1939)
HUMMEL (1778-1837)

HAYDN (1732-1809)
Rohrau

MOZART (1756-91)
Salzburg

WOLF (1860-1903)
Windisch-Graz

ITALY

YUGOSLAVIA

Brahms [p.27] was Schumann's protégé and was caught up in the events of his decline. A fine pianist, he wrote powerful and passionate music in his youth, becoming more sombre and autumnal later. He was in his forties when he produced his First Symphony, following this fairly quickly with three more. He also wrote in the other classical forms of sonata, quartet and concerto, contributing fine examples to each. Among his other music are many songs and a *German Requiem*.

All these composers found their audience in a reasonably prosperous middle class. However, against the trend in this as in much else, Wagner [p.109] discovered his own greatest supporter in a monarch, King Ludwig of Bavaria, who had the enthusiasm and resources to make possible the building of the Bayreuth opera house that remains the Mecca of Wagnerians.

Wagner was wholly a man of the theatre, who gained wide experience in a variety of posts before producing a series of masterpieces from *The Flying Dutchman* to *Parsifal*; to mention only two others of his music dramas, *Tristan and Isolde* and *The Mastersingers*, is to realise the range of his musical vision. Wagner's ideal of a 'unified art work' that was to point the way to the future has never been as fruitful as he hoped. But his rich musical language and the profound psychological resonances of his music dramas ensure them a unique place in history.

But if Wagner represents the New German School which saw the symphony and sonata as outdated, we have seen that this was not so for all his contemporaries and even for later composers. Thus, Bruckner [p.29] and Mahler [p.23], who both greatly admired Wagner, devoted much of their creative gifts to composing symphonies. Bruckner's often have an epic quality, while some of Mahler's incorporate the voice and his Eighth uses large vocal forces to staggering effect. Mahler's music can be as epic as that of Bruckner,

Above: *A cover of the song by Richard Strauss (1864-1949), entitled* 'Heimkehr' *('Homeward'), Op. 15, No. 5, published in Leipzig c.1885.*

Below: *Scene from Kurt Weill's* The Threepenny Opera, *directed by Colin Graham, in a 1976 production by the short-lived English Music Theatre.*

as in that work, or quietly intimate and even childlike, as in his *Wunderhorn* songs and parts of the First, Third and Fourth Symphonies. Yet there is often a tension and unease, and we may note that he once consulted the psychologist Freud. He said 'My time will come', and rightly: for he has never been as popular as he is today, particularly with young listeners.

Richard Strauss [p.65] was another who idolised Wagner, but he followed him more closely. His symphonic poems (including *Don Juan* and *Also sprach Zarathustra*) and his operas (among which are *Salome, Elektra* and *Der Rosenkavalier*) owe much to Wagner in their instrumentation and evocation of atmosphere. Strauss lived right on through Nazism and World War II, and though his operas betray no sign of the times, such late works as the *Metamorphosen* for strings and the *Four Last Songs* with orchestra seem to bid a tender farewell to a vanished age. Another composer of the same generation was Hugo Wolf [p.191], who died young but left a large body of songs whose psychological insight make them especially valuable. They may be less melodious than Schubert's but they compensate for this by their acute sensitivity to every verbal nuance and an outstanding sense of mood and character.

The next leading figures of the German-speaking world are Schoenberg and his pupils Berg and Webern. Schoenberg [p.207] began as a late Romantic akin to Mahler but went on to an intensity of expression and an extremity of language that suspends the traditional key system. In the 1920s he finally devised the method called serialism which ordered notes in a new way altogether. Such uncompromising works as his Five Piano Pieces, Op.23, Wind Quintet and Violin Concerto often met with bitter opposition, but no one doubted his courage and a later slight mellowing of style won over some former detractors. For many people, his unfinished opera *Moses and Aron* is his masterpiece. Berg [p.209] composed the operas *Wozzeck* and *Lulu*, and is more approachable, not least in his Violin Concerto and songs: Webern [p.211], on the other hand, is elusive, writing music of great finesse but forbidding concentration.

The political events of the 1930s had a profound effect on German-Austrian music. Arnold Schoenberg left for the United States, and so did younger men such as Hindemith and Weill. Hindemith turned from an early avant-gardism towards a lofty view of art exemplified by his opera *Mathis der Maler*, from which he also made a symphony, and his song cycle *Marienleben*. Kurt Weill wrote the vivid *Threepenny Opera* and the infamous *Rise and Fall of the City of Mahagonny* (which was given a lively reception at its first performance) with Brecht in the 1920s. Later, in the United States of America, he provided music for a number of successful Broadway shows.

*Domenico SCARLATTI
(1685-1757)*

Member of a musically prolific Italian family, whose father Alessandro played a vital role in the development of opera, Domenico was to become equally important in the history of keyboard music. Born in Naples (in the same year as Bach and Handel) he studied at first with his father, and for a while seemed set to become an opera composer himself. But in the course of moving between noble and ecclesiastical patrons in various Italian cities, periods serving at the Portuguese and Spanish courts, and two years as an opera harpsichordist in London, his pre-eminence at the keyboard became apparent. He once took part in a contest with Handel, whose superiority at the organ was conceded, but whom he equalled at the harpsichord. He wrote over 550 pieces for this instrument, grouped under the modest title of 'exercises' (actually *Essercizi*, from his prolonged Spanish sojourns), but really proto-sonatas of very forward-looking construction. He introduced a new freedom of style, paralleled by innovatory playing techniques such as crossed hands, which opened a fresh expressive world for the instrument which was to dominate drawing-rooms until the pianoforte finally took over. J.C.

Above: *The German composer Paul Hindemith (1895-1963) was also a teacher and, from 1946 onwards, very active as a conductor in Europe.*

Above: *An anonymous 16th-century painting of pioneer Italian composer Giovanni Pierluigi of Palestrina, always known by the name of his birthplace.*

It may be because of World War II that there are no major German-Austrian figures from the next generation. Soon after the war, Hans Werner Henze (b. 1926) began to make a name for himself, chiefly in opera, but his radical politics then led him away from a cultivated style to work in an advanced and sometimes shocking idiom and to leave Germany. Henze is among many composers today who have turned at times to the old forms of opera, concerto and symphony but find something new and disturbing to say within them.

Possibly the most exciting German figure today is Karlheinz Stockhausen. He was initially a composer of the advanced avant-garde, working in a complex serial idiom that baffled and antagonised the ordinary music-lover. But such works have gradually given way to a more directly appealing kind, relating to a kind of visionary mysticism: *Mantra, Stimmung* and the opera *Donnerstag aus Licht* (1981) show this progress. In Stockhausen's own text, the angel-hero of *Donnerstag* finally declares: 'I have fallen in love eternally with Mankind, with this Earth and her children.'

Any attempt to sum up the overall character of German-Austrian music must involve generalities, but perhaps we can note that Germany has given us fine intellectual achievements such as Bach's polyphony and the closely argued form of the fugue. On the other hand a work such as Mozart's orches-

tral serenade *Eine kleine Nachtmusik* represents the elegant poise of Classicism already turning towards the prettiness of Rococo style. The contrast here is such as we may find between a sober North German church and a prettily decorated Austrian one. The powerfully self-expressive aspect of the German personality was firmly controlled in Bach's time, but came to the fore in the nineteenth century and is perhaps symbolised in Beethoven's genius, that of Wagner and possibly most recently in that of Stockhausen. C.H.

ITALY

Italian music has always favoured melody, a fact which is most obvious in songs and other vocal forms such as opera, but is also evident in the melodious instrumental writing of Vivaldi in his violin concertos. Operas and concertos belong to Baroque times, but the first major names in Italian music are those of the Renaissance composers Palestrina and Victoria, the latter Spanish by birth, who wrote sacred choral music in Rome during the sixteenth century. At the same time secular pieces called madrigals were composed by Palestrina and others including Andrea Gabrieli, Gesualdo, Marenzio and Monteverdi. Madrigals were written for a small group of unaccompanied voices and often were about love or happiness.

The expressive character of madrigals, together with a wish to revive ancient traditions

of musical drama, provided a starting point for opera, which emerged in Florence around 1600. (Though already discussed in Part Two of this book, it appears again here since it is so central to Italian music.) Monteverdi's *Orfeo* in 1607 is the first major operatic landmark, a work that tells the Orpheus and Eurydice legend in expressive vocal declamation (recitative) and melodious arias. The singers are supported by an orchestra of strings, wind and keyboard instruments which also plays alone in some sections such as the overture, and such writing was in turn made possible by Italian skills in making and playing instruments. Monteverdi [p.81] went on to write several more operas, culminating in his *Coronation of Poppea*, a sophisticated tale of intrigue set in Nero's Rome.

Besides other church music – settings of the Mass, polyphonic motets and so on – Italy now also had a sacred equivalent of opera in the oratorio, in which singers took various roles but did not wear costumes or move about a stage. In the oratorios of Carissimi there was also a chorus who could be actors (for example, victorious Israelites or guests at a feast) or simply comment on the action.

Comedy, absent from the earliest operas, was soon cultivated in Rome and established a trend towards the *opera buffa* style. This was lighter and more topical than the *opera seria* with its gods and historical personages, and it suited the audiences in new public opera houses that opened first in the wealthy city of Venice, which had twelve by the end of the century. Here such men as Cavalli (Monteverdi's pupil) and Cesti could succeed with tuneful and spectacular productions. Cesti's *Il Pomo d'oro* (1667), actually written for the Viennese court, had a large orchestra, dancing and lavish sets calculated to impress a distinguished audience.

Instrumental music flourished above all with the instruments of the violin family whose makers included such names as the Amati family, da Salò and finally Antonio Stradivari. There were chamber sonatas for violin with accompaniment and 'trio sonatas' for two violins, string bass and keyboard. In the orchestral field there were concertos ranging from solo pieces for one instrument and orchestra to *concerti grossi* in which two groups of players were juxtaposed. Solo concertos usually had three movements, as they do today, but *concerti grossi* might have four or more. The names of Vivaldi [p.11] and Corelli [p.19] stand out in these two forms, and between them they had a profound influence on the German composers Bach and Handel.

This last fact is symbolic of a historical trend. For while German-Austrian composers learned much about instrumental writing from the Italians and then went on to lead the way in this field, Italian music came to centre increasingly on opera and other vocal forms. During the eighteenth century – except in the case of Mozart, who was at home in every form – the main streams of musical creation divided.

Most singers in early Italian operas were men, since women were banned from the stage. Men whose treble voices were preserved by surgery took women's roles and often those of men too – Monteverdi's Nero among them. During the eighteenth century the best of these *castrati* (like Farinelli and Nicolini) were fine actors with brilliant voices which they could also use with subtlety. They achieved great renown, and opera composers welcomed their ability to embellish music with ornaments and runs. But as the appearance of women on stage became acceptable, they were eventually superseded.

The art of singing came increasingly to dominate opera. Plots were often set by several composers and were so well known that they became unimportant, and the quality of music itself gave way to audience

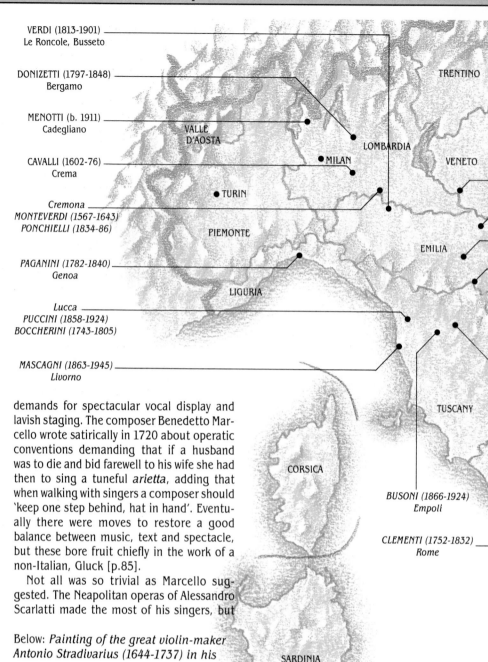

VERDI (1813-1901)
Le Roncole, Busseto

DONIZETTI (1797-1848)
Bergamo

MENOTTI (b. 1911)
Cadegliano

CAVALLI (1602-76)
Crema

Cremona
MONTEVERDI (1567-1643)
PONCHIELLI (1834-86)

PAGANINI (1782-1840)
Genoa

Lucca
PUCCINI (1858-1924)
BOCCHERINI (1743-1805)

MASCAGNI (1863-1945)
Livorno

VALLE D'AOSTA
LOMBARDIA
MILAN
TRENTINO
VENETO
TURIN
PIEMONTE
EMILIA
LIGURIA
TUSCANY
CORSICA
BUSONI (1866-1924)
Empoli
CLEMENTI (1752-1832)
Rome
SARDINIA

demands for spectacular vocal display and lavish staging. The composer Benedetto Marcello wrote satirically in 1720 about operatic conventions demanding that if a husband was to die and bid farewell to his wife she had then to sing a tuneful *arietta*, adding that when walking with singers a composer should 'keep one step behind, hat in hand'. Eventually there were moves to restore a good balance between music, text and spectacle, but these bore fruit chiefly in the work of a non-Italian, Gluck [p.85].

Not all was so trivial as Marcello suggested. The Neapolitan operas of Alessandro Scarlatti made the most of his singers, but

Below: *Painting of the great violin-maker Antonio Stradivarius (1644-1737) in his workshop at Cremona, by Edgar Bundy (1862-1922).*

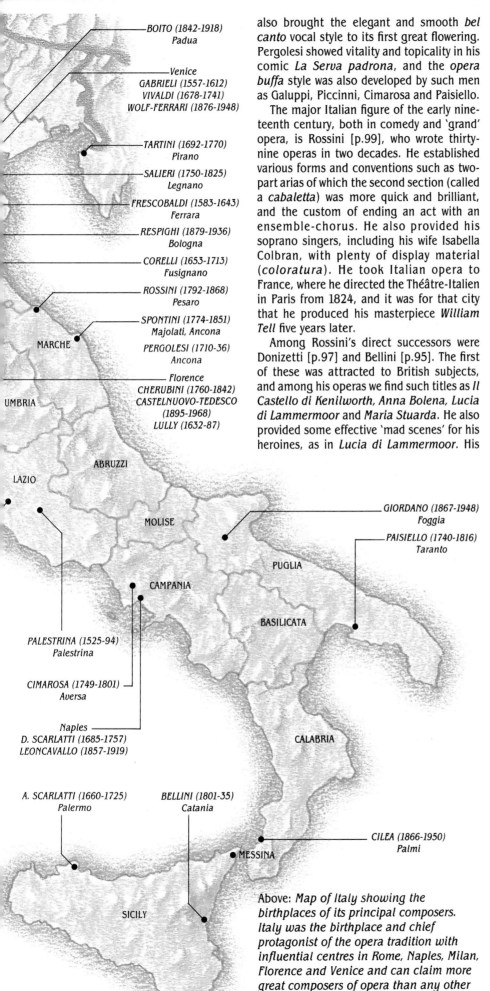

BOITO (1842-1918)
Padua

Venice
GABRIELI (1557-1612)
VIVALDI (1678-1741)
WOLF-FERRARI (1876-1948)

TARTINI (1692-1770)
Pirano

SALIERI (1750-1825)
Legnano

FRESCOBALDI (1583-1643)
Ferrara

RESPIGHI (1879-1936)
Bologna

CORELLI (1653-1713)
Fusignano

ROSSINI (1792-1868)
Pesaro

SPONTINI (1774-1851)
Majolati, Ancona

MARCHE

PERGOLESI (1710-36)
Ancona

Florence
CHERUBINI (1760-1842)
CASTELNUOVO-TEDESCO
(1895-1968)
LULLY (1632-87)

UMBRIA

ABRUZZI

LAZIO

MOLISE

GIORDANO (1867-1948)
Foggia

PAISIELLO (1740-1816)
Taranto

PUGLIA

CAMPANIA

BASILICATA

PALESTRINA (1525-94)
Palestrina

CIMAROSA (1749-1801)
Aversa

Naples
D. SCARLATTI (1685-1757)
LEONCAVALLO (1857-1919)

CALABRIA

A. SCARLATTI (1660-1725)
Palermo

BELLINI (1801-35)
Catania

CILEA (1866-1950)
Palmi

MESSINA

SICILY

Above: *Map of Italy showing the birthplaces of its principal composers. Italy was the birthplace and chief protagonist of the opera tradition with influential centres in Rome, Naples, Milan, Florence and Venice and can claim more great composers of opera than any other country.*

also brought the elegant and smooth *bel canto* vocal style to its first great flowering. Pergolesi showed vitality and topicality in his comic *La Serva padrona*, and the *opera buffa* style was also developed by such men as Galuppi, Piccinni, Cimarosa and Paisiello.

The major Italian figure of the early nineteenth century, both in comedy and 'grand' opera, is Rossini [p.99], who wrote thirty-nine operas in two decades. He established various forms and conventions such as two-part arias of which the second section (called a *cabaletta*) was more quick and brilliant, and the custom of ending an act with an ensemble-chorus. He also provided his soprano singers, including his wife Isabella Colbran, with plenty of display material (*coloratura*). He took Italian opera to France, where he directed the Théâtre-Italien in Paris from 1824, and it was for that city that he produced his masterpiece *William Tell* five years later.

Among Rossini's direct successors were Donizetti [p.97] and Bellini [p.95]. The first of these was attracted to British subjects, and among his operas we find such titles as *Il Castello di Kenilworth, Anna Bolena, Lucia di Lammermoor* and *Maria Stuarda*. He also provided some effective 'mad scenes' for his heroines, as in *Lucia di Lammermoor*. His

*Bedřich SMETANA
(1824-84)*

First Czech composer of truly national character, he had little formal training but thrived in a musical family, playing in a string quartet at five and on the piano in public at six, and composing by eight. But it was all instinctual, and he later told Liszt that musical theory was still a closed book to him at seventeen. Under suspicion for taking part in the anti-Austrian uprising of 1848, he spent some years in Sweden teaching and conducting, then toured as a concert pianist; but in 1863 he was back in Prague working on operas with a Bohemian (Czech) orientation. His second opera, the sparkling and comic *The Bartered Bride*, brought a rich melodic gift to bear upon local folk and dance idioms, and was a huge success. Now an established national figure, he completed eight operas altogether, but is also much admired for his six symphonic poems called *Má Vlast (My Country)*, especially *Vltava*, which traces the course of a great river. But he never heard these pieces, or his last three operas and the two String quartets, all of which were composed after he became deaf in 1874. He finally went insane and died in an asylum, but was buried as a national hero. J.C.

Below: *The great Spanish mezzo-soprano Isabella Colbran (1785-1845) who first appeared in Italy in 1806 and married Rossini in 1822.*

comedies *L'Elisir d'amore* and *Don Pasquale* are firmly in today's repertory. Bellini is rather more subtle: this composer who died young left fewer operas than Donizetti, but his tragic *Norma* provides a fine role for a singer-actress, while both *La Sonnambula* and *I Puritani* explore different expressive worlds to advantage.

Two major figures between, Verdi and Puccini, bring the story of Italian music into the present century. Verdi [p.93] produced the first of his many operas in 1839 and his last in 1893. His stirring youthful music became a symbol of Italian nationalism, but it was also because of its fervour, melodiousness and dramatic power that *Nabucco* (1842) was performed not only in Italy but also within a decade in cities as far afield as Berlin, Constantinople, St Petersburg, and London. *Macbeth*, *Rigoletto*, *Il Trovatore* and *La Traviata* mark further increases in Verdi's dramatic range, and there is psychological depth in the latter tale of a courtesan who renounces her young lover and dies. He found an epic style in *Simon Boccanegra* and *Don Carlos*, and crowned his long career with the Shakespearean operas *Otello* and *Falstaff*.

A new style called *verismo*, with realistic plots set in simple surroundings, was established in the 1890s by Mascagni [p.103] (*Cavalleria Rusticana*) and Leoncavallo [p.101] (*I Pagliacci*). This was inherited by Puccini [p.107] in such works as *La Bohème* (1896), set in a milieu of young and impoverished Parisian artists. But the chief Puccini characteristic is his moving portrayal of heroines who sacrifice themselves for love: among these are Tosca and Madam Butterfly in the operas of those names. However, Princess Turandot in his last opera is a strong and ruthless character until she is conquered by love. Puccini was a fine melodist who wrote sympathetically both for voices and for orchestra as well as having a powerful theatrical flair; what more may we ask of an opera composer? But his work seems to end an era, and sadly no Italian composer since his time has as yet made a major contribution to the international repertory, although we may note the names of such men as Dallapiccola, Nono and Berio, who have worked in opera and other fields since World War II and used the advanced musical language first explored by Schoenberg. C.H.

FRANCE

Until about five hundred years ago France was a divided territory, and its early musical history touches on the work of musicians of many kinds. In medieval times there were troubadours, famous poet-musicians such as William of Aquitaine, who flourished around 1100, and Bernart de Ventadorn. There were also innumerable humbler minstrels, or *jongleurs*. In churches and cathedrals sacred music was cultivated, and as choirmasters of

Above: *The painting 'The Musical Society' by Fr. Puget (1622-94) gives a vivid impression of musicians and music-making in France in the 17th century.*

Below: *The Ricordi edition of the libretto of Puccini's last opera,* Turandot, *which he left unfinished at the end of his career. His death marked the end of an era.*

Notre Dame in Paris both Léonin and Pérotin advanced the development of vocal polyphony in up to four parts. The theory of music, including rhythm and notation, was developed by Philippe de Vitry in his book called *The New Art* early in the fourteenth century: he also wrote vocal pieces. Guillaume de Machaut was the composer of the first known polyphonic Mass setting.

In the fifteenth century the Burgundians Dufay, Binchois and Ockeghem contributed variously to both sacred and secular music, and another Burgundian, Josquin Desprez (*c.* 1450-1521), is a major figure of his time who brought into both secular and sacred music a sense of chordal progression and structural proportion that was largely new. This clarifier

and innovator was in his lifetime called 'the Michelangelo of music'. French music such as his was now often known in other countries, not least because in the sixteenth century it was already being printed in Paris, Avignon, Lyon and other cities.

By the seventeenth century music was dominated by the taste of the royal court in Paris with its chapel and one hundred and fifty musicians. Under the 'Sun King' Louis XIV in this *grand siècle*, there were sacred works, songs (*airs de cour*) and ballets and in due course the operas of Lully [p.199], born an Italian but becoming French and the King's preferred composer. Lully's *tragédies lyriques*, written from 1673 onwards, form the first operatic repertory outside Italy; and though like Italian operas of the time they tell conventionally of gods and heroes, we know that their tunes were sung in the streets of Paris, and recent performances have brought them convincingly to life.

The chief successor to Lully was Rameau. His opera *Hippolyte et Aricie* (1733) made a deep impression on audiences with its powerful story and skilful writing for voices and for orchestra. There is a dance element in this and others of his operas and opera-ballets that reflects a Gallic taste for the elegant and chic – a Rococo stylishness which we also find in the harpsichord pieces of the time written by Couperin, Daquin and Rameau himself.

Besides opera, there were public concerts, and the foundation of the Concerts Spirituels in 1725 gave a boost to orchestral playing, as did that of a later series called Concerts de la Loge Olympique in 1769, for which Haydn and Mozart wrote symphonies. Several foreign composers succeeded in Paris at this time: one was Gluck, whose *Orfeo ed Euridice* reached Paris in 1774 and who then wrote other operas for the French capital. Later,

Carl NIELSEN
(1865-1931)

Above: *English National Opera production of* Orpheus in the Underworld *by Offenbach with fantastic new stage decor by the cartoonist Gerald Scarfe.*

Cherubini, Spontini, Rossini and Meyerbeer all lived in Paris and contributed to the development of both 'grand' and comic opera, just as Chopin did in the field of piano music. Although the events of the French Revolution (1789) had been violent and disturbing, they actually seem to have stimulated the arts, so that in the first half of the nineteenth century Paris was something of a Mecca to musicians of all kinds with its opera houses, concert halls and elegant *salons* in which some of the most cultivated men and women in Europe met to discuss the arts. Chopin wrote to a Polish friend: 'I have *everything* in Paris.'

Though France gained much from all these brilliant immigrants, the time was ripe for another native composer of genius. Berlioz [p.13] was a doctor's son who as a boy adored both music and literature and went on to write a programmatic *Fantastic* Symphony (1830) that described the dreams of a jilted lover attempting suicide by opium. This work is a milestone marking the beginning of the Romantic era which lasted into our own century, a period in which composers worked with a new intensity of self-expression and evocation of mood. Berlioz, a 'lark as big as an eagle', as the poet Heine called him, wrote virtually nothing that was not inspired by a literary text. His other major works include a 'dramatic symphony' with voices called *Romeo and Juliet* and the epic and lengthy opera *The Trojans*, which was never performed complete in his lifetime. Other subjects inspiring his music were Benvenuto Cellini's autobiography in his opera of that name, Byron's *Childe Harold* in his symphony with viola *Harold in Italy*, and Goethe's *Faust* in his 'dramatic legend' *The Damnation of Faust*. That he was a master of the orchestra is demonstrated by such music as the *Royal Hunt* and *Storm* in *The Trojans*.

This arch-Romantic once declared that music was 'the art of causing emotion by combinations of sounds' to carry a listener 'to infinite regions'.

Though Berlioz's own operas did not become popular in his lifetime, French opera flourished. Gounod's [p. 219] *Faust* (1859) and Bizet's [p.87] *Carmen* are masterpieces of dramatic flair and vocal-orchestral elegance, with the Bizet work (his last before his death at thirty-six) going the deeper of the two in its portrayal of passion in a contemporary Spanish setting. Other names are those of Ambroise Thomas, who wrote a *Mignon* and *Hamlet*, and the German-born Offenbach [p.175], the latter a brilliant composer of operettas including *Orpheus in the Underworld*. Saint-Saëns [p.61] too wrote operas, among them *Samson and Delilah*, but is today better remembered for his vivid instrumental work *The Carnival of the Animals*. A lyrical style is a feature of Massenet's [p.89] operas *Manon* and *Werther*, as well as Fauré's *Pénélope* and the operettas of Messager.

By the end of the nineteenth century instrumental music of all kinds was once again flourishing, though there were (and still are) few French symphonies. Debussy

Denmark's major composer, he started at fourteen as a trumpeter in a military band, but then obtained a scholarship and studied at the Copenhagen Conservatory, became an orchestral violinist, and eventually a conductor. Hardly known beyond his own country until after World War II, he produced music in various traditional genres, including the opera *Saul and David*, but his greatest impact outside Denmark has come from the six symphonies. These have the special quality of spanning two worlds, providing an accessible and expansive late-romantic framework while drawing upon contemporary chromatic and experimental trends without ever actually becoming atonal. At their best they have a sort of lithe majesty, a broad but exciting sweep that is never overtly nationalistic but which nevertheless cannot easily be confused with the work of any other composer. Four of the six symphonies have names, and while these only indicate moods, titles such as *The Inextinguishable* and *Sinfonia Espansiva* do say something of the composer's optimistic outlook. There was also a streak of boyish daring, as when he instructs the side-drummer in his Fifth Symphony to improvise in such a manner as to drown the rest of the orchestra! His Violin, Clarinet and Flute concertos are fine works, and amongst the various tone-poems is *Helios*, a lovely tribute to the sun inspired by a Mediterranean holiday with his wife in 1903. J.C.

Paul TORTELIER
(b. 1914)

Distinguished French cellist, conductor and composer who studied at the Paris Conservatoire, where he won first prize for the violoncello in 1930. Five years later he was appointed principal cellist with the Monte Carlo orchestra, and in 1937 he went to the USA to take up an appointment with the Boston Symphony Orchestra. After World War II he returned to Paris to become principal cellist with the Société des Concerts du Conservatoire, and in 1947 embarked upon his career as a soloist with many of the world's leading orchestras. He made his English début in London in 1947 with a performance of *Don Quixote* by Richard Strauss. He spent some time in Israel before accepting a professorship at the Paris Conservatoire. His many compositions include two

cello concertos, a double cello concerto and works for the instrument unaccompanied. He has also written an *Israel Symphony*. He has made a number of outstanding recordings from his wide repertoire and is a brilliant teacher, giving many lecture recitals and master classes at home and abroad. In recent years, he has enhanced his formidable reputation still further by creating a chamber music group with his wife, herself a cellist, his daughter Maria de la Pau, who is a pianist, and his son Yan Pascal, violinist and conductor. Among his most enduring recordings are those of the Bach unaccompanied Cello Suites, the Beethoven Cello concertos as well as a *Don Quixote* recorded in 1975 and a 1973 recording of the Elgar Cello Concerto with Boult. R.H.

Left: *Portrait of the composer and teacher Luigi Cherubini (1760-1842). As director of the Paris Conservatoire from 1822 he showed a very fickle mind as to whom he would enroll.*

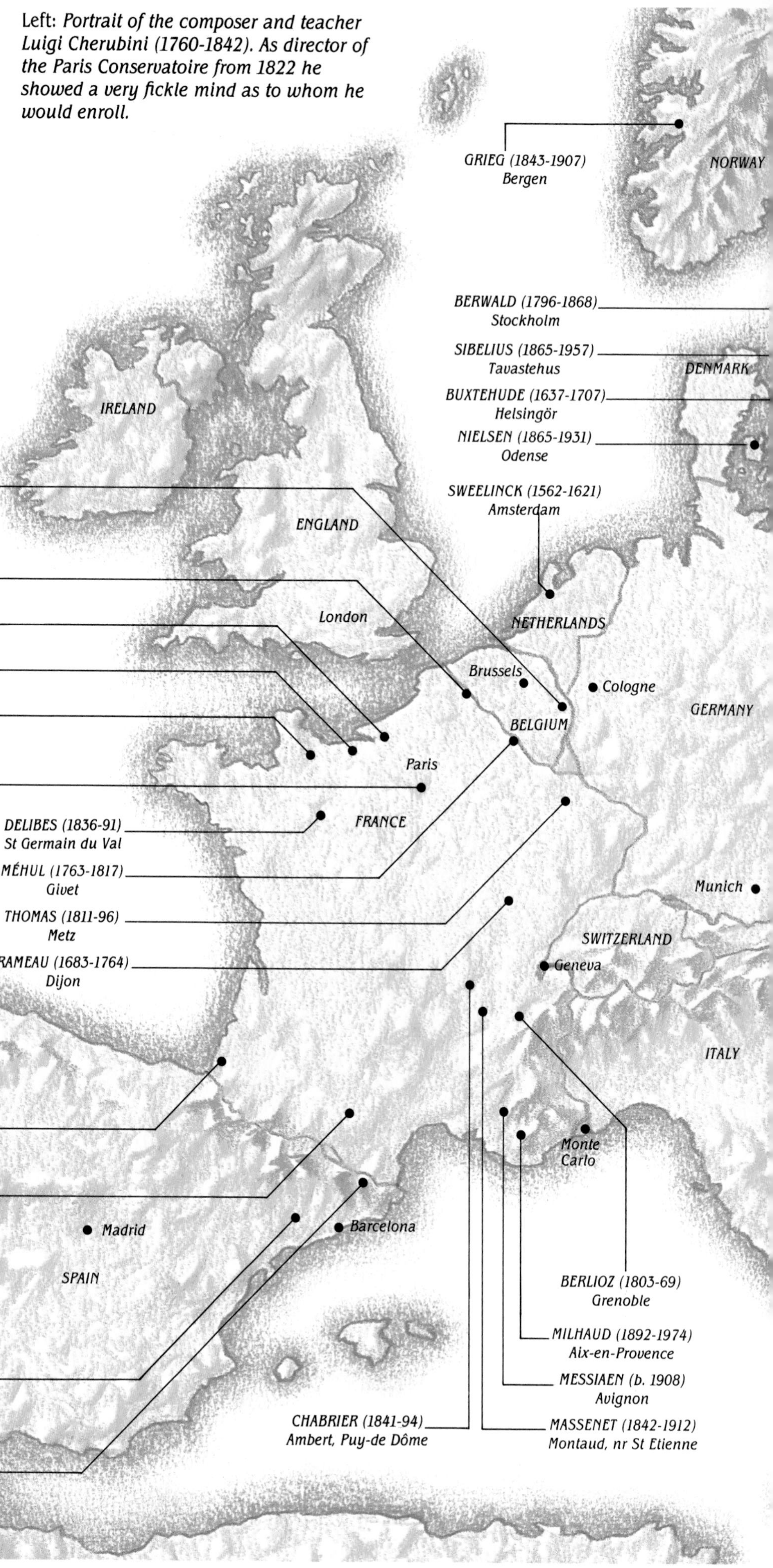

GRIEG (1843-1907)
Bergen

NORWAY

BERWALD (1796-1868)
Stockholm

SIBELIUS (1865-1957)
Tavastehus

DENMARK

BUXTEHUDE (1637-1707)
Helsingör

NIELSEN (1865-1931)
Odense

SWEELINCK (1562-1621)
Amsterdam

IRELAND

ENGLAND

NETHERLANDS

Liège
FRANCK (1822-90)
GRÉTRY (1741-1813)

LALO (1823-92)
Lille

London

BOÏELDIEU (1775-1834)
Rouen

Brussels

Cologne

SATIE (1866-1925)
Honfleur

GERMANY

AUBER (1782-1871)
Caen

BELGIUM

Paris
SAINTS-SAËNS (1835-1921)
BIZET (1838-75)
DUPARC (1848-1933)
POULENC (1899-1963)
GOUNOD (1818-93)
DEBUSSY (1862-1918)
M-A CHARPENTIER (1634-1704)
ADAM (1803-56)
D'INDY (1851-1931)
IBERT (1890-1962)
COUPERIN (1668-1733)
LECOCQ (1832-1918)
CHAUSSON (1855-99)

Paris

FRANCE

DELIBES (1836-91)
St Germain du Val

MÉHUL (1763-1817)
Givet

THOMAS (1811-96)
Metz

Munich

RAMEAU (1683-1764)
Dijon

SWITZERLAND

Geneva

ITALY

RAVEL (1875-1937)
Ciboure, St-Jean-de Luz

Monte
Carlo

FAURÉ (1845-1924)
Pamiers, Ariège

Madrid

Barcelona

SPAIN

BERLIOZ (1803-69)
Grenoble

MILHAUD (1892-1974)
Aix-en-Provence

GRANADOS (1867-1916)
Lerida

MESSIAEN (b. 1908)
Avignon

FALLA (1876-1946)
Cadiz

CHABRIER (1841-94)
Ambert, Puy-de Dôme

MASSENET (1842-1912)
Montaud, nr St Etienne

ALBÉNIZ (1860-1909)
Camprodon, Catalonia

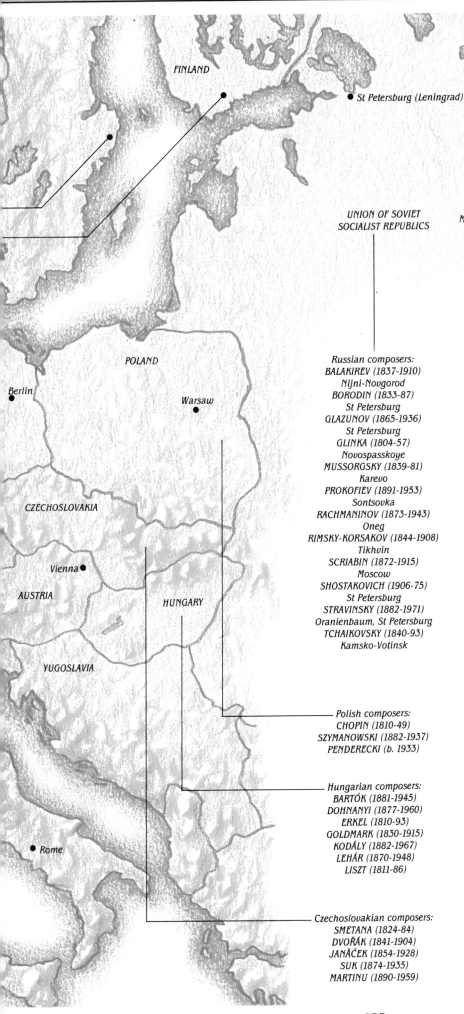

FINLAND

● St Petersburg (Leningrad)

UNION OF SOVIET
SOCIALIST REPUBLICS

● Moscow

POLAND

Berlin ●

Warsaw ●

CZECHOSLOVAKIA

Vienna ●

AUSTRIA

HUNGARY

YUGOSLAVIA

● Rome

Russian composers:
BALAKIREV (1837-1910)
Nijni-Novgorod
BORODIN (1833-87)
St Petersburg
GLAZUNOV (1865-1936)
St Petersburg
GLINKA (1804-57)
Novospasskoye
MUSSORGSKY (1839-81)
Karevo
PROKOFIEV (1891-1953)
Sontsovka
RACHMANINOV (1873-1943)
Oneg
RIMSKY-KORSAKOV (1844-1908)
Tikhvin
SCRIABIN (1872-1915)
Moscow
SHOSTAKOVICH (1906-75)
St Petersburg
STRAVINSKY (1882-1971)
Oranienbaum, St Petersburg
TCHAIKOVSKY (1840-93)
Kamsko-Votinsk

Polish composers:
CHOPIN (1810-49)
SZYMANOWSKI (1882-1937)
PENDERECKI (b. 1933)

Hungarian composers:
BARTÓK (1881-1945)
DOHNANYI (1877-1960)
ERKEL (1810-93)
GOLDMARK (1830-1915)
KODÁLY (1882-1967)
LEHÁR (1870-1948)
LISZT (1811-86)

Czechoslovakian composers:
SMETANA (1824-84)
DVOŘÁK (1841-1904)
JANÁČEK (1854-1928)
SUK (1874-1935)
MARTINU (1890-1959)

Nicolai RIMSKY-KORSAKOV
(1844-1908)

An aristocratic naval officer with musical inclinations, he drifted into composition, became one of 'The Five' devoted to musical nationalism, achieved fame as a master of orchestral colour, and ended as the senior figure in Russian music, with a strong influence on the early work of his pupil Stravinsky. Although still serving in the navy, his reputation as a promising composer led to his appointment in 1871 as professor of composition at St Petersburg Conservatory. However, being largely self taught and normally working by ear, he knew very little theory and had to undertake secret studies in order to keep ahead of his students. But he succeeded, and became a respected teacher as well as an admired composer. Most widely known for his richly scored *Scheherazade* and the brilliant *Spanish Caprice*, he wrote symphonies and chamber music as well as colourful overtures, suites and fantasias – plus fifteen operas. These last include *The Snow Maiden*, *Sadko* and *Tsar Saltan*, and exult in exploiting the magic and pageantry of Russian legends and fairy tales. Despite his family background, R-K showed some sympathy for revolutionary students in 1905 and was officially censured, an episode that gave rise to his satirical last opera *The Golden Cockerel*. Apart from his own compositions, he arranged and orchestrated the works of other composers, most notably his friend Modest Mussorgsky's *Boris Godunov* and *Night on the Bare Mountain*.J.C.

Left: *Outline map of Europe showing the birthplaces of many of its outstanding composers. Detailed maps show well endowed areas of Germany & Austria (p.126-7), Italy (p.130-31) and Great Britain (p.140-41). Beyond Central Europe we have also listed composers from Poland, Hungary, Czechoslovakia and Russia. The map gives a good sense of the spread of musical activities in Europe, with Vienna an obvious centre, Germany a solid bulwark and the tentacle lines spreading out to France and Spain in the West, the now separatist bloc in the East and Great Britain in maritime isolation on the fringes.*

[p.165] made his name in 1894 with his orchestral *Prélude à l'Après-midi d'un faune* for orchestra: here was an evocation of a dreamy forest scene that sounded a new and compelling note in music, one of suggestion rather than statement that relates to the work of French poets and painters of the time. His opera *Pelléas et Mélisande* is a mysterious love story set in a medieval castle that has the same calculated ambiguity and poses as many questions as it answers. With his flexible and evocative harmonic language, his sure but unconventional sense of form and his wonderful ear for instrumental sound, Debussy is a great figure of modern music. Some of his later works, like the piano *Etudes* and the ballet *Jeux* have only come to be appreciated today, seventy years after his death. But other pieces, from his piano piece *Clair de lune* to his orchestral triptych *La Mer*, have long been popular; the latter is in effect an impressionistic symphony.

Ravel [p.73], the composer of *Bolero*, is a somewhat different figure. Though his harmony is advanced, he is in some ways closer to classical ideals. He often used dance styles, as in *Bolero* and the *Pavane for a Dead Infanta*, and classical structures, as in his piano Sonatine, String Quartet, Piano Trio and two piano concertos. But he too could be impressionistic, for example in his piano *Miroirs* and *Gaspard de la nuit*, in which a player of great agility and subtlety must make the instrument shimmer and dazzle by turns. He wrote well for the voice too, and his two operas, *L'Heure espagnole* and *L'Enfant et les sortilèges*, sparkle with humour and humanity.

A move towards a new simplicity, wit and Gallic directness was stimulated by the eccentric but charmingly individual Satie [p.167] and came to fruition after World War I with the group of composers called 'Les Six'. Of these, only three are at all well known today, and of these only one remained faithful to the original ideals, for while Honegger and Milhaud [p.159] eventually moved away from brevity and simplicity towards a more epic utterance, it is only Poulenc [p.195] who never lost these qualities. He was a fine melodist with a quintessentially French charm and wit which make his *Mouvements perpétuels* for piano (written when he was only nineteen) both delightful and individual. There is, of course, a greater depth in his Organ Concerto, his religious works and the operas *La Voix humaine* (for a single woman singer bidding an anguished farewell to her lover on the telephone) and *Les Dialogues des Carmélites*, but the direct melodiousness of all this music is part of its strength. Two other composers sharing something of the Les Six aesthetic are Ibert and Françaix.

Among living French composers, the senior figure is Messiaen [p.123]. A devout man who was for many years a church organist, he has often chosen religious subjects, and specifically Catholic ones, for his organ

and piano music as well as orchestral works. His music has an extraordinary power and personality, and it has taken its place in the modern repertory despite often being lengthy and difficult to perform. Other stimuli to his inspiration have been Indian culture, most notably in the *Turangalîla* Symphony (1948), and birdsong: one enormous piano work is actually called *Catalogue d'oiseaux*. There is an ecstasy and passion in Messiaen's music which can suggest religious revelation or a simple eroticism, possibly

Above: 'Les Six', composers (left to right) Tailleferre, Milhaud, Honegger, Durey, Poulenc and Auric with Marcelle Meyer (centre) and Jean Cocteau (rear). Painted by Jacques-Emil Blanche.

both at the same time. Duruflé, Jolivet and Dutilleux are others who have brought individual voices to French music.

Boulez is a younger figure than any of these. He studied with Messiaen and in the 1950s became a leader of the European avant-garde with such works as his *Le Marteau sans maître* for voice and ensemble, piano sonatas and *Structures* for two pianos; these were followed by orchestral pieces including *Pli selon pli* (1962), a vocal setting of the poet Mallarmé. He is also a conductor of international repute, and by no means only in contemporary music – he has conducted Wagner's *Ring* cycle at Bayreuth. Today he directs the music research institute IRCAM in Paris, but may have slowed as a creator.

The character of French music is hard to define. It is usually recognisable as such, yet seems to have many and varied strains. One of these is represented by the exuberance and expansiveness of Berlioz and Messiaen, another by the poise and sheer charm of Couperin, Massenet and Poulenc, another by the controlled yet intense sensuality of Bizet's *Carmen* and Ravel's *La Valse* and *Bolero*, another by the Baroque dignity of the Lully and Rameau operas, and yet another by the intellectual passion of Boulez. And where do we place the elusive but undeniably great figure of Debussy? But we should perhaps be grateful for such stylistic riches, which perfectly balance the contributions to music made by the other nations. C.H.

RUSSIA AND EASTERN EUROPE

Despite inheriting a rich store of folk music together with that of the Orthodox Church, it was not until the nineteenth century that Russian composers acquired a voice of their own. Indeed, her first major composer, Glinka, was called 'the father of Russian music' by his immediate successors. He studied abroad and then returned to write his

David OISTRAKH
(1908-74)

Russian violinist who first impinged on the musical world when he won First Prize in the International Competition in Brussels in 1937. He had studied at the Odessa Conservatory, graduating in 1926. The next year performed the Glazunov Violin Concerto in Kiev under the composer's direction. Went to Moscow and taught at the Conservatory there. Played in Paris and London in 1953 and went to the USA in 1955. His remarkable technique and his great sense of historical style brought him high acclaim in the sixties whenever he played or recorded. In Russia he was a figurehead in the violin world, helping younger players and working with their leading composers in encouraging the widening of the violin repertoire. Among his star pupils was his son Igor (b. 1931), who has had a spectacular career of his own and whom many consider to be as fine a violinist as his father. P.G.

Modest MUSSORGSKY
(1839-81)

Despite showing early musical promise and coming from a well-off family, this most vital and original of the Russian nationalist composers seemed destined in his youth for a military career. But he eventually met Balakirev and his circle, resigned his army commission and turned seriously to music, meantime scraping a living in various minor government posts, his family's wealth having disappeared. His life now became one of uncompromising devotion to his art, particularly an obsession with the idea of making vocal music echo the inflections of ordinary speech. He tackled several operas, but his naturalistic ideals were most strikingly implemented in his only complete one, *Boris Godunov*, a sweeping epic concerned as much with Russia and its people as with the self-tortured Tsar Boris. Likewise, his *Songs and Dances of Death* have a gripping power of direct expression. Instrumentally, *Pictures at an Exhibition* is a masterpiece of descriptive piano music (but usually heard in Ravel's orchestration), while *Night on the Bare Mountain* is an ever-popular orchestral showpiece, although mostly know in Rimsky-Korsakov's rearrangement. Mussorgsky's own orchestration and harmonies were once regarded as crude, hence the various polishing operations by others, but the originals are gradually becoming accepted on their own terms. However, his early confidence finally became overwhelmed by alcohol, and he died of a stroke at forty-two. J.C.

Left: *Tsar Nicholas I attending a performance of the opera in the self-indulgent, pre-revolutionary days of Russian monarchy, before the curtain finally came down.*

Above: *One of the principal glories of the Russian ballet, Tchaikovsky's* Swan Lake, *being performed here in spectacular style by the great Margot Fonteyn and Michael Somes.*

opera *A Life for the Tsar* in 1836 with such innovations as a wedding chorus in quintuple time (a common metre in Russian folk music but almost unknown in the West) and an imitation of the Kremlin bells. 'We northerners feel differently', he declared, so sounding a note of conscious nationalism that was to have an effect on several other countries besides his own.

The group of composers called 'The Five' followed Glinka's example: these were Borodin, Cui, Balakirev, Mussorgsky and Rimsky-Korsakov. Each brought something individual to music but emphasised its Russianness, though Cui (half-French) was more cosmopolitan than the others.

Borodin's [p.51] *Prince Igor* and Mussorgsky's *Boris Godunov* are operatic masterpieces, the first being highly colourful but the second going deeper in its portrayal of a tormented ruler. Mussorgsky's [p.137] *Pictures at an Exhibition* (1874) is for piano but is often heard in Ravel's orchestral version. Balakirev wrote picturesquely both for orchestra and for piano: his pianopiece *Islamey* is a virtuoso showpiece. Rimsky-Korsakov [p.135] composed operas and much else including the vivid orchestral pieces *Scheherazade* and *Capriccio espagnol*.

Tchaikovsky [p.31] stood a little apart from The Five, although he too sometimes used themes from folk music and demon-strates an equal Russianness in works as different as his ballets (*Swan Lake, The Sleeping Beauty* and *The Nutcracker*) and his *Pathetic* Symphony. Among other works, his First Piano Concerto is immensely popular today, as are his richly textured Violin Concerto, the opera *Eugene Onegin* and the tone poem *Romeo and Juliet*. In all these we may salute a master craftsman and melodist possessing abundant charm.

Other countries now found their own musical voices. Czechoslovakia (as it is now) produced Smetana [p.131], the composer of the opera *The Bartered Bride*, and Dvořák [p.127], who wrote *Slavonic Dances*, a fine Cello Concerto and nine symphonies culminating in the *New World* Symphony (1893) with its rich outpouring of melody.

Though Poland had a figure corresponding to these men in Moniuszko, his operas and other music are not widely known, and the outstanding composer of the period is Chopin [p.163]. However, his is a special case among nationalists, for he was half French and chose to live in Paris. Almost all his music is for piano solo, and its range of expression is astonishing; while his nocturnes and waltzes may suggest elegant Parisian *salons*, his mazurkas and polonaises evoke his native country.

The twentieth century saw the emergence of other masters. In Czechoslovakia, Janáček [p.113] produced a series of powerful operas and instrumental works including a sinfonietta with parts for twelve trumpets, and Martinů also wrote operas of importance. Szymanowski gave Poland a major opera in his mysterious *King Roger*. The Hungarian composer Bartók [p.157] wrote challenging but magnificent string quartets; his music is exciting with its folk-influenced irregular rhythms and culminated in a showpiece *Concerto for Orchestra* (1943)

Among the Russians, Scriabin was a brilliant pianist and something of a mystic who wrote piano sonatas and symphonies which are only beginning to be appreciated today. Conversely, Rachmaninov [p.59] has always been popular and his piano concertos always attract an audience, though we should remember his other fine music including three symphonies, choral works and songs. Stravinsky [p.77] changed the course of music with his thrilling pre-war ballets including *The Rite of Spring* (1913), and then moved towards a neo-classical style in such different works as *Pulcinella* and *Oedipus Rex* and finally into serialism. Prokofiev [p.37] lived abroad and then in the Soviet Union, while Shostakovich [p.39] was

---

Pablo CASALS
(1876-1973)

Spanish cellist, conductor, pianist and composer who received his first music lessons from his father, who was an organist. After trying nearly all the instruments of the orchestra by the time he was twelve, Casals chose the cello, and went to Madrid to enrol at the Royal Conservatory. His career really began in the street cafés of Barcelona, but in 1895 he accepted a post as solo cellist with the Paris Opera. In 1898 he appeared as soloist at Lamoureux concerts in Paris and at the Crystal Palace in London. A highly successful tour followed in 1901, and from that time on his reputation grew slowly but steadily. He placed Bach's unaccompanied suites, which had been regarded hitherto merely as academic exercises, firmly in the platform repertoire. In 1919 he formed his own orchestra in Barcelona, and the famous collaboration with Cortot and Thibaud further enhanced his international reputation. He was a staunch opponent of the Franco régime, and in 1939 he declared that he would not return to Spain until the end of totalitarian rule. He made his home on the French side of the Pyrenees, establishing the Prades Festival in 1950. R.H.

---

brought up in Soviet society: though much of their music has a brilliant, witty style, there are dark depths in Shostakovich that may reflect a despair at political pressures.

Today the Soviet Union has avant-garde composers represented best by Schnittke, Other contemporary figures are Penderecki from Poland, formerly avant-garde but now writing more traditionally in forms including sacred music, and Lutosławski whose Third Symphony (1983) is the latest of many works to win acclaim. C.H.

SPAIN

The Iberian Peninsula, which also includes Portugal, has always had its music, often enriched by the Moorish influence that has remained – as it has in architecture – from lengthy periods of Arab settlement. In the sixteenth century the composers Morales and Victoria are important in church music, but both worked also in Italy. Antonio Soler (1729-83) wrote keyboard sonatas, while Martin y Soler (1754-1806) – no relation – was an opera composer who spent much of his life outside Spain.

Spanish opera had appeared with the light-hearted *zarzuelas* of the seventeenth

Below: The Spanish composer Manuel de Falla (1876-1946), writer of La vida breve, El Amor brujo *and* El Sombrero de tres picos.

Below: Spanish composer, Enrique Granados, born 1867 and died in World War I in 1916 when his ship was torpedoed by a German submarine.

century but only reached its peak in the late nineteenth with composers such as Barbieri and Bretón. Pedrell, Albéniz and Falla also wrote *zarzuelas*, but are better known for other things. For it was now that a real renaissance occurred in Spanish music. Pedrell was the teacher of both Albéniz and Falla; Albéniz [p.153] wrote splendidly decorative piano music and Falla [p.69] ballet music and opera as well as the exotic and evocative *Nights in the Gardens of Spain* for piano and orchestra. But his major work, a 'scenic cantata' called *Atlántida*, was left unfinished at his death in 1946, and although Ernesto Halffter made a completion and it was produced in 1962 it has not yet been revived. Granados (also a Pedrell pupil) wrote piano music, including the famous *Lover and the Nightingale*, and the opera *Goyescas* (1916), which was inspired by Goya's paintings. C.H.

SCANDINAVIA

'The North is most decidedly entitled to a language of its own.' Schumann's famous remark was made about the Danish musician Gade but it could equally apply to that other Dane, Nielsen – or to Grieg, Berwald and Sibelius, who were respectively Norwegian, Swedish and Finnish.

These figures belong to the nineteenth and twentieth centuries. Of course there had been Scandinavian composers before, but not recognisably so: for example, Buxtehude (1637-1707) the Danish organist, worked within the German tradition that made him a precursor of Bach. But when Gade (1817-90) wrote his *Nordic Pictures* and *Nine Songs in Folk Style* he was asserting his nationality. Grieg [p.55] went further, and when Gade actually thought his Second Violin Sonata 'too Norwegian' he retorted that his next would be even more so. Grieg's music to Ibsen's play *Peer Gynt*, his *Holberg Suite* and Piano Concerto are imbued with a northern freshness that he learned from folk art; it perhaps comes out even more strongly in his many short piano pieces and songs.

Sweden had an original figure rather earlier in Berwald (1796-1868), but he cannot be classed with the nationalists. He lived for some years in Berlin and Vienna, returning to Sweden in middle life, and besides writing

Above: *Norwegian composer Edvard Grieg (1843-1907), a small man who mainly wrote musical miniatures apart from his Piano Concerto and the well-known* Peer Gynt *music.*

Below: *The great Finnish composer and national hero Jean Sibelius (1865-1957) portrayed in the younger romantic days of 1894 in an aquarelle by A. Gallen-Kalella.*

music directed an orthopaedic institute and a glassworks. His four symphonies – among them the *Sinfonie singulière* (1845) – and chamber music show an individual mind (and ear) at work, but he had no obvious successors and now seems rather a lonely figure.

Finland has also produced only one well-known composer, but he is a major figure of the early twentieth century. Sibelius [p.35] had a long life (1865-1957) but wrote virtually nothing after 1930; his seven symphonies, symphonic poems including *En Saga* and *Tapiola, Karelia Suite* and Violin Concerto all variously demonstrate a ruggedly individual and compelling gift. The symphonies in particular show a special structural and tonal mastery as well as an abundance of atmosphere ranging from the warmth of the Third to the thrilling power of the Fifth or Seventh. At the same time, the Fourth and Sixth Symphonies have brooding mystery that we also find in *Tapiola*.

Nielsen [p.133], born in Denmark a few months before Sibelius, is also a symphonist with six symphonies to his credit. His musical personality is complex and quirky, sometimes grand and forbidding and elsewhere cosily simple with an assertive humanity. His operas *Saul and David* and *Maskarade* symbolise this range, the one being epic as befits the biblical story and the other a sophisticated romantic comedy of intrigue. The dramatic yet personal aspect of Nielsen's music is represented too in his Flute and Clarinet Concertos and his Wind Quintet, works in which solo instruments seem transformed into individual characters – as is the aggressive side drum in the Fifth Symphony, who at one point must improvise 'as if at all costs he wants to stop the progress of the orchestra'.

The later twentieth century has as yet produced no figure of the stature of those already mentioned, but we may mention the Swedish musician Blomdahl (1916-68) and the Estonians Tubin (1905-82) and Pärt (b. 1935), the former a symphonist and the latter an imaginative minimalist with a keen ear for sound.C.H.

BRITAIN

From the minstrels of King Alfred the Great's court who sang 'loud to the harp' to Britten and the Beatles in our own century, Britain has always been rich in music. However, there was a period when the country had fewer composers than performers. Cathedrals and churches have fostered a fine tradition of sacred choral music and singing, and there are folksongs and dances of many kinds, while the brass band movement of Wales and other industrial areas is yet another manifestation of the British love of music-making.

We can gain a glimpse into the state of British music as early as the thirteenth century in the round 'Sumer is icumen in', a cheerful greeting to summer in six vocal

Edward ELGAR
(1857-1934)

Inevitably fixed in the public mind as composer of *Land of Hope and Glory*, this son of a music-shop proprietor learnt to play violin and organ in his youth, produced works for the entertainment of family and friends, played an active part in the musical life of the West-Midlands, composing cantatas, chamber works, songs and other pieces as he went, and finally shot to fame with the *Enigma Variations* just before the turn of the century. He was soon at the centre of British musical life, knighted, showered with honours, and richly creative right through the Edwardian age until just after World War I, when his haunting, elegaic Cello concerto was followed by the death of his wife, from which he never really recovered, except in a final spate of enthusiasm for recording his works. His Catholicism produced *The Dream of Gerontius*, while the crown of his splended orchestral writing came with *Falstaff*, two symphonies, and the Violin Concerto. But despite *Falstaff*, the *Cockaigne* (*In London Town*) overture, and the patriotic marches, Elgar was no nationalist when it came to stylistic sources, since he drew openly on Germanic models. Nevertheless, his own inimitable melodic stamp dominates for most of the time, and after decades of post-Edwardian disdain he can now be appreciated as a great international composer in his own right, who somehow sounds very English as well. J.C.

parts that may have been written by a monk in Reading; in its combination of skilful craft and earthy vigour it looks forward to Chaucer in the next century. By the fifteenth century we already know some musicians by name, among these being John Dunstable, who probably served the Duke of Bedford at his court in France; he may have been the first composer to provide liturgical music with an instrumental accompaniment. Several kings were noted for their skill in music, including Henry V and Henry VIII; both composed and the latter played keyboard instruments, as did his daughter Elizabeth I.

In Elizabethan times, and a little beyond her reign, much lively music was written for the virginals – a kind of harpsichord – by Byrd, Morley, Bull and Farnaby among others, using such forms as dances and variations. The lute had its music too, fine instruments being made in England, and Dowland was among the many composers who wrote songs to its accompaniment. The unaccompanied vocal madrigal was imported from Italy but was then Anglicised with a new freshness and topical texts. One major madrigal collection by twenty-five composers called *The Triumphs of Oriana* (1601) was dedicated to Queen Elizabeth: it was edited by Morley and among the other contributors were Tomkins, Wilbye and Weelkes. Music also had its place in the theatre, and there are several songs in Shakespeare's plays.

Church music underwent a change when Henry VIII declared a degree of independence from Rome in 1534 and the spirit of Protestantism gradually spread to Britain. English words now often replaced Latin and required new music, usually in a plainer style, while harmonised Anglican chant superseded unaccompanied plainchant. Tallis composed English hymns that are in use today, but he and his pupil Byrd also wrote church music to both Latin and English texts. Byrd's *Great Service*, in up to ten polyphonic parts, sets English words in a rich and noble style. Tallis, Byrd and Byrd's own pupil Gibbons also wrote English anthems, with or without accompaniment: perhaps the most famous by Gibbons is called *This is the record of John*.

A dramatic form of the early seventeenth century was the masque, a spectacular musical play that did not aspire to the status of opera, which was sung throughout. Henry Lawes contributed music to Milton's *Comus*, produced at Ludlow Castle in 1634, and there were many lavish masque productions in London. Although the Puritan period (1649-60) brought some disapproval of extravagance, the tradition of theatrical spectacle was too strong to be suppressed, and with the Restoration a new zest for music swept the country. Charles II ordered 'the Composers of his Chappell to add Symphonys etc, with Instruments to their Anthems', according to the composer Blow, with the result that one diarist thought the music 'better suiting a tavern, or playhouse, than a church'. At the same time, the diarist Pepys could join in songs or play his recorder among ordinary people in London hostelries.

The outstanding musician of the late seventeenth century was Purcell [p.83], who trained as a choirboy in the Chapel Royal and then became the organist of Westminster Abbey. He composed much church music as well as festive odes for court or other celebrations – one called *Hail, bright Cecilia* (1692) praises the patron saint of music with five solo singers, a chorus and an orchestra including trumpets and drums. His opera *Dido and Aeneas*, written for a London girls' school, is a masterpiece of music drama but stands alone in his output, most of his work for the theatre being music (sometimes very elaborate) to accompany plays such as *King*

Below: *Arundel manuscript depicting David (on his harp) and other musicians, as imagined by a 15th-century illustrative artist.*

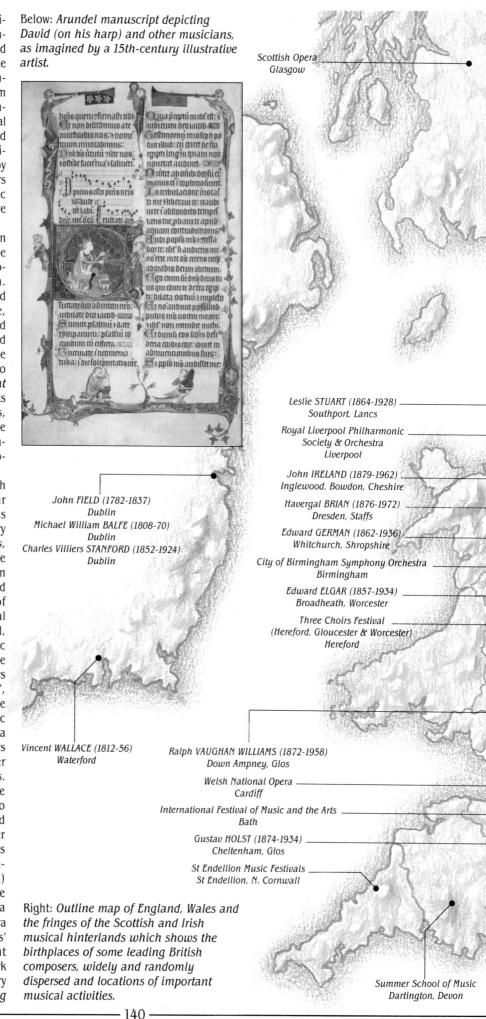

Right: *Outline map of England, Wales and the fringes of the Scottish and Irish musical hinterlands which shows the birthplaces of some leading British composers, widely and randomly dispersed and locations of important musical activities.*

Scottish Opera
Glasgow

Leslie STUART (1864-1928)
Southport, Lancs

Royal Liverpool Philharmonic
Society & Orchestra
Liverpool

John IRELAND (1879-1962)
Inglewood, Bowdon, Cheshire

Havergal BRIAN (1876-1972)
Dresden, Staffs

Edward GERMAN (1862-1936)
Whitchurch, Shropshire

City of Birmingham Symphony Orchestra
Birmingham

Edward ELGAR (1857-1934)
Broadheath, Worcester

Three Choirs Festival
(Hereford, Gloucester & Worcester)
Hereford

John FIELD (1782-1837)
Dublin
Michael William BALFE (1808-70)
Dublin
Charles Villiers STANFORD (1852-1924)
Dublin

Vincent WALLACE (1812-56)
Waterford

Ralph VAUGHAN WILLIAMS (1872-1958)
Down Ampney, Glos

Welsh National Opera
Cardiff

International Festival of Music and the Arts
Bath

Gustav HOLST (1874-1934)
Cheltenham, Glos

St Endellion Music Festivals
St Endellion, N. Cornwall

Summer School of Music
Dartington, Devon

Edinburgh International Festival
Edinburgh

Below: *William Byrd (1543-1623), who studied under Thomas Tallis, was frequently prosecuted under the edicts of Elizabeth for his Roman Catholic beliefs.*

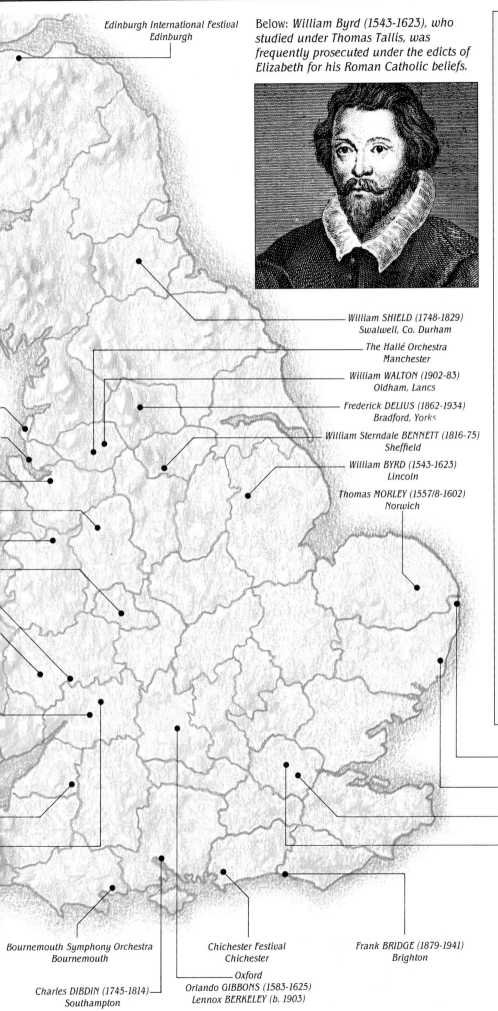

William SHIELD (1748-1829)
Swalwell, Co. Durham

The Hallé Orchestra
Manchester

William WALTON (1902-83)
Oldham, Lancs

Frederick DELIUS (1862-1934)
Bradford, Yorks

William Sterndale BENNETT (1816-75)
Sheffield

William BYRD (1543-1623)
Lincoln

Thomas MORLEY (1557/8-1602)
Norwich

Frederick DELIUS
(1862-1934)

English composer, born of émigré German parents in Bradford, lived for a while in America, studied in Germany, had strong affinity with Scandinavia, but finally settled near Fontainbleau in France. His music is as fluid as his national identity, since it has a dreamy, drifting, improvisatory quality which is a law unto itself. His titles seem to indicate tone-paintings: *Summer Night on the River, Paris – Song of a Great City, On Hearing the First Cuckoo in Spring, Sea Drift.* But such pieces are rhapsodic evocations of the feelings associated with their subjects rather than programmatic sketches, and are written in a style which, while employing a sort of post-Wagnerian harmony, is absolutely unique to Delius. He was very much his own man, and while there are a couple of concertos and some chamber pieces amongst the rhapsodies, tone-poems, songs, works for chorus and orchestra, and six operas, he rarely followed conventional compositional rules. Even his *Mass* and *Requiem* deny their titles by using humanistic (even atheistic) Nietzchean texts. He was forty before his music received any recognition, and then in Germany before England, but largely due to the championship of Sir Thomas Beecham, and later of Eric Fenby (who helped the composer during his last blind and paralysed years), he now has a firm place in British musical affections. J.C.

Benjamin BRITTEN (1913-76)
Lowestoft, Suffolk

Aldeburgh Festival of Music and the Arts
Aldeburgh

Thomas TALLIS (c. 1505-85)
Greenwich

London
John DOWLAND (1563-1626)
Henry PURCELL (c. 1659-95)
Thomas ARNE (1710-78)
William BOYCE (1711-79)
Samuel ARNOLD (1740-1802)
Henry Rowley BISHOP (1786-1855)
Arthur SULLIVAN (1842-1900)
Arnold BAX (1883-1953)
George BUTTERWORTH (1885-1916)
Arthur BLISS (1891-1975)
Peter WARLOCK (Philip Heseltine) (1894-1930)
Gerald FINZI (1901-56)
Michael TIPPETT (b. 1905)

Bournemouth Symphony Orchestra
Bournemouth

Chichester Festival
Chichester

Frank BRIDGE (1879-1941)
Brighton

Oxford
Orlando GIBBONS (1583-1625)
Lennox BERKELEY (b. 1903)

Charles DIBDIN (1745-1814)
Southampton

Arthur and _The Fairy Queen_ which were nearer the accepted masque tradition.

After Purcell's death in 1695 came a period in which there were few notable British creators of music. The reasons for this relate partly to the Hanoverian succession; the German ruler George I ascended the throne and at much the same time his compatriot Handel [p.185] came to Britain to dominate the musical scene, writing Italian operas for London though at the same time carrying on the Purcellian tradition (which he evidently knew well) in English royal odes, anthems and eventually the oratorio _Messiah_ in 1742. There were native composers: Arne [p.171] who composed _Rule, Britannia_ (1740) and (with others) a ballad opera called _Love in a Village_. Other later names are those of three Irishmen: John Field (1782-1837) [p.53], whose piano style influenced Chopin, and the opera composers Balfe and Wallace. Sterndale Bennett (1816-75) was admired by Mendelssohn and Schumann (who called him 'a glorious artist'), but did not fulfil his youthful promise. Samuel Wesley and his son S.S. Wesley were active and influential in church music. But broadly speaking, for the century and a half from Handel's arrival in Britain to the Savoy Operas of Gilbert and Sullivan the country was weak in native talent. Indeed, in the early nineteenth century the German composer Mendelssohn, adored both by the Royal Family and the public, became the major musical influence in Britain, just as Handel had been.

However, the renaissance of British music since then has more than compensated for the fallow years. Sullivan's [p.217] light operas, written to Gilbert's libretti over about twenty-five years from 1871, delighted the public and made a fortune for both men and their impresario D'Oyly Carte. Next, Elgar [p.159] emerged from provincial obscurity to become the voice of Edwardian England with his _Enigma Variations_ (1899), _Pomp and Circumstance_ marches, and the orchestral pictures _Cockaigne (In London Town)_ and _Falstaff. The Dream of Gerontius_ was hailed in 1902 by Richard Strauss as music by 'the first English progressive'. Two symphonies

and two concertos, one for violin and one for cello, show this complex composer in a range of moods from ceremonial to elegiac.

Other composers followed Elgar and re-established British music internationally. Delius [p.141] was a visionary who excelled in the evocation of atmosphere and mood, not least that of nostalgia: the popular orchestral piece _On Hearing the First Cuckoo in Spring_ (1913) gives a clear idea of this aspect of his style, though there are larger works too which sound a more epic note such as his _Mass of Life_. Vaughan Williams [p.121] was a conscious (but not blinkered) nationalist whose nine symphonies include a _London Symphony_ and who wrote very late in life an opera on Bunyan's _The Pilgrim's Progress_ which was produced in 1951. Holst is best known for _The Planets_ (1916), a work of power and exuberant virtuosity; but a certain quiet intensity of feeling is more characteristic of this thoughtful, visionary man and is to be noted in his choral _Hymn of Jesus_, the opera _Sāvitri_ and the orchestral tone

Above: _London production of the Andrew Lloyd Webber musical_ The Phantom of the Opera _with Sarah Brightman and Michael Crawford in the leading roles._

poems _Egdon Heath_ and _Hammersmith_.

The next generation or so gave British music further important names. Walton [p.215] dazzled the musical world with a series of vivid youthful works from _Façade_ to the oratorio _Belshazzar's Feast_ and his First Symphony, though his later years were less productive. Tippett [p.117] developed far more slowly, but after his oratorio _A Child of Our Time_ in 1941 he has gone from strength to strength and proved an artist whose stature is still hard to assess: his four big operas and his choral–orchestral _The Mask of Time_ (1984) bring the 'classical' side of British music right up to date.

Britten [p.111] is probably the outstanding figure in this century and perhaps in all English music. This immensely gifted and hardworking composer was a thorough professional and proud of the fact. He revitalised British opera single-handed with his _Peter Grimes_ in 1945 and went on to compose several more operas culminating in _Death in Venice_, completed in 1973. He often wrote for children, either as listeners or performers, in works as different as his _Young Person's Guide to the Orchestra_ and _War Requiem_; yet there is nothing childish about his achievement in a large number of works in all genres (save the more epic kind of symphony) of which most have entered the repertory.

In the last thirty years or so, Britain has seen no lessening of musical activity. There has been a steady raising of standards of performance and musical education as well as a rise of several new musical names among

Constant LAMBERT
(1905-1951)

While still a student at the Royal College of Music, where he was taught by Vaughan Williams, Lambert was introduced to Diaghilev by the painter Edmund Dulac. With his uncanny gift for recognising unusual talent the Russian impresario immediately commissioned the young man to write a ballet. The result was _Romeo and Juliet_, which opened at Monte Carlo in May 1926, and was the first work to be written by an English composer for Diaghilev's company. By the time it appeared, Lambert had already achieved a certain notoriety as reciter in Walton's _Façade_. But other compositions of his own followed, in which the influence of jazz could be clearly seen, including his well-known choral work, _Rio Grande_. In 1930 Lambert returned to ballet with the formation of

the Carmargo Society, whose principal conductor he became. Among many distinguished productions under his baton was that of _Job_ by Vaughan Williams. Although Lambert now found little time for composing, in 1936 he gave the first performance of his unjustly neglected concert masque, _Summer's Last Will and Testament_, which was followed two years later by his brilliant ballet score _Horoscope_. A wit, bon viveur, conductor and writer (_Music Ho!_ is as readable now as it was when it was first published in 1934), who had sufficiently wide-ranging tastes perhaps to bring together popular and classical music through a clear understanding of the jazz language, Lambert's early death robbed music in Britain of a colourful and richly talented personality. R.H.

Above: *Many young American composers studied with Nadia Boulanger: (l. to r.) Virgil Thomson, Walter Piston, Herbert Elwell and Aaron Copland.*

composers. Men such as Bennett, Maxwell Davies and Birtwistle have been active in opera and other music theatre (including film) as well as purely instrumental pieces. But for the ordinary music-lover, other names and styles are vastly better known and seem likely to continue so, for democracy has brought major and influential changes in public taste that we cannot ignore.

Thus the group of four Beatles emerged from Liverpool in the early 1960s to conquer the pop music world with a freshness and imaginative invention expressed in a series of musical numbers culminating in the masterly album *Sergeant Pepper's Lonely Hearts Club Band* (1967); not long after that they disbanded, but individual members have continued to make music. Pink Floyd are a longer-lasting group possessing real imagination and sensitivity, to judge by such albums as *The Dark Side of the Moon* (1973). But the shooting of the Beatle John Lennon in 1980, together with the violent deaths of other rock musicians such as Brian Jones of The Rolling Stones and the various drug or sex allegations which may involve such popular artists as Boy George and Elton John remind us of the perils of an art and life-style that aims at an intense appeal to the impressionable young. On the other hand, Andrew Lloyd Webber (b. 1948) works in a style midway between pop and 'classical' and must be one of the most successful musicians ever in terms of earnings: his musicals *Evita, Cats* and *The Phantom of the Opera* are all running at the time of writing and have already made their mark in history. C.H.

AMERICA

A mixture of European settlers brought the first classifiable music to the North American continent in the sixteenth and seventeenth centuries: Dutch and English with psalms and hymns and Germans and Moravians with instrumental bands and a tradition of organ-building. Soon the 'new found land' had its patriotic songs and by the eighteenth century Boston and other big cities prided themselves on their opera, concerts and home music: almost every young lady and gentleman, one Philadelphia newspaper declared in 1810, could 'charm their neighbours with something that courtesy calls music'. A New Yorker, McDowell, studied in Europe and returned to be Professor of Music at Columbia University: one critic in 1900 called him 'the greatest of American composers'. But his style was European; and a much more recognisably American figure was Charles Ives [p.145], brought up by a bandmaster father 'mainly on Bach and Stephen Foster'. Ives pulled no punches and constantly challenged the ear, which he said he 'had to pull . . . hard'. He wrote pieces simultaneously using several musical ideas with differing keys and speeds, or having optional sections (marked 'to play or not to play'), or demanding two conductors – like *Central Park in the Dark* (1907). His Fourth Symphony (1916) mixes dance rhythms with hymnlike sections and national tunes like *Marching through Georgia*. Most of his music was unknown for many years, and he never heard a full orchestra play his music until he was seventy-five.

Aaron Copland [p.25] has suggested that Ives was 'too far in advance of his own', a fact probably also true of the only other composer at all like him, Ruggles, whose *Sun-*

Heitor VILLA-LOBOS
(1887-1959)

The most prolific Latin-American composer, with works in many of the conventional categories plus a broad range of compositions inspired by the folk music of his native Brazil. Largely self-taught, he joined bands of wandering instrumentalists in his youth, then performed in cafés, theatres and night clubs, finally playing the cello in orchestras and the piano as a soloist. Always fascinated by his country's indigenous music, he set about exploring popular idioms and collecting folk melodies, pursuing his investigations right into the Amazonian heartland. Although also influenced by French music, he absorbed the native Brazilian influences so thoroughly that his lyrical, free-flowing, rhythmically varied style blends with an imaginative use of instrumental colour to produce a music that could never be other than South American. Curiously, J.S. Bach was also an important influence, causing him to produce his *Bachianas Brasileiras*, a series of nine pieces in baroque form but using Brazilian ideas, of which the lovely No. 5 for soprano and eight cellos is very popular. His sixteen *Chôros* are also intriguing, being pieces for a widely contrasting range of performers and echoing his early experiences with the native bands. There are also twelve symphonies, ten concertos, piano music, orchestral suites, and much else to explore in the output of this colourful composer. J.C.

Treader for orchestra (1933) had to wait thirty years for its première. By this time Copland himself was an acknowledged master, having studied in Paris and returned in 1924 seeking a style 'that could speak of universal things in a vernacular of American speech rhythms . . . music with a largeness of utterance'. He achieved this in such works as his ballets *Billy the Kid, Rodeo* and *Appalachian Spring*, where the mood can be snappy, countrified, cleanly spacious and homely by turns. Bernstein has called him 'the best we have'.

Jazz is a major strand in American music, and not only in the case of black musicians such as Joplin and Ellington. Gershwin came from the same Brooklyn Jewish background as Copland but developed differently, writing songs of lasting quality for musical shows as well as larger-scale works including his *Rhapsody in Blue*, Piano Concerto, and the black opera *Porgy and Bess* (1935). Other major song composers were Berlin, Kern and the ultra-sophisticated Cole Porter.

Thomson, Sessions, Harris and Barber are among 'symphonic' composers of this generation, but the next outstanding figure after Gershwin to bridge the gap between serious and popular styles is Bernstein [p.119] (b. 1918). His musical *West Side Story* is still popular thirty years after it was first produced, and more recent pieces such as his *Mass* for the Kennedy Arts Centre in Washington and his opera *A Quiet Place* (1983) show that his busy international career as a conductor has not dimmed his flair and expressive intensity.

An avant-garde movement in music has its septuagenarian senior figure in Cage, who has specialised in various 'happenings' with various degrees of chance, including one notorious piece called *4'33"* (1952) in which no sound is heard at all; he has declared that 'everything we do is music'. More academic (though not in a pejorative sense) are Carter and Babbitt, both of whom have composed ingenious and challenging scores; the degree of independence given to the players in such a work as Carter's Third String Quartet makes the work dauntingly difficult to perform.

A much younger avant-garde movement links with styles that have been variously labelled as post-modernism and minimalism. A minimalist must make much out of little, and Philip Glass's opera *Einstein on the Beach* begins with nearly four minutes of a sequence of three primary triads in C major repeated over and over again, but there is nothing minimal about its overall duration of

Arthur FARWELL (1872-1952)
St Paul, Minnesota

Roy HARRIS (1898-1979)
Chandler, Oklahoma

Scott JOPLIN (1868-1917)
Texarkarna, Arkansas

Henry COWELL (1897-1965)
Menlo Park, California

Below: *The English National Opera's 1987 production of* Akhnaten. *This is an opera set in ancient Egypt, and was written by the young minimalist American composer Philip Glass.*

Above: *Outline map of the United States of America showing the birthplaces of many of its principal composers, both in the academic field and in the sphere of popular music. An obvious bias towards* the East Coast clearly has its basis in the immigratory history of the country with most newcomers from Europe obviously settling in the most developed and populated areas.

four and a half hours without intermission; for reasons which have little to do with music, the audience at the 1976 New York production was invited 'to leave and re-enter the auditorium quietly, as necessary'. Glass's 1984 opera *Akhnaten*, set in ancient Egypt, has a similar timelessness, and a sympathetic critic has suggested that he 'has tuned in to man's most primitive and elemental impulses – the beat of the human heart and the bodily cycles of breathing and movement'. But what some listeners find soothing others find infuriating, and another commentator called *Akhnaten* 'anti-music written for people who have to dope themselves to be able to respond to it'. Reich and Adams are others using minimalist techniques, and the latter's orchestral *The Chairman Dances* has won over many doubters.

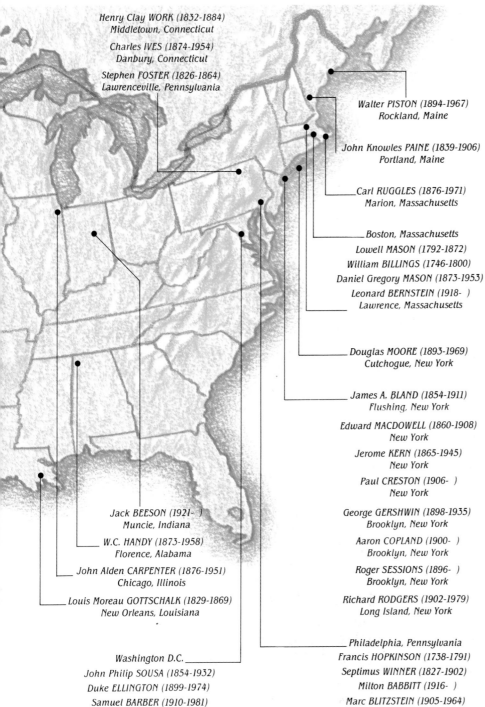

Henry Clay WORK (1832-1884)
Middletown, Connecticut

Charles IVES (1874-1954)
Danbury, Connecticut

Stephen FOSTER (1826-1864)
Lawrenceville, Pennsylvania

Walter PISTON (1894-1967)
Rockland, Maine

John Knowles PAINE (1839-1906)
Portland, Maine

Carl RUGGLES (1876-1971)
Marion, Massachusetts

Boston, Massachusetts
Lowell MASON (1792-1872)
William BILLINGS (1746-1800)
Daniel Gregory MASON (1873-1953)
Leonard BERNSTEIN (1918-)
Lawrence, Massachusetts

Douglas MOORE (1893-1969)
Cutchogue, New York

James A. BLAND (1854-1911)
Flushing, New York

Edward MACDOWELL (1860-1908)
New York

Jerome KERN (1865-1945)
New York

Paul CRESTON (1906-)
New York

George GERSHWIN (1898-1935)
Brooklyn, New York

Aaron COPLAND (1900-)
Brooklyn, New York

Roger SESSIONS (1896-)
Brooklyn, New York

Richard RODGERS (1902-1979)
Long Island, New York

Philadelphia, Pennsylvania
Francis HOPKINSON (1738-1791)
Septimus WINNER (1827-1902)
Milton BABBITT (1916-)
Marc BLITZSTEIN (1905-1964)

Jack BEESON (1921-)
Muncie, Indiana

W.C. HANDY (1873-1958)
Florence, Alabama

John Alden CARPENTER (1876-1951)
Chicago, Illinois

Louis Moreau GOTTSCHALK (1829-1869)
New Orleans, Louisiana

Washington D.C.
John Philip SOUSA (1854-1932)
Duke ELLINGTON (1899-1974)
Samuel BARBER (1910-1981)

Charles IVES
(1874-1954)

An insurance broker and part-time composer who has become the father-figure of American music, he studied at college but learnt most of what he needed from his lively-minded bandmaster father. Ives absorbed all the sights, sounds, music and mystical Emersonian ideas surrounding a stimulating New England childhood, and regurgitated them in a great flood of seemingly chaotic music when he grew up. The early *Song for Harvest Season*, for instance, gives voice, trombone, cornet and organ pedals each a different key. His works leap from excruciating dissonance to a hymn-tune or piece of ragtime; orchestral groups play from opposite sides of the hall; incompatible idioms and/or tempos are heard simultaneously; and so on. He tried anything and everything, and incidentally employed polytonality, quarter tones, serialism and aleatory effects ahead of all the European pioneers. But his music is so difficult that performances of the bigger works were long delayed. The vast Fourth Symphony required a team of copyists to decipher it, and Stokowski needed two assistant conductors to help perform it fifty years after it was penned. An eccentric genius with no time for musical conventions or niceties, Ives poured all the complexities and chaos of life into his music, and made his own rules from beginning to end. J.C.

Latin America has had various musical traditions, including opera since the eighteenth century, and Argentina's Teatro Colón in Buenos Aires (opened in 1857) is today a major international centre. The best known Latin American composer is the Brazilian Villa-Lobos [p.143], whose popular guitar music is only one part of a vast output that includes twelve symphonies and numerous concertos as well as the Bach-inspired *Bachianas Brasileiras* for various performing combinations. The Argentinian composer Ginastera (1916-83) lived his last years in Europe and was stylistically advanced for his time in such works as his Violin Concerto of 1963; his opera *Bomarzo*, set in sixteenth-century Italy, was banned in his native country because of its overt sexuality. Its première was in Washington in 1967. C.H.

Artur RUBINSTEIN
(1886-1982)

Celebrated Polish pianist who became an American citizen at the age of sixty, but whose musical genius showed itself at a very early age: he was five when he gave his first public recital in Warsaw. After a period of study under Rozycki he was taken by his sister to play for Joachim in Berlin, who agreed to pay for his musical training. He studied technique under Bartsch and Breithopf, and one of his professors of composition was Max Bruch. In 1897 he performed a Mozart piano concerto, with Joachim conducting, which was so well received that further engagements in Dresden, Hamburg and Warsaw followed immediately. He returned to his studies, this time under Paderewski in Switzerland, before visiting Paris in 1905, where he gave six recitals and performed with the Lamoureux Orchestra, and London where he received an equally rapturous welcome. Extensive overseas tours followed and the following year he went to the USA to perform in New York and Philadelphia. He spoke eight languages fluently, and served as an interpreter during the Great War as well as giving many charity recitals with the violinist Ysaÿe. He became an exponent of the music of Falla, but his reputation as one of the greatest pianists of the twentieth century rests with his mastery of the classics, and especially of works by his compatriot Chopin. His recorded repertoire is dominated by enduring readings of the mazurkas, nocturnes, waltzes and the orchestrally accompanied works. To which any collector of great piano performances would add his recordings of Beethoven, Brahms, Falla, Liszt, Mozart and Rachmaninov, all of whom he played with a mixture of assured brilliance and sensitivity. R.H.

PART FOUR

CHAMBER MUSIC

Below: *The English Chamber Orchestra under its principal conductor, Jeffrey Tate, at the Queen Elizabeth Hall, London, 1987.*

For many people the term 'chamber music' is somewhat off-putting. They associate it with a highly intellectual kind of music-making designed for small audiences consisting of experts and feel that it probably offers little to the ordinary listener. This feeling has no real justification, and it is a great pity if it prevents the exploration of what is a wonderful repertory to which most of our favourite composers have contributed. Sometimes one wonders if it has something to do with the word 'chamber' itself, which to English ears may sound antiquated and even sinister – perhaps because we think of Madame Tussaud's waxwork Chamber of Horrors, or of the Star Chamber in which trials were held long ago in the Palace of Westminster.

In fact the term comes from the Italian *musica da camera* and means no more than 'room music' – music intended for domestic surroundings and not a public hall or the open air. This implies a smallish number of players and listeners, and is linked to the nature of the music itself, which must be suitable for these circumstances. In practice we do not use it for a single performer such as a pianist, and reserve it for ensemble playing – that is, where musicians play together. The number of players ranges from two to ten, and each has his own 'part' or musical line: this is not the same as an orchestra in which several violins or cellos may play in unison. Another feature which makes chamber music different from, say, a concerto with its star soloist is that each performer is equal with the others.

This point leads us on to the next, which is that originally much chamber music was simply intended for the enjoyment of the players themselves and not really designed for audiences. There is a parallel here with games, for which we also use the word 'play', just as the French and Germans do with their words *jouer* and *spielen*. Although countless amateur groups meet to play chamber music just for their own enjoyment, such music today is commonly performed or recorded by professional ensembles with listeners in mind.

Even so, a performance of chamber music often still seems to represent a kind of exchange between a small group of musicians more than something deliberately directed at an audience, and perhaps this is because its composers have themselves seen it above all in that way. For this reason it usually has more subtlety and delicacy than orchestral works, operas and concertos where big sweeping effects are needed to win over a public. The storm in Beethoven's *Pastoral* Symphony is overwhelmingly effective when played as intended by a symphony orchestra with drums and trombones, but we cannot imagine it occurring in his *Spring* Sonata for violin and piano, for it would be out of place, and even out of scale, in a chamber work. Someone once made a musical joke out of arranging Tchaikovsky's *1812* Overture for a small ensemble of recorders and other delicate instruments: inevitably this thrilling music sounded ridiculous played by such small forces. We do not

Below: *A warm summer evening has taken 'chamber' music out of doors? 'Konzert am Kurbayer ischen Hofe' was painted by Peter Jakob Horemans (1700-76) in 1771.*

turn to chamber music for epic utterances or grand effects, but rather for qualities which are more personal and intimate. It is no coincidence that Beethoven chose the medium of the string quartet for the deep musical thoughts of his last years.

The history of chamber music goes back as far as music itself. The Old Testament tells of King Nebuchadnezzar's Babylonian band of 'cornet, flute, harp, sackbut, psaltery, dulcimer, and all kinds of music'. In ancient Rome wealthy households often had servants skilled in music who could join together to provide entertainment or just a background to conversation. The Middle Ages saw a steady development in the craft of making and standardising instruments – an important factor since they can only play together if in tune – and also in playing skills, with guilds of musicians existing by the eleventh century.

By Renaissance times it was fashionable for the wealthy and educated to have some skill in domestic music-making. In Britain Henry VIII played the lute, recorder and keyboard instruments, and his daughter Queen Elizabeth also liked music and played the virginals; this fact was widely known, and at a pageant in her honour at Kenilworth Castle in 1575 she was pleasantly surprised by the appearance of a construction in the form of a dolphin in which 'a consort of Musicke was secretly placed, the which sounded'. Similarly in 1591, at Eltham near London, she enjoyed 'the musicke of an exquisite consort, wherein was the Lute, Bandora, Base-violl, Citterne, Treble-violl, and Flute'. It was for these instruments that the British composer Thomas Morley arranged some 'consort lessons' eight years later; a consort was an ensemble, and the word is of course related to 'concert' with its exactly similar sense of performers joining together to make music.

Most European rulers, nobles and wealthy merchants now had musicians in their households, some of them brought expensively from abroad: thus the British lutenist John Dowland travelled widely before joining the Danish court with a high salary in 1598. Louis XIV of France had many court musicians including a *maître de la musique de la chambre du roy* who was responsible for the

Luigi BOCCHERINI
(1743-1805)

A composer who turned out an astonishing quantity of music which nearly always seems very attractive when heard, but who is known to the general public by just one movement, and to confirmed music-lovers by only a handful of works. Cellist son of an Italian double-bass player, he toured as a virtuoso performer before settling in Spain for eighteen years, then spent ten years as court composer to William II of Prussia, finally returning to Madrid and dying in poverty for lack of a patron. A contemporary of Haydn and resembling him in both outlook and music, his somewhat less virile style caused him to be known as 'Mrs Haydn'; but his melodies are splendid and his harmony often striking. The Minuet from one of his 113 string quintets is universally recognised (Op. 13:5 in E major), the B flat Cello Concerto is becoming well known, various chamber works with a guitar part are now quite popular, and a few of the 91 string quartets have found their way on to recordings. But there are also 20 symphonies, 60 trios, and another 40 quintets for various instrumental groups, plus much church music and some operas. J.C.

Above: *Henry VIII was a talented amateur musician who played several instruments, including the harp and lute, and also a composer. The gentleman with him was not a music critic but the court jester.*

Right: *A somewhat unusual chamber ensemble perhaps involved in some sort of 16th-century jam-session. This impression of 'Le Concert allemand' was painted by an unknown French artist of the time.*

performance of music when he rose, retired to bed or ate meals; and when the Restoration took place in England in 1660 Charles II returned from exile in France to appoint his own numerous court musicians in London. Many British composers wrote chamber music at this time, among them Purcell, who held a court appointment and composed fantasies for three to seven viols and trio sonatas (dedicated to the king) for two violins and accompaniment. Another figure of this age is the Italian composer Corelli (1653-1713), who wrote his own trio sonatas while in the service of Queen Christina of Sweden at her court in Rome. This Baroque period of about 1600-1750 saw chamber music come fully of age, with its own forms of which the chief was the four-movement sonata for two or more instruments. Bach, Handel, Telemann, Cou-

perin and Vivaldi are all major figures here, and Bach's multi-sectional *Musical Offering* (1747) for flute, two violins, string bass and keyboard represents a pinnacle of the polyphonic art of the time.

In the classical era from 1750 to 1830 the great German-Austrian figures of Haydn, Mozart, Beethoven and Schubert all contributed extensively to the chamber repertory. Haydn may with justice be called the father of the modern string quartet, and he wrote over eighty quartets as well as much other chamber music. All these composers were themselves skilful string ensemble players. Together with their great skill, such individual qualities as Haydn's vitality and humour, Mozart's grace and humanity, Beethoven's vigour and contemplation and Schubert's melodious yet mysterious warmth have made

Above: *Early chamber music was more of a natural domestic activity (in higher social circles) than the serious art form it is today. `The Concert after the Meal' by Ambrosius Benson (1495-1550).*

the chamber works of each of these men central to the repertory.

In the Romantic period that followed, some artists turned away from classical forms such as the sonata, a form which includes the majority of chamber works such as trios, quartets, quintets and so on, which are simply sonatas for three or more instruments. We do not associate Berlioz, Chopin or Liszt with chamber music, nor do we look for it in the work of opera composers such as Rossini, Wagner or Verdi, though, as it happens, most of these men produced at least

Louis SPOHR
(1784-1859)

Child prodigy German violinist who became a noted conductor and composer, serving in, touring with, and directing various European orchestras, giving recitals with his harpist-pianist first wife, and finally settling as court conductor at Cassel. He composed a great deal of music in various genres, including 11 operas, 9 symphonies, 15 violin concertos and 34 string quartets. One of the operas was a *Faust*, which greatly influenced Weber, while his *Zemire und Azor* of 1819 anticipated Wagner in its use of leitmotivs to propel the drama by means of music rather than action. Later, he became a protagonist for Wagner's own operas although, curiously, he found romanticism distasteful and preferred classical traditions despite the progressive tendencies in his own music. He was less ambiguous in politics, his liberal sympathies in 1848 causing the feudalistic Elector to refuse him leave, which he took nevertheless and thus provoked a long legal battle. But whatever his fortunes with German princes, he delighted Queen Victoria and always enjoyed great success in England following his first London appearance in 1820. He made a great impression then with the *Gesangszene* violin concerto (No. 8 in A minor), which remains popular to this day, together with a few other concertos and a small number of chamber works. J.C.

Above: *Music at the wedding feast of Sir Henry Unton, an oil painting of* c. *1596 by an unknown artist which gives a clear picture of the kind of chamber ensemble in common use in those times.*

some works of this kind. We find it rather in composers who were in their time considered more conservative, such as Mendelssohn, Schumann and Brahms, together with Weber and Spohr. Mendelssohn wrote his vivid Octet for eight string players at sixteen, while Brahms composed his wonderfully autumnal Clarinet Quintet near the end of his life. These composers are, as it happens, all German; but others such as the Russians Borodin and Tchaikovsky and the Czechs Smetana and Dvořák wrote string quartets and other chamber works. So did Grieg and (later) Niel-

sen and Sibelius in Scandinavia. With such names as these, we are already talking about twentieth-century music, and French composers Franck, Fauré, Debussy and Ravel bring us to a time rather closer to our own. The string quartets of Debussy and Ravel are both early masterpieces, often coupled together in recordings. Poulenc is another Frenchman, belonging to the next generation, whose contribution to chamber music was considerable.

The present century has seen a number of influential masters contributing to chamber music, including Schoenberg and his pupils Berg and Webern as well as Bartók, Stravinsky and Prokofiev. The British composers Elgar and Vaughan Williams also figure here, as do the later Englishmen Walton, Tippett and Britten. Shostakovich is a major Soviet com-

poser with fifteen string quartets and much else in his chamber catalogue. In the United States we have Ives, Copland, Carter and Cage. France has given us Messiaen and Boulez, and a new progressive Soviet school headed by Schnittke has continued to explore the medium as have the Polish composers Lutosławski and Penderecki. The German Stockhausen has written a number of chamber works plus some which push the definition of this genre challengingly outwards, such as his *Mikrophonie I* (1964) with its parts for tamtam (gong) plus electronic sound manipulators. Julian Lloyd Webber's *Variations* (1977) for cello and six-piece rock band make a quite different kind of challenge in reminding us of the interplay between musicians which is a feature shared by classical chamber music and jazz. C.H.

From the seventeenth century and often earlier, skill in domestic music-making was considered a social asset, and in Henry Peacham's *The Compleat Gentleman* (1622) the reader is told that he should be able to read a musical part at sight and 'to play the same upon your Violl'. In Jacobean England, Orlando Gibbons wrote dances and fantasias for strings; this latter form was also used by the young Purcell in 1680, but his trio sonatas for two violins and accompaniment of about the same time aimed at 'a just imitation' of Italian masters like Vitali and Corelli who made important steps towards establishing definite chamber music forms, as did Vivaldi and (in Germany) Bach, Handel and Telemann a generation later. Bach wrote sonatas for one instrument with accompaniment including examples for flute, violin and *viola da gamba*, but his crowning chamber achievement is undoubtedly his *Musical Offering* (1747) in which a 'royal theme' given him by Frederick the Great (a keen amateur flautist and composer) is treated in nine sections including ingenious canons, fugues and a trio sonata for flute, violin and accompaniment. Handel also wrote violin sonatas and trio sonatas, sometimes in a four-movement pattern. Telemann's *Parisian* Quartets (1737) for flute, violin, cello and harpsichord represent a move towards the lighter world of the Rococo, as do the *Concerts royaux* by

Above: *An early writer of music for the chamber ensemble was Orlando Gibbons (1583-1625), British composer of many dances and fantasias that built on the foundations of the small instrumental ensembles of the early Italian masters such as Corelli and Vitali. In 1619 he was given the official post of 'chamber musician to the King'.*

the French composer Couperin which are essentially entertainment music for the light though cultivated tastes of an aristocratic listener.

The trend towards a less learned sounding style, or at least an art that concealed art, reached its apogee with the Classical era that begins with the early quartets of Haydn, by 1755 a resourceful young musician skilled in all the forms of his time. He used the ensemble of two violins, viola and cello first for *divertimenti* and later in a four-movement form that was to become standard, with a brisk allegro in sonata form followed by a melodious slow movement, a minuet and a vivacious finale. (Sometimes the minuet comes second.)

By 1772 Haydn had written nearly thirty quartets, and after a gap of nine years he returned to the form with the six Quartets, Op. 33, which he said were 'in an entirely new and special manner', though his varied but always recognisable idiom had been developing before then. After this he wrote over thirty more works in this form and medium, of which the *Emperor* Quartet, Op. 76, No. 3, with its famous slow-movement set of variations on the *Austrian Hymn* is just one of several which have since been given nicknames. His invention and wit are no less evident in his piano trios of which No. 23 in G major has the vivacious 'Gipsy Rondo' finale. Mozart also belongs to this era, and his six string quartets dedicated to Haydn (1782-85) are as remarkable as anything he wrote; among his copious output of chamber music we can only single out masterpieces such as the String Trio, the Quintet for Piano and Wind, the Clarinet Quintet and the String Quintet (using two violas) in G minor, all of which belong to his last decade.

In the Vienna of Beethoven and Schubert, the first thirty years or so of the nineteenth century, chamber music was usually still performed domestically by amateurs, but by now there were also a few professional ensembles such as the Schuppanzigh Quartet (named after its leader) who gave premières of music by Haydn and these two later men. Both were inspired to write fine quartets: Beethoven's seventeen works in this form are among his greatest, and his last (between Op. 127 and Op. 135) belong to a final creative period in which he explored new worlds of thought and feeling. But he wrote chamber works throughout his career and indeed his official Op. 1 was a set of piano trios: his most celebrated work for this medium is his last, the *Archduke* Trio dedicated to his friend and patron the Archduke Rudolph. There are also violin sonatas (including the *Spring* and the *Kreutzer*), and five for cello which sound yet

Left: *Josef Haydn (1732-1809) helped to finalise the classical four-movement format of the 19th century and the inevitable sonata-form of the 1st movement.*

Above: *A romantic but nicely detailed impression of Haydn and his Esterházy quartet providing enlightened entertainment for his noble employers. He liked to play with eminent contemporary composers.*

Below: *The young Mozart (1756-1791) plays a duet with his sister Maria Anna watched by their father Leopold under a portrait of their mother. Painted by Johann Nepomuk della Croce, c. 1780-81.*

Isaac ALBÉNIZ
(1860-1909)

A child prodigy who played in public at four and had a *pasodoble* performed by a military band at seven, this composer-pianist became the first Spaniard of note (with his contemporary Granados) to take the native music of his own country seriously as the inspiration for original compositions. Much travelled (he ran away from home and crossed the Atlantic at thirteen), he studied at Leipzig and Brussels, worked with Liszt, d'Indy and Dukas, lived for a while in London and more permanently in Paris, toured extensively as a concert pianist, and composed songs, operas, *zarzuelas*, a piano concerto, and the orchestral rhapsody *Catalonia* as well as the solo piano music on which his fame now rests. There is a vast range of piano pieces, culminating in the great twelve-part *Iberia*. This richly textured and exuberant work draws heavily on Andalusian folk melody and may be regarded as Albéniz's masterpiece; with his *Suite Española*, it has attracted others into producing orchestral versions. But despite the pianistic emphasis, five of his operas were performed in the 1890s, at which time he was commissioned by an English banker to produce an operatic trilogy based on the King Arthur legend. But this was never finished. J.C.

another expressive note, together with various other pieces. Schubert's rich melodic gift is even more spontaneous than Beethoven's and found expression in several masterpieces among which we may list the sunlit Piano Trio in B flat and *Trout* Quintet (scored unusually for piano, violin, viola, cello and double bass), the mellow *Arpeggione* Sonata (written for an instrument now obsolete and played today by cellists) and the Octet for strings and wind, while the *Death and the Maiden* String Quartet and the String Quintet of his last year (1828) explore a more sombre vein. But for all the depth of some of these works, there was nothing self-consciously intellectual about Schubert's approach to chamber music, and he wrote waltzes and minuets for quartet as well as these more formal pieces.

The successors of these men include Mendelssohn, Schumann and Brahms. All wrote

Above: *Portrait by von Kloeber of Beethoven (1770-1827), whose output of string quartets, especially the later ones, is generally considered to be a great peak of chamber music writing.*

Above: *Schubert's Piano Quintet,* The Trout, *is one of the most popular chamber music works ever written. Here in the first variation of the Andantino the piano has the melody while the strings embellish.*

Below: *The romantic genius of chamber music Robert Schumann (1810-56) with his wife Clara to whom he dedicated his Piano Quintet.*

string quartets, and also for the increasingly popular combination of piano with strings. One of Mendelssohn's most delightful pieces is the fresh yet abundantly skilful string Octet he wrote at sixteen, while his later Piano Trio No. 1 in D minor shows a more dramatic side. Schumann's Piano Quintet is a big piece with a demanding piano part; dedicated to his pianist wife Clara it shows the passionate, rich and impulsive nature of his gift. He also wrote violin sonatas and partnered the piano with other less common instruments like the oboe and cello. Brahms was his protégé: a more sober artist who composed sonatas for violin, cello and clarinet, piano trios and quartets, a Piano Quintet and two string quintets, the later wonderfully lyrical Clarinet Quintet and two string sextets. His Trio for Violin, Horn and Piano was probably the first work for that combination. His fine craftsmanship and warm melodic vein place him among the great composers, though there is rarely the sheer spontaneity we find in Schubert, whom he greatly admired.

The nationalist composers of Eastern Europe brought a new folk-orientated note to the chamber repertory and an additional individuality that reflected the Romantic period to which they belonged. The Second String Quartet of Borodin is tender and seductive, its 'nocturne' slow movement sounding like a love song. A similar heartfelt quality permeates Tchaikovsky's First Quartet (one of three). His string sextet *Souvenir de Florence* has a predictably southern warmth, but his Piano Trio written in memory

of a friend is alternately elegiac and triumphant; a decade later, Rachmaninov was to write his own powerful and large-scale *Elegiac Trio* (1894) on hearing of Tchaikovsky's death. Such personal elements find their way also into the Czech composer Smetana's First Quartet, with its subtitle *From my Life,* and later the two quartets by his compatriot Janáček, of which the second is

called *Intimate Letters* and was inspired by his love for a young girl; he also gave a programmatic aspect to his Wind Sextet *Mládi (Youth).* Even the *American* Quartet by Dvořák has its folk and programmatic element, here evoking the music of his émigré compatriots in Iowa and that of the local Indians as well as birdsong; this work and his Piano Quintet are alike beloved for their abundant tunefulness and warmth of spirit, while the *Dumky* Piano Trio is at times more poignantly nostalgic.

Grieg and Sibelius are among Scandinavians who each wrote one string quartet, the former composer saying of his that 'it strives towards breadth and soaring flight'. Sibelius's Quartet in D minor is a sometimes gentle work in five movements with the subtitle *Voces intimae.* Nielsen contributed more to the chamber repertory: four quartets, a quintet for mixed wind and strings called *Serenata in vano* and a Wind Quintet (1922) for five friends in which each instrument represents a 'personality'. In France, Franck gave the world a Piano Quintet of much grandeur and a superbly lyrical Violin Sonata as well as a Quartet (his last chamber work) that deserves to be better known than it is; Fauré too wrote fine chamber music including sonatas for violin and cello. Debussy and Ravel each composed one string quartet: both works are celebrated youthful masterpieces brimful of feeling. Debussy also wrote sonatas for violin and cello and one surpassingly beautiful one for flute, viola and harp. Ravel's ethereally lovely Introduction and Allegro (a septet) also features the harp. His magnificent Piano Trio, written at the start of World War I, ranges from delicacy to the overwhelming triumph of its conclusion, while his later Duo for violin and cello and Violin Sonata breathe a fascinating world-weari-

**Gabriel FAURÉ
(1845-1924)**

French composer, organist and teacher whose music has come to epitomise all that is intimate, balanced and delicate – an art situated at the opposite pole from effusive late-romanticism, yet offering its own quietly intense beauty. Studying under Saint-Saëns at the Niedermeyer School rather than at the conventional Paris Conservatoire, Fauré eventually became professor of composition at the latter, and finally its director (1905) until his retirement in 1920. This seemingly mild man's appointment as director provoked so much conservative opposition that resignations came from all directions, leading to the comment that he resembled Robespierre in needing a 'daily cartload of victims'. But otherwise his life was one of quiet teaching and composing, apart from the final aural trauma of deafness which clouded his last years, but failed to inhibit composition. Essentially a miniaturist who disliked the chore of orchestration, Fauré is famed principally as a songwriter (he has been called the French Schumann), but his considerable output of chamber and piano works – the latter sometimes very challenging – deserves attention, while his most popular work on a larger scale is the *Requiem*, a choral piece of great beauty. Definitely a composer for the odd hour of very refined enjoyment. J.C.

ness. Poulenc has a charm and tenderness all of his own evident in his late-period sonatas for clarinet, flute and oboe, while a jazzy vein features in some earlier pieces such as the Sonata for Horn, Trumpet and Trombone.

Among other more modern masters, Bartók and Shostakovich stand out as contributing much to the string quartet repertory with six and fifteen works respectively; others of the Russian composer's works include his Piano Quintet and Piano Trio No. 2, while Bartók's thrilling Sonata for Two Pianos and Percussion and *Contrasts* for Violin, Clarinet and Piano are for rare if not unique combinations more accessible via recordings than in the concert hall. Schoenberg, Berg, Webern, Stravinsky, Hindemith, Vaughan Williams, Ives, Copland, Messiaen, Britten, Tippett, Boulez and Stockhausen are among other twentieth-century figures whose work seems sure to endure. Several musicians (Schoenberg, Ravel and Boulez among them) have used a chamber ensemble to partner a singer in a vocal work. The British ensemble called the Fires of London often performs pieces designed as 'music theatre'. Today's musical scene also includes many chamber orchestras, perhaps of some twenty players, such as that of Stuttgart in Germany, the Italian group I Musici and the Academy of St Martin-in-the-Fields and English Chamber Orchestra.

Above: *Two modern British masters of chamber music, Michael Tippett (b.1905) and Benjamin Britten (1913-76); a picture taken at Tippett's 60th birthday celebrations in January 1965.*

Below: *The Russian composer Dmitri Shostakovich (1906-75) was a modern writer who dedicated much effort to writing chamber music, including fifteen string quartets and a Piano Quintet.*

The music of the great composers of the past is accessible to us because it is 'recorded' in the old sense of the word, that is, written down in a form allowing it to be recreated by performers today. We do not have to rely on others for accounts of its quality but are in a position to judge it afresh for ourselves with each generation – and indeed its ability to stand this test is in itself a mark of greatness. With performers the story is different, or has been until the present century and the immense technological achievement of recording: we can only read contemporary accounts of the playing of Bach or Chopin, and of chamber ensembles. One which many listeners would dearly love to hear has no official name: it is the string quartet whose members played for their own domestic pleasure and included both Haydn and Mozart.

By the beginning of the nineteenth century there were a few named groups of professional players. One in Vienna which performed music by Haydn, Beethoven and Schubert was the string quartet named after its leader Ignaz Schuppanzigh (1776-1830) and in which during its heyday the other players were usually Sina (or Holz), Weiss and Linke. Schuppanzigh was an amiable, plump man whom Beethoven liked to call 'my lord Falstaff', and he was on good terms with all three of these great composers. His quartet was formed by 1805 and still further

improved when the wealthy music-loving diplomat Count Razumovsky authorised him to assemble 'the finest string quartet in Europe'. The Schuppanzigh Quartet gave the first performances of most of Beethoven's quartets and also that of Schubert's A minor Quartet which was dedicated to its leader.

Schuppanzigh also played outside Austria, taking Beethoven's music as far afield as Russia. Another ensemble was the Müller

Above: *The violinist Yehudi Menuhin with his sister Hephzibah and the French cellist Maurice Gendron contributed some classic performances with their recordings of the two Schubert Piano Trios.*

Quartet of four brothers: they made their début in Hamburg in 1831 and then took a repertory mainly of Haydn, Mozart and Beethoven to several European countries includ-

ing Germany, France, Denmark, the Netherlands and Russia; the family tradition continued when the four sons of their leader Karl Müller in turn formed a touring string quartet of their own twenty-five years later. A cellist called Valentin Müller, perhaps unrelated, joined the Maurin Quartet which played Beethoven to French audiences in 1852. In Britain, a London violinist and violist called Joseph Dando gave a series of quartet concerts from 1836 to 1842 at the Hanover Square Rooms; at this time he himself played the viola and the other players were Henry Blagrove, Henry Gattie and Charles Lucas, though he returned to the role of first violinist in a later series of performances. The Dando Quartet introduced quartets by Mendelssohn and Schumann to British audiences.

The most notable ensemble of the next generation was still a string quartet, the Joachim Quartet which was led by Joseph Joachim and was active (with some changes in personnel) from 1869 to 1907. He founded it with Berlin colleagues and their command of Beethoven and Brahms (both of whom they played complete) was acknowledged in all the major European centres. All the instruments were by Stradivari, as is the case with the Cleveland Quartet today. The Busch Quartet founded by Adolf Busch in 1919 performed a repertory similarly based on the great Viennese masters, while the Busch

Chamber Players which he also led were famous in Bach and Handel. The great violinist Yehudi Menuhin was a Busch pupil, a fact that reminds us that we now reach musicians of our own time: Menuhin himself and his pianist sister Hephzibah have themselves played as a chamber duo since 1934, in such works as the sonatas of Mozart and Beethoven.

The Busch Quartet and the Menuhins are among the many fine ensembles of the first half of this century whose art is still available to us via recordings. So are the Léner Quartet from Hungary, fine in Debussy and Ravel as well as the classical repertory, and the Hungarian String Quartet, who, although using the same basic repertory, were major advocates of Bartók. The Kolisch Quartet, active from 1922 to 1939, was unusual in playing the standard repertory from memory and also bravely gave premières of Schoenberg's Third and Fourth Quartets, Berg's Lyric Suite and Bartók's Fifth Quartet at a time when these masters were misunderstood or opposed. Other well-known quartets are the Budapest, Pro Arte, Loewenguth, Italian and Griller, the latter (1928-61) being all-British. The Amadeus Quartet (1947-87) is now also sadly part of history following the recent death of its violinist Peter Schidlof; this distinguished group were noted for their refinement in a wide repertory and for the continuity of personnel over four decades.

Left: *One of the most celebrated regular string quartets of recent times has been the Amadeus Quartet, founded in 1947 and disbanding in 1987 on the death of their violinist Peter Schidlof, without whom they felt unable to continue.*

Below: *The Allegri String Quartet has been active in the concert and recording field for over twenty years with a slightly changing personnel but a continuity of style. They mainly play the well-established repertoire.*

*Béla BARTÓK
(1881-1945)*

A brilliant lad whose mother taught him piano and then contrived a route leading him to formal studies in Budapest, this intense and serious-minded pianist/composer eventually became a key figure in twentieth-century music. Often employing a raw, spiky dissonance, his music nevertheless remains melodically Hungarian at root and was eventually characterised by a uniquely vital rhythmic thrust. His six string quartets and the rarefied and mysterious *Music for Strings, Percussion and Celesta* are regarded almost in awe by aficionados. At first under the spell of Richard Strauss, Liszt, Debussy and the early Stravinsky, Bartók was profoundly affected by the explorations of Hungarian peasant music which he began with Kodály in 1905. He became totally absorbed by the various folk idioms, and eventually received official support for his researches, in the meantime pursuing his career as a pianist and producing music increasingly influenced by what he had found in rural southeast Europe. But Fascism then drove him to the USA (1940), where his health faltered and he seemed unwanted. However, encouragement came in due course, prompting the magnificent *Concerto for Orchestra* in 1943, and his Third Piano Concerto and a Viola Concerto in the year of his death. J.C.

Among today's quartets, one of the most senior and most admired is the Juilliard Quartet (1946), of which the leader Robert Mann was latterly the only remaining founder-member: they have given powerful performances of the classical and modern repertory including new American works. Other quartets of great distinction, some more recently formed with younger players, include the Prague (1955) from Czechoslovakia, the Borodin from Russia, the Melos from Germany and the Delmé, Lindsay, Alberni and Endellion from Britain; the La Salle and Arditti Quartets have excelled in difficult new music.

This list of ensembles has inevitably concentrated on string quartets. There is a 'chicken and egg' situation in which the preponderance of string quartets composed has

Above: *The Beaux Arts Trio, a talented and unified group formed in 1955 to operate in the specialised field of the Piano Trio repertoire. The pianist Menahem Pressler is now the only original member.*

led to the formation of ensembles reflecting the richness of this one repertory and composers have tended to direct their thoughts to this medium for practical reasons: duos, trios and so on are less common, while regularly-working unusual combinations of instruments such as those required by Brahms's Horn Trio or Debussy's Sonata for Flute, Viola and Harp are even rarer – though it must be said that both these works have led to others for the same combination, for example the Horn Trio written in 1954 by Lennox Berkeley. Several ensembles, such as the

Above: *Other kinds of music have their own chamber ensembles, with the Philip Jones Brass Ensemble not only delving in the existing brass repertoire but very active in finding new compositions.*

Music Group of London, Melos Ensemble and Nash Ensemble, have been deliberately flexible as to personnel and accordingly can programme a wide range of chamber music. Others such as the Philip Jones Brass Ensemble have to a large extent generated their own repertory with new commissioned works or arrangements of classics. After string quartets, probably the commonest regular ensemble is that of a piano trio: among these the Beaux Arts Trio from America (founded 1955) is the best known, in a repertory including all the trios of Mozart, Beethoven, Schubert, Brahms and Dvořák as well as modern works such as Ravel's Trio; of its original members only the pianist Menahem Pressler remains. The Italian Trio di Trieste, founded in 1933, is also well known for a number of recordings including trios by several composers from Brahms to Ravel. The artists Jacques Thibaud, Pablo Casals and Alfred Cortot were each famous as individual performers, but also occasionally joined forces from the 1920s onwards and produced some fine recordings, including one of Schubert's B flat major Trio (1926) that is widely considered a classic. Similarly the violinist Fritz Kreisler recorded the complete Beethoven violin sonatas with the pianist Franz Rupp and Grieg's Third Violin Sonata with Rachmaninov at the keyboard.

The last twenty years or so has seen the appearance of a number of 'chamber orchestras' of some twenty players appropriate for the performance of Baroque music, Mozart's concertos and much else, sometimes with informed attempts at combined authentic-

Darius MILHAUD
(1892-1974)

Above: *Composers have always delighted in writing for the pleasingly sonorous combinations of woodwind and brass. The Netherlands Wind Ensemble is able to operate in a wide and varied repertoire.*

ities of pitch, instrumental construction, string material and the like. The Stuttgart Chamber Orchestra founded in 1945 by Karl Münchinger was a pioneer in this field, as were the Italian group I Musici formed by twelve eighteen-year-old students led by Felix Ayo in Rome in 1952 (which Toscanini called 'a perfect chamber orchestra') and the Solisti di Zagreb, an ensemble founded in 1954 by twelve expert players under the leadership of the cellist Antonio Janigro. Such chamber orchestras as the Vienna Concentus Musicus (founded 1953), and in Britain the English Chamber Orchestra (from 1960, formerly the Goldsbrough Orchestra), the Academy of St Martin-in-the-Fields founded in 1959 by Neville Marriner and the London Sinfonietta

founded in 1968 by David Atherton and Nicholas Snowman to promote twentieth-century music are now a regular and important part of the musical scene, as are the London Classical Players whose recent Beethoven symphony recordings under the conductor Roger Norrington have been widely praised. Finally, chamber ensembles of various sizes have also played their part in a newish tradition of 'music theatre' stemming largely from Schoenberg's *Pierrot lunaire* (1912) for voice and ensemble: among the best known to British audiences is the Fires of London, founded as the Pierrot Players in 1967 by Peter Maxwell Davies and Harrison Birtwistle. C.H.

Below: *The chamber orchestra, smaller than the normal symphony orchestra, was first envisaged to operate in the Baroque field. Established groups like the London Classical Players find music of all periods for 'authentic' performance.*

Coming from an affluent and cultivated French-Jewish background, this extraordinarily prolific and adaptable composer studied at the Paris Conservatoire, where he felt in sympathy with modern French music (worshipping Debussy) but reacted against heavy Germanic influences (hating Wagner). He was deeply affected by Latin-American music in Brazil and by jazz in the USA, absorbed everything like a musical sponge, and eventually produced a total of about 450 works in practically every genre one could imagine, while spending much of his life in a wheelchair due to arthritis. Milhaud, whose special aptitude and interest was in polytonal effects, applied these (and any other modern ideas which came to hand) largely to the practical business of producing music for commissions, never in response to profound inspiration or in the pursuit of aesthetic creeds. His output is thus both very diverse and of rather variable quality, often fun-poking (e.g. Cocteau's ballet *Le Bœuf sur la toît*), sometimes revolutionary (*La Création du monde*, using a seventeen-piece jazz-band), occasionally very impressive (the opera *Christophe Colomb*). But it is nearly always exuberant, with noisiness set against the quietly pastoral, often with an underlying folk-like melancholy, and always with a touch of charm. J.C.

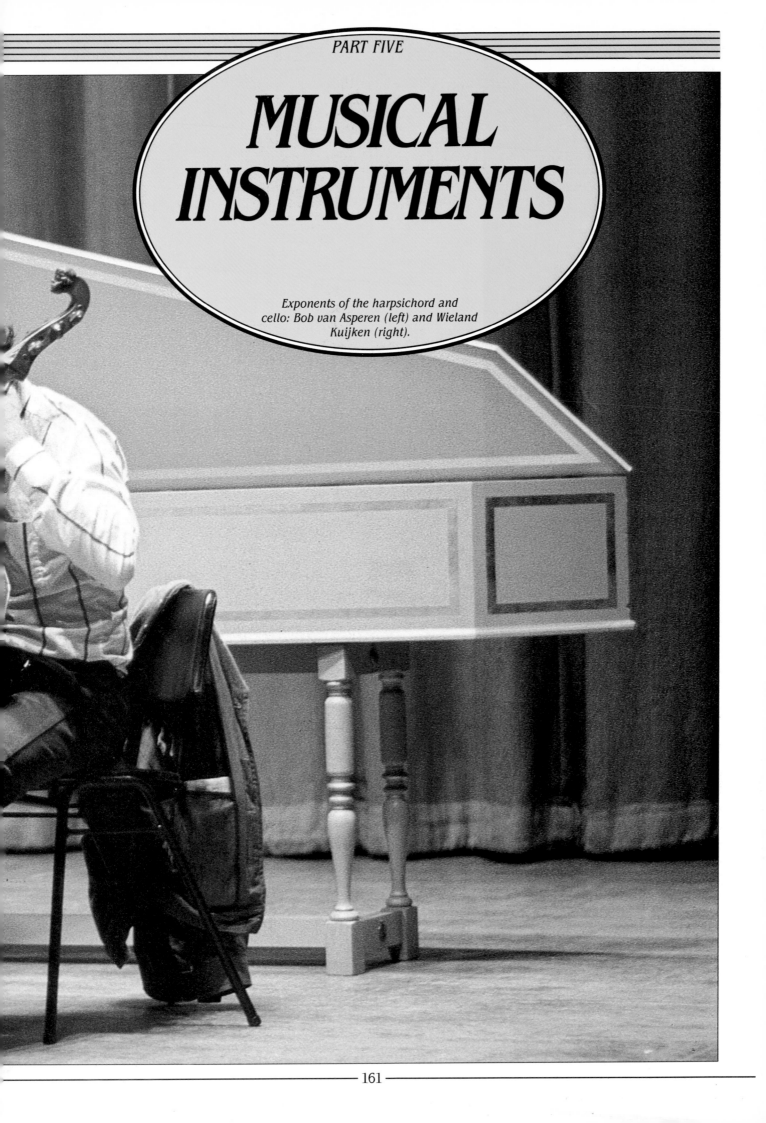

PART FIVE

MUSICAL INSTRUMENTS

Exponents of the harpsichord and cello: Bob van Asperen (left) and Wieland Kuijken (right).

Musical instruments are many and bewilderingly varied, particularly if we take into account the multifarious array of folk instruments from all over the world. They are usually classified today according to a method devised in 1914 by the scholars Erich Hornbostel and Curt Sachs. This has four main categories, each named by a term ending with 'phone', a suffix deriving from the Greek word for voice, *phone*. (A fifth category has been added since – see below.)

All these categories define the way in which vibrations are set up by a player to make a musical sound. In the case of *idiophones*, the instrument itself vibrates through being struck by a beater (e.g. a triangle or xylophone) or part of itself (castanets, cymbals). *Membranophones* have a stretched area of skin that is struck or rubbed, and include drums. *Chordophones* have vibrating strings which may be bowed, plucked or struck, as respectively with the violin, harp and piano.

Aerophones have a vibrating column of air and include all wind instruments. The fifth category recently added is that of *electrophones*, electronic instruments such as synthesisers and domestic organs in which sound is generated by electronic means and delivered through loudspeakers.

ORCHESTRAL INSTRUMENTS: THE STRINGS

The standard instruments of the symphony orchestra all fall into the first four of these categories. The foundation of the orchestra is provided by the strings, who outnumber the wind and percussion; and the orchestra's leader is the first violinist who usually sits immediately to the conductor's left and may assist him with advice about technical matters such as bowing. The bowed string family consists of violins (usually divided into roughly equal groups of 'firsts' and 'seconds'), violas, cellos and double basses, the numbers involved becoming progressively smaller as we go from higher to lower instruments. All these instruments are made of wood and are hollow, having a large number of separate parts, about seventy for a violin. Different woods are used, the string side or belly perhaps being of spruce while the back is of a harder wood such as maple and the fingerboard (under the strings) of ebony. The four strings themselves are of gut, nylon or metal; for example the violin's highest string (E) is usually of steel while the other three have a gut core wound round with metal. Bows are commonly of Pernambuco wood, with rosined horsehair that is tightened by a screw mechanism and drawn across a string (occasionally two) to set it in vibration and produce a note. The player's left hand 'stops' a string (presses it against the fingerboard) to determine the vibrating length and thus the note played, or he can

Left: *The violins made by Antonio Stradivari in Cremona are sought after by both collectors and virtuosi and when an instrument like 'The Lady Blunt' is up for auction fantastic prices are reached.*

Above: *An anonymous 19th-century Italian painting of the great violin virtuoso Niccolò Paganini (1782-1840) from the Conservatory of St Peter at Paiella, Naples.*

Jascha HEIFETZ
(1901-1986)

At the age of three Heifetz received his first lessons from his father, who was a highly accomplished violinist, and graduated from the Wilno School of Music when he was eight. He made a number of appearances as a child prodigy and was then admitted to the Imperial Conservatory at St Petersburg. When he was twelve he toured Russia, Germany and Scandinavia with considerable success, and a year later played in Berlin with the Berlin Philharmonic Orchestra, in Vienna under Safonov and at Leipzig at the Gewandhaus under Nikisch. After the 1917 Revolution he left the Soviet Union with his family and emigrated to the USA, making his début there the same year. His first appearance in London was at the Queen's Hall in 1920, after which he toured the Far East and Australia. Further visits to Europe followed, and in 1926 he visited Palestine where he gave a number of free concerts for the Jewish colony. By this time he had become a naturalised American citizen, and his reputation as one of the outstanding violinists of his generation was already firmly established. In 1939 he commissioned a concerto from William Walton: during the latter stages of his career he devoted an increasing amount of his time to chamber music. R.H.

Frédéric CHOPIN
(1810-49)

Idol of the Paris salons, this fastidious Franco-Polish composer, raised in a comfortable Warsaw family, was moved to tears by music as an infant and picked out tunes on the piano almost as soon as he could stand. Playing in public by seven (his first polonaise published at eight) and commencing formal studies in composition at twelve, his pianism simply flooded out. Not, however, in the grand Lisztian manner, but with a new type of singing intimacy and poetic nuance, via music of fresh yet subtle harmonic richness in which ornamentation and *rubato* became functional necessities rather than indulgent excursions. This blossoming of the piano's expressive powers materialised in a stream of mostly small pieces (mazurkas, studies, preludes, nocturnes, waltzes, polonaises, ballades, impromptus, scherzos, etc), nearly all of which have remained in the active repertoire. Such is their suggestive power – or so strong is the romantic notion of a doomed artist – that endless attempts have been made to link the music with events in Chopin's life: his departure from Poland as the Russians marched in, his love-affair with the French novelist George Sand, a relentless decline of health, with blood splashing on the piano keyboard, and so on. But whether or not any of this is in the scores, the music itself is surely immortal. J.C.

also bow the 'open' (unstopped) string. A string or strings can also be plucked with the fingers in the effect called *pizzicato*. 'Harmonics' with their ethereal tone are reproduced in a special way, the bowed string being just touched at a point called a node, and there are other occasional effects such as using the bow near the bridge for a glassy tone (*sul ponticello*).

The *violin* itself is the treble instrument of the string family. It has strings tuned in perfect fifths upwards from the G below middle C

Above: *Sir Yehudi Menuhin made his mark as a child prodigy of the violin in 1924 and recorded the Elgar Violin Concerto with the composer conducting when he was in his teens and Elgar in his 70s.*

Below: *Two of the most famous violinists to come out of Russia are David Oistrakh and his son Igor, both equally acclaimed as interpreters of the great classics and the music of their own country.*

– G, D, A, and E. The low G is of course its bottom note and the usable compass upwards is about three and a half octaves. The instrument dates from the sixteenth century and was fully established by the seventeenth, when it also took its place in the orchestra. One of the most famous early makers was Antonio Stradivari from Cremona, Italy; among famous performer-composers have been Corelli and Paganini.

The *viola* is tuned a fifth below the violin, with strings playing (in rising order) C, G, D and A. It is unique among standard orchestral instruments in that its music is written in the alto clef, which has middle C as the third line on the stave. Its length is about 16 or 17 inches compared with the violin's fourteen or so. It has a mellow tone that is attractive and unmistakable; but there is far less solo music

Above: *Jacqueline du Pré, who died at the age of 42 in 1987 after illness had halted her career at 26, will be remembered as a natural genius of the cello, and a great interpreter of the Elgar concerto.*

Above: *The double basses are generally providing the solid foundations of the modern orchestral sound, but the instrument is capable of a melodic solo as many composers have proved.*

Above: *The French cellist Paul Tortelier, in addition to being one of the great virtuosi of the day, is admired as a discerning teacher and a composer of some delightful music.*

written for it than the violin, though as it happens several composers have played it, including Mozart, Hindemith (who gave the première of Walton's Viola Concerto) and Britten. In chamber music it is indispensable. Its compass is not less than the violin's but in general not more than two and a half octaves are used orchestrally.

The *cello* (or violoncello) is tuned one octave below the viola, i.e. starting on the C below the bass clef with G. D. and tenor A as the other strings. Its role as a bass instrument largely obscured its fine melodic aspects and (with a good player) considerable agility until Bach and Haydn wrote solo works for it and then in the nineteenth century Beethoven wrote his five sonatas and Dvořák his Cello Concerto, while Brahms gave it a prominent solo in his Second Piano Concerto. Since then it has flourished as a solo instrument, and even in the orchestra string melodies are sometimes 'sung' not by violins but by unison cellos in their upper register, say the octave or so upwards from middle C.

The *double bass* is a little different from the other bowed strings in its shape and its tuning in fourths, not fifths, both of which reflect its links with the older string family of viols. The standard tuning in fact is E, A, D and G – the upper string G being the note at the bottom of the bass clef; but some basses have a fifth string (or another device fitted to the E string) giving the note C below the standard low E. Double bass music is written an octave higher than played to avoid leger lines and to facilitate reading. The instrument can play up to middle C and beyond, but normally it provides a harmonic bass to the string family: just occasionally a melodic solo can be very effective, as in the funereal slow movement of Mahler's First Symphony. Elsewhere the bass can be deliberately comic – a famous example is the 'elephant' music in Saint-Saëns's *Carnival of the Animals*.

The *harp* is different from the bowed strings in that its strings are always plucked and it has a totally different construction. The player does not stop his strings as a violinist does, but instead has many more of them, basically one for each note in his compass of six and a half octaves. We say 'basically' because there are just seven notes in each octave, the instrument being tuned to the rather unusual scale of C flat major, but the pitch of each string can be raised by either a semitone or whole tone by means of a pedal mechanism. This allows the use of any key and in a sense makes the harp a fully chromatic instrument, but its construction and nature nevertheless belong to the standard scales of classical tonality. This lovely instrument has a history as old as music itself, in East and West alike; the modern pedal harp is however the invention of the French maker Sébastien Érard, patented by him in 1810. The harp can play

Mstislav ROSTROPOVICH
(b. 1927)

Russian cellist, pianist and conductor who made his public début in 1942 during his student days at the Moscow Conservatory. His formidable gifts were immediately apparent, and within only a few years he was recognised as one of the greatest cellists of his day not only within the USSR, but throughout the world. Prokofiev, Shostakovich and Benjamin Britten, who became a close personal friend, wrote works especially for him. He made his London début in 1955: Jack Brymer described Rostropovich as 'that magnificent cellist who looks very much like a bank clerk, but plays like an angel'. In 1960 he was appointed professor of the violoncello at the Moscow and Leningrad Conservatories. His courageous public support for the novelist Solzhenitsyn brought him into disfavour with the Soviet authorities and he was refused permission to leave the USSR. However, after an invitation to conduct the Vienna opera in 1974 he and his wife were given exit visas, in theory for two years, but in fact on permanent exile. They were stripped of their Soviet citizenship four years later. Meanwhile, in 1977, Rostropovich was appointed Artistic Director of the Aldeburgh Festival, and later the same year conducted the National Symphony Orchestra in Washington. It is as a conductor that this gifted Russian musician has enjoyed an outstanding second career in opera houses and concert halls all over the world, conducting and recording both orchestral music and opera. He also happens to be a most accomplished pianist. R.H.

Claude DEBUSSY
(1862-1918)

Arguably the greatest French composer since Berlioz, this dandyish, self-centred man (who caused two women to attempt suicide and was threatened with a thrashing by Maeterlinck concerning the opera *Pelléas et Mélisande*), became the apostle of an impressionistic music which has been seen as presaging some aspects of twentieth-century atonalism, due to its heavy dependence on dissonant chordal relationships and on a specially delicate layering of textures. After some youthful piano studies and a turbulent period at the Paris Conservatoire, he travelled in Russia, eventually won the Prix de Rome, and then immersed himself in Wagner, whom he dismissed with Gallic spleen in due course. Impressed by the texture of Javanese music, absorbed by Mussorgsky's vocal writing, admiring the Symbolist poets, and attracted by Erik Satie's musical iconoclasm, he leapt to fame in 1894 with the allegedly 'formless' *Prélude à l'Après-midi d'un faune*. Disdaining most other music, Debussy evolved his own means of providing what he called a 'sonorous halo', which in the case of his piano works involved the biggest step since Chopin away from percussive effects in favour of colour shaped by pedalling. His approach in all genres was something quite new, and whether it be via the shifting visions of waves and clouds in *La Mer*, or the hazy evocations witnessed in *Images*, that 'halo' is certainly now something to reckon with.
J.C.

Above: *The harp is one of the oldest of all musical instruments and the modern instrument is a valuable and beautiful object with a considerable repertoire of music available.*

chords and melodies, indeed both in combination, and its music is written on two staves like that of the piano. It also has a celebrated and uniquely recognisable effect called a *glissando* in which the player draws his finger quickly over the strings in a sweep of sound. Mozart wrote a Concerto for Flute and Harp, and more recently French composers such as Debussy and Ravel used the instrument to great effect. Britten wrote a Suite for harp solo for the Welsh player Osian Ellis and arranged folk songs for voice with harp accompaniment. In the orchestra the harp usually stands alone.

WOODWIND

The standard woodwind instruments of the symphony orchestra, chamber music and the solo repertory are the flute, oboe, clarinet and bassoon. Each of these has smaller or larger (i.e. higher- or lower-pitched) relatives; thus the piccolo is a small, high flute and the cor anglais or English horn an alto oboe, while the bass clarinet and contrabassoon (double bassoon) are larger and deeper versions of the standard instrument. In all these instruments, as aerophones, the main principle is the same – an air column inside a pipe is made to vibrate by the player's breath and the speed of vibration (frequency) determines the pitch of the note. The player's fingers and the holes in the pipe allow him to vary the length of the air column used and so alter the note itself – broadly speaking (because for notes in the upper registers there is an additional need for techniques such as overblowing and cross-fingering which use the acoustic phenomenon called the harmonic series), the shorter the air column, the higher the note that is produced. The elaborate systems of metal keywork that we see on modern instruments are aids to fingering – not least because the fingers of two hands cannot cover the whole

length of an instrument, even a small one.

The *flute* is played by directing the breath across the edge of a hole near the end of the instrument, which is held sideways. The tube (pipe) itself is cylindrical, and the compass is three octaves upwards from middle C: after his first octave the player 'overblows' to obtain the octave higher and then uses cross-fingerings to go beyond that; the modern flute with its elaborate keywork is the work of the maker Theobald Boehm in the nineteenth century. Though flutes are woodwind instruments and were once of wood, today they are usually of a metal such as silver or even gold. The instrument has brilliance in its upper register and often mystery in its lower range: it is well exploited by Debussy in his tone poem *L'Après-midi d'un faune*, which begins with a flute solo, and the same composer later wrote a haunting sonata for the unusual combination of flute, viola and harp. The *piccolo* is a small brother of the flute and pitched an octave higher: to save the use of leger lines, its music is written an octave below the sounding note; it is brilliant in the orchestra but has few melodic solos, though the Russian composer Shostakovich has given it some in his symphonies.

The *oboe* is a double reed instrument with a conical tube (opening out towards the open end or bell) and a compass from the B flat below middle C to the F or G above the treble stave. Its tone is penetrating and expressive, in fact 'reedy'; it was one of Handel's favourite instruments, and in the twentieth century Richard Strauss and Vaughan Williams wrote oboe concertos. The *cor anglais* is an alto oboe and is pitched a fifth lower; it is longer than the oboe and its bell is unusual in being globular. Its wistful and sometimes melancholy tones are heard to advantage in such music as the slow movement of Dvořák's *New World* Symphony and Sibelius's orchestral 'legend' called *The Swan of Tuonela*, in which it perfectly evokes the dying swan sailing on the dark waters of a lake.

The *clarinet* is a single-reed treble instrument of cyindrical bore, with a range of three and a half octaves that allows it to go higher than the oboe while also having the alto range of the cor anglais. In practice the highest notes are not very much used, being difficult and shrill, but the lower register has a warm, liquid sound and as a whole the instrument produces a smooth, slightly hollow tone that becomes progressively more penetrating above the treble stave. The instru-

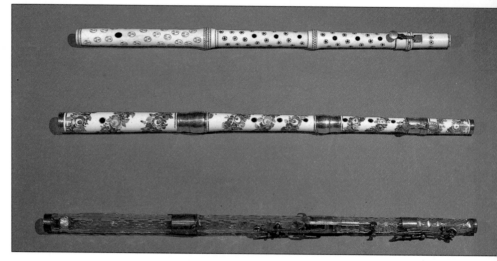

Above: *The flute, once generally made of wood, is today usually made of metal, often of silver or gold. But it could be in ivory, porcelain or crystal, as are these beautiful instruments above.*

Below: *There have been many fine flute soloists but no one has ever achieved more popularity than James Galway who combines easy virtuosity with a personal commitment and style.*

Léon GOOSSENS
(1897-1988)

Third son of a highly-gifted musical family, Léon Goossens was introduced to the oboe at an early age by his father, who was principal conductor of the Carl Rosa Opera Company in Liverpool. His first professional engagement was at the age of twelve in a performance of *Till Eulenspiegel* with the Liverpool Philharmonic under a somewhat surprised Thomas Beecham. When his family moved to London in 1911 Goossens entered the Royal College of Music: in 1913 he was invited by Henry Wood to join the Queen's Hall Orchestra, becoming the first oboist a year later. After serving in the 1914-18 war he returned to the orchestra and in 1923 was appointed professor of oboe at the Royal College of Music. In 1924 he joined the Royal Academy of Music and formed the Philharmonic Trio, which toured successfully throughout Europe. He made his US début in 1928, and when Beecham founded the London Philharmonic Orchestra in 1932 he became principal oboist. Bax, Bliss, Britten, Hindemith, Poulenc and Vaughan Williams all wrote for Goossens, and Elgar left an incomplete movement of an unfinished suite composed specially for him. After 1945 he gave up orchestral playing completely to concentrate on solo work and teaching. What Segovia has done for the guitar in the twentieth century and Casals for the cello, Goossens has achieved for the oboe: his influence on a whole generation of British musicians has been incalculable. In his lifetime the oboe changed from an ugly duckling into a swan. R.H.

Top: *The oboe, formerly known as the hautboy, has a double reed and has been the most regular orchestral representative of the woodwind family since it was wholly accepted in the 17th century.*

Below: *Other important members of the woodwind section are the clarinets, the most favoured solo instrument as well, and the bassoons which provide the bass line and a certain amount of comedy.*

Erik SATIE
(1866-1925)

This eccentric Franco-Scot is known as much for his manner – and for his influence on other French composers – as for his own creations, which comprise mostly short piano pieces but also encompass some pre-talkies film music and a few orchestral and stage works. The latter include *Parade*, a ballet produced by Diaghilev in 1917, with story by Cocteau, décor by Picasso, and music using jazz rhythms aided by the sounds of a typewriter, a siren, and a steamship whistle. From a musical family, he made his living at first by playing in cafés and writing music for Montmartre entertainers. He befriended Debussy in the 1890s, studied for a while with Roussel and d'Indy, and eventually became the spiritual focus for a group of defiantly modern young composers known as Les Six. They were attracted by his irreverent attitude and the extreme economy of his music, and also by the surrealistic titles he was apt to give his works, such as *Morceaux en forme de poire (Pieces in the form of a pear)* or *(Véritables) préludes flasques – pour un chien (Limp preludes for a dog)*. Perhaps his best-known piano pieces are the early *Gymnopédies*, which, like various others, have been orchestrated from time to time. J.C.

ment was only established in Mozart's lifetime, and his Concerto and Clarinet Quintet are famous, as are the concertos by Weber and the Quintet by Brahms. There are two versions, one pitched 'in B flat' and the other 'in A', and to save difficulty their music is written in such a way that the same fingering is used for a written note whichever instrument is played – that is, a written C will sound as B flat on one instrument and A on the other. The *bass clarinet* is pitched an octave lower; because of its length it is bent at both ends so that it resembles a tenor saxophone. It is also a 'transposing instrument': so a clarinettist can turn to the bass clarinet during an orchestral work and play the same notes in the treble, which will now come out just over an octave lower.

The *bassoon* with its double reed has a long tube which is bent back on itself and a compass of just over three octaves upwards from the B flat below the bass stave. The tone is reedy yet mellower than that of the oboe; as a melodic instrument it comes into its own in the tenor range. The bassoon can sound comic (as in Dukas's *The Sorcerer's Apprentice*), or gloomy (Tchaikovsky's *Pathetic* Symphony); a famous very high solo occurs at the beginning of Stravinsky's *Rite of Spring*. As with the clarinet, there are concertos by both Mozart and Weber. The *contrabassoon* plays an octave lower and really only occurs in certain orchestral music from Beethoven's *Choral* Symphony onwards. Its deep tone is unmistakable. There is a solo at the start of Ravel's Piano Concerto for Left Hand, and another in his *Beauty and the Beast* in the suite called *Ma Mère l'Oye*.

Other woodwind which occasionally play in the orchestra include the bass (really alto) flute, the bass (really baritone) oboe and small high clarinets. Last but certainly not least there is the *alto saxophone* – woodwind though made of metal – that figures in some symphonic music, for example by Rachmaninov and Vaughan Williams.

BRASS

Trumpets, horns, trombones and tuba are powerful instruments but can also be used gently. Here the air in a metal tube is set in vibration by air passing through the player's compressed lips. This tube will have a fundamental note and others related to it in the 'harmonic series' which can all be pitched by changes in lip vibrations; for notes other than these the player uses valves or (for the trombone) a slide mechanism which effectively alter the length of the air column. All these instruments can also be muted by a 'stopper' fitted into the open end or bell. Incidentally, all have genuine solo capacity and have had concertos written for them: for example the Trumpet Concerto by Haydn, Mozart's horn concertos, Rimsky-Korsakov's for trombone and Vaughan Williams' for tuba.

The *trumpet* is a treble instrument with a range of two and a half octaves roughly corresponding to that of a treble voice. It has a military sound, and so usually plays brilliant passages or melodies of a rather noble kind; but it is just right for such music as the 'Sword' motif in Wagner's *Ring* cycle of music dramas.

The *horn* is mellower and more romantic than the trumpet (though it can be very powerful, too), and is also pitched lower, with an alto range for melody playing plus a bass register going down well below the stave. The horns in an orchestra (usually four in all) often play in sustained chords than can fill a texture to good effect. It would be hard to find any orchestral works lacking horn solos; but perhaps it is the German and Austrian composers from Beethoven through to Strauss and Mahler who have made the most of this beautiful and versatile instrument.

Above: *The saxophone, made in various shapes and sizes, combines brass and woodwind characteristics. It was designed for brass and military band use but often adds extra colour to the modern orchestra.*

Below: *French trumpet virtuoso Maurice André is foremost among those who have explored and recorded the once neglected repertoire of the baroque trumpet concerto. He owns over 80 trumpets.*

Below: *The horn, generally referred to as the French horn because it evolved in that country, has developed from a straight instrument used in hunting to one of the most complex members of the orchestra, difficult to play but capable of a fine range of tonal effects.*

Below left: *A leading exponent of the French horn today is the Australian Barry Tuckwell, first horn of the London Symphony Orchestra for 13 years but now known as a distinguished soloist.*

Below right: *The trombone, earlier known as the sackbut, is to the brass what the cellos are to the string section, while the tuba is regarded as the brass equivalent of the double bass.*

Louis Moreau GOTTSCHALK
(1829-69)

Remarkable pioneering composer/musician who wrote much that was well ahead of its time, and helped to bring a new awareness of national strains of American music. Like so many American composers he seems to have had a split creative personality. Finishing his musical training in Paris from 1842-6, he then began to earn a fabulous reputation as a successor to Liszt, a pianist of great virtuosity writing pieces for his own performance that were entirely in the European romantic drawing-room tradition. He was also a great showman, extravagantly dressed and extrovert in manner. After successful tours of France, Switzerland and Spain he returned to America in 1853 for a grand tour there; and now he found a very individual strain of music that had its sources partly in the black dances he heard in his native New Orleans, partly in the Latin-American rhythms he heard in South-America and the West Indies. He wrote some remarkable piano pieces that were an early foretaste of the music that was to emerge as ragtime; and works like his *La Nuit des Tropiques* which seem incredibly modern even now. They are full of Spanish rhythms and an obvious inspiration for many pieces written later by such composers as Aaron Copland and George Gershwin. P.G.

Beethoven brought the *trombones* into the standard symphony orchestra, and their entry at the height of the storm in his *Pastoral* Symphony is famous. Trombone tone is always recognisable, but can be many things: noble, solemn or even frightening as in Stravinsky's *Rite of Spring*. Melodies are often surprisingly effective, for good players produce many subtleties of tone and dynamics. Orchestras usually have three trombones, covering the tenor and bass registers: modern instruments often have a basic tenor range and a valve device giving them access to deeper notes. Of course, trombones are also important in military bands.

Finally, the *tuba* is the deepest of the brass and has a wide conical bore that relates it to the bugle family and gives it a round tone. It rarely has orchestral solos and comes into its own more in a military band, where it may be

MODERN ORCHESTRAL INSTRUMENTS

The modern orchestra is a perfectly balanced combination of string, woodwind and brass instruments underpinned by a vast assortment of percussion and a few colourful additions like the harp, the xylophone and the piano. The main body of sound comes from the strings – violins (usually split into 1st and 2nd), violas, cellos and basses, capable of a warm, wide-ranging and flexible totality of sound that is eminently satisfying in its own right and frequently heard alone. The colourful possibilities of the orchestra are extended by the very personal sounds of the various woodwind instruments – piccolo, flute, oboe, cor anglais, clarinet, bassoon – also capable of varied and colourful music-making on their own. The brass add strength and solidity and can be strident or gentle. Adding the essential element of rhythm comes an immensely varied range of percussion instruments, with the tuned timpani at their core, with which the modern composer delights in demonstrating his ingenuity. The permutations of sound of which this varied collection of musical voices is capable are vast.

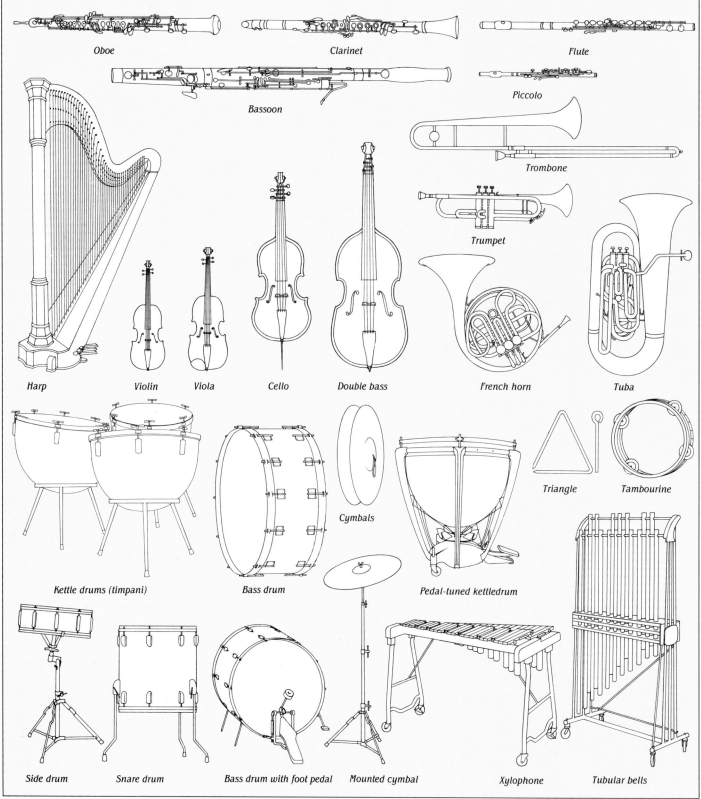

Oboe

Clarinet

Flute

Bassoon

Piccolo

Trombone

Trumpet

Harp

Violin

Viola

Cello

Double bass

French horn

Tuba

Kettle drums (timpani)

Bass drum

Cymbals

Pedal-tuned kettledrum

Triangle

Tambourine

Side drum

Snare drum

Bass drum with foot pedal

Mounted cymbal

Xylophone

Tubular bells

Above: *The timpani were the first percussion instruments to become a regular part of the orchestra, providing not only rhythm, but, being tunable, also an additional harmonic voice.*

Below: *The modern percussion section has become extensive and varied, often occupying the efforts of several musicians to manipulate a range of both standard and unconventional instruments.*

Thomas ARNE
(1710-1778)

In that interim period between the heyday of Purcell and the first golden age of British music and the rebirth that was heralded by the emergence of Elgar and a new national awareness, there was little to boost the spirit of English music. One composer who battled to get his music on the stages of Drury Lane and Covent Garden in the face of a long-lasting dominance by the mighty Handel was Thomas Arne. Fighting, in the first place, against his father's wish that he should become a solicitor, he studied music in his spare time and soon began to produce substantial pieces 'after the Italian manner'. The first of these was *Rosamond* in 1733. This was followed by the masques *Dido and Aeneas* (1734), the important *Comus* (1738) and *Alfred* (1740) with its popular air 'Rule, Britannia'. On the strength of these he was appointed resident composer at Drury Lane where he produced such operas as *Thomas and Sally* (1760), *Love in a Village* (1762) and *Artaxerxes* (1762), a favourite of Haydn's, which was included in the Covent Garden repertoire into the nineteenth century. He also wrote a fine set of symphonies. His works have been described as having an agreeable straight-forwardness and honourable simplicity and well repay revival. P.G.

called by the delightful and appropriate name of bombardon – a smaller tenor version being the equally well-named euphonium.

PERCUSSION

Percussion instruments are all struck in some way, as their name implies. This department of the orchestra, with its splashes and bangs, is sometimes affectionately called 'the kitchen', but like a cook's spice rack it provides a very important element in an orchestral 'cuisine'. We tend to associate percussion with modern music, but it had an essential part in medieval times and even earlier, as it is in folk music all over the world today. Purcell, Bach and Handel used *timpani* (kettledrums), with their bowl over which is stretched a skin tuned by tightening or loosening with a screw or pedal device. The use of three or more different sized timpani

in an orchestra allows a player to play melodic motifs with, of course, an accompanying rhythmic impact. Unlike the timpani, the *side drum* and *bass drum* do not play notes of definite pitch: but the smaller instrument naturally has a higher and brighter effect than the thud of the big bass. All drums can play rolls, achieving a 'sustained note' effect by rapid repeated beats on the skin. The timpani or side drum player holds a stick in each hand, but the timpanist's has a felt head while the side drummer's is wholly of wood; the bass drummer has a single felt-covered stick, used even for a roll which other players may execute with two hands. The *tambourine* is also a drum; it is small and hand-held with jingles around its edge and can be struck, shaken or rubbed.

The *triangle, cymbals* and *gong* or *tam-tam* are all of metal. The first of these takes its name from its shape and is suspended and

struck with a beater to give a high 'ting' or even a roll. Cymbals are large metal plates of a special shape; they can be clashed or a single cymbal suspended for a roll. The tam-tam is a great plate of beaten bronze which has an awesome sound, whether played softly or loudly – a crescendo roll to *forte* is literally shattering in effect. One wooden idiophone is the *castanets*, clappers with a handle that are held in the hand and shaken – almost all musical evocations of Spain feature this sound so associated with that country and its folk dancers.

A group of tuned percussion includes the *celesta* (dealt with in the section below explaining a keyboard instrument), the *xylophone* with its row of wooden bars laid out like a keyboard and its metallic equivalent the *glockenspiel* – in the case of these last two the player has a beater in each hand to play and can do so with surprising agility.

In one sense, nearly all instruments are ancient: familiar instruments such as the harp, trumpet and drum all have a fairly clear ancestry that can be traced back as far as music itself. Even the piano, considered as an instrument in which the strings are struck by hammers, has a forerunner in the dulcimer which originated a thousand years ago in the Middle East. Only the electrophones such as the synthesiser and ondes Martenot can be said to be wholly modern, though even the latter has been in use for sixty years. The reasons are simply that the principles of making musical sounds are as old as Nature itself and (with the exception of electricity) have been available to all from time immemorial: they are just different ways of creating vibrations to produce notes of definite or indefinite pitch.

Names of instruments should be used in a broad way. No one suggests that the trumpet placed in the Egyptian tomb of King Tutankhamun in the fourteenth century BC was identical with a modern valve instrument, or that the transverse flutes called the *ti* and *ch'ih* of the Chou dynasty in China (about 1050-255 BC) resembled those of a symphony orchestra. But they are near enough to have the same name as our modern instruments, just as the tenth-century organ of Winchester Cathedral with its 40 notes, 400 pipes and 70 perspiring bellows-pumpers is in every important principle the same as a modern one with air provided by a motor.

Possibly the oldest instruments of all are those of percussion, where in some cases little or no material is required to make

Above: *Detail inside a kylix from Vulci showing early Greek end-blown flute player and dancer. Dating back to 520-10 BC, it emphasises the antiquity of the art of music-making.*

music. In Ethiopia 'earth drums' have existed where the air in holes dug in the ground is made to vibrate by beating over them, and Indian literature also mentions such drums. Here music was probably linked with religious ritual, and perhaps language, too – African drums are also used to send signals. Drums

Below: *King David, renowned as a harp player, is depicted directing the Biblical String Quartet, probably as an accompaniment to psalms, in a thirteenth-century fresco on wood from the cathedral in Siena.*

were played by the Mesopotamians from some three thousand years before the Christian era, as were the clappers by dancing girls that are precursors of castanets; later this culture had tambourines and cymbals and bells.

Even at this time, plucked string instruments were made in Mesopotamia to a high standard of workmanship. Harps with up to twelve strings were sometimes decorated with precious metals such as silver and even gold, and the lyre and lute also appeared. Animal horns were hollowed out and blown as 'trumpets' giving perhaps three or four notes according to lip vibration. Wind instruments with a double reed and a pair of pipes are known from 2000 BC and were adopted first by the Egyptians and then by the Greeks as the *aulos*, a sharp-toned instrument which is the ancestor of the modern bagpipe. The Greeks consecrated the thrilling sound of the *aulos* to Dionysus, the god of wine and impulse, while the other chief instrument of ancient Greece, the much gentler *kithara* or lyre, was dedicated to Apollo, the god of reason and balance. The lyre was similarly inherited from Mesopotamia and Egypt, where the Greek musical theorists and geometrician Pythagoras, studied in the sixth century BC. All these instruments came down to ancient Greece and Rome to remain as a Middle Eastern legacy to Western Europe. They also belong to biblical music and the Jewish communities of the Old Testament, for Moses was born in Egypt and studied music there. The Hebrew 'trumpet' of ram's horn called the *shofar* was used for ceremo-

nials. Their double-reed wind instrument called the *halil* and the *aulos* are the same, just as King David's 'harp', the *kinnor*, is the Greek lyre the *kithara*. By the time of Christ, the Jewish Temple in Jerusalem had an orchestra of twelve players of lyres, harps and cymbals, to which two *halil* performers were added for some feast days. But after the destruction of the Temple in AD 70, the Jews gave up the use of instruments in worship as a symbol of sorrow. Even in the early Christian church singing was normally unaccompanied, and only in medieval times did the pipe organ begin to find its now regular place. The organ itself has its prototype in the hydraulically pumped organ of Ctesibius of Alex-andria in the third century BC, and came to Europe via Byzantium (now Constantinople), the eastern capital of the Christian Church.

The bowed instruments of the violin family are related to such older ones as the lute; for this also has a wooden body hollowed out for resonance and a set of tightened and tuned strings over a fingerboard that are stopped by the fingers to give further different pitches. The earliest known use of a bow with horsehair or something similar to draw sound from the strings is in the tenth century, in instruments such as the *rebec* (from the Arabic *rabàb*), which commonly had three strings and could be held upright or (later) to the chin like a modern violin.

*Niccolò PAGANINI
(1782-1840)*

A violinist and composer of such virtuosity and strange character that history tends to look upon him more as a legend than as a flesh and blood character. His beginnings were ordinary enough; the son of a poor shopkeeper who did his best to have him taught both on the mandolin and the violin. On this latter instrument he showed incredible ability and was playing in public at the age of eleven. At eight he had composed his first Violin Sonata and thereafter kept up a steady flood of works including several fine concertos. Oddly he has remained best known for one haunting theme from a set of violin pieces that was used as the basis for variations by Rachmaninov and others; that and the *La Campanella* movement from his B minor concerto, transcribed by Liszt. From around 1805 his fabulous reputation as a violinist grew worldwide as he was rapturously received by audiences everywhere, who were fascinated by his dazzling technique and his repertoire of tricks. He suffered from a lung disorder and became more gaunt and eccentric in appearance over the years so that many thought him in league with the devil. Although considered a miserly character he was generous in his help to such composers as Berlioz, from whom he commissioned *Harold in Italy* (for viola). However, he was not pleased with it because the solo part was too small. P.G.

Above: *King David performing on a primitive harp which shows that even in those times the principles of amplification were understood and implemented by the use of a soundbox.*

Right: *The modern guitar virtuoso Julian Bream also explored the possibilities of the lute and its extensive repertoire and did much to revive interest in music of the Elizabethan era.*

Many instruments, such as the flute or cello, are essentially melodic. For this reason they do not normally play on their own, since Western ears expect harmony as well as melody, and single notes without 'chords' can sound incomplete; for the same reason, songs are traditionally accompanied by the piano. But the piano itself can supply both melody and harmony, as is symbolised by the notation of its music on two staves showing treble and bass. This in turn reminds us that the pianist uses two hands to play notes, unlike the violinist who only uses the fingers of his left for this purpose, while his right arm moves the bow. Yet another thing related to the use of two staves instead of just one is that the compass of the piano is far greater than that of instruments which play in a certain range, such as treble for flute or violin and tenor/bass for cello or bassoon; the piano can go higher than the violin and lower than the double bass. The use of two staves also applies to the celesta, although it only plays higher notes. The organist actually has his music written on three staves, since besides using his hands on keyboards he must also use his feet on a pedal board that is laid out like a keyboard with 'black' and 'white' notes, though usually these are not coloured and they must be suitable for feet rather than fingers.

The chief forerunner of the piano was the *harpsichord*, which resembles a piano with its keyboard and overall shape but in which the strings are plucked instead of being struck by hammers. This is the instrument that Bach usually expected to play in a keyboard concerto, some of his Preludes and Fugues and other solo keyboard music, and as a *continuo* harmonic backing in, say, a *Brandenburg* Concerto. It makes a sound very different from that of a piano; the chief limitation is that altering the touch makes no difference to the dynamic level (that is, volume of sound). Modern harpsichords are made to exacting technological standards, but naturally make no attempt to change this basic characteristic of the instrument; similarly modern composers like Henze and Dodgson who have written for it design their music to dispense with such effects as crescendo.

The *pianoforte* was fully established early in the eighteenth century by Bartolomeo Cristofori (1655-1730) and takes its name from its ability to play both 'soft and loud', and to graduate the dynamics between. Its music really belongs to the nineteenth century and beyond, and many of Beethoven's keyboard works (like the *Moonlight* Sonata) and such Romantic music as Chopin's nocturnes and Rachmaninov's preludes depend on this ability, as well as the all-important sustaining pedal (on the right) which lifts the felt dampers from the strings and allows them to sound even when a note is released by the finger. (The left pedal – the 'soft' pedal – moves the hammers in such a

Vladimir HOROWITZ
(b. 1904)

Russian-born pianist whose studies at the Kiev Conservatory under Tarnowsky and Blumenfeld were interrupted by the aftermath of the Russian revolution. In the turbulent conditions of the time his 1920 public début went largely unnoticed, but later recitals in Kharkov and other major Russian cities slowly established his reputation. He frequently performed with the violinist Nathan Milstein, who became a close personal friend, but it was a spectacular series of solo recitals in Leningrad in 1923 that launched his European career. His reception on the Continent was ecstatic, but a poor choice of concert halls caused a débâcle in London and he vowed never to return to England. Fortunately his second visit in 1930 was much more auspicious: in the meantime he had made his American début in 1928 where he met his idol, Rachmaninov. He decided to settle in the USA, and in 1933 married Toscanini's daughter. In 1936 his career as an international musical celebrity was cut short by illness and it was not until three years later that he resumed his concert career. A second retirement came in 1953 although he continued with a busy recording schedule. He returned to the concert platform in New York in 1956, and in his eighties he gave a series of remarkable recitals, including a memorable return visit to Moscow. P.G.

Above: *The clavichord was the immediate ancestor of the piano. The strings were first struck with hammers instead of being plucked as in the harpsichord. The instrument above is of German origin, 1767.*

Below: *The pianforte answered the need for a keyboard instrument in which the volume of sound could be regulated and the touch more easily graded. The modern grand has a richly varied sound.*

Jacques OFFENBACH
(1819-80)

A German-Jew, born in Cologne, Offenbach was to spend most of his life in Paris and became French by adoption. In Paris he established himself as a virtuoso cellist but his main ambition was to write for the theatre. He found it difficult to break into the operatic and dramatic world, so in 1855 he opened his own small theatre which he called Les Bouffes-Parisiens and here produced many short pieces which pioneered a new form of comic opera that was to become known as operetta. His first great success was *Orphée aux Enfers (Orpheus in the Underworld)* in 1858 which caught the public imagination by its satire, its tunefulness and its famous can-can. Among the hundred and more operettas that he wrote and produced after this, the world best remembers *La Belle Hélène, La Grande Duchess de Gérolstein, La Périchole* and *La Vie Parisienne*, all full-length works replete with melody and still staged. Despite his success in the field of operetta, Offenbach's final ambition was to write a grand opera. He worked on this during his final years of illness but died before he could see *Les Contes d'Hoffmann* performed. P.G.

Above: *The harpsichord originated in Italy and survived early rivalry from the piano to become an instrument with a special repertoire of its own. Illustrated is a Flemish two-manual instrument.*

Below: *The age of electronic wizardry has seen the dominance of older instruments lost to the wider possibilities of tone, colour, and endless permutations of sound that the synthesiser can offer.*

way as to mute the tone.) In the nineteenth century the piano underwent many improvements: the keyboard has been progressively extended, the speed of the action increased, and metal frames introduced which allow greater string tension and consequent increased brilliance. The present range is seven octaves plus three semitones, with the note middle C just to the left of centre. Most notes have three strings tuned in unison; in the lower two octaves there are only two or (for the lowest notes of all) one.

The *organ*'s ancestry goes back 2000 years. It has sets of pipes which may vary in length from a few inches to over 30 feet and are supplied with wind by an electric motor; these are designed so that the instrument as a whole has many different tone colours that are selected by the operation of 'stops' and can be used alone or in combination. There are two or more keyboards (manuals) plus a pedal board so that a melody and its accompaniment, or two or more voices in a poly-

phonic texture, may each have its own kind of sound. An electronic organ which creates its sounds not acoustically but through electronic synthesis has the same capacity to produce a wide range of tone, though here it will emerge from loudspeakers rather than pipes activated by wind pressure. Small electronic organs and simple keyboards designed for home use work on similar principles, and the player has the advantage that he may listen through headphones and be inaudible to anyone else.

Synthesisers with digital technology offer even more facilities including the ability to create wholly new sounds and to record and copy music without the use of microphones or magnetic tape.

Finally, the celesta, an instrument resembling a small upright piano with a usual compass — of four octaves upwards from middle C. Instead of strings it has metal bars, which are struck by hammers covered with felt, and there is a sustaining pedal.

The organ is a wind and keyboard instrument in one. The keys of its two or more manuals and pedal board activate a mechanism that supplies wind under pressure to pipes which then 'speak' with musical notes.

The earliest known organ was the invention of Ctesibius (or Ktesibios) of Alexandria in around 270 BC. An instrument of this kind, as described by the Greek physicist Hero of the same city some decades later, was worked by water pressure, a piston activated by a lever forcing air into a water chamber and then into the pipes to make them sound.

In time, organs became increasingly elaborate and especially fine instruments were prized not only for their music but also for their technology and expensive ornamentation. They could be given as princely gifts and the Byzantine Emperor Constantine V presented one in 757 to the Frankish King Pépin III, the father of Charlemagne. The instrument took its place in Christian worship at about this time; the one at Winchester Cathedral in England during the tenth century had forty keys (notes) and ten pipes to each and required seventy men to work the bellows that provided the air pressure. There were also much smaller instruments, some being portable and carried with a shoulder strap: the player provided the wind with one hand operating a bellows and fingered a small keyboard with the other.

With the addition of the pedal board in the fourteenth century and the construction of multiple keyboards (manuals) provided with a variety of stops (see below), the organ became essentially the instrument known to Renaissance and Baroque musicians. The church organs on which Bach played and for which he composed so much of his music had many ranks of pipes designed to produce certain kinds of tone that could be used alone or

Above: *The organ of St Eustache in Paris in an aquarelle of 1801. The organ is a typical baroque instrument which was played by a number of distinguished French composers resident there.*

in combination: the small levers to bring these into actions are called 'stops'; rather confusingly, the same word is used both for the row of pipes with its characteristic sound and the device that brings it into use. The fine Schnitger organs of North Germany and Holland, dating from Bach's lifetime (1685-1750) had up to four manuals and sixty stops, the longest and thus deepest-sounding pipe being 32 feet and the shortest a mere 12 inches.

The organ repertory is extensive, but more patchy than that of, say, the piano or violin. There are Renaissance organist-composers — such as the Englishman John Bull, Frescobaldi in Italy and Jan Sweelinck in Amster-

dam — whose organ fantasias are carefully worked out treatments of a single musical idea. In Baroque times, Bach himself towers among all other musicians with his mass of solo works such as toccatas, fantasias, chorale preludes and fugues and the six trio sonatas (*c.* 1727) in which the player's two hands each on a different manual and his feet on the pedal board have parts of nearly equal difficulty. Handel also wrote a series of vigorous organ concertos.

The major classical composers left little for organ: for example, there are no major works from Haydn, Beethoven or Schubert, though all professional players perform the magnificent and dramatic F minor Fantasia, K608, that Mozart composed in the last year of his life for a mechanical organ in a clock and wish he had written much more for their instrument. Among Romantic composers, both Liszt and Brahms wrote a few important pieces, Liszt's Fantasia on the name of Bach (treated as the notes B flat, A, C and B natural) being a thrilling blend of Baroque splendour and Romantic passion. But the chief organ composers of the later nineteenth century are often little known in other music: there are the Germans Reubke (who died young but left one fine sonata), Rheinberger and Karg-Elert. France and Belgium have Franck as a major name with his *Pièce héroïque* and *Trois chorals*, together with Saint-Saëns (whose so-called *Organ Symphony* of 1886 has a part for the instrument), Widor and Vierne; the latter composed six solo 'symphonies' between 1899 and 1930.

The twentieth century has also seen individual works of distinction, among which are Schoenberg's Variations on a Recitative, Vaughan Williams's Preludes on Welsh Hymn Tunes and Poulenc's Organ Concerto with timpani and string orchestra, the latter taking its initial inspiration from a Bach fan-

Above: *The Belgian composer César Franck (1822-90) held several important posts as organist in Paris from 1848 and wrote music for the instrument which greatly advanced playing techniques.*

Above: *Camille Saint-Saëns (1835-1921), the distinguished French composer, was organist at Saint-Merry and other churches in Paris from 1853 after studying at the Conservatoire as an organ scholar.*

Right: *An interior view of the magnificent chapel of King's College, Cambridge, dating back to c. 1461, showing the fine organ that has provided the background to a great tradition of choral singing.*

Franz LISZT
(1811-86)

Son of a Hungarian farm superintendent, this pianistic prodigy made his first concert appearance at nine, was studying in Vienna at ten, and by twelve was off on a round of European tours which lasted until 1847. Flamboyant in the grand manner, he aimed for a keyboard wizardry to match that of Paganini on the violin. Settling first in Paris, he was influenced by his friends Berlioz and Chopin, then operated for some years from Geneva (where he settled with Countess d'Agoult), before spending a decade as *Kapellmeister* at Weimar (with Princess Sayn-Wittgenstien now in tow), where he aided Wagner, Berlioz and others with important opera productions. From 1860 he lived on and off in Rome, where he took minor clerical orders despite his active sex life and an undying vanity. He insisted on adulation, yet once his greatness was acknowledged he could be abundantly painstaking and generous in helping others, be they pupils or fellow-composers. After 1847 he concentrated on making Weimar into a great musical centre, and spent much more time composing. He invented the symphonic poem, created two programme symphonies, several concertos, various liturgical pieces, and diverse orchestral and vocal works, plus a vast quantity of solo piano music, ranging from the *Hungarian Rhapsodies*, via *Consolations* and *Transcendental Studies*, to the B minor Sonata. And there were numerous piano transcriptions which promoted the music of others. J.C.

tasia but going on to be highly individual and exciting. The outstanding single name here is that of the French composer Olivier Messiaen (b. 1908). He was for half a century the organist of the Trinité Church in Paris and has written numerous highly individual works of which most have a powerful and visionary religious theme and some are lengthy; the *Livre du Saint Sacrement* (1984) is a recent example. Messiaen's music, once thought over-colourful and too saturated with emotion, has in recent years won over most of the doubters and few organists do not have at least a few of his pieces in their repertory. After Bach, perhaps only he can withstand the test of a one-composer recital. C.H.

Although the manufacture and use of instruments are as old as music itself, instrumental music as such took a long time to acquire the kind of independent life represented by, say, the organ works of J.S. Bach, Haydn's string quartets and the nine symphonies of Beethoven. It is true that the ancient Greeks had some independent instrumental music, like the programmatic *Pythic Nome* played by the aulete Sakados in 586 BC which had five movements and described a fight between the god Apollo and a dragon. But this kind of art was largely lost by the Middle Ages, when instruments were used principally to accompany something else such as singing or dancing.

As the language of music developed, it became less dependent on words or bodily movements. The need was for forms that would carry the musical thought in a meaningful way. William Byrd (1543-1623) unconsciously emulated the Greek piece mentioned above when he wrote a harpsichord piece called *The Battle*; here a story provided a shape, but in his many pairings of two dances as a 'pavan and galliard' for the same keyboard instrument he was anticipating Bach's instrumental suites consisting of a longer sequence of dances and other movements. Byrd's sets of variations similarly opened up the way for later composers: one for a five-part consort of viols called 'Browning my dear' has twenty variations on the

song theme of this name. His Dutch contemporary Jan Sweelinck wrote the first fully worked-out organ fugues (polyphonic 'essays' on a subject given out at the start) and delighted Amsterdam audiences with organ recitals at which he played variations and dances and folksongs.

By the late seventeenth century, the major and minor scales were fully established: there were 'but two Keys in Musick', as Purcell put it. Unlike the older church modes, each had its associated harmony, the three principal chords being the tonic on the first degree (note) of the scale, the subdominant on the fourth and the dominant on the fifth. Both Purcell and Bach excelled in the form called a chaconne, in which the theme is not a melody at all but a sequence of chords; Brahms was to use it much later in the finale of his Fourth Symphony. Harmonies now progressed in a meaningful way from bar to bar, and chord sequences were henceforth closely related to bar lines in what may be called 'harmonic rhythm'. The advances in instrumental music depended not only on composers and performers but also on fine inventors and craftsmen, sometimes working as families – the Ruckers with their harpsichords in Antwerp, the Stradivaris making violins in Cremona and the organ-building Schnitgers and Silbermanns in Germany, the latter firm also making clavichords and pianos.

Below: *The art of violin-making was developed in Italy, notably in Cremona, by the Stradivari family in the late 17th century when the instrument achieved its early perfection of form and construction.*

Below: *An outdoor concert pictured in 16th-century Italy which shows a sophisticated ensemble of instruments – spinet, lute, flûte à bec and bass-viol – providing a harmonious blend of voices.*

Above: *Obvious enjoyment in a modern interpretation of Schubert's* Trout *Quintet: Zubin Mehta at the piano, Perlman and Zukerman (violins), Du Pré (cello) and Barenboim (double bass).*

Ferruccio BUSONI
(1866-1924)

Prodigy son of musical parents, gave his first piano recital at seven, and went on to become a virtuoso performer renowned for his Lisztian grandeur. But pianism was paralleled by an urge to teach, compose, conduct and theorise. He held teaching posts in Finland, Russia and the USA before settling in Germany, where his intellectualism was more acceptable than in his native Italy. An apostle of 'Young Classicism', he advocated a system of multiple scales and microtonal intervals, and welcomed the early experiments in electronic music, but stopped short of such things in his own compositions. These cover a wide range of conventional genres, including several operas and a great deal of solo piano music. The earlier works tend to be classic-romantic in manner, and the later ones more harmonically adventurous, with the vast Piano Concerto of 1904 providing a watershed. Complete with choral finale, this seems to draw upon all that is grandiose in Bach, Beethoven and Liszt, yet is clearly of this century. Later, his music became more coolly intellectual, as in the *Fantasia Contrappuntistica* for one or two pianos. This is still derivative (from Bach) but offers an extraordinary transformation into pure Busoni. His opera *Doktor Faustus* also provides a fascinating musical short-circuit between the nineteenth and twentieth centuries. J.C.

Andrés SEGOVIA
(1893-1987)

Although the guitar was once highly regarded, by the time Segovia came on the scene it had become little more than a folk-art instrument. He resisted family pressure to study a more conventional instrument and instead devoted himself to restoring the guitar to its proper status in the world of music. There were no opportunities for formal training, so he developed his own playing techniques while taking general studies at the Granada Music Institute. He also set about expanding the repertoire by producing numerous arrangements and transcriptions of works by Bach and Haydn and other classical composers, as well as some by contemporary Spanish composers such as Granados and Albéniz. He gave his first concert in Granada in 1909, and within a few years he embarked upon a series of tours which took him all over the world. As his reputation grew, so other composers wrote music specially for his instrument, among them Turina, Torroba, Ponce and Castelnuovo-Tedesco. His technical mastery, musicianship and unparalleled gifts as a teacher made him a legendary figure in his own lifetime; many classical guitarists owe him a debt. R.H.

Solo and consort (chamber) music abound from Baroque times. Solo pieces were usually for a keyboard instrument such as the organ or harpsichord, and later the piano, which could provide harmony as well as melody; but the unaccompanied violin and cello suites of Bach and Telemann's fantasias for flute alone prove that this does not have to be the rule and, incidentally, show that even a single melody line can imply clear harmonic progressions, for example (but not only) in arpeggio figures that spell out the notes of chords.

Besides the forms already mentioned such as suites, fugues and variations, the Classical period of Haydn, Mozart, Beethoven and Schubert also saw the rise of the sonata to a position of unsurpassed eminence in instrumental music. This is a substantial structure in three or four movements, of which the first and longest is usually fairly fast and in 'sonata form': this has a three-part shape, with the first part or 'exposition' laying out two main contrasted ideas, the second ('development') elaborating and enlarging on them in some way and the third ('recapitulation') restating them. The second movement of a sonata is normally slow and lyrical, and the finale vivid and sparkling; if there are four movements (as in most symphonies) the third is a minuet or scherzo. The word sonata is only applied to music for one or two instruments; but a trio, quartet or quintet and even a concerto or symphony remains a sonata as regards this overall shape.

The instrumental repertory is vast and contains music for many instruments and combinations. For practical reasons, some combinations such as the string quartet are far commoner than others, and in turn ensembles consisting of these instruments are formed and attract composers to create yet more works for them. A few musicians have liked to write for unusual combinations, paying the inevitable price in rarity of performances. Percy Grainger wrote a *Random Round* for six pianists playing on two pianos and several works for 'elastic scoring' that left some choice of instruments to the players, while the *Chôro No. 7* by Villa-Lobos is for flute, oboe, clarinet, saxophone, bassoon, gong, violin and cello. But for most people, the piano, the organ, the string quartet and of course the symphony orchestra can say all that musical creators need to say; and the 'language' of instrumental music is surely as rich as that of vocal works. C.H.

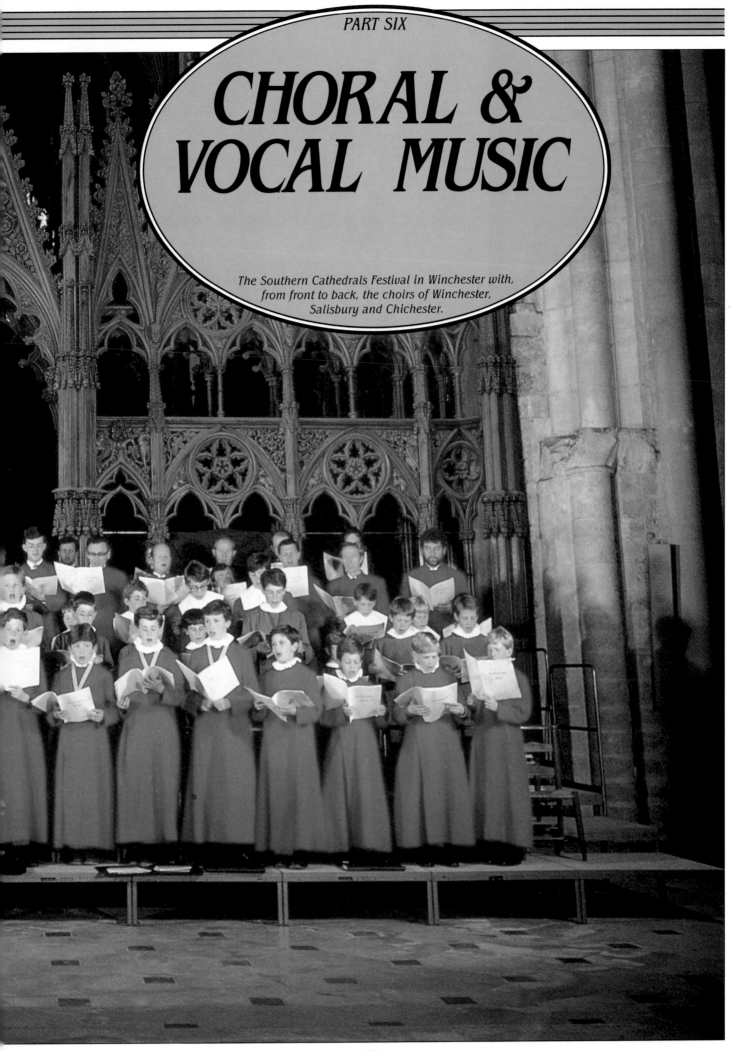

PART SIX

CHORAL & VOCAL MUSIC

The Southern Cathedrals Festival in Winchester with, from front to back, the choirs of Winchester, Salisbury and Chichester.

Whether in madrigals or choral symphonies, opera or oratorio, religious worship, sea shanties or rugby songs, choral singing is central to music. For while certain types of singing such as love songs and lullabies belong obviously to the solo voice, others seem to call out for the joining together of many. The chief thing here is a unanimity of spirit and emotion which a group of people can only express by making music. There is something stirring about such self-expression, especially when it is spontaneous, and since the voice requires no training to be used at a basic level, a raw and sometimes overwhelming force can be present that carries away the singers themselves as well as those who hear them.

Since the beginning of history, religion has used voices to unite people. In the third millennium BC, the Sumerians of Mesopotamia had choral singing in their temples; and later the Greeks similarly sang at weddings and funerals, while in India there were choral hymns. In the time of Christ the Temple in Jerusalem had a choir, and the Christian Church therefore inherited a tradition of choral singing in worship. In the sixth century Pope Gregory the Great set about establishing the melodies and general style of plainchant unison singing so that it could be uniform all over the Christian world. As new melodies were added the need for a system of notation became clear and by the tenth century and the appearance of polyphony (part-singing) this need became absolute: thus it is largely to choral singing that we owe our system of writing music down. Choirs have continued to play their part in church

Above: *The spontaneous pleasure of group singing is well caught in this delightful French painting by an unknown artist of the 16th century. Madrigal and glee singing was a popular pastime of the period.*

music ever since. It was the Sistine Choir of the Pope's chapel at the Vatican that Mozart heard in 1770 at the age of fourteen; their celebrated performance of Allegri's beautiful polyphonic *Miserere* was supposed to be their exclusive property and the music was a fairly well-kept secret, but Mozart went home after the service and wrote it down from memory.

Secular choral singing has often been untrained. People simply joined together in unison song, and we may think for example of medieval villagers in a dance, or sailors singing a shanty with a rhythm that helped them to pull a rope, or King Henry V's soldiers who were reputed to have improvised the *Agincourt Song* after their victory in battle. But a more trained vocal skill is evident in the madrigal groups of Renaissance times, first in Italy and later elsewhere, including England. It became a social accomplishment to be able to read a vocal part in madrigals and other ensemble music. Purcell could write his anthems and choral odes, and Handel his oratorios such as *Messiah*, in the

Johann Sebastian BACH
(1685-1750)

knowledge that choirs could sing them, and the same was true of Bach's cantatas and Passions in Germany.

Eighteenth-century Britain had a number of choral societies such as the Canterbury Catch Club which was founded in a tavern in 1779 and refreshed its members with 'gin punch and mutton pies' between renderings of catches (cheerful rounds for male voices) and the rather similar songs called glees. A more aristocratic and dignified singing club was the Anacreontic Society founded in London in 1766, to which Haydn once paid a visit; its members included a few professional musicians. It is a strange fact of musical history that the melody *Anacreon in Heaven* composed for this society by the English singer and organist John Stafford Smith (1750-1836) has become that of the American national anthem, *The Star-Spangled Banner*. As far afield as India, the British members of the Catch Club of Calcutta met weekly to sing at 10 p.m. and ended their meetings at sunrise, with an interval at 2 a.m. for 'a kettle of burnt champagne'.

These convivial and masculine societies in turn led to others with still higher purposes, like the Edinburgh Harmonists' Club founded in 1822, and the Huddersfield Choral Society of Yorkshire, founded in 1836 – another advance in this latter case being that women were also admitted as members. It was a group such as these, the Birmingham Festival Choral Society formed in 1811, that allowed Mendelssohn to give the première of

Left: *'A Village Choir' by Thomas Webster (1800-68); a delightful portrayal of choral endeavours in the village church where lies the strength of this British tradition.*

Right: *The famous Mormon Tabernacle Choir was founded in 1847 a few weeks after the first Mormon pioneers reached Utah in the far west.*

Above: *A performance of Haydn's* The Creation *in the old Vienna University in 1808. It had first been publicly performed in Vienna in 1799 and was immediately well received. Aquarelle by B. Wiegand.*

his oratorio *Elijah* in that city's Town Hall in 1846. Here the sacred and secular wings of choral singing met to excellent purpose.

Although many of these examples have been British, similar developments have taken place in other European countries and in the United States. Everywhere today, fine choral societies are to be found. They are usually composed of amateur singers, and it is a mark of their dedication and good training, usually under professional chorusmasters, that they can participate on an equal basis with solo singers and orchestras in major works of the repertory such as a Mass by Bach or Beethoven, a Handel oratorio, Beethoven's *Choral* Symphony, the Requiem of Berlioz or Verdi, Mahler's Eighth Symphony and Sir William Walton's *Belshazzar's Feast.* C.H.

As a composer Bach was practical and industrious, knew his own value and constantly sought to improve it by study and application. Although, after his father's death in 1695, he was a pupil with his elder brother and may later have had some organ lessons with Georg Böhm, he was virtually self-taught. At fifteen he became a chorister at Luneberg and in 1793 was appointed violinist in the court orchestra of the Duke of Weimar. He left in the same year to become organist in Arnstadt and in 1705 travelled to Lübeck to hear the great Buxtehude play. In 1707 he moved to Mühlhausen where he married his cousin Maria Barbara then returned to Weimar the next year where he was court organist for the next nine years. In 1917 he became *Kapellmeister* to the court of Prince Leopold of Anhalt-Cöthen. In 1720 his first wife died and the following year he married Anne Magdalena Wilcken. His final move was to Leipzig where he succeeded Kühnau as the Cantor of St Thomas's Church, a post he held until the end of his life. In 1747 he visited the court of Frederick the Great at Potsdam where his son C. P. E. Bach was harpsichordist. In 1749 his eyesight began to fail and after an unsuccessful operation in 1750 he became totally blind. On his death not a single monument was erected to his memory; his music lay neglected for some eighty years.

Some celebrated choirs are now part of history. Until time travel is invented, we can never hear the Levite choir of biblical times that was appointed to sing 'with joy' by King David when the Ark of the Covenant was carried into Jerusalem, nor their successors from the same Levite tribe who sang in the Temple in the time of Christ. In the 1st century AD Seneca described gigantic Roman choirs, but we know little of what, or how, they sang. The choir set up by St Augustine in Canterbury (where he was the first archbishop) in about 600 was apparently 'a flourishing singing school', but we can only imagine how it may have sounded. The same must be said of the Roman Schola Cantorum organised by Pope Gregory the Great at this time, with its boy and men singers who received training as well as performing, and who later also took part in secular feasts. The famous Sistine Choir in the Vatican was named after the man who founded it (and built the chapel itself) in the fifteenth century, Pope Sixtus IV: its strength in 1625 was fixed at thirty-two singers, by this time including adult male sopranos (castrati). This was also the size during the fifteenth century of the choirs of King's College, Cambridge, and Magdalen College, Oxford; and we know that between twenty and thirty-five members were usual in English cathedrals such as Westminster Abbey, Durham and Winchester.

Such religious choirs, including those of many other European churches and cathedrals, have a long lineage. That of the Chapel Royal in England during Purcell's lifetime (the late seventeenth century) had forty-four members, but mostly they remained small, as the number of choir stalls in cathedrals indicates. Even Bach's Lutheran choir at St Thomas's Church, Leipzig, which performed his Passion music and cantatas, consisted of only about thirty-six singers, and at a London performance of Handel's *Messiah* in 1758 the chorus was of thirteen men and six boys.

Choirs grew rapidly outside churches, even in sacred music, and three hundred singers took part in a Handel Festival at Westminster Abbey in 1784. This was the time of the founding of major choral societies in the German-speaking countries such as the Viennese Tonkünstler-Sozietät, founded in 1771 when Mozart was a boy, and the Berliner Singakademie (1792). The National Festival Chorus of France in 1794, celebrating the achievements of the Revolution a few years before, had the participation of no less than 2400 voices. The English 'catch clubs' (see above) led indirectly to the foundation of choral societies such as those of Huddersfield and Birmingham, the latter giving the first performance of Mendelssohn's oratorio *Elijah* in 1846. The Vienna Singakademie (founded in 1858) had Brahms as its conductor for a while, though his *German Requiem* and *Alto Rhapsody* were first performed by the city's other great choir, the Singverein der Gesel-

Above: *Psalms of Penitance by Orlande de Lassus (1532-94) sung in the private music chapel of the Duke of Bavaria. Miniature from the 16th-century Mielen-Codex in the Bavarian State Library.*

Below: *The Wandsworth Boys Choir was much admired by Benjamin Britten and was frequently used for performances and recordings of his choral works, as well as in works by other composers.*

George Frideric HANDEL
(1685-1759)

Son of an unmusical barber-surgeon, he received some lessons from the local organist, studied law at Halle University, then set off to build a musical career. He became violinist, then harpsichordist, at the Hamburg Opera and stepped in to provide music for an abandoned libretto, leading in 1705 to his first opera, *Almira*. This was followed by three others before he went off to Italy to soak up ideas and influences. He became *Kapellmeister* at Hanover in 1710, but that same year visited London where he was invited to write *Rinaldo*. This being a success he moved permanently to England, was granted a royal pension, and spent the next thirty-five years at the centre of London's operatic life, composing some forty Italian operas. But the *opera seria* style eventually drifted out of fashion, so in the 1830s he turned increasingly to his own special brand of oratorio, producing nearly thirty and usually playing an organ concerto or two during the intervals. A large, voracious, animated man, Handel's health declined in later years and he eventually went blind; but he was idolised in England and long regarded as supreme among composers. Even today there can be few who have not heard of the *Messiah* (or indeed the *Water Music*), while the famous *Largo*, although originally a satirical aria in a comic opera, is now one of the world's great tunes. J.C.

Below: *The famous Vienna Boys Choir has a history going back to 1498 when a chapel was founded by Emperor Maximilian. The present choir was reformed in 1924 by Josef Schmitt.*

Above: *The long choral tradition of King's College, Cambridge, and the acoustics of their fine chapel have produced a unique style. The choir with Sir David Willcocks and the English National Orchestra.*

schaft der Musikfreunde, founded in the same year.

Any listing of choirs today must be highly selective. There are several well-established and large municipal choral bodies like the London Bach Choir, the Oratorio Society of New York and the various European choirs already mentioned above. Boys' choirs, consisting of treble voices only, are doubtless led by the justly celebrated Vienna Boys Choir (Wiener Sängerknaben) whose lineage goes back as far as 1498, though the Texas Boys Choir are also fine. Russian choirs are noted for their fine basses, whether in Orthodox church music or (as with the Don Cossack Choir) secular song. The Jubilee Singers of Tennessee have toured the United States of America and Europe with spirituals and other

religious music, and the Mormon Tabernacle Choir of Utah is also impressive in a similar tradition. Festivals of music in British cities such as Brighton and Edinburgh often assemble fine choral bodies on an annual basis. Smaller groups such as the BBC Singers, of which the celebrated tenor Peter Pears was a member in the 1930s, the John Alldis Choir, the Ambrosian Singers and the King's Singers can tackle unfamiliar or challengingly contemporary music and often do so with success. Several orchestras such as the Hallé, Montreal Symphony and BBC Symphony have their own choral bodies who can join them in performances of works requiring big vocal forces. There is no sound more thrilling than the combined forces of a great orchestra and a great choir. C.H.

The human voice is the oldest means of making music and also the only 'instrument' that is more commonly used for another purpose, in this case speech. In this aspect it reminds us of the significant truth that music, like speech itself, is a form of self-expression and communication. And of course it is normally employed in a combination of speech and musical notes, although it can also be used wordlessly – as happens with the women's choirs in Holst's *Neptune* (in *The Planets*) and Debussy's *Sirènes*, the last of his orchestral *Nocturnes*.

Producing the voice is a complex action of which we are usually unaware, although the training of singers must take it fully into account. Breath is supplied under pressure by the lungs via two small vibrating folds of muscular tissue within the larynx at the top of the trachea (windpipe) called the vocal cords (not 'chords' as some people think) to the

resonating cavity of the mouth, nose and upper part of the throat. Changes in pitch are made by changing the tensions of the vocal cords: as they become more tense the pitch rises. The quality, volume and colour of tone depend on many factors, only some of which are fully controllable; thus one person's untrained voice may be very pleasant but a good pianist or violinist may make a poor sound when he tries to sing. Singing requires more air supply than ordinary speech, and singers work to develop their lung capacity. The nineteenth-century bass Luigi Lablache could, in a single breath, sing a long note from soft to loud and back again, drink a glass of wine without breathing, sing a twelve-note scale while trilling on each note and finally blow out a candle with his mouth open.

Beyond the musical aspect of singing, the singer must also enunciate words with their

Below: *A 16th-century portrayal of music-making in Verona, the singers led by musicians playing the plucked lute, the bowed rebec (the later four-stringed variety) and the psaltery.*

Above: *The singers in this 14th-century manuscript read music from a parchment roll whilst singing in the unison style of plainchant or plainsong that dated from Roman times.*

Below: *Swedish soprano Elisabeth Söderström and German contralto Marga Höffgen during a performance of Beethoven's* Missa solemnis, *his version of the high mass first heard in 1824.*

vowels and consonants in a way that in broad terms resembles what we do in normal speech but has significant differences – try, for example, saying the word 'night' and then singing it as a long note, or doing the same with 'boat' and 'bound', to see how vowels which are impure (these are called diphthongs) need special treatment. In fact the 'i' of 'night' is 'ah' followed by 'ee': the singer sustains the 'ah' part of the diphthong until the very last moment.

The standard vocal ranges are four in number. Broadly speaking, a bass voice has a compass extending about two or three notes either side of the bass clef (stave) (1), and the tenor is a fifth higher (2). These are exclusively men's voices; the alto (whether male or female) or contralto range is from about the G below the treble clef (stave) to the E on its top space (3), while the soprano and a boy's treble have from middle C upwards to the A or

Right: *20th-century-styled prima donna Joan Sutherland, one of many great opera singers to come from Australia, in the leading role of Marie in Donizetti's* La Fille du Régiment, *a forerunner of operetta.*

Franz SCHUBERT
(1797-1828)

Twelfth child of a self-employed Austrian schoolmaster, he joined the resident choir-school of the Imperial Court chapel in Vienna at eleven, immediately outstripped the principal music teacher's instructional capacity, played violin and piano with ease, and wrote his first symphony just before he left at sixteen. He then taught at his father's school for a few years, but in 1817 adopted a bohemian existence, living in lodgings with artistic, literary and musical friends, all the time composing at a prodigious rate in practically every major genre: some 200 works, plus 600 songs drawing upon the verses of 91 poets. These songs, from the simple perfection of *Gretchen am Spinnrade* (composed at seventeen) to the relentless chill of the *Winterreise* cycle from the year before his death, are now regarded as one of the supreme achievements of the human spirit. Yet had it not been for the support of the many loyal friends which the shy Schubert attracted, even these would have languished (like most of his music) unknown outside Vienna until decades after his tragically early death. He never married, and asked little more of life than the freedom to create music, an activity to which he brought unparalleled melodic gifts. But so often is that music tinged with sadness that people will forever wonder what emptiness there may have been in his heart. J.C.

even the C above the treble stave (4). These categories and ranges are useful for choirs, but solo singers will often have a wider range. Soloists also subdivide the categories further, and we should remember that such labels as baritone (between tenor and bass) and mezzo/soprano and alto) imply different kinds of tone as well as different pitch ranges. Even within a single range there are different kinds of voice, say between a lyric tenor in a French operetta and a *Heldentenor* (heroic tenor) suitable for the role of Wagner's Siegfried, or for that matter a Welsh folk singer. There are other examples, for instance an Italian bass in comic opera will not make the same kind of sound as a Russian singing the title role in Mussorgsky's *Boris Godunov.* C.H.

'Since singing is so good a thing, I wish all men would learn to sing.' So said William Byrd in 1588, and he added: 'The exercise of singing is delightful to nature and good to preserve the health of man. It doth strengthen all the parts of the breast, and doth open the pipes. It is a singular good remedy for a stuttering and stammering in the speech . . . There is not any music of instruments whatsoever comparable to that which is made of the voices of men.' These are encouraging words, as are those of a moralising French proverb: '*Bouche qui mord à la chanson ne mord pas à la grappe* – A mouth occupied with song is not occupied with the grape.' And one of Shakespeare's characters, Armado in *Love's Labour's Lost*, says to another, 'Warble, child, make passionate my sense of hearing.' In a more ribald mood, James Joyce wrote in his novel *Ulysses* that 'tenors get women by the score'.

But what is song? Obviously it is music made with the voice or voices. It resembles speech in that it usually has intelligible words – though the voice can be used wordlessly – but goes beyond it in adding a variety of elements of music such as pitch, dynamics (i.e. volume) and fairly definite metrical rhythm with its aspects of duration and accent.

Like birds and animals, who use their calls or 'voices' for many different reasons such as courtship or warning, people have sung since time immemorial – a mother crooning a lullaby to send a child to sleep is one obvious example, and work songs and religious ritual chants are others. In ancient Greece and Rome, solo singers performed to the accompaniment of a quiet instrument such as the lyre, while choruses sang in unison accompanied by the sharp, reedy sound of the double pipe or aulos. As for Jewish and Christian traditions, the Bible is full of references to song – 'O come, let us sing unto the Lord . . . O sing unto the Lord a new song', cries the Psalmist.

Folk song is as old as music itself, but art songs that were composed and written down appeared later. Medieval times gave us the courtly love songs of the French troubadours and *trouvères* and the German *Minnesinger*, while in Germany during the late Renaissance the Mastersingers took pride in their guilds and song competitions. Here great musical skill might be displayed, both in the creation and in the performance of songs, and Wagner's celebrated opera of this name portrays their world and a real historical person in the

Below: *The revival of ancient fashions in music has been a fruitful part of the modern scene, with groups such as The Mastersingers (here featuring Alan Opie and Penelope Mackie) abounding.*

Robert SCHUMANN
(1810-56)

Raised in a bookish atmosphere which encouraged much reading of romantic literature, this introspective and deeply sensitive German showed early musical aptitudes, but was obliged to study law before adopting his true vocation. Then, seemingly a future pianist, he invented a finger-clamping device which inadvertently injured his hand, thus releasing more energy for composition, which had already commenced around 1830 with the *Abegg Variations* and twelve *Papillons* pieces for piano. He also became a music critic, was the first to recognise Chopin's genius, and in 1834 (when he was composing *Carnaval*) founded his own periodical to promote the cause of Romanticism against Philistines of all kinds. He wrote with both passion and sympathetic understanding, adopting pen-names to represent opposed sides of his own nature. In 1840 he married the pianist Clara Wieck against fierce opposition from her father, who regarded Schumann as an impractical idealist. But the union evoked a flood of music, first songs (including the great *Dichterliebe* cycle), then orchestral and chamber works, and led on to a busy life interspersed with spells of mental instability. The latter finally led via hallucinatory episodes to attempted suicide and thence to two final years in an asylum: a sad end for a man whose expressive ideals were only intermittently appreciated in his own time. Clara outlived him by forty years and became a lifelong friend of Brahms. J.C.

Above: *A famous painting by Julius Schmid (1854-1935) imaginatively recaptures the atmosphere of a Viennese evening with the composer Franz Schubert at the piano entertaining at a social gathering.*

Below: *Vera Lynn, the Forces' Sweetheart of the Second World War, broadcasting to the troops on the occasion of the victory in Europe in 1945. Her singing of songs like 'We'll meet again' had an incalculable effect on British war morale.*

character of Hans Sachs. Skill was also needed for the group singing of madrigals, with words usually about nature or love, that was a social accomplishment in Italy and Elizabethan England.

Song and drama joined hands in the new form of opera that appeared in Italy in around 1600 and went on to conquer the world. An operatic aria is simply an 'air' or solo song, and of course many operas such as Verdi's have magnificent choruses also. At the same time songs to sacred words featured in Bach's Passion music and church cantatas.

The German *Lied* is a form of art song that came into its own with the over 600 songs of Schubert composed in the early part of the nineteenth century. Other composers, such as Schumann, Brahms, Wolf, Strauss and Mahler, followed him in setting poems to music for solo voice and piano in a way that brought out every shade of meaning in a text. Sometimes the form is strophic like that of a hymn, with each verse of a poem repeating the same melody; elsewhere a song may be through-composed without such repetition. For sheer melody, Schubert is unsurpassed, while for psychological penetration of a text we might look to the songs of Wolf.

Something akin to *Lieder* is found in the *mélodies* of French composers such as Fauré and Debussy, and the English art song has a number of distinguished exponents from Quilter to Britten; in Russia, Tchaikovsky and Rachmaninov have written beautiful songs.

Finally, it goes without saying that folk songs and the songs of popular music are often of the highest quality. Patriotic choral songs like national anthems or the Socialist *Internationale* can be rousing indeed. The wartime songs sung in Britain by Vera Lynn (such as 'We'll meet again') had an immense appeal and a genuine power to cheer and comfort in times of adversity, and for a more recent generation protest songs like 'We shall overcome' have had the same kind of force.

*L*ied is the German word for song, but as we use it today it has come to mean something more specific. Unlike, say, an operatic aria, a *Lied* is intimate in character. It was originally designed for performance in domestic surroundings, has German words and is for a single voice with piano. The piano part of *Lieder* is more than mere accompaniment, and many great pianists such as Benjamin Britten, Alfred Brendel, Daniel Barenboim and Sviatoslav Richter have joined with distinguished singers in their performance. The origin of the lied lies in German folk song, but although several composers wrote songs to German words before Franz Schubert wrote his six hundred and more lieder, the fully-fledged form really only emerges with the work of that great Viennese composer during the early nineteenth century.

Lieder singers in Schubert's time were often amateur musicians, far removed in kind and skill from the major operatic artists of this period who enjoyed international reputations. Indeed, Schubert himself was one of them. However, other singers were professional artists. Johann Michael Vogl, who gave the first performances of Schu-

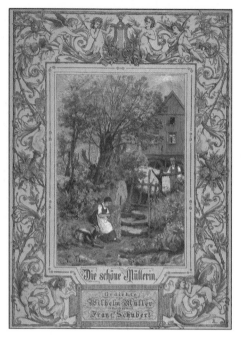

Above: *Franz Schubert, the supreme writer of German* Lieder, *had his major achievement in song-cycles like* Die schöne Müllerin, *written in 1823 but not publicly performed until 1856.*

bert's song cycle *Die Winterreise*, was better known to the public as an opera singer who performed no less than 130 roles; similarly Pauline Anna Milder-Hauptmann, for whom Schubert created the lengthy song with clarinet *obbligato* called *The Shepherd on the Rock*, owed her fame more to her creation of the title role in Beethoven's opera *Fidelio*.

But as the lied grew in artistic stature, singers increasingly devoted their skill to this new kind of song in which interpretative subtlety had to respond to every nuance of a text. In turn, the skill of such artists as these inspired composers after Schubert such as Schumann, Brahms and Wolf. Thus Brahms wrote his *Magelone Romances* in the 1860s for the baritone Julius Stockhausen, who brought lieder from the salon into the concert hall by giving the first public performance of Schubert's cycle *Die schöne Müllerin* in Vienna in 1856. Stockhausen and Brahms joined in a voice-and-piano partnership to perform lieder such as Schumann's *Dichterliebe (The Poet's Love)* cycle in 1861. Stockhausen was also a conductor, and must have been a musician of unusual intelligence, for in 1863 he was chosen in preference to Brahms for the conductorship of the Philharmonic Society in Brahms's native city of Hamburg and conducted Schubert's *Great* C major Symphony there at his first concert. As a lieder singer born just within Schubert's lifetime (1826), he was evidently quite out of the ordinary. Sir George Grove declared that 'the rich beauty of his voice, the nobility of the style, the perfect phrasing, the intimate sympathy, and, not least, the intelligible way in which the words were given – in itself one of his greatest claims to distinction – all combined to make his singing of songs a wonderful event'.

These details emphasise the important point that fine lieder singers are characteristically people of high musical attainment and sensitivity as well as having fine voices. The form itself seems to demand this. Perhaps because of this thoughtful, even introspective, aspect of their art, which requires them to think about it as well as sing beautifully, some lieder singers have been fine teachers of the interpretation of lieder and so helped the growth of the art itself. Julius Stockhausen himself was one such teacher, as was his pupil, the Dutch baritone Johannes Messchaert; another was the Polish soprano Marcella Sembrich, who after an operatic career turned to the lieder repertory, became an American citizen and taught in the USA. These latter two names also remind us that the performance of German lieder is by no means reserved to singers who have German as their mother tongue.

Left: *Robert Schumann was the worthy successor to Schubert in the* Lieder *world. This is an illustrated 1860 edition of his 'Mondnacht' from his cycle* Liederkreis, *written in 1840.*

Hugo WOLF
(1860-1903)

Many lieder singers have also been famous in opera. When we compare the interpretative needs of opera performance with those of lieder we find something like a parallel between the different demands placed upon an actor by the theatre and film work: the first requires broad and well-projected effects while the second commonly relies on small yet compelling gesture and facial expressions. It is perhaps for this reason that the art of lieder singing has been especially well served by the gramophone, with the microphone faithfully recording innumerable vocal subtleties that might be lost on a concert hall or opera house. Yet this point should not imply a conflict: as with actors, musical artists can offer flexibility and many fine singers have been equally at home in these different forms of music-making. One thinks of sopranos such as Lotte Lehmann, Elizabeth Schumann and Elizabeth Schwarzkopf, of the British contralto Kathleen Ferrier, of the tenors Karl Erb and Peter Pears, of the baritones Heinrich Schlusnus and Dietrich Fischer-Dieskau, and of the bass-baritone Hans Hotter. It is a mark of the versatility of these artists that they have excelled in musical forms that are so different – the one perhaps somewhat larger than life, the other a kind of vocal chamber music.

GREAT LIEDER SINGERS

Lotte Lehmann (1888-1976) studied in Berlin and made her name in opera, where Puccini had a high regard for her as his Suor Angelica and Richard Strauss chose her as his first Dyer's Wife in *Die Frau ohne Schatten*; one of her most famous roles was the Marschallin in his *Der Rosenkavalier*. It was mainly after her first maturity that she turned to the lieder repertory, to which she brought a keen dramatic sense tempered by the intimacy of the song form, a sympathy with the pianists who partnered her and great literary sensitivity.

Above: *The great singer Lotte Lehmann (1888-1976) holds a master class with a young Grace Bumbry the attentive pupil and the well-known accompanist Ivor Newton at the piano.*

Elizabeth Schumann (1888-1952) (soprano) was born in Germany and also began her career in the opera house, where she was renowned for her roles in Mozart and both Johann and Richard Strauss. She made her home in New York from 1938 and many of her lieder recitals and recordings date from this latter part of her career. She recorded lieder by the four major composers Schubert, Schumann (no relation), Brahms and Wolf, and by Mahler also: among her famous performances are Schubert's *Du bist die Ruh'*, *Horch, horch, die Lerch'* and the final *Des baches Wiegenlied* in the cycle *Die schöne Müllerin*, in which the mill-stream sings a lullaby to the love-lorn drowned youth. She also distinguished herself in Schumann's cycle *Frauenliebe und Leben (Woman's Life and Love)*. Her ability to bring a light touch and humour to song was evident in such songs as Wolf's *In dem Schatten meiner Locken* and *Mausfallensprüchlein*.

Elizabeth Schwarzkopf (b. 1915) is another German soprano whose birthplace, Jarotschin, is now actually in Poland. Although pursuing a brilliant career in opera, she came to lieder early, making her début recital in 1942 in Berlin. Together with the German baritone Dietrich Fischer-Dieskau she is the principal lieder singer of the decades following World War II. Her farewell major recital tour was in 1975, the year in which she reached sixty, but a dozen years after that she remains active as a teacher in many centres, including British ones; in 1953 she married Walter Legge, the British music director of EMI records and founder of the Philharmonia Orchestra, who himself had founded a London Lieder Club twenty years previously

Just about the closest approach to the 'mad genius' of popular imagination to be found among major composers, he spent his whole life upsetting everyone, continually sponged on others, held the most extreme views, and finally went insane – all the time producing a stream of exquisitely perfect songs. His father (an Austrian leather merchant) gave him some musical instruction, he studied at the Vienna Conservatory for eighteen months until his (disputed) expulsion, tried his hand unsuccessfully at teaching and conducting, then turned to music criticism. In this he adopted a fanatical pro-Wagner, anti-Brahms stance which made him many enemies. In 1897 he suffered psychotic delusions that he had been appointed director of the Vienna opera in place of Mahler, spent a year in an asylum, after his release wandered aimlessly before attempting suicide, and was finally recommitted until his death. His 240 songs (and the lovely *Italian Serenade* for strings) represent his alter ego. Wolf's acute sensitivity to a wide range of poetry – especially that of Mörike, Eichendorff and Goethe – led him to evolve what has been called the 'psychological song', in which music and verse interpenetrate so intimately and exactly that many regard him as the ultimate and supreme exponent of the German *Lied*. J.C.

and suggested many of her programmes. Schwarzkopf has been greatly admired, perhaps most of all in Wolf's lieder, in which she was often partnered by the pianist Gerald Moore and in which she could convey the subtleties of the text and its musical clothing to a degree unparalleled by others. However, elsewhere her very intelligence and meticulous preparation could occasionally deprive her singing of the feeling of spontaneity and freshness which some songs by, say, Schubert need. But her vocal quality was beyond question: here was 'a lustrous, powerful lyric soprano, full-toned, warm and flexible'. Her modesty was recalled by Gerald Moore: 'as we stand to bow she called to me, "was I in tune?"'. He added that it seemed quite unfair that anyone could look so ravishing and sing so beautifully.

Above: *Kathleen Ferrier (1912-1953) became one of Britain's favourite singers before her tragic death. At the first Edinburgh Festival in 1947 she sang Mahler's* Das Lied von der Erde.

Above: *The great British composer Benjamin Britten at Glyndebourne in 1946 discussing with his friend and interpreter Peter Pears the production of his latest opera* The Rape of Lucretia.

Right: *Victoria de Los Angeles, Elizabeth Schwarzkopf and Dietrich Fischer-Dieskau singing the Mozart terzetto 'La Partenza' at the 'Homage to Gerald Moore' concert at the Festival Hall in 1967.*

Elena Gerhardt (1883-1961) was born in Leipzig but settled in Britain in 1934 and took British nationality. Her first public recital was on her twentieth birthday and she first sang in England three years later. During World War II she took part in many London concerts and she also recorded extensively. Her voice was at first soprano, but it deepened to mezzo-soprano with the years; and this (together with her powerful chest register) allowed her convincingly to perform songs usually given only by male singers, such as Schubert's *Der Atlas* with its strong portrayal of a poet carrying a world of grief on his shoulders, and – even more unusually – the same composer's tragic song cycle *Die Winterreise*. The first volume of records produced by the Hugo Wolf Society (founded in 1931 by The Gramophone Company) consisted of nineteen Wolf lieder sung by her with the partnership of the pianist Coenraad van Bos. Nearly forty years ago the authors of *The Record Guide* declared that in lieder this artist 'developed a mastery of phrasing, enunciation and tone colour which have set a standard difficult approach', and more recently a critic has said that 'she gave herself completely to her art, making every song that she sang into a part of her own warm and rich personality'. She was also a teacher: one of her pupils was the soprano Victoria de Los Angeles and another was the tenor Peter Pears.

Kathleen Ferrier (1912-53) was a contralto singer who became one of Britain's best loved artists both for her vocal quality and art

and for her warm and forthright personality. Her courageous fight against cancer is still remembered, and many admiring and affectionate tributes came her way after her early death from friends such as Benjamin Britten (for whom she created the title role in his opera *The Rape of Lucretia*) and the critic Sir Neville Cardus. Cardus declared that England had had 'only one truly great singer since the war, and her name was Kathleen Ferrier', and for him this was a voice 'which seemed as though classic shapes in marble were changing to melody, warm, rich-throated, but chaste'. Her tonal combination of mellowness and purity was unusual: a laryngologist who examined her throat called it a beautiful example of vocal architecture. Those who heard her in lieder (sometimes accompanied by the conductor Bruno Walter) regret that she recorded far too little of this repertory, although her performance of a song such as Schubert's *Die junge Nonne* with its final cry of 'Hallelujah' shows us how she could grasp the psychology of the poem in which a young woman renounces love to devote herself to Christ. The lyrical *An die Musik* and the ebullient *Der Musensohn* are other Schubert songs in which she gave fully of her art, as she also did in Brahms's songs with viola *obbligato* called *Geistliches Wiegenlied* and *Gestille Sehnsucht*. However, her repertory was not large, and arguably she lacked the vocal lightness that would have given her even more interpretative resource; Bruno Walter thought that she was at her best in 'music of spiritual meaning'.

Karl Erb (1877-1958) is doubtless the German tenor with the highest reputation in lieder. Unusually for a singer, he was self-taught; he sang chiefly in opera until he was in his early fifties, when he gave up the stage and devoted himself to recital and concert work, continuing to sing until a surprisingly late age. He recorded a great deal of the repertory, including its major composers Schubert, Schumann, Brahms and Wolf. Erb was above all a fine musician, with a 'soft-grained yet powerful' voice of slightly nasal timbre that he used with high intelligence; his diction and, still more importantly, his evident literary understanding of his texts were of an equal quality.

The British tenor Peter Pears (1910-86) was born in Surrey and studied at the Royal College of Music. He sang with the BBC Singers in the mid-1930s, and at this time formed his lifelong friendship and artistic partnership with the composer Benjamin Britten. Britten wrote major operatic roles and many songs for him, including settings of the German poet Hölderlin which may perhaps be classed as lieder. The two men made a magnificent partnership in lieder recitals, performing the major cycles of Schubert, Schumann's *Dichterliebe* and much else including various Wolf songs and (on one single occasion) some by Webern. They also recorded extensively; and when Britten was latterly unable to play after suffering a stroke, Pears also worked with the American pianist Murray Perahia, recording the Schumann *Liederkreis* cycle of twelve songs as

Henri DUPARC
(1848-1933)

Here is a composer who probably holds the record for leaving behind the least music compatible with posthumous fame, and who also spent the last forty-eight years of his life away from his native land (France), detached from music and indifferent both to his past and to his friends. He studied piano and composition as the favourite of César Franck's select group of early pupils, but a strong self-critical vein prompted him to destroy most of his early works. A symphonic poem, *Lénore*, and a few small piano pieces survive, but Duparc's fame rests entirely upon a dozen or so of the sixteen songs which he composed before 1885, the year in which a breakdown and subsequent incurable mental illness (but by no means insanity) caused his abandonment of music and withdrawal to exile in Switzerland. These songs, whose style can be regarded as paralleling that of Symbolism in literature, have an intense yet subtle restraint, coupled with an intimate blending of music and verse, which does for French vocal music what Hugo Wolf's songs did for the German *Lied*. An English listener could well start by trying *Chanson triste* (poet: Lahor), *L'Invitation au voyage* (Baudelaire) and *Phidylé* (de Lisle). J.C.

Clara BUTT
(1873-1936)

English contralto who studied first in Bristol and then, from 1889, at the Royal College of Music. She made her London début as Ursula in Sullivan's *Golden Legend* at the Royal Albert Hall in December 1892. Three days later she sang the part of Orpheus in a student production of Gluck's opera at the Lyceum Theatre, a role to which she returned later under Beecham at Covent Garden in 1920. However, it was as a concert artist and not as an opera singer that she achieved considerable fame, with a commanding stage presence to support a voice of great warmth and beauty. Elgar composed *Sea Pictures* for her, presented with much success at the Norwich Festival in 1899, also the patriotic piece *Spirit of England*, which appeared in 1916. Clara Butt toured extensively, giving ballad recitals with her husband, the baritone Kennersley Rumford. In 1920 she was created a Dame Commander of the British Empire in recognition of her services during World War I. She made a number of recordings in her later years when her voice was well past its prime, which do much less than justice to one of the outstanding singers of her generation. R.H.

---

well as the same composer's groups of songs, Op. 40 and Op. 90. His voice was personal in quality (not everyone cared for it) but it was used with consistently luminous intelligence and musical sensitivity. After Pears's death Dietrich Fischer-Dieskau wrote that 'singers of such spirituality are rare . . . [this artistry] never ceased to inspire our wonder', and Elizabeth Schwarzkopf called him 'a very English Englishman . . . [who became] one of the major German lieder singers'.

Several baritone singers have been distinguished in lieder. We could name a number, from Gerhard Hüsch (1901-84) – for many a model of style in Schubert and Wolf – to men of a much more recent generation like Hermann Prey and Olaf Bär. But the outstanding figure among living baritones is Dietrich Fischer-Dieskau (b. 1925). His repertory of well over a thousand songs takes in virtually all the major cycles and individual

songs of the four greatest lieder composers, and he has also performed lieder by Strauss and other composers who are rather less well known in this field, such as Mendelssohn, Loewe and Liszt – whose German songs make up the majority of the seventy or so that he wrote. He has probably recorded more lieder than any other singer, some more than once, affording connoisseurs a fascinating glimpse into vocal and artistic changes that have taken place over a career that goes back forty years. A man of considerable culture and literary intelligence, he has also published a study of Schubert's songs. A certain weighty seriousness of tone is an asset in many songs, if less appropriate to others; but he uses his big voice with delicacy. The critic Alan Blyth has declared that his art embodies 'a perfect marriage of tone and words, an almost flawless technique and an unerring ability to impart the right colour and nuance to a

phrase'. What more can be said.

Bass and bass-baritone singers of lieder do not have quite the same quantity of repertory available to them as tenors and baritones, for the voice itself cannot suggest the youth in love needed for, say, Schubert's *Die schöne Müllerin*. But other cycles, such as the same composer's *Die Winterreise* or his sombre and ghostly song *Der Doppelgänger* are admirably suited to a register of voice that can suggest world-weariness. The Austrian bass-baritone Hans Hotter (b. 1909) is splendid in these works and at home also in Schumann's military-style *Die beiden Grenadiere* with its description of two of Napoleon's defeated soldiers returning to France who hear the news of their emperor's downfall. Famous also in opera, not least as Wagner's Wotan, Hotter was also able to reduce his naturally full tone when needed and to sing with flexibility and a degree of lightness. C.H.

There is a story of a Swiss music critic some forty years ago who attended a song recital at which a very inadequate soprano was partnered by a distinguished accompanist. His newspaper review the next morning consisted of nothing but praise for the first nineteen of its twenty lines – but unfortunately this praise was devoted entirely to the pianist. No mention was made of the singer until the last sentence, which read: 'At the soprano was Madame Schmidt'.

This story is not intended to illustrate unkind music criticism but to show just how subordinate the role of the pianist-accompanist in a song recital was once thought to be. There were plenty of concert notices like that (which was the point of the critic's joke), but the roles were usually reversed and the accompanist mentioned as a kind of after-thought – sometimes even when the performance was of the violin sonatas by Mozart and Beethoven which are actually marked 'for piano and violin'! There is some justification for this in the use of the word 'accompany' itself, for the *Concise Oxford Dictionary* defines it as, among other things, 'go with, escort, attend . . . (mus.) support (singer, player, chorus) by performing subsidiary part'.

For reasons already implied in connection with *Lieder* in the previous section of this book, many musicians today choose instead to refer to the pianist in a song recital as the singer's partner. At times we should go further and call the pianist an equal, in keeping with his stature and the demands of the music. When Ferrier is 'accompanied' by Bruno Walter, Fischer-Dieskau by Barenboim or Brendel or Pears by Britten, the keyboard player is doing much more than 'escorting' the voice: he is co-interpreting the song. Furthermore the nature of the piano writing in a Schubert song cycle or such a work as Schumann's cycle *Dichterliebe*, as well as countless individual songs by these and other composers, simply forbids us to think of it as a 'subsidiary part'. Indeed, the Schumann work just mentioned ends with a complete little 'movement' for piano solo that acts as an epilogue to its sixteen songs: it is over a page of slowish music that has not been heard before, which crowns the cycle in a way that is quite magical. Again and again, too, the piano brings a programmatic and atmospheric element to a song which clothes and illuminates the vocal line with its text – the sound of the village dance in the ninth song of the Schumann ('*Das ist ein Flöten und Geigen*'), or (to take examples from Schubert) the lime-tree's rustling leaves in *Der Lindenbaum* in *Die Winterreise* and the galloping horse in the terrifying night ride of *Erlkönig*.

Having said all this, we must admit that sometimes the 'accompanist' in a song is required only to be just that. Schubert's lengthy song 'The Shepherd on the Rock' has boring pages of a mere chordal pattern for

Above: *An aquarelle of Johannes Brahms (1833-97) as accompanist in the Boesendorfer-Saal of the Liechtenstein-palais in Vienna. Brahms followed a tradition as a great German* Lieder *writer.*

the pianist, and the chief reason is that in this particular piece a clarinet performs as well as the voice and piano, and there simply isn't enough interesting material to go around. Many Victorian ballads with piano give a fairly subordinate role to the keyboard, as do some French *mélodies* – repeated chords for the right hand above sustained bass notes are a common accompaniment device that supplies harmony and some sense of movement. Really basic accompaniment is best illustrated by the punctuating keyboard chords that can go with vocal recitative in oratorios

and operas (even Mozart's), or the kind of keyboard support for a voice or melodic instrument which is used in Baroque music, dignified only with the word 'continuo' and written just as bass notes with figures showing the chords to add above them.

The pianists already mentioned above have all been major artists in their own right. For a professional piano accompanist of the first rank, who confined his work almost wholly to this kind of partnership, there is no better example than the British performer Gerald Moore (1899-1986). He had a long career of some forty years during which he worked with many of this century's finest singers and instrumentalists; he also gave master classes on accompaniment in many of the world's musical centres and was awarded the Hugo Wolf Medal of Vienna in 1973. He wrote two

Francis POULENC
(1899-1963)

Raised in an artistic and musical family, this light-hearted Frenchman was taught piano by his mother at five, was composing the odd piece by seven, and joined the Satie/Cocteau circle in his teens to become a member of 'Les Six', whose aim was to draw upon popular idioms and be irreverently 'modern'. But while his modernism certainly followed a pattern of charm and transparency, with pieces mostly conceived on a small scale, he generally abjured twentieth-century expectations by writing old-fashioned melodies and harmonies, albeit in music having a brittle, sometimes brash quality. Thus at one time fashionable critics turned their noses up at Poulenc, because he would persist in writing tunes. He also developed a strong lyrical vein, with an emphasis on vocal works which include nearly 150 songs, many now greatly admired. He agreed with one critic who declared him to be part monk and part street-arab, the former represented in his religious works, and in the opera *Dialogues des Carmélites*, the latter summed up by his comic opera *Les Mamelles de Tirésias*, an audacious sexual farce. But whether it be music for Diaghilev's ballet *Les Biches*, the song cycle *Le Bestiaire*, or one of the many sets of piano pieces, there is always something pleasing to pick from the profuse output of this smiling Parisian. J.C.

Above: *The celebrated German baritone Dietrich Fischer-Dieskau accompanied by the equally celebrated pianist Gerald Moore – a partnership which produced many masterly performances.*

Below: *Great Austrian tenor Richard Tauber (1892-1948) started his career in grand opera but is mainly remembered for his supremacy in the field of Viennese operetta, particularly in the works of Franz Lehár.*

books on accompaniment and some memoirs modestly titled *Am I Too Loud?*.

Moore's modesty also led him to call Benjamin Britten the greatest of accompanists; but Britten mainly worked with the tenor Peter Pears and only rarely with other artists. Another accompanist-composer is the German Aribert Reimann (b. 1936), who often partners Fischer-Dieskau and has also composed *Lieder* for him which they have performed. The Austrian pianist Jörg Demus (b. 1928) has also partnered Fischer-Dieskau and other singers, including the soprano Elly Ameling and the tenor Peter Schreier.

Janet Baker wrote of Gerald Moore in 1967 when he retired: 'Only those of us fortunate enough to have worked with the indescribable, incomparable and irreplaceable Gerald Moore can appreciate his art to the full.' C.H.

PART SEVEN

MEDIEVAL & RENAISSANCE MUSIC

'The Sense of Hearing' by Abraham Bosse (1602-76) captures the flavour of 17th-century music-making.

Medieval music – the music of the Middle Ages – was rich but in many respects unorganised. After the end of the Roman Empire the preservation of music in its more cultivated forms was largely in the hands of the Church, the only recognised international authority. The medieval church inherited the Gregorian plainchant singing named after the sixth-century Pope who gave it a clear role in worship, and this was developed and elaborated under the Emperor Charlemagne two hundred years later. To the original Latin chants of psalms and the like, church musicians now gradually added new devotional words and music to go with them in forms now known as sequences and tropes. From these in turn came church music plays in which the Gospel stories of Easter or Christmas were set to music and dramatised. As music became more elaborate, ways were found to write it down, and it was the Italian choirmaster Guido of Arezzo who in about 1030 perfected a stave system of four lines from which he could train singers to read: the notes were placed on or between the lines just as in today's five-line stave. It was he also who developed a kind of tonic sol-fa to name the notes of a scale and the intervals between them; indeed, the names Re, Mi and Fa are from his system.

Outside the Church, music initially depended on minstrels of all kinds, professional itinerant all-round entertainers variously called *jongleurs* in France, *Gaukler* or *Spielmänner* in Germany, gleemen in Britain and so on. They gathered at public festivals, Church councils or princely weddings and by the eleventh century they had guilds at which they exchanged skills (like juggling) and songs; the Italian poet Petrarch called them 'very hardworking and cheeky beyond measure'. But music-making spread to the wealthier and more educated classes: King Alfred the Great was skilled in music, and Duke William of Aquitaine (1071-1127) was among the first of the troubadours, southern French poet-musicians and sometimes crusaders creating courtly love songs – as was his great-grandson Richard Coeur de Lion, later King Richard I of England; Northern France had an equivalent in the *trouvères*. While for obvious reasons the music of ordinary minstrels was not written down, much less preserved, the troubadours and the *trouvères* together left about 1,000 songs in a notated form.

However, as yet neither secular nor sacred music had a way of showing rhythm, or for that matter the speed of music. We can often deduce a rhythm, of course, from the words of a troubadour song or a hymn; or in the case of dance songs from the idea of bodily

Right: A band of Flemish musicians of the 15th century. This is a typical waits band of the period; the musical instruments are all portable.

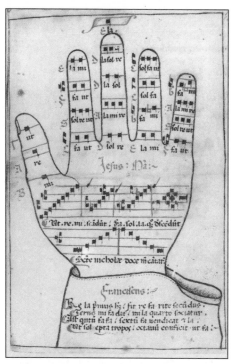

movement. But as little by little the art of harmony and polyphony came into music, this became necessary. For example, in the style called 'St Martial organum' there were two vocal parts sung simultaneously of which the upper had quick notes and the lower slower ones: synchronisation was essential. Borrowing rhythmic patterns from poetry could help in some cases but not in all. In the thirteenth century the German theorist

Left: The Benedictine monk and musical theorist Guido d'Arezzo (c. 990-c. 1050) was responsible for early naming of notes and demonstrated the positions of the then current six-note scale with the 'Guidonian hand'.

Right: Early monastic music-making; the monks reading a manuscript of the time such as this miniature drawing illuminates, showing the 4-line stave which was common until the end of the 15th century.

Jean-Baptiste LULLY (1632-87)

Son of a Florentine miller, his style as a strolling player so impressed a visitor that he was taken to France at fourteen where he worked in a noble household, eventually becoming leader of the resident string band. At twenty he moved into the service of Louis XIV as a ballet dancer and violinist, where he made a great impression and received rapid advancement. In 1658 he began composing his own ballets, and within another four years was in charge of the whole royal musical establishment. In 1664 he began a fruitful collaboration with Molière in producing comedy-ballets, then for the last fourteen years of his life concentrated on opera, having obtained exclusive rights to present operatic productions. Since music in seventeenth-century France was totally dominated by the Court, Lully thus became for practical purposes the founder of French opera, which he shaped with enormous skill into something distinct from the popular Italian variety. He was an acute politician who saw to it that his rather rigid ideas held sway, but if much of his music now seems rather ponderous, one may still find gems scattered through his thirty or so principle works. By a nice irony, he died from a poisoned foot, caused by stabbing it with a staff while beating time when performing a *Te Deum* in celebration of the king's recovery from an illness. J.C.

Left: *The famous Harley manuscript of 'Sumer is icumen in', one of the first English partsongs, a canon for four voices which dates back to* c. *1240; with alternative Latin words.*

Franco of Cologne produced his treatise called *The Art of Measurable Song* in which he distinguished notes of varying length relative to each other: the double long, long, breve and semibreve. The basic unit was the breve (literally 'short'), corresponding to the modern crotchet. (It is a paradox that we seem to have speeded music up since then so that the semibreve equalling four crotchets is now a long note.) Early in the next century this system was extended by Philippe de Vitry in his book called *The New Art*; he added extra note values such as the minim and semiminim (respectively half and a quarter of a semibreve) and time signatures for duple and triple time.

It is doubtless wrong to imagine that these theorists were the inventors of rhythmic notation. Indeed a piece of music of the mid-thirteenth century proves that it was known in England at that time. The round 'Sumer is icumen in' – in other words, 'summer is coming' – is in no less than six vocal (i.e. polyphonic) parts and joins a secular vitality to the skill of the Reading monk who copied (and very probably wrote) it. This round is a major landmark in medieval music, and not only for reasons of its advanced technique – implying also, incidentally, that there was now an equivalent performance skill. Even more importantly, it shows that the learning of church musicians that had hitherto been restricted to liturgical use could be coupled with a fresh secular spirit of individuality, humour and life-affirmation. In this single English round of the thirteenth century we may see the new mode of thought that brought about the Renaissance. C.H.

The word renaissance means 're-birth', but its use by historians implies rather a re-shaping of human thought. When it started to occur during the fourteenth century it was as if Europe were throwing off a malaise that had affected it ever since the fall of the Roman Empire and gaining a new confidence and strength. Paradoxically, this strength came partly from facing disasters such as the loss of the liberated Holy Land in 1291, the Hundred Years' War which began in 1337 and the Black Death that killed one in four Europeans. Even the Church was awry: rival Popes claimed the divine office and the Englishman John Wyclif attacked the papacy and some doctrines and demanded a return to purely Biblical teaching.

The arts reflected this new spirit of defiant optimism. In Italy Giotto's paintings spoke of Christianity 'in terms of human feeling' and Boccaccio's *Decameron* showed young Florentines during the plague devoting themselves to love, literature and music. Secular songs of this time bubble with a vitality expressed in catchy tunes and brisk rhythms. Even in church music the blind Italian composer Francesco Landini could bring a new expressiveness – 'no one had ever heard such beautiful, almost heart-breaking harmonies' wrote a contemporary in 1389. It is said that once when Landini was playing the organ a nightingale came to perch above his head.

In France the composer Guillaume de Machaut (*c*. 1300-77) seems to symbolise the first musical flowering of the renaissance and its so-called New Art. More of his music survives than of any other composer of his period, and beyond that he shows a wider range of style; like his *trouvère* predecessors he was a poet as well as a musician, a courtier who served in Prague and Paris and wrote expressive love songs. He was also a priest whose sacred music includes a *Messe de Nostre Dame* which is the first known complete polyphonic setting (in four vocal parts) of the Mass. Machaut was a master of smooth harmony but deliberately used discord in his Mass to evoke the Crucifixion; and melody itself played a major part in his style. His art left mere ingenuity behind to become one of sound and the senses, and he once wrote of a new piece, 'I have listened to it several times and it pleases me very well'. He also stated that words and music had to have real feeling if they were not to be false.

New ideas also appeared elsewhere. In the monastery of Montserrat in Spain folksong melodies, pilgrim songs and dances were collected in around 1400 in a manuscript now called the *Red Book*. The Tyrolean knight Oswald von Wolkenstein (*c*. 1377-1445) travelled widely as a *Minnesinger* and wrote songs in which instruments had more to play than was usual: he has been called the first composer of *Lieder*. The English carol, in

Left: *The tomb and monument of Francesco Landini (c. 1335-97), blind organist, lutenist and composer who was organist of the church of San Lorenzo in Florence and an exponent of 'ars nova'.*

Below: *The musicians and composers Guillaume Dufay (c. 1400-74) and Gilles Binchois (c. 1400-60) with portative organ and harp pictured in a 15th-century miniature by Martin Lefranc.*

verse form and often vigorous, has its most notable example in the *Agincourt Song (Deo gratias Anglia)* celebrating Henry V's famous victory in 1415.

The Englishman John Dunstable was a leading figure of the fifteenth century who, like many other musicians of his time, composed both sacred and secular music for a noble employer, in this case the Duke of Bedford who became Regent of France in 1422: his song to Italian words 'O rosa bella' shows his mastery of flowing melody. Guillaume Dufay from the north of France was perhaps influenced by Dunstable; his four-voice Mass *Se la face ay pale* is so called because it uses the tune of his own (secular) ballade to those words and has been called 'a stunning example' of his mastery of large-scale structure. The scholar Howard Brown has claimed that 'Dufay formed the central musical language of the Renaissance' and points to his shapely melodies and harmonic progres-

Below: *Anonymous 17th-century portrait of a musician with bass-lute from the Ashmolean Museum, Oxford, generally thought to be Claudio Monteverdi (1567-1643), pioneer of Italian music.*

sions, qualities that were vitally important to the development of forms which form the basis of later music.

Prominent musicians were often French or from the Netherlands: men such as Antoine Busnois, Johannes Ockeghem, Jacob Obrecht and Heinrich Isaac. But the towering figure of the late Renaissance, who more than anyone brought it to the threshold of the Baroque era, is Josquin Desprez (c. 1440-1521). He may have studied with Ockeghem (on whose death in 1497 he wrote an elegy called *Nymphes des bois*, but also learned the Italian virtues of clarity and vitality during a period as a cathedral chorister at Milan. As with so many musicians of the time, his surviving music is wholly vocal and both sacred and secular. It is clear and purposeful in melody and harmony, and sensitive to words in such matters as word-painting; for example, a descent into the grave in his motet *Absalom, my Son* is paralleled by the use of steadily flatter keys. Such techniques earned a special name: *musica reservata*. His little four-part song *El grillo (The Cricket)* sparkles with life and wit in its depiction of a cheerful, songful and industrious insect. Josquin has been praised by many, during and

Giovanni Pierluigi da PALESTRINA (1525-94)

In his late teens Palestrina was organist and choirmaster in the cathedral of his native city, from which he took his name, but when his bishop became Pope he moved to Rome (1551) as choirmaster of the Julian Chapel at the Vatican. In 1554 he published a book of masses dedicated to the Pope, who died the following year. His successor, Marcellus II, held office for only three weeks, but one of Palestrina's most celebrated masses is dedicated to his memory. Soon after Pope Paul IV was elected, for reasons which are not at all clear, Palestrina was dismissed. He then became *maestro di capella* of St John Lateran, for which church he wrote his *Lamentations*. After holding a number of important appointments in Rome he entered the service of Cardinal Ippolito d'Este in 1557, and four years later returned to the Julian Chapel, this time as its director. Then followed a most unhappy time in which he lost his wife and two sons as a result of epidemics. He vowed to enter the priesthood, but a few weeks later married the widow of a rich fur merchant, whose fortune enabled him to spend his remaining years in great comfort, and to publish no fewer than sixteen collections of his music. 'Worldly cares of any kind are adverse to the Muses', he once observed, '. . . especially those arising from a lack of private means.' R.H.

after his lifetime. 'He is the master of the notes by which others are mastered', exclaimed Martin Luther; and he has also been compared to Michelangelo (1567), called 'the father of polyphonic music' (1711) and 'the Beethoven of his time' (1983).

The poet Ronsard claimed in 1560 that the composer Jean Mouton (c. 1459-1522) was Josquin's pupil, and if this is so an unbroken line of teacher-pupil contacts (via Adrian Willaert in early sixteenth-century Venice, Cipriano de Rore and Marc'Antonio Ingegneri) links him with the great Italian figure of the early Baroque, Monteverdi. It is tempting to think so, for many of Josquin's innovations found their full realisation a century after his death, and he has been called the first composer whose music appeals to our modern sense of the art. C.H.

For centuries the music of medieval and renaissance times was known only to a handful of scholars, and their studies of manuscripts rarely led to actual hearing of the compositions concerned. The reasons were manifold: it was unclear what speeds and even rhythms might have been intended, what pitch would be appropriate, and what if any accompaniment might have been intended for, say, a song melody. Beyond all this, hardly any medieval instruments survived, least of all in a playable form. Pictures or carvings of instruments with their instrumentalists were fairly common, but showed so many discrepancies that few facts could be ascertained; for example, a painter might for artistic reasons refrain from showing the puffed-out cheeks of a wind player.

Little by little, this situation has changed. Today many more scholars are themselves practising musicians, and vice versa, so that to the erudition and painstaking research of the musicologist a new and vital imaginative (yet reasoned) element has been added of a kind that only a practical playing musician can provide. Universities and other institutes of higher education now include performance practice in music studies in a way that was almost unimaginable until about a generation ago.

Above: *Queen Elizabeth I portrayed in a miniature of the period (c. 1560) playing the lute. This was an accomplishment expected of all educated persons in England of that time.*

Below: *A detail from a fresco by Simone Martini – showing aulos and lute players. This scene is taken from the story of the life of St Martin, in the church of S. Francesco at Assisi.*

What we now know with reasonable certainty is that the music of the Middle Ages strove for brilliance rather than refinement, and that although this changed progressively with the Renaissance the subtle playing styles of today were neither achieved nor sought for. Contrasting tones were liked, so that while we today listen to a string quartet with instruments all from one family a medieval ensemble might have been very mixed. It could for example have had a folk fiddle such as a rebec or a *vielle* (hurdy-gurdy) which was held on the player's lap, portable organ, recorder and drums or jingles.

Medieval instruments were categorised as soft, for indoor use, or loud, for outside: recorders (end-blown flutes) and plucked string instruments such as the psaltery (held in the hands) were among the former group, while the latter included brass, drums of various kinds, bagpipes with their drones, and from about the thirteenth century shawms, which were double-reed woodwind precursors of the oboe and resembled a bagpipe chanter. Outdoor music was often used for dances and was then lively and of a popular kind, but ceremonial occasions for the nobility had more dignified music often featuring trumpets and bigger drums. The nobility were also more likely to have access to the kind of indoor playing, say with the lute, that might divert a more courtly audience. The lute originally came from the Arab world, just as the recorder did from Italy, but all instruments could be made locally to standards varying from rude to refined.

It may seem at first as if music for the human voice must have been the same in medieval and renaissance times as it is today, but if we reflect on the vast difference in singing style between, say, an American country singer, a Welsh choir and an Indian popular vocalist we realise that this line of thought yields little. Doubtless 'country styles' were rougher than courtly ones, but it is difficult to go much beyond this.

Still, both in instrumental and vocal music – and the two often go together, particularly in secular pieces – we have some plausible idea at least of performance. David Munrow's Early Music Consort have recorded an album called *Instruments of the Middle Ages and Renaissance* that features musicians playing replicas of old instruments in a variety of lively music, and a vocal-instrumental group called the Early Music Quartet directed by Thomas Binkley has recorded a series called *Music of the Middle Ages*, and some *Secular music circa 1300*: here are troubadour songs and much else. The Schola Cantorum Londoniensis have recorded some *Music of the early Middle Ages* under Professor Denis Stevens. An expert string player as well as a musicologist, Professor Stevens himself represents the new breed of scholar-performer so necessary to bring the older forms of music back to life.

Thomas TALLIS
(c. 1505-85)

Although little is known about his early life and background, it is clear that at the time of the Dissolution, Thomas Tallis was organist at the Abbey of the Holy Cross at Waltham. He left in 1540 and, after a short time at Canterbury, became a gentleman of the Chapel Royal in 1542 where he remained, serving under four sovereigns, for the rest of his long life. In 1575 Elizabeth I granted letters patent to Tallis and William Byrd which gave them for twenty-one years the sole right to print music and music paper. This should have proved lucrative but, in fact, involved them in a loss during the early years. They published jointly thirty-four *Cantiones sacrae* that year, and Tallis went on to compose a great deal of church music which shows technical command of a very high order, and sustained inspiration. His 40-part motet *Spem in alium* and the splendid five-part *Lamentations of Jeremiah* are two of the most outstanding vocal works in the repertoire. Tallis also made important contributions to the development of keyboard music, but only a part of his output survives. The splendid tune used by Vaughan Williams in his *Fantasia on a theme of Thomas Tallis* (1910) comes from the *Whole Psalter* written in 1567. R.H.

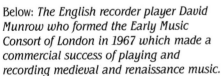

Below: *The English recorder player David Munrow who formed the Early Music Consort of London in 1967 which made a commercial success of playing and recording medieval and renaissance music.*

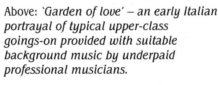

Above: *'Garden of love' – an early Italian portrayal of typical upper-class goings-on provided with suitable background music by underpaid professional musicians.*

It is certain that actual performances of medieval and renaissance music, whether vocal or instrumental, went further than the written notes in the way of improvised ornamentation and rhythmic flexibility. This practice survived well into Baroque times and the eighteenth century, not least with opera singers, and still does up to a point today, for example in jazz. Once again, there is no alternative to intelligent and imaginative guesswork and though all accept the necessity for flexibility it is not always that everyone will find a particular performance convincing. Old manuscripts do not tell us what instruments or voices are expected to perform, much less the exact style of delivery for the written notes. But as Thomas Binkley puts it, 'a virtuoso instrumentalist would not be satisfied simply to play a drone'; thus improvisation and even inspiration must have a place in any performance of old music that

can hope for something like conviction.

Throughout this whole early period, and above all as we come to the Renaissance, performance becomes progressively less conjectural. The notation from which musicians must read is increasingly detailed over such matter as rhythm, pitch and the voices and instruments required. Within the last ten years or so, new and outstanding performances particularly of vocal music available on record have made a considerable impression even on listeners to whom music before 1600 was previously a closed book. Such works as Josquin's *Missa pange lingua* and the British composer Thomas Tallis's motet in forty vocal parts *Spem in alium*, as performed by The Tallis Scholars under their director Peter Phillips, show signs of achieving classic status and even general popularity, and could herald a vogue for the music of the late Renaissance period. C.H.

PART EIGHT

READING & USING MUSIC

Practice makes perfect ... A member of the BBC Symphony Orchestra alone with violin and score.

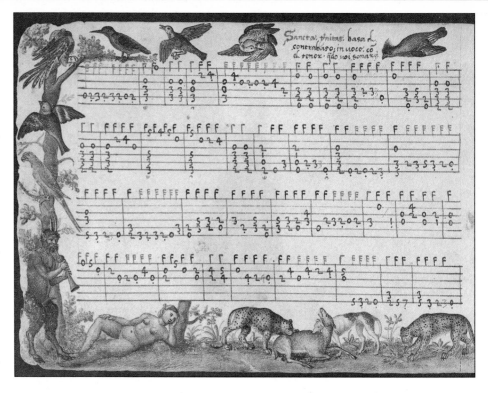

Everyone knows what music is. Or do they? In fact the word is not all that easy to define. People have to agree if a definition is to be useful; and yet we often say 'That's not music' about anything that we don't like even when it is sung or played on a musical instrument. 'Uproar's your only music', wrote the poet Keats in 1818.

So where can we agree about what sounds are, or can be, musical ones? Poets can find them in Nature: Byron wrote of 'the deep sea and music in its roar', and Longfellow declared, 'I hear the wind among the trees/ Playing the celestial symphonies'. And where does music come from? 'All music is from heaven', declared the American composer Charles Ives; but 'Music is the creation of man' was the opinion of the writer H.R. Haweis in a book published in 1871. For Shakespeare in *Twelfth Night* music was 'the food of love', and the composer Berlioz thought that 'music can give an idea of love . . . they are the two wings of the soul'.

Perhaps we should at this point consult the reference books in search of a sober definition of music. But if we look up 'music' in the 20-volume *New Grove Dictionary of Music and Musicians*, we find . . . nothing at all! The *New Oxford Companion to Music* and the *New Harvard Dictionary of Music* are equally silent on the subject, and so are other respected music books. It is amazing that while telling us much about every aspect of music, these reference books seem in a conspiracy of silence about what it actually is. An ordinary *Concise Oxford Dictionary* is more informative. 'Art of combining sounds with a view to beauty of form and expression of emotion; sounds so produced; pleasant sound, e.g. song of bird, murmur of brook, cry of hounds.' That last example seems doubtful, to say the least – but there it is, it seems that music can be anything that is 'music to our ears', whether man-made or otherwise.

However, for the purposes of this book, let's stick to music of the man-made kind, which can be written down and sung or played by musical instruments. A good working definition, with which most people might agree, is that music is organised sound.

A composer creates a musical structure rather like an architect designs a building. The idea for its general style and shape is at first in his head, and then he realises it in detail using basic materials such as notes of different lengths, pitches, tone colour and volume, and may write it down in musical notation. Then a performer or performers brings this musical score to life just as a builder constructs the building designed by the architect, going from instructions written on paper to the actual thing itself.

That's one parallel. Another is to think of a composer's use of his language with its notes, chords, phrases, movements and complete works as resembling a dramatist's use of letters of the alphabet, words, sen-

Below: A circular canon for counter-tenors. Composers were always trying to find new and novel ways of giving written music a physical appearance that gave a vivid impression of the end-product.

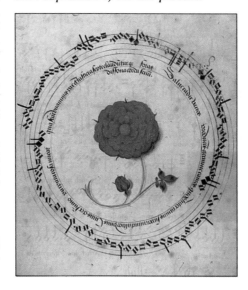

Above: Early Italian lute tablature or notational system as introduced into Europe from c. 1500 on. Many systems have been used since to facilitate the playing of particular instruments.

tences, scenes, acts and finally a complete play. The composer's music is then performed by musicians – 'played', indeed, using the same word for both arts – just as the play is played by actors.

THE BASIC ELEMENTS

The fundamental elements of music include pitch, duration, dynamics, texture and tone colour. From these parameters we derive the larger features of melody, harmony, rhythm and form, and quality of sound.

Let's take the basics first, one by one. *Pitch* is the 'what note is it' aspect of music. To say that a note is 'middle C' – the C near the middle of the piano keyboard and be-

tween the treble and bass clefs, scientifically identified as C', with the little stroke showing its place in the Helmholtz notation – is to define its pitch. That pitch is simply the frequency of vibration that corresponds to this note, in this case 256 cycles (oscillations) per second, or 256 Hz (for Hertz). The note an octave above, also a C (C'' in Helmholtz notation), will vibrate twice as fast and sound correspondingly higher. It's not necessary to remember the Helmholtz nomenclature, though it is useful to theorists, and the reason is that musicians manage quite well with just the seven letter names from A up to G. But there are a few modifications of them which we need to recall: for example, C *sharp* is a half tone (a semitone) above C, and D *flat* is the identical note half a tone below D. *Tones* and *semitones* are measures of pitch difference. The octave (say C to the next C above) is divisible into six tones and, of course, twelve semitones. The pitch of tones is shown by their position on the five-line *stave* with its *clef* sign telling us how high or low the stave is placed, e.g. treble or bass register.

Duration is the 'how long is a note' aspect of music. There are many measures of duration – or more specifically relative duration – for the speed (tempo) of the music must be established, for example at 60 crochets to the minute, or 40 (slower), or 90 (faster) and so on. The *crotchet* is the standard median duration and others relate to it by multiplying or dividing by two. Thus a *minim* is twice as long as a crotchet and a *semibreve*

Arnold SCHOENBERG
(1874-1951)

Although he learnt violin and cello as a boy, and received some instruction in counterpoint from Zemlinsky, this revolutionary and hugely influential Austrian-Jewish composer was mostly self taught. During a period spent scoring music for others, and then as conductor of a cabaret, he produced his first major composition, *Transfigured Night* (1899), a chromatic but voluptuous piece of late-romantic string writing. Then, composing and teaching in Vienna and Berlin (with Berg and Webern among his pupils), he generated a series of increasingly dissonant works. These ranged from string quartets to the massively conceived *Gurrelieder*, while the ensuing period (1908-12) saw the creation of completely atonal works such as *Erwartung, Five Orchestral Pieces* and *Pierrot Lunaire*, a song cycle employing a kind of swooping speech. Many of Schoenberg's works produced a hostile response, but he fought fanatically for 'the emancipation of dissonance' and believed that tonality must give way to different types of expressiveness. In 1923 he formally spelt out this 'Second Viennese School' philosophy as a system of 12-tone serial composition, which he continued to employ (but not always) after his exile to the USA in 1933. Until his death he worked on the unfinished opera *Moses and Aron*, which embodies his Jewish faith but has also been seen as a moving allegory of his own lonely mission in an uncomprehending world. J.C.

Above: *A page from a 15th-century antiphonary; early notation of Gregorian choral plainsong in a typically lavishly decorated manuscript preserved in the famous Laurentian Library in Florence.*

four times as long; a *quaver* is half as long as a *crotchet* and a *semiquaver* a quarter as long. Another way of altering a note's value (duration) is to put a dot to the right of it, which adds half its length, and so a dotted minim is equal to a minim and a half.

Dynamics or volume is the 'how loud is a note' aspect of music. We indicate it by marking such as *piano* for soft and *forte* for loud – these are usually abbreviated in a musical score as *p* and *f*. Words such as *crescendo* and *diminuendo* tell a performer to get louder or softer. There are also marks to show if notes are to be accented.

Texture and *tone colour* are to do with the 'what does it sound like' aspect of music. Texture, say in orchestral music, may be thick or thin, rich or delicate and so on. Tone colour is simply the kind of sound a composer or performer chooses: imagine the G above middle C sung by a tenor and then by a soprano, or played by a trumpet and then a violin. The 'same' note changes when we change the producer of it, and beyond that a singer or player can make that one note sound in many ways, and no two voices or instruments will produce identical sounds anyway, which is just one reason why a per-

former always contributes something creative. The reasons why different tone colours are produced by different voices or instruments are physical. The vocal chords of a singer cannot make the same sound as the struck string in a piano, and can be explained scientifically, just as a scientist using an oscilloscope with its visual display on a screen can see and analyse the different wave formations made by musical sounds.

MELODY

Melody is the arrangement of notes (pitches) in a sequence forming a theme or tune, or a word for the theme itself. But the rhythmic aspect is important too, namely the duration

Above: *A 13th-century plainsong manuscript which is preserved in the Assisi Biblioteca Comunale. Such books, hand-written on vellum, maintain a remarkable freshness of appearance.*

Below: *A song by Felix Mendelssohn (1809-47), 'Reiselied' with words by Heinrich Heine in a lavishly romantic illustrated edition of 1860 which is well-suited to the Victorian spirit of the work.*

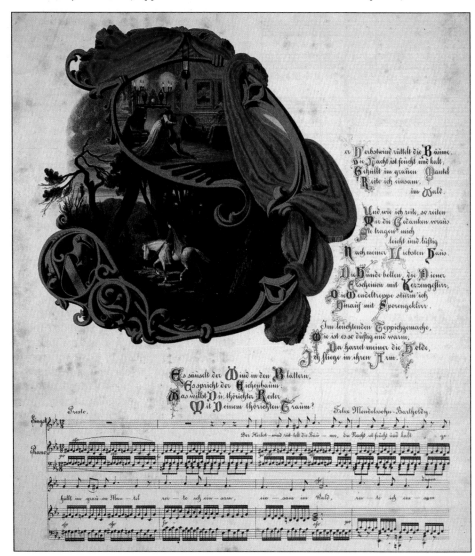

pitch. The chief note of a key, on which melodies usually end, is the *tonic*, the first note of a scale, which in C major or minor would be C.

HARMONY

In melodies, notes at various pitches are arranged in sequence, as it were horizontally. In harmony they are arranged vertically and 'simultaneously' as chords. Harmony is a younger art than melody, and in some non-Western music (such as Indian) it does not exist at all as we understand it. The force of *key* or tonality in Western music is like that of gravitation in physics: that is, having chosen his key the composer will order his melody and harmony around the notes which belong in it. Harmony is not merely a matter of individual chords, for the progression from one chord to another is governed by an artistic logic just as is the movement from one note to another in melody. In practice the two go hand in hand. To see what this means, look at a hymnbook and see how the chords under the tune progress along with the tune itself and are related to it: it would be unthinkable, for example, for a tune in D major to end on D but be harmonised with a chord of B flat. Each note of a major or minor scale has an associated three-note chord or triad made by adding the third and fifth scale degree above it – say E and G above C, or G and B above E, in the key (and scale) of C major.

RHYTHM

The word rhythm really means 'flow', the pattern of movement in time that is made by music. Besides the durational aspect of rhythm, i.e. how long the notes last, there is the important matter of *metre*, the pattern of beats which is as fundamental to music as the human pulse is to life, representing as it does the heartbeat itself. Music too is measured in *beats* and the *bars* which are regular groups of them, and our ears like to 'feel the beat' of music: certainly without it we could not march, dance, or tap a foot, and a conductor would have little use for his baton. We hear music commonly in groups of two beats (with the first of the two more accented) or three (with a similar accent on the first). The time signature at the start might be 2/4 (two crochets in a bar) in the first case, 3/4 in the second; and more complicated time signatures often come down to the same thing, for example 6/8 being two dotted crotchet beats to a bar. The bars (the American word 'measures' explains their function) which make up a piece of music also show where the strong first beat in a group occurs, after the bar line. Bars are useful practically for other reasons also, and if a choir director or conductor wants to start in the middle of the music, he can say 'from bar 80' or whatever it is. We also use the word 'rhythm' to identify a particular rhythmic

Nadia BOULANGER
(1887-1979)

According to the American composer Virgil Thompson there is a Boulanger pupil in every American town. An exaggeration, no doubt, but the number of pupils, American and English, who have passed through her hands is formidable indeed. During her own days at the Paris Conservatoire, where she studied composition under Gabriel Fauré, she won first prizes in harmony, counterpoint, fugue, organ and accompaniment, and in 1908 she came second in the Prix de Rome with her cantata *La Sirène*. She returned to the Conservatoire in 1909 as a teacher, and took up further posts at the École Normale de Musique in Paris (1920) and the American Conservatory at Fontainbleau (1921), of which she became director in 1948. She also made frequent visits to the USA, teaching at the Juilliard School and elsewhere. Nadia Boulanger was prominent among those who rediscovered the music of Monteverdi in the early years of this century, and she also championed Fauré's cause by conducting many performances of his *Requiem* long before it came to occupy a permanent place in the choral repertoire. Of her own compositions she was much more dismissive: 'not bad, but useless', was her characteristically modest verdict. R.H.

Anton WEBERN
(1883-1945)

Unlike his friend Alban Berg, with whom he studied under Arnold Schoenberg from 1904, this scholarly Austrian came to composition with a full musicological endowment, having started under the eye of his pianist mother, then moving via proper academic stages on to a university doctorate. He worked as a conductor at various centres until 1917, directed the Vienna workers' symphony concerts for twelve years, and was musical adviser and conductor with Austrian Radio from 1927 to 1938. He worked in obscurity during World War II, and was shot accidently in 1945. But this moderate career was paralleled by a revolutionary creative process. Webern extended the logic of Schoenberg's 12-tone doctrines into every sphere of composition, eventually applying serial principles to counterpoint, dynamics and tone-colour. At the same time, he explored a world of small forms, employing a distillation of delicately poised tiny phrases in pieces sometimes lasting only a minute or so. He allocated the various notes of a phrase to different instruments, so that his music is more dependent than that of any previous composer on colouristic as opposed to thematic/harmonic structure. Being totally without consonant resting points, it is difficult to appreciate and has remained unpopular with concert audiences. Nevertheless, a whole generation of post-1950 serialist composers were indebted as much to him as to Schoenberg himself. J.C.

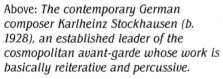

Above: *The contemporary German composer Karlheinz Stockhausen (b. 1928), an established leader of the cosmopolitan avant-garde whose work is basically reiterative and percussive.*

idea, like the four-note one at the start of Beethoven's Fifth Symphony.

FORM

Form involves a large-scale organisation of durations: how long various sections are in relation to the whole. But it is much more besides: the organisation of themes in a musical work belongs to the realm of melody, while the distribution of keys, textures and tone colours belongs to harmony and other elements of the musical whole. In a sense form is the summing up and synthesis of everything else that makes up a musical work: the whole of which all else is a part.

QUALITY OF SOUND

By this we just mean what the music sounds like; we do not use the word 'quality' in the sense of evaluating how good it is, for that is a matter for private taste, or if you like expert opinion – or both. When a composer speaks of sound quality he may well mean its nature, whether it is for one instrument or many, gentle or powerful in volume, soothing or harsh in tone colour. Performers searching for a particular kind of sound have different ways of doing so: the pianist changes his touch or uses the sustaining pedal, the organist alters the registration (stops) and the violinist or cellist uses his bow differently or puts on his mute to muffle the tone a little. Singers have especially wide resources as to the way a single note or a whole melody may be made to sound, and the very words themselves have their effect on this too. Perhaps the biggest mystery of all is how sound assumes a recognisable identity. Clearly people's voices are recognisably different, but it is less easy to explain why two people playing the same clarinet can make it sound different; or even how two different pianists can be identified. It is all part of that valuable asset called style. C.H.

PART NINE

RECORDED MUSIC

The latest technology. The manufacture of compact discs at Disctronics in the United Kingdom.

IONIZED AIR

The storage of music for re-creation at leisure is an ancient dream, first realized in a limited way when groups of bells were made to ring in sequence by automatic means. This led eventually to the musical-box, and finally to a wide range of 'mechanical instruments', some of which attracted the attention of serious composers. But such devices could never accurately reproduce individual flesh-and-blood performances; and even the music of Haydn, Mozart and Beethoven sounded stilted when re-created by a pattern of pegs set in a-rotating barrel. The facility to relive real musical events had to await the coming of the gramophone, with one special exception: the piano-roll. This once had quite a vogue because of its capacity for presenting the interpretations of individual pianists as they would have sounded if the performers were seated at the replay instrument. A number of virtuoso players were attracted by the medium, while, in one very striking case, a piano-roll of George Gershwin enabled the composer to play the solo part in a recording of his *Rhapsody in Blue* some forty years after his death.

These days it is taken for granted that recording is the obvious way to tackle such an enterprise, but in its early years the gramophone's musical applications were not taken too seriously. The devices were actually known as Talking Machines and were promoted as office dictating aids, and when commercial recordings did come along they were of humorous monologues and the like. That was in the first decade after 1877, the year in which the Frenchman Charles Cros theorised and the American Thomas Edison demonstrated that acoustical waves in the air could be translated into replayable traces on a moving surface. The phonograph which Edison used for this was very primitive, but by speaking loudly at a small diaphragm which activated a needle, he managed to transmute the sound of his voice into a series of minute undulations impressed on a spiral groove around a rotating tin-foil cylinder. Then, by placing a similar stylus in the same groove, he caused a further diaphragm to vibrate in sympathy and thus re-create some semblance of what he had recorded.

Ten years or so later, Emile Berliner promoted the idea of discs instead of cylinders, and for the first time there was serious talk of recordings being used for musical entertainment in the home. Berliner called his system the gramophone (although 'phonograph' remained the generic term in America), and his first records, pressed in hard rubber and of 7-inch diameter, rotated at 70rpm and played for about two minutes. In this last respect they offered no advance over Edison's cylinders, but their flat format meant that it was much easier to take an impression of the original groove and press its pattern on to mass-produced copies. Berliner also arranged that his grooves were 'lateral-cut', giving side-to-side motions of the needle

Above: *John Culshaw (1924-80), classical recording manager with Decca (1956-67) and producer of the first complete recording of Wagner's* Ring, *at the console with members of the Decca recording team.*

Below: *Behind the scenes at 1976 recording of the Berlioz* Requiem *at the Invalides in Paris. Producer John McClure with conductor Leonard Bernstein. Stuart Burrows, rear, and editor Peter Gammond, right.*

instead of the vertical vibrations employed by Edison. The latter 'hill-and-dale' system was to play an important part on disc records too during the thirty turbulent years that elapsed before the cylinder finally disappeared in the 1920s, after the arrival of electrical recording. By that time, the issue of 10-inch or 12-inch two-sided lateral-cut records, pressed in hard-wearing (but hissy) 'filled' shellac, for rotation at 78rpm and giving a maximum of some four minutes per side, was universal.

But the die had been cast much earlier, and well before the end of the acoustic era the gramophone disc had generated a worldwide industry linked with music. However, from the very beginning the realities of taste and commerce dictated that 'classical' music should engage only a small portion of total

recording activity, and the catalogues were dominated by banjo solos, comic songs, sentimental ballads and military bands although the great Sousa himself often conducted the latter. The first ever recording of a classical artist was offered by Edison in 1888 at the launch of his 'improved' phonograph (now using wax as the recording medium). This was the child-prodigy pianist Josef Hofmann, to be followed by Liszt's pupil and one-time son-in-law Hans von Bülow playing a Chopin mazurka. The next year found Brahms playing a *Hungarian Rhapsody* into a phonograph horn in Vienna. The piano is barely discernible through the accompanying background noise, but we do hear the composer signing off by gruffly shouting his own name.

William WALTON
(1902-83)

Son of a choirmaster and himself a choirboy at Oxford's Christ Church Cathedral school, he was soon at home on the piano as a boy but received no formal training in music after sixteen, at which age he wrote a piano quartet. However, he picked up some hints on composition from a few eminent people and eventually eased himself into a composing career, starting with what was conceived as a private entertainment for friends – *Façade*. Written for a small ensemble to accompany poems read by Edith Sitwell, its exuberant, parodying manner was so successful that he produced a suite for full orchestra (1926) which shot him to fame. This was preceded by his lively *Portsmouth Point* overture, and followed by the Viola Concerto, with Paul Hindemith as soloist at the first performance. The dramatic choral/orchestral *Belshazzar's Feast* followed in 1931, then his fine First Symphony and the Violin Concerto. World War II saw much film music, culminating in *Henry V*, with his opera *Troilus and Cressida* following in 1954. Other music in various genres (from ceremonial, via ballet to chamber) came from the pen of this very self-critical composer, who was knighted in 1951. Although *Façade* and some dabblings in the jazz idiom gave Walton an early avant-garde image, his music is essentially romantic/lyrical, with a combination of melancholy and rhythmic impetus which is all his own. J.C.

Above: *An early phonograph. Thomas Edison first invented the means of recording but preferred the cylinder for many years. Emile Berliner came along ten years later with the flat disc.*

Below: *Earnest consideration at a Decca* La Bohème *session. Singers Tonini, Panerai, Pavarotti and the recording team with (front) Karajan, producer Ray Minshul, Freni, Harwood and Ghiaurov.*

Nearly all the instrumental recordings are dreadful by modern standards, and while the later acoustical period produced some reasonable chamber music records, it was not really until the electrical age that a recorded orchestra became worth listening to for pleasure. Today, the prime role of such recordings is to provide small insights into aspects of interpretation, especially when a composer is involved. Grieg recorded some of his piano miniatures in 1903, Debussy enthusiastically acted as accompanist in a recital of his own songs in 1904, and the ageing Saint-Saëns tackled some of his own piano music in 1905. The piano sound is very limited on these recordings, but it so happened that the singing voice – easily focused into the mouth of a recording horn –

generally had a much more worthwhile impact. Thus it transpired that in those experimental days the trained opera singer was the perfect recording artist to represent classical music. The legendary Adelina Patti was already sixty-three when she first recorded, Lilli Lehman fifty-seven, and Nellie Melba forty-three; but while Tetrazzini, Galli-Curci, Chaliapin and Caruso all came from a later generation, we could not have heard any of them in their prime were it not for the pioneering recordists. But the vocal emphasis did sometimes get out of hand, with as many versions of some arias from competing famous singers as we have today of orchestral works from competing famous conductors.

Classical music-lovers started to get fretful, and despite the technical difficulties the

recording companies dipped a careful toe or two into purely instrumental waters. The year 1910 saw Beethoven's *Moonlight* Sonata – albeit severely cut to occupy just two sides – from Mark Hambourg, and in 1911 Paderewski tackled some Chopin. The first-ever symphonic records (Beethoven Nos 5 and 6) appeared in 1913, to be followed a year later by another No. 5 featuring the prestigious Nikisch conducting the Berlin Philharmonic. But as was the way in early acoustical days, Nikisch had to manage with extraordinarily limited instrumental forces, which excluded even the timpani, yet was still obliged to constrain the dynamics into a virtually continuous *mezzo-forte* to avoid 'blast' at one extreme or disappearance into surface hiss at the other. So much for Beethoven's great challenge to Fate! Yet Nikisch seems to have been pleased enough, even though Toscanini said later that the recording was a travesty of the conductor's concert hall view of the work.

It might be thought that if a symphony was barely suitable as gramophonic fare, then operas would be impossible. Yet individual singers were so successful that it was deemed manageable to attempt at least some semblance of a complete opera, albeit with the instrumental support heard only vaguely in the background. Thus as early as 1906 a version of *Il Trovatore* was offered on eighteen sides. But it was short on consistency, as no less than sixteen singers had shared the five principal roles over a three-year recording period. But 1907 saw the first recording of a major work under the direction of its com-

Above: *The Brahms Double Concerto under serious discussion between Peter Andry, violinist David Oistrakh, cellist Mitislav Rostropovich, Carson Taylor and conductor George Szell.*

Below: *David Tudor and John Cage are seen here at rehearsals in London's Royal Albert Hall prior to performing in a concert in 1972. These figures are two of the greatest exponents of modern electronic music.*

poser, *Pagliacci* conducted by Leoncavallo, after which there was a boom in opera recording on the Continent, including complete versions of *Faust, Die Fledermaus, Carmen* and *Roméo et Juliette*. Some of these came on 14-inch two-sided hill-and-dale discs, which very wealthy Parisians could play on a special twin-turntable, with side-sequences arranged so as to cover complete acts without a break.

Then war intervened, and after 1918 the acoustical system had reached its zenith. In the case of orchestral music, it at last became feasible to avoid the use of tubas in place of string-basses, or of Stroh violins (bowed instruments with horns) to augment the fiddles. Somewhat wider dynamics also became manageable, but the ubiquitous 4-minute side was still inclined to influence tempi and dictate severe cuts. Symphonies known to last 40 minutes in the concert hall would somehow still find themselves conveniently accommodated on six 4-minute sides. But there was an ever growing and increasingly discriminating record-buying public acquiring a taste for the classics, and gradually the whole business became more serious minded.

Then, with orchestral recordings already being issued at an unprecedented rate, the electrical process arrived in 1925, opening up a whole new sonic world. The microphone allowed sounds of much wider frequency range to be picked up with less colouration, from performers sensibly disposed in more agreeable acoustic settings, while the resulting 'audio' signals could be amplified and adjusted to achieve properly controlled behaviour at the cutting stylus. But while the actual recordings were much better, most people continued to use their existing acoustical gramophones for replay, and were often unimpressed by the new sound. However, a matching revolution came eventually with the introduction of electrical 'pickups' coupled to amplifiers and loudspeakers, a transition which coincided with the burgeoning early days of radio whose components and technology provided the necessary back-up. Soon, new levels of musical and audio awareness went hand in hand as improved sound quality was paralleled by expanding record catalogues, and the 1930s saw the first glimmer of what was to become the hobby of hi-fi in the LP years after 1950.

Meanwhile, musicians at all levels moved on from a cautious conservatism and began to take records and radio far more seriously. Playing to a microphone started its relentless climb towards parity with playing to an audience. The first electrical recording of a symphony (Tchaikovsky No. 4) appeared at the end of 1925; Leopold Stokowski, always an enthusiast for better recorded sound, produced a flood (as it seemed then) of epoch-making records with the Philadelphia Orchestra; chunks of Wagner were recorded 'live' at Bayreuth; Richard Strauss conducted

Arthur SULLIVAN
(1842-1900)

Sullivan was one of those composers whose creative life was a tug between the call of the classical musical field and the popular theatre. Beyond the sparkling concert overture 'Di ballo' (which is very much in the vein of his operettas, anyway) his serious works tend to be neglected; tuneful and worthy but seldom inspired – the oratorio *The Golden Legend* and other choral works; his symphony; several sets of incidental music; an opera, *Ivanhoe*, and a vast number of songs. Many of these in the most maudlin Victorian vein, like 'The lost chord', had considerable success at the time. Queen Victoria, amongst others, looked to him for serious endeavour, which gave him a constant feeling of guilt when success in the popular theatre demanded so much of his time. The world, however, is grateful that his partnership with the playwright and humorist W.S. Gilbert (1836-1911), led to the delightful and immortal operettas that were to become known as the Savoy operas – *Trial by Jury*, *HMS Pinafore*, *The Pirates of Penzance*, *Patience*, *Iolanthe*, *Princess Ida*, *The Mikado*, *Ruddigore*, *The Yeomen of the Guard* and *The Gondoliers*. Initially inspired by Offenbach, Sullivan showed true genius in these works and this is how the world remembers him. P.G.

Above: *The musical world of Karlheinz Stockhausen (b. 1928) is largely built upon the new possibilities opened up by the West German electronic music studio in Cologne and similar facilities. The result is such a title as* Kontra-Punkte.

some of his own music on record; Rachmaninov played in his own concertos; and in London, Gustav Holst directed the LSO in an electrical version of his *Planets*. Very notably, the ageing Elgar evinced an almost childlike enthusiasm for the gramophone record, and in his last years conducted or oversaw recordings of all his major works. He was the first front-rank composer to do this, and while the creators of music are not necessarily its best interpreters, it is useful and important to hear how any composer views his own scores. Stravinsky, Britten, Bernstein, Copland and others followed suit in the LP age, while conductors having close links with particular composers (such as Boult with Vaughan Williams and Beecham with Delius) have also been enabled to leave their special imprints for posterity.

The next great event in recording history was the long-playing record of 1948-50, which coupled a lower speed with narrower grooves to escape from that ubiquitous 4-minute prison, at the same time permitting a wider dynamic range by virtue of its silent background. Also, the new printed sleeves provided 'programme notes' of the sort one might get at a concert. These were and are frequently the only source of infor-

mation easily available to record buyers concerning the music they love, and their continual production has created a whole new means of musical education to complement the more serious approach to listening engendered by hearing complete movements, often complete works, at one sitting. Adding to the appeal of such sittings, stereo came along in 1958 by putting different musical waveforms on the LP's two groove walls, which then each moved at 45° to the record surface, a sort of modern halfway house between Edison and Berliner. This brought further dimensions of clarity and space to reproduced musical sounds, which made it easier than had been possible in all the eighty years since Edison to imagine oneself looking through a large open window into the concert-hall. At one point in the mid-1950s it seemed that tape might provide the road to stereo, but while it had been in use for some years in making professional master-recordings, it was not until the early 1980s that mass-produced tape copies (in cassette form) finally matched the LP in sales, by which time Compact Discs had arrived. These latter provide a more permanent silence behind the pianissimos, and an even cleaner and clearer presentation of up to 75 minutes of music. But, alas, their digital mode of recording means that there is no longer a groove to carry those representations of actual musical waveforms which have fascinated record-lovers since recording began.

But whether it be via visible wavy grooves or invisible digital codes, the music itself is

now available with a richness and proliferation that would have seemed miraculous in 1877. This has altered the whole way in which musical careers are shaped and musical taste is formed. The huge popularity of Mahler, for instance, could never have arisen if his symphonies depended only on concert hall performances. Indeed, the statistics of record sales, radio audiences and concert attendance show that the vast majority of listening to classical music now takes place in front of loudspeakers, in contrast with the situation a century ago, when it *all* took place in front of musicians. It was once said of Enrico Caruso that one could not be sure whether he had been made by the gramophone, or the gramophone by him. Today, that could almost apply to the whole music business. Many conductors and not a few orchestras are known as much from their recordings as

100 CLASSICAL RECORDINGS

A list of LP recordings that have been highly acclaimed since their first appearance; the date of which is given in brackets [56]. Such a choice is bound to be highly personal but here represents a cross-section of the preferences of the contributors to this book.

Records such as these tend to remain in the record companies' catalogues, but there are always a few that are out of circulation. We have given preference to recordings that are currently or recently available but where the first choice is not available an alternative recording is given. When the original choice is not available on CD an alternative CD version is given. As this is the medium we are most likely to have around for some years to come, this makes the list of practical use as well as of academic interest. Record numbers (which tend to get outdated) are not given (just the record label) but they can be found by referring to the current *Gramophone* LP or CD listings. Record labels are indicated as follows: ARG = Argo; CBS = CBS[Columbia]; DEC = Decca[London]; DGG = Deutsch Grammophon; EMI = EMI[Angel]; ERA = Erato; O-L = L'Oiseau-Lyre; PHI = Philips; RCA = RCA[Victor]. Availability of a CD version is indicated by the symbol ◯. The sign ◊ indicates that a listed item is not currently available and points to an available alternative. ◊◊ indicates a CD option.

Note that Nos 99 and 100 – operetta and *zarzuela* – are collections. P.G.

J.S. BACH
1 Cello suites – Casals – CBS [36/9]◊ Tortelier – EMI [63]◯
2 Magnificat – Gardiner – PHI [85]◯
3 *St Matthew Passion* – Klemperer – EMI [62] ◊◊ Corboz – ERA [83]◯

BARTÓK
4 Concerto for Orchestra/Dance Suite – Solti – DEC [65]◯

BEETHOVEN
5 Symphony No. 3 *Eroica* – Klemperer EMI [61]◯
6 Symphony No. 6 *Pastoral* – Kleiber – DEC [54]◊ Klemperer – EMI [58]◯
7 Symphony No. 7 – Karajan – DGG [63]◯
8 Piano Concerto No. 5 *Emperor* – Kempff/Leitner – DGG [55]◊ Arrau/Davis – PHI [86]◯
9 Late String Quartets – Busch Quartet – EMI [38]◊ Berg Qt – EMI [83/4]◯
10 Piano Trio No. 7 *Archduke* – Ashkenazy/etc – EMI [87]◯
11 *Fidelio* – Klemperer – EMI [61]◊
12 *Missa solemnis* – Toscanini – RCA [54]◊

BELLINI
13 *Norma* – Callas/Serafin – EMI [54]◯

BERLIOZ
14 *La Damnation de Faust* – Solti – DEC [82]◯

BERNSTEIN
15 *West Side Story* – Bernstein – DGG [85]◯

BERWALD
16 Symphonies 3 & 4 – Ehrling – DEC [68]◊

BIZET
17 Symphony in C – Beecham – EMI [58]◯
18 *Carmen* – Los Angeles/Beecham – EMI [60] ◯ ◊◊ Abbado – DGG [78]◯

BRAHMS
19 Piano Concerto No. 1 – Curzon/Szell – DEC [62]◊ Ashkenazy/Haitink – DEC [83]◯

BRITTEN
21 *Serenade* – Pears/Brain/Britten – DEC [54]◯
21 *Peter Grimes* – Britten – DEC [59]◯
22 *War Requiem* – Britten – DEC [63]◯

BYRD
23 Masses – Phillips – GIMELL [86]◯

CHOPIN
24 Waltzes – Rubinstein – RCA [55]◯

DEBUSSY
25 *Pelléas et Mélisande* – Karajan – EMI [79]◯

DELIUS
26 Shorter Works – Beecham – EMI [56/8]◯

DONIZETTI
27 *La Fille du Régiment* – Sutherland/Bonynge – DEC [68]◯
28 *Lucia di Lammermoor* – Sutherland/Bonynge – DEC [72]◯

DVOŘÁK
29 Symphony No. 8 – Kertesz – DEC [63] ◊◊ Dohnanyi – DEC [86]◯

ELGAR
30 Introduction & Allegro/Serenade/etc – Barbirolli – EMI [63]◯
31 Cello Concerto/*Sea Pictures* – Du Pré/Baker/Barbirolli – EMI [65]◯
32 Violin Concerto – Menuhin/Elgar – EMI [32] ◊◊ Kennedy/Handley – EMI [84]◯
33 'The Miniature Elgar' – Collingwood – EMI [64]◊ 'Miniatures' – Del Mar CHANDOS [76]◯

FAURÉ
34 *Requiem* – Rutter – CON [85]◯

GERSHWIN
35 *Rhapsody in Blue/American in Paris* – Gershwin [25]/Thomas – CBS [76]◯
36 *Porgy and Bess* – Maazel – DEC [76]◯

HANDEL
37 *L'Allegro, Il Penseroso* – Gardiner – ERA [81]◯
38 *Messiah* – Davis – PHI [66]◯

HAYDN
40 Symphony No. 88, 98 – Jochum – DGG [63]◊ 93, 94, 96 – Davis PHI [80]◯
40 *The Creation* – Marriner – PHI [80]◯

HUMPERDINCK
41 *Hansel und Gretel* – Karajan – EMI [54]◯

LISZT
42 Piano Concertos 1 & 2 – Richter/Kondrashin – PHI [61]◯
43 Piano Music - Curzon – DEC [63]◊ Bolet – DEC [81]◯

MAHLER
44 *Das Lied von der Erde* – Ferrier/Walter – DEC [52]◯
45 Symphony No. 2 – Klemperer – EMI [63] ◊◊ Rattle – EMI [87]◯
46 Symphony No. 4 – Klemperer – EMI [62]◊ Maazel – CBS [85]◯
47 Symphony No. 9 – Karajan – DGG [81]◯

MASCAGNI
48 *L'Amico Fritz* – Freni/Prêtre – EMI [69]◯

MILHAUD
49 *Le Bœuf sur le Toît* (& Auric, Françaix, Satie) – Dorati – PHI [67] ◊◊ w. *Création du Monde* – Bernstein – EMI [78]◯

MONTEVERDI
50 Madrigals – Boulanger – EMI [37] ◊◊ Madrigals, Bk 4 – Rooley – O-L [86]◯
51 *Selve morale e spirituale* – Parrott – EMI [84]◯

MOZART
52 Symphony No. 25 & 29 – Britten – DEC [78]◊ 29, 35, 40 – Marriner – PHI [71]◯
53 Symphony No. 39 & 40 – Beecham – PHI [54/55]◊ 39 & 41 – Davis – PHI [83]◯
54 Piano Concertos 20 & 27 – Curzon/Britten – DEC [83] ◊◊ 20/27 – Perahia – CBS [76]◯
55 Piano Concertos No. 20 & 24 – Haskil/Markevich – PHI [61]◯
56 Piano Concertos 23/24 – Kempff/Leitner – DGG [60]◊ 23/27 – Brendel/Marriner – PHI [75]◯
57 Piano Concertos (Cpte) – Perahia – CBS [76-8]◯
58 Clarinet & Bassoon Concertos – Brymer/Brooke/Beecham – EMI [58 & 59]◯
59 Horn Concertos – Brain/Karajan – EMI [54]◯
60 Piano Quartets – Curzon/Amadeus – DEC [52]◊ Beaux Arts/Giurranna – PHI [84]◯
61 Requiem Mass – Hogwood – O-L [84]◯
62 *Così fan tutte* – Böhm – EMI [63]◊ Haitink – EMI [87]◯
63 *Don Giovanni* – Giulini – EMI [59]◯
64 *Le Nozze di Figaro* – Kleiber – DEC [55]◊ Marriner – PHI [87]◯
65 *Die Zauberflöte* – Beecham – EMI [37]◊ Solti – DEC [71]◯

MUSSORGSKY
66 *Pictures at an Exhibition* – Maazel – EMI [63]◯

NICOLAI
67 *The Merry Wives of Windsor* – Heger – EMI [63]◊

PUCCINI
68 *La Bohème* – Los Angeles/Beecham – EMI [56]◯
69 *Madama Butterfly* – Tebaldi/Serafin – DEC [58] ◊◊ Karajan DEC [75]◯
70 *Tosca* – Callas/Sabata – EMI [53]◯

RACHMANINOV
71 Piano Concerto No. 2 – Rachmaninov/Stokowski – RCA [29]◊ Ashkenazy – DEC [72]◯

RAVEL
72 *Daphnis et Chloë* – Dutoit – DEC [81]◯

ROSSINI
73 String Sonatas – Marriner – ARG [67] ◊◊ Furi – DGG [86]◯

74 *Il Viaggio à Reims* – Abbado – DGG [85]♡

SAINT-SAËNS
75 Piano Concerto No. 2 – Ousset/Rattle – EMI [82]♡

SCHUBERT
76 Symphonies No. 3 & 5 – Beecham – EMI [59]♡
77 Symphony No. 9 – Furtwängler – DGG [56]♡
78 String Quintet – Casals/etc – CBS [55] ◊◊ H. Schiff/Berg Qt – EMI [83]♡
79 Piano Quintet *Trout* – Curzon/Vienna – DEC [58] ◊◊ A. Schiff/Hagen Qt – DEC [85]♡
80 *Die schöne Müllerin* – Fischer-Dieskau – DGG [72]♡
81 Lieder – Schumann – EMI [27/49] ◊◊ Ameling – PHI [84]♡

J. STRAUSS
82 *Die Fledermaus* – Krauss – DEC [50]◊ C. Kleiber – DGG [76]♡

R. STRAUSS
83 *Le Bourgeois Gentilhomme* – Krauss – DEC [52]◊
84 *Capriccio* – Sawallisch – EMI [58]♡
85 *Elektra* – Solti – DEC [67]♡
86 *Der Rosenkavalier* – Karajan – EMI [57]♡

SULLIVAN
87 *Trial By Jury/HMS Pinafore* – Sargent – EMI [58/60]♡
88 *The Pirates of Penzance* – Godfrey – DEC [58]♡
89 *Pineapple Poll* – Mackerras – ARABESQUE [62]♡

TCHAIKOVSKY
90 Symphony Nos. 4-6 – Mravinsky – DGG [57]♡

VAUGHAN WILLIAMS
91 Symphony No. 4 – Vaughan Williams – EMI [37] ◊◊ Boult – EMI [68]♡
92 Symphony No. 5 – Barbirolli – EMI [63]◊ Haitink – EMI [87]♡

VERDI
93 *Un Ballo in Maschera* – Callas/Votto – EMI [57]♡
94 *Simon Boccanegra* – Abbado – DGG [77]♡
95 Requiem – Giulini – EMI [64]♡

WAGNER
96 *Tristan und Isolde* – Furtwängler – EMI [53] ◊◊ Bernstein – PHI [81]♡
97 *The Ring* – Solti – DEC [59/63]♡ or *Die Walküre* (Act 1) – Walter – EMI [35]

WEBER
98 *Der Freischütz* – C. Kleiber – DGG [73]♡
COLLECTIONS
99 OPERETTA – Schwarzkopf – EMI [59]♡
100 ZARZUELA – Los Angeles – EMI [68]◊

from their concert appearances, while the performing standards set by recordings are such that opera stars have even been booed in the theatre for not living up to the reputation they have created in the recording studio. The whole business of making stereo recordings – especially of opera – has become an art in its own right, with recording producers as a new breed of impresario. The economics of stage productions or the performance of large-scale choral/orchestral works often require that there must be parallel recording sessions, and so on.

Thus the gramophone and its offshoots are now an inextricable part of music itself, and the future is likely to see ever closer ties between performance and recording in all their aspects. The dominance of television and the arrival of video opera recordings with stereo sound (now also on video CDs) points to a time when we may complement the sounds of music by displaying the full theatre stage or concert platform across a large flat screen at the end of the domestic sitting-room. Also, although unsuccessful when promoted as quadraphony in the 1970s, attempts to provide a 'surround-sound' effect may be revived in some more viable form via digital means, so that the listener will be convincingly transported *through* that stereo window into the acoustic of concert hall or church at the touch of a button.

But with recordings of any sort, and however sophisticated they may be, there will always be that specific domestic privilege of which Hilaire Belloc wrote in 1929:

> If, at the Opera, you're in the stalls
> You dare not bolt until the curtain falls.
> But, with the gramophone, it needs no skill
> To stop the noise at once, and when you will.

J.C.

Below: *The studio set up for orchestral recording with Rudolf Kempe and the Dresden State orchestra and soloists Max Rostal (violin) and Paul Tortelier (cello).*

Charles GOUNOD (1818-93)

Son of artist parents and himself no mean draftsman, he chose the stave in preference to the paintbrush at thirteen, having studied music with his pianist-artist mother. He went on to the Paris Conservatoire and won the Prix de Rome in 1839, spending the statutory three years in Rome where he investigated ancient Italian church music, that of Palestrina in particular. Accordingly, back in Paris he became an organist and choirmaster, and for some years seemed destined for the priesthood. But the balance again tipped in favour of music, and from 1851 he tried his hand at opera, eventually achieving success with *Faust* in 1859. So exactly did this meet the needs of the time, and so perfect an example was it of creamily melodic yet well orchestrated and staged sentimentality, that Gounod never managed to equal it. His *Romeo and Juliet* came near in some respects, but *Faust* remains the one among his thirteen operas which automatically equates with his name. He also composed some charming songs and a large quantity of religious music, of which the *St Cecilia Mass* is sometimes heard. And in the Mendelssohnian tradition he produced oratorios for British festivals, having spent the years 1870-75 in England, where he founded what became the Royal Choral Society. He was a gushing, pushy man, who kissed everyone in sight. J.C.

GLOSSARY OF MUSICAL TERMS

Throughout a musical score the composer needs to add some instructions so that the interpreter knows how he would like the work performed – which is no guarantee that his wishes will not be totally ignored. The universal language of music was long accepted as being Italian and therefore the majority of musical terms need translating. Later composers have taken a nationalistic stance and put the instructions in their own language which further complicates matters for the score reader. The basic glossary of musical terms given here offers Italian; French and/or German (where there is an exact equivalent); and (where necessary) English (or American) alternatives.

The most essential instructions are those concerning the speed of the performance and this is conveyed by such words as:

Moderato [It.], **Modère** [Fr.], **Gemässigt** [Ger.]. At a moderate, average sort of speed. This can only be vaguely assumed as people's ideas of moderation are inclined to vary. In practical terms one might think of it as a walking pace, neither hurried nor dragged out.

Allegro [It.]. Literary, meaning 'cheerful, light-hearted' so that, while not specifically a term of speed, it is generally taken to mean something faster than *moderato*; but not too fast. A movement or composition of a bright nature. Somewhat less than *allegro*, i.e. less lively and therefore generally slightly slower and somewhere between *allegro* and *moderato*, comes **Allegretto** [It.].

Vivace [It.]. Lively, vivacious, and therefore at sprightly rate – at least a brisk trot.

Presto [It.], **Schnell** [Ger.]. Quickly; definitely at a running pace. And if to be played really fast then **Prestissimo** [It.], **Rasch** [Ger.] – fast.

Moving in the other and slower direction we have:

Andante [It.], **Gehend** [Ger.]. Going smoothly, i.e. at a very steady, ambling sort of pace. Somewhere between, slightly faster than *andante*, slightly slower than *moderato*, comes **Andantino** [It.) – at a gentle speed.

Adagio [It.]. Somewhat slower than *andante* but not so emphatically slow as

Largo [It.], **Large** [Fr.]. Definitely slowly and in a stately sort of manner. But not the ultimate in slowness which is usually indicated by

Grave [It.]. At a very slow and solemn pace; or

Lento [It.], **Lent.**, **Lenteur** [Fr.], very slowly.

All such instructions tend to get freely interpreted by star conductors and virtuoso musicians. Toscanini would play a Haydn movement marked *allegro molto*, i.e. 'very brightly', at a speed which some would consider to be verging on *presto*. The result suggested

that it was Haydn who knew what he meant rather than Toscanini. On the other hand Mozart would perhaps mark a slow movement of one of his concertos *adagio* (e.g. K488) but a case can be made for performers who find it holds together better if taken a little faster than *adagio* suggests.

At certain points the composer might require some change or temporary adjustment of tempo such as:

Accelerando [It.], **Beschleunigt** [Ger.], **Pressez** [Fr.]. Becoming faster, accelerating.

Allargando [It.]. In a slower and more spacious manner, perhaps suggesting more emphasis and therefore somewhat louder.

Rallentando [It.], **Allonger** [Fr.] (generally abbreviated to **Rall.**). A temporary slowing down at some point; likewise **Ritardando** [It.] [generally abbreviated to **Ritard.** or **Rit.**], a gradual and usually temporary slowing down, usually at the end of a phrase or section; the opposite being

Stringendo [It.]. A gradual speeding up. After such adjustments, temporary or more prolonged, an indication of a return to the original speed will be indicated by

A tempo, at the [normal] speed.

If it is a matter of holding or lingering over one note, a **Tenuto** is asked for by writing the abbreviation **ten.** Over the note. If a more definite pause or stop is wanted a sign known as a **Fermata** [It.], **Fermate** [Ger.], **Point d'orgue** [Fr.] is used over the note, written thus ⌢. This would hold the note for at least twice its normal length.

The manner or style of playing, beyond matters of speed, might be indicated by the use of some of the following:

Agitato [It.]. In an agitated or hurried manner.

Bravura [It.]. With dash, energy, with a flourish, asking for brilliant execution.

Cantabile [It.], **Gesangvoll** [Ger.]. Literally, in a singing manner, lilting, with musical expression.

Espressivo [It.]; **Furioso** [It.]; **Grandioso** [It.]; **Grazioso** [It.]. All self-explanatory by their straightforward translation into English – expressively, furiously, grandiosely and gracefully.

Legato [It.]. In a flowing manner with the notes almost blending into one another; the opposite of which is

Staccato [It.], **Gestossen** [Ger.], **Sec** [Fr.]. With the notes played crisply and sharply, so that they sound separated.

Leggiero [It.]. Lightly.

Portamento [It.]. Gliding from one note to the other, an exaggerated *legato* with the notes connected, giving a slurred effect. Used especially of string playing or vocal music where it is possible to move from one note to another without a perceptible break.

Scherzando [It.]. In a light-hearted, jocular manner. A piece or movement in this vein is called a *scherzo*.

Dynamics are indicated by a range of volumes from *pianissimo* to *fortissimo* **Piano** [It.] (usually simply written as *p*) means softly; **Forte** [It.] (*f*) means loudly. Hence the *pianoforte*, an instrument able to play both softly and loudly. A greater degree of softness is indicated by *pp*, *ppp* and so on; of loudness by *ff*, *fff* and so on. The word *mezzo* means moderately, so moderately soft and moderately loud are indicated by *mp* and *mf*. A temporary move from soft to loud or loud to soft is indicated by *fp* or *pf*. A gradual increase in loudness is asked for by the word **Crescendo** [It.); or the opposite by **Descrescendo** [It.]. More emphatically, a dying away to virtually nothing might be indicated by the word **Diminuendo** [It.] or **Smorzando** [It.]; or specifically to nothing by **Calando** [It.] or **Morendo** [It.].

Further common words that might be encountered are:

A cappella or Alla cappella [It.]. Choral music without instrumental accompaniment.

Ad libitum [It.] (*ad lib.*). To be freely interpreted or (of a certain passage) optionally used.

Arco or coll'arco [It.]. With the bow. Generally a return to normal string playing after a passage of *pizzicato* (qv) or some other device.

Arpeggio [It.], **Arpège** [Fr.]. A chord played so that the notes sound one after the other – like a harp – or a chord split into quavers or semiquavers, etc.

Cadenza [It.]. A virtuoso solo passage.

Col legno [It.]. An instruction to play with the back of the bow.

Da capo [It.] (*D.C.*). Repeat from the beginning; or **Dal segno** [It.] (*D.S.*). Go back to a specific point indicated by a sign.

Glissando [It.]. A continuous ascending or descending move from note to note.

Pizzicato [It.]. To pluck the strings with the fingers.

Sordino [It.]. A mute; hence, to play with a mute – *con sordino*.

INDEX

PICTURE CREDITS